M. 11.14

Stephan Pl

Gow

ege

ANTIOCH

CITY AND IMPERIAL
ADMINISTRATION IN THE
LATER ROMAN EMPIRE

ANTIOCH

CITY AND IMPERIAL
ADMINISTRATION IN THE
LATER ROMAN EMPIRE

J. H. W. G. LIEBESCHUETZ

Lecturer in Classics
in the University of Leicester

OXFORD
AT THE CLARENDON PRESS
1972

Oxford University Press, Ely House, London W. 1

GLASGOW NEW YORK TORONTO MELBOURNE WELLINGTON
CAPE TOWN IBADAN NAIROBI DAR ES SALAAM LUSAKA ADDIS ABABA
DELHI BOMBAY CALCUTTA MADRAS KARACHI LAHORE DACCA
KUALA LUMPUR SINGAPORE HONG KONG TOKYO

PRINTED IN GREAT BRITAIN
AT THE UNIVERSITY PRESS, OXFORD
BY VIVIAN RIDLER
PRINTER TO THE UNIVERSITY

PREFACE

This book began as a thesis for the Ph.D of London University. The topic and general approach were suggested by my teacher, the late Professor A. H. M. Jones. I was supervised by Professor A. D. Momigliano. My studies were assisted by the Lloyd Scholarship of University College and the Lincoln Shelley Studentship of the University of London. I am grateful to Professor R. Browning for encouragement and help, and to Professor A. F. Norman for lending me voluminous notes of work on Libanius which was at that time entirely unpublished. At a later stage Professors G. Downey and J. Lassus helpfully answered requests for information. Dr. R. O. Davies, Dr. E. J. F. Primrose, and Professor R. E. F. Smith enabled one ignorant of Russian to learn from papers of Professor G. L. Kurbatov. Professor E. Kirsten provided me with a copy of his study, 'Die byzantinische Stadt'. Mr. P. R. L. Brown advised on the conversion of the thesis into a book.

The Research Board of Leicester University gave a grant towards the preparation of the final text. I owe a debt of gratitude to Professor A. Wasserstein and my colleagues in the Classics Department at Leicester for offering me a congenial and stimulating academic environment.

The two maps were drafted by Mr. T. Garfield. They include information taken from *Westermanns Atlas zur Weltgeschichte* (Braunschweig, 1965), 40, no. 3; R. Mouterde and A. Poidebard, *Le 'Limes' de Chalcis* (Paris, Geuthner, 1945), Map 1; G. Tchalenko, *Villages antiques de la Syrie du Nord* (Paris, Geuthner, 1953), vol. 2, Pl. XXXV; vol. 3, 57, fig. 7 (by H. Seyrig). Mr. F. A. Holmes read the proofs. Margaret and Rachel Liebeschuetz performed much arid and arduous work for the completion of the manuscript. All errors and omissions are my own.

J. H. W. G. L.

Leicester
April 1971

CONTENTS

MAPS
(*at end*)

The Territory of Antioch

Antioch, Communications and Frontier Defence in Syria

ABBREVIATIONS

Prosopographical References

O. Seeck has distinguished holders of the same name by Roman numerals placed after the name. These numerals are used in Foerster's edition and in most subsequent work on Libanius, including the present book.

A.J.A.	*American Journal of Archaeology*
A.J.P.	*American Journal of Philology*
Book of the Prefect	*The Eparchicon* of Leo the Wise
B.R. Syria	*B.R. 513 Geographical Handbook Series: Syria*
Bruns	C. G. Bruns, *Fontes iuris Romani antiqui*
B.Z.	*Byzantinische Zeitschrift*
C.E.R.P.	A. H. M. Jones, *Cities of the Eastern Roman Provinces*
Chr.	U. Wilcken and L. Mitteis, *Chrestomathie der Papyruskunde*
C.I.G.	*Corpus Inscriptionum Graecarum*
C.I.L.	*Corpus Inscriptionum Latinarum*
C.J.	*Codex Justinianus*
Cl. Phil.	*Classical Philology*
Cl. Rev.	*Classical Review*
Coll. Avell.	*Epistulae imperatorum pontificum aliorum . . . Avellana quae dicitur Collectio (C.S.E.L. xxxv)*
C.S.L.	*comes sacrarum largitionum*
C.T.	*Codex Theodosianus*
D.A.C.L.	Cabrol and Leclercq, *Dictionnaire d'archéologie chrétienne et de liturgie*
Ec. H. Rev.	*Economic History Review*
E.L.F.	*Julian, Epistulae, Leges, Fragmenta*, ed. J. Bidez and F. Cumont
E.S.A.R.	*An Economic Survey of Ancient Rome*, ed. T. Frank
F.I.R.	see under *Leges Saeculares*
G.C.	A. H. M. Jones, *The Greek City*
I.G.	*Inscriptiones Graecae*
I.G.L.S.	*Inscriptions grecques et latines de la Syrie*
I.G.R.R.	R. Cagnat, *Inscriptiones Graecae ad res Romanas pertinentes*
I.L.S.	H. Dessau, *Inscriptiones Latinae Selectae*
J.E.A.	*Journal of Egyptian Archaeology*
J.H.S.	*Journal of Hellenic Studies*
Joh. Eph. V. SS. Or.	John of Ephesus, *Vitae Sanctorum Orientalium*
J.R.S.	*Journal of Roman Studies*
J. Theol. S.	*Journal of Theological Studies*
Leges Saeculares (F.I.R. ii², 759–98)	*Fontes Iuris Romani Ante-Iustiniani*, vol. 2, 759–98

L.R.E.	A. H. M. Jones, *Later Roman Empire*
Mansi	J. D. Mansi, *Sacrorum conciliorum nova . . . collectio*
Not. Dig. Or.	*Notitia Dignitatum Orientalis*
Nov.	*Novella*
O.G.I.S.	W. Dittenberger, *Orientis Graecae Inscriptiones Selectae*
P.A.E.S.	*Publications of the Princeton University Archaeological Expedition to Syria 1904–5 and 1909*
P.A.P.S.	*Proceedings of the American Philosophical Society*
Pat. Or.	*Patrologia Orientalis*
P.B.S.R.	*Papers of the British School at Rome*
P.G.	J. P. Migne, *Patrologia Graeca*
P.L.	J. P. Migne, *Patrologia Latina*
P.P. Gal.	*praefectus praetorio Galliarum*
P.P.O.	*praefectus praetorio orientis*
P.U. Cpl.	*praefectus urbi* (Constantinople)
P.U.R.	*praefectus urbi* (Rome)
P.S.I.	*Papiri greci e latini*, Florence, 1912–
P.W.	Pauly–Wissowa(–Kroll), *Real-Encyclopädie der classischen Alter-tumswissenschaft*
Rev. bibl.	*Revue biblique*
Rh. M.	*Rheinisches Museum für Philologie*
S.E.H.H.W.	M. Rostovtzeff, *Social and Economic History of the Hellenistic World*
S.E.H.R.E.	M. Rostovtzeff, *Social and Economic History of the Roman Empire*[2]
T.A.P.A.	*Transactions of the American Philological Association*
V.D.I.	*Vestnik drevnei istorii*
V.L.U. ist.	*Vestnik Leningradskogo universiteta* (*istor. sektsiya*)
V. Mel.	*Vita Sanctae Melaniae Iunioris*
Y. Cl. St.	*Yale Classical Studies*

INTRODUCTION

THE fourth century A.D. was an age of change. The first decades saw the restoration of the stability of the Roman Empire, after a long period of anarchy, through the reforms of Diocletian and Constantine. The last quarter witnessed the battle of Adrianople, the entry of the Visigoths into the empire, and the beginning of the chain of events which culminated with the destruction of the empire in the West and its preservation in the East.

The well-being of the empire and the condition of its cities were linked. The state of its cities can be used as an index of the state of the part of the empire in which they were situated. Of all the provincial cities Antioch is by far the best known. This is largely due to the survival of the writings of the Antiochene orator Libanius. The letters and speeches of Libanius contain a great store of varied information which has been made accessible by the work of a succession of excellent scholars, notably Reiske, Sievers, Seeck, Pack, Petit, and Norman. The evidence of Libanius can be supplemented by the sermons of his pupil John Chrysostomus, by the *Chronicle* of John Malalas, and by archaeological remains.

From the point of view of the social historian the literary sources have a severe disadvantage: they were not originally composed for the purpose of informing later generations of the circumstances of the lives of their authors. Letters or speeches were occasioned by specific and often exceptional circumstances. The persistent routine of economic life and administration is simply taken for granted. Hence a reconstruction of the economy and government of Antioch based on Antiochene sources alone will be very incomplete. The historian must try to fill the gaps as well as he can by analogy with conditions elsewhere in the empire.

Parts of the picture remain sketchy in spite of this. It is possible to observe the basic stability of city life in the East but not to trace in detail the economic activities required to maintain large urban populations. We can describe the principal civic authorities but the detail of how city and territory were administered escape our knowledge.

The reforms of Constantine and Diocletian enabled the imperial administration to intensify its control of cities. At Antioch the consequences of the new system can be studied at close quarters. Libanius provides evidence of the selfishness and incompetence of the local oligarchy. The failings which provoked interference by the imperial governors are plain to see. But it is also clear that the interventions weakened the institutions of local self-government and thus made further extension of imperial control inevitable. We can observe how the municipal oligarchy lost control of the government of the city to the imperial governors and watch the development of new institutions adapted to the changed situation.

These trends in the public life of Antioch are of more than local interest. They represent a situation which has arisen at many periods of history: the problem of how to reconcile effective civic self-government with the claims of the centralized administration of the state within which the cities are situated. Placed in their immediate historical context, the developments at Antioch can be seen to be part of a larger pattern: the transformation of the classical world into that of the Middle Ages.

I

THE LIFE AND WRITINGS OF LIBANIUS

I. THE LIFE[1] AND PERSONALITY OF LIBANIUS

LIBANIUS was born in 314, two years after the defeat of Maxentius and the conversion of Constantine. Both parents belonged to leading families of Antioch. 'In this very great city', he was to recall, 'my family was one of the greatest—in education, in wealth, in public-spirited spending on shows and games, and in the eloquence which opposes the presumption of provincial governors. Some believe that my great-grandfather came from Italy. They have been misled by a speech of his composed in the language of the Italians. He did indeed know Latin, but he was not therefore an immigrant. And he was distinguished not only by knowledge of Latin but also by the power of divination.' The family of Libanius' father had lost property but his maternal uncles assisted his widowed mother in the upbringing of her children, and were leading figures in the council of the city. During the first forty or fifty years of Libanius' life members of his family, their kinsmen by marriage, and other close associates played a prominent role in the public life of Antioch. This family background left a lasting impression on Libanius' mind, even though he chose not to follow in the footsteps of his forefathers and occupy a leading position in the council of Antioch. He preferred

---

[1] On the life of Libanius see: L. Petit, *Essai sur la vie et la correspondance du sophiste Libanius* (Paris, 1866), in sympathy with the classical conventions of Libanius' writings and sensitive to the difference between courtly rhetoric and servile flattery; G. R. Sievers, *Das Leben des Libanius* (Berlin, 1868), a sound and thoughtful basis for the study of Libanius, though its chronology of the letters is superseded by Seeck's later study; O. Seeck, *Die Briefe des Libanius zeitlich geordnet* (Leipzig, 1906), fundamental for chronology and prosopography of Libanius' life; R. Foerster and K. Münscher, s.v. Libanius, *P.W.* xii. 2, cols. 2485 ff., contains a bibliography; P. Petit, *Libanius et la vie municipale à Antioche au IVe siècle après J.-C.* (Paris, 1955), a very good book containing a reliable and comprehensive exposition of the material and an authoritative discussion of its significance; A. F. Norman, *Libanius' Autobiography—Oration I* (Oxford, 1965), text, translation, and enlightening commentary.

B

to give his life to the heritage of Greek literature and to become a sophist.[1]

'I had reached my fifteenth year when there entered into me a fierce passion for the art of rhetoric. As a result the attraction of country life held no further interest for me. I sold my pigeons— pets that can become an obsession with a boy. I rejected chariot races and all kinds of stage shows. But the behaviour which produced the greatest astonishment among young and old alike was that I kept away from gladiatorial combats.' For five years he did little but study, following now the guidance of one teacher, now of another, but pursuing all the time his own longing to memorize as much as possible of the ancient authors.[2] Then at the age of twenty he decided to go to Athens to study at that recognized centre of Greek culture. Libanius' departure for Athens was the decisive act of his life. It represented rejection of the life of a civic politician and acceptance of that of a sophist. He made the decision public and final by allowing his mother to sell family property.

Libanius remained in Athens for four years (336–40). His gifts earned him a great reputation; he was offered an appointment and accepted it, but the jealous machinations of rivals forced him to give it up.[3] He left Athens in 340, and for the next fourteen years lived the unsettled life of a sophist who had not yet established firm roots anywhere, although his reputation already assured him of students and appointments. He spent three years at Constantinople, until rivals, allied with the proconsul, threatened his life; then he followed a summons from the council of Nicaea to open a school in their city. A little later, he accepted an invitation from Nicomedia to live and teach there. Afterwards he described these years as the happiest of his life. Here Julian, later emperor, made the acquaintance of Libanius' writings. He was not allowed to hear the outspokenly pagan sophist but managed to obtain copies of orations, which he admired greatly and used as models for his own.[4]

Then in 349 the fame of Libanius' achievements at Nicomedia and especially his panegyric of the Emperors Constantius and Constans resulted in his being recalled to Constantinople, where he received an official appointment with an imperial salary.

---

[1] *Or.* i. 1–5.   [2] *Or.* i. 8.   [3] *Or.* i. 16–27.
[4] *Or.* i. 30–75; on Julian: J. Bidez, *La Vie de l'empereur Julien* (Paris, 1930); A. J. Festugière, 'Julien à Macellum', *J.R.S.* xlvii (1957), 53–8.

Although he was reasonably successful at Constantinople and honoured with presents from the emperor, he was not happy. In the summer of 353 he managed to obtain leave to pay a visit to Antioch—the first after seventeen years. 'I saw the streets and gates of which I was so fond, I saw temples and colonnades and the time-worn walls of my home; I saw my mother now grey-haired, her brother not yet without a child, my elder brother already a grandfather. I saw the crowd of my schoolfriends, some as governors, others as advocates, and my father's friends now reduced to a few; the city seemed strong in the number of educated citizens; I was glad and apprehensive at the same time.' He need not have been. The visit proved a triumph.

He returned to Constantinople but could not settle down there any more. Early in 354 he was back at Antioch. All was not plain sailing. Libanius was on temporary leave of absence from his duties at Constantinople and he had to engage in a good deal of intrigue and to write numerous letters, full of pitiful descriptions of ill health, before he obtained the emperor's permanent permission to stay at Antioch. At the same time he was struggling to get pupils and an official appointment. Finally, all was well.[1] Libanius' vagabond existence was over; never again did he leave the city. In the year 355 begins the first series of the surviving letters, and with it our information on life at Antioch.

When Libanius returned home after an absence of eighteen years he found Antioch under the harsh rule of the Caesar Gallus, who was governing the Eastern provinces while his uncle the Emperor Constantius was occupied by the usurpation of Magnentius in the West. Gallus had clashed with the council, of which Libanius' uncle Phasganius was a member, over its failure to deal with the famine. The councillors were under arrest and their leaders threatened with death. Soon after Libanius' arrival Gallus connived at the lynching of the consular of Syria, and some time later allowed his soldiers to kill the praetorian prefect of the East and the quaestor Montius.[2]

The recall and execution of Gallus in 354 closed a chapter in Antiochene history. With short interruptions, the city had been

[1] *Or.* i. 96 ff. and Norman's commentary; Norman, 'The Family of Argyrius', *J.H.S.* lxxiv (1954), 44–8; P. Wolf, *Vom Schulwesen der Spätantike* (Baden Baden, 1950), 41.
[2] E. A. Thompson, *The Historical Work of Ammianus Marcellinus* (Cambridge, 1947), 54–71.

the residence of a ruler since 333, when Constantius, then Caesar, made his headquarters there. After he became emperor in 337, on the death of his father Constantine, he spent the winter of 338–9 at Antioch, and the city remained his residence until in 351 the murder of his brother and fellow emperor, Constans, forced him to leave for the West.[1] A little later he appointed Gallus. After the departure of Gallus, Antioch gradually lost its pre-eminence in the East, which had never been official, to Constantinople. Constantius and Julian were to make Antioch their residence for short periods. Valens resided there for seven years. But Theodosius, Libanius' last emperor, never came to Antioch at all.

This loss of imperial distinction was regretted by the people of Antioch, and Libanius from time to time expresses his dislike of Constantinople, the upstart rival of his native city. However, the conditions which had produced the pre-eminence of Antioch had not been favourable to the prosperity of its people. The needs of the Persian War had compelled Constantius to spend so much time at Antioch. Almost every spring from 337 until about 351, Persian armies had crossed the Tigris and invaded Mesopotamia. Constantius had been obliged to lead his forces against them in summer and drive them back. In 359 the Persians again invaded the empire on a very large scale and captured Amida. In 360 Constantius returned to Antioch to take command but could not prevent the loss of further fortresses.[2] Then in 363 came Julian's Persian campaign, and at last Jovian's peace treaty on terms unfavourable to the empire.[3]

These endless and often indecisive campaigns in Mesopotamia must have had a direct effect on the condition of Antioch, for it was the duty of the city to provide supplies for the army and to transport them over a long distance to the scene of war.[4] These heavy expenses, incurred over so long a period, seriously, and according to Libanius permanently, weakened the economic resources of the council of the city.[5]

Owing to the survival of much of Libanius' correspondence we are well informed of the first ten years of his life at Antioch

---

[1] O. Seeck, s.v. Constantius, *P.W.* iv. 1, cols. 1044–94.
[2] Ibid., cols. 1047–8, 1053–4, 1055, 1061–2, 1063–4, 1091–3.
[3] A. Piganiol, *L'Empire chrétien*, 146.
[4] See below, p. 90.   [5] *Or.* xlix. 2.

(354–64). The climax of this period was the brief rule of Julian and his stay at Antioch (July 362–March 363). The emperor, besides being an admirer of Libanius' writing, was by this time his personal friend. All the causes which Libanius had at heart flourished through Julian's support. 'I laughed and danced, joyfully composed and delivered my orations; for the altars received their blood offerings, and smoke carried the savour of burnt sacrifices up to heaven, the gods were honoured with their festivals which only a few old men were left to remember, the art of prophecy came again into its own, that of oratory to be admired. . . .' Later Libanius was saddened by Julian's difficulties with the people of Antioch, difficulties caused by lack of public spirit among the city councillors in time of famine and also by the strength of Christian feeling among the population as a whole.[1]

After 365 we have no more letters and we depend for information on the scrappy and disjointed information of the *Autobiography*. From 370 to 377 the Emperor Valens was at Antioch, perhaps again because of disputes with Persia. Military operations now took place in Armenia and affected Antioch less. Libanius narrowly escaped implication in the terrible magic trials following the Theodorus affair, a frightening demonstration of the power which the fear of magic practices exercised at the time, not only over the uneducated, like Valens, but over Libanius as well.[2]

In the year 378 Valens was killed in the battle of Adrianople, and the struggle for the life of the empire against the barbarians began. Some years later Libanius addressed a speech to the Emperor Theodosius, 'On avenging Julian', in which he argued that the disaster of Adrianople was the punishment of the gods for failure to avenge the supposed murder of Julian.[3] With this opens the later series of surviving speeches dealing with public affairs. For the years 388 and 390–3 the speeches are

---

[1] *Or.* i. 119–32; citation from Norman, *Libanius' Autobiography*; Sievers, *Leben*, 85–124; Bidez, *Vie de Julien*, 277–90; G. Downey, 'The economic crisis at Antioch under Julian the Apostate' in *Studies in Honor of A. C. Johnson* (Princeton, 1951), 312–21.

[2] *Or.* i. 171–8; Amm. xxix. 1. 1–44, 2. 1–11.

[3] *Or.* xxiv. 1. Norman, *Libanius, Selected Works* i. 501 shows that c. 13 refers to the Theodorus conspiracy of 371, not the murder of Gratian in 383 as suggested by I. Hahn, *Klio* xxxviii (1960), 225–32.

supplemented by letters. The picture of Antioch which we can reconstruct from this information is a gloomy one, as might be expected in view of the circumstances of the empire in these years.

A number of events stand out in this period. In 382 during a famine Libanius protested to the *comes orientis* Philagrius in the presence of an angry crowd about the public beating of some bakers.[1] It was probably in 383–4, when Proculus, the son of Tatian (later praetorian prefect), was governor, that Libanius received the honorary title of praetorian prefect.[2] This title gave powerful official standing to his influence in the town and outside it. It is probably no coincidence that the remarkable speeches of social criticism began to appear in these years. In 384–5 Icarius was *comes orientis*. Libanius' relations with him, at first very good, steadily deteriorated. The speeches inspired by this relationship contain a characteristic mixture of personal grievance and social good sense.[3] In the summer of 385 the praetorian prefect Cynegius stayed at Antioch while on his way to Egypt. Though a fanatical Christian, he was extremely polite to the pagan sophist, but part of his policy, the destruction of pagan temples, was hateful to Libanius.[4]

In 387 an imperial edict which once more demanded new taxes brought about a riot, in the course of which paintings and statues of the imperial family were overthrown. The famous Riot of the Statues was only a brief affair, but afterwards the city waited in fear and trembling for the emperor's punishment.[5] In April 388 the pagan Tatian succeeded Cynegius as praetorian prefect and remained in office until summer 392. Libanius was still alive to see his successor Rufinus pay a brief visit to Antioch. The letters are full of complaints of ill health and expectation of death. It is thought that he died some time in 393.[6]

The last years of Libanius' life were not happy. He appears to have been isolated at Antioch. His family no longer played an important part in local affairs; the governors were unfriendly. No sooner had he succeeded in obtaining the right to settle his property on his illegitimate son Cimon than attempts were made to force the son into the council. Similar attacks were directed

[1] *Or.* i. 205 ff., xxix. 6, xxxiv. 4.
[2] *Or.* i. 212, ibid. 221–4; on the title: P. Petit, *Byzantion* xxi (1951), 293.
[3] *Or.* i. 225 ff., xxvi–xxix.   [4] P. Petit, op. cit. 285–310.
[5] *Or.* i. 252–4, ix–xxiii; Joh. Chrys. *Hom. ad pop. Ant.* 21 (*P.G.* xlix. 15–222).
[6] Seeck, *Briefe*, 446–7.

against two assistants. Libanius himself was plagued with an accusation of treason which was dismissed and then resumed several times. In addition, the tide was running strongly against 'logoi' and in favour of Latin and Law. Libanius also suffered severely from gout. In 389 he lost his closest friend Olympius, in 391 the woman with whom he had lived for many years, and in 392 Cimon. But while Libanius was unhappy and an invalid there is no reason to suppose that his mind had deteriorated. The last speech which can be dated, that written against Florentius, perhaps at the instigation of the praetorian prefect Rufinus, shows the same qualities of accurate social observation and sympathy, and the same defects of personal prejudice and abuse, as the writings of earlier and happier years.[1]

While many of Libanius' political attitudes are those that might be expected of a member of his class, the landowning municipal aristocracy, his interest and observation extended further. This was partly the result of a strong sensibility towards the sufferings of others, which gave him sympathy with people like the shopkeepers or the peasants. He felt an urge to right their wrongs, although he would not have met them socially, nor thought of claiming the same legal rights for them as he would claim for men of his own class. But perhaps it was his profession even more than his sensitive nature that led him to observe his own class with a certain detachment. His decision to go to Athens with a view to becoming a sophist had involved a readiness to break with Antioch for the sake of 'logoi', and when he returned he was separated from members of his family and class by the fact that he was immune from their curial obligations.

Libanius' character shows many of the marks of the performing artist's temperament. The sight of an audience causes him to rejoice 'as Achilles rejoiced at the sight of his armour . . .'. He lists his requirements for happiness: 'a healthy body, a mind at rest, frequent declamations and applause at every one, pupils queueing up, pupils making progress, study at night, the sweat of performance at noon, distinctions, goodwill, love . . .'. He was oversensitive to slights, quick to feel that his worth was not recognized and to turn from friendship to enmity at a supposed insult. The *Autobiography* suggests a man morbidly concerned with himself, though we must allow for the fact that some of this concern is

---

[1] *Or.* xlvi; P. Petit, *Historia* v (1956), 499–500.

really a matter of style, drawing attention to similarities between Libanius' life and that of the great sophist Aristides, as described in the *Sacred Discourses*.[1]

Nevertheless, in comparison with Aristides, Libanius is very markedly a professional man, a professor rather than an artist. This is, I think, characteristic of the changed times. The extravagances of the great display artists had been shorn just as their rhetoric had become less diffuse. Aristides did little or no teaching, but travelled to speak at great festivals throughout the Hellenic world.[2] In the fourth century most of the festivals had long ceased. They were pagan, and in any case the cities lacked the funds to engage in cultural display, just as they could no longer afford display buildings. Libanius made many speeches at Antioch, and was admired as a creator and declaimer of speeches, but the greater part of his time was spent in the service of a regular paid post. Teaching was the central activity of Libanius' life; this involved him in many activities besides education, particularly wire-pulling. The result was to bring him in closer touch with his surroundings and with reality.[3]

One consequence of Libanius' close connection with education was that a matter of great concern to Aristides, the ancient conflict between rhetoric and philosophy, was of no interest to him. To one who was engaged in teaching the Hellenic tradition in the face of rivalry from Latin and Law, and criticism if not hostility from Christianity, rhetoric and philosophy were allies. Moreover, for Libanius the term 'philosopher' had lost much of its association with systematic thinking or reasonable understanding, and had come to describe a highly moral and self-controlled person—approaching the Christian ideal of saintliness.[4]

---

[1] i. 88, 51; G. Misch, *A History of Autobiography in Antiquity*, tr. by E. W. Dickes (London, 1950), vol. 2. 554–63; C. Behr, *Aristides and the Sacred Tales* (Amsterdam, 1968). Admiration and imitation of Aristides: Lib. *Ep.* 631, 1534, *Or.* lxi, lxiv, *Decl.* xlvi; R. Pack, *C.P.* xlii (1947), 17–20.

[2] On travels: A. Boulanger, *Aelius Aristide* (Paris, 1923), 111 ff.; on festivals: ibid. 28–37; in the Later Empire *private* patronage might take their place: A. Cameron, 'Wandering Poets', *Historia* xiv (1965), 470–509.

[3] P. Friedländer, *Johannes von Gaza und Paulus Silentiarius* (Berlin, 1912), 98–9, compares Libanius' praise of Antioch with Aristides' of Smyrna: '... von Antiochien kann man sich ein ungefähres Bild machen, von Smyrna nicht.'

[4] *Ep.* 123, Eustathius, a philosopher, ought to pray that Libanius' opponents are changed from their present perversity, Libanius not being a philosopher can pray that they remain as foolish as they are. Virtues of a philosopher: *Or.* xlii. 3,

While Libanius no longer sees philosophers and sophists as rivals, an unmistakable distinction between the sophistic and the philosophic outlook persists into this period.[1] Libanius is as unmistakably a sophist as Synesius, who in social background resembles Libanius, is a philosopher. Such arguments as those of Synesius' book on dream interpretation are quite strange to Libanius' thought.[2] It is also significant of the two ways of thought that Synesius wrote a political allegory, while Libanius scarcely used this type of writing.[3] Synesius' reaction to the offer of a bishopric is characteristic of the philosophical attitude lacking in Libanius. Libanius would have sympathized with Synesius' reluctance to divorce his wife in order to fit himself for consecration, but Synesius also hesitated because he might be asked to give up the philosophical doctrine of the everlasting nature of the world. Only if this and other truths were granted him, could he accept the priesthood and then only with the reservation that whereas he would be φιλομυθῶν in public, to his congregation, he would continue φιλοσοφῶν at home.[4] Libanius felt under no moral obligation towards any systematic doctrine and he does not make a distinction between different levels of thought.

It was not Libanius' habit to think systematically or consistently on any topic.[5] Libanius was of course well acquainted with the phrases of Hellenistic political theory[6] but he uses them as part of his rhetorical armoury, not because they are part of a systematic view of the world which he believes to be true. Thus in his panegyrics on the Emperor Julian[7] he maintains that the soldiers who proclaimed Julian Augustus had been instigated by

7–9. Egyptian philosophy: ibid. 16; cf. Amm. xxii. 16. 17 ff.; Lib. *Ep.* 720. Pythagoras mentioned with Plato or Aristotle: *Ep.* 1466, 1496, *Or.* xv. 28, xvi. 47. On conflict of Philosophy and Rhetoric, H. von Arnim, *Dio von Prusa* (Berlin, 1898), 4–114; Boulanger, op. cit. 210–65.

[1] See the very acute remarks of H. I. Marrou, *S. Augustin et la fin de la culture antique* (Paris, 1938), 169–73.

[2] Chr. Lacombrade, *Synésios de Cyrène* (Paris, 1951), 150–69.

[3] Ibid. 111–21. There are very few examples of allegorical interpretation of the classics in Libanius, though these occupied a central place in Julian's reform of paganism. Julian, unlike Libanius, was a philosopher; cf. Bidez, *Vie de Julien*, 248–60.

[4] Chr. Lacombrade, op. cit. 212–28; Synesius, *Ep.* 105.

[5] L. Harmand, *Libanius, discours sur les patronages* (Paris, 1955), 111–13, constructs an un-Libanian synthesis from diverse passages.

[6] F. Dvornik, *Early Christian and Byzantine Political Philosophy* (Washington, 1966); N. H. Baynes, *Byzantine Studies and Other Essays* (London, 1955), 48 ff., 168 ff.

[7] *Or.* xii. 59, xiii. 34; but also after Julian's death: xviii. 104.

a divinity. This is not meaningless flattery. Clearly, the gods might be expected to approve and support the accession of Julian. But it would be quite mistaken to conclude that Libanius was committed to a philosophy which elevated the rule of any emperor to the position of the chosen Vice-regent of God on earth. In fact, in the eyes of Libanius,[1] as indeed of Julian himself,[2] the ideal role of the ruler would seem to have been closer to that of civic magistrate than that of Hellenistic monarch.

Libanius' political outlook cannot be reconstructed from the commonplaces of political theory which he quotes, but only by observing his attitude in concrete cases. If we do this we note that the only branch of government toward which Libanius feels genuine emotion is city government. He cannot ignore the importance of the emperor and of his officials, but he really attributes to them only the negative function of keeping the cities safe to govern themselves.[3] In spite of his own formal Roman citizenship, he considers himself a citizen of Antioch, and although most governors come from his own class in the Greek East, he looks upon the administration as Roman and, to some extent, foreign.[4] There is no trace of that deep involvement with Rome which Western Christian writers like Augustine or Jerome felt almost in spite of themselves. It is characteristic that in the *Antiochicus* Libanius' sketch of the history of his native city stops short with the arrival of the Romans. Not a single Roman emperor is mentioned by name and only Diocletian and Galerius by allusion. That one capital of the empire was Constantinople made the empire no less Roman and no more agreeable. Constantinople was a rival city of Antioch. In the affairs of the empire as a whole, in its death struggle against the barbarians, he was only marginally interested. He praises Julian in the panegyrics,

---

[1] *Decl.* v. 84, 85, *Or.* l. 19, xxv. 57; Dvornik, op. cit. 669.

[2] Julian, *Or.* i. 10B, 14A, 16A, 45D; *Or.* ii. 88B–89A; *Ep. ad Them.* 261–2; *Misop.* 344D; cf. Dvornik, op. cit. 665.

[3] Petit, *Libanius*, 182–3.

[4] *Ep.* 668 (vol. 10, 609, l. 22), 825 (vol. 10, 745, ll. 18–21), 1004 (vol. 11, 133, ll. 10–11), 238, *Or.* xv. 25, x. 14. Contrast Aristides' *Roman Oration* (*Or.* xxvi); Boulanger, *Aristide*, 348 ff.; J. H. Oliver, 'The Ruling Power', *Trans. Am. Phil. Soc.*, n.s. xliii. 4 (1953), 871 ff. Aristides' appreciation of Rome's achievements does not exclude a sense of the immense superiority of Hellenic civilization. Libanius once praises Roman generosity with her citizenship, *Or.* xxx. 5, but he does not feel a Roman. On the reduced moral ascendancy of Rome in the fourth century: Bidez, *Vie de Julien*, 40 ff.

mistakenly, for not taking Gothic mercenaries on his Persian campaign. But his object is rhetorical, to contrast the civilized behaviour of Julian, who disdained to employ barbarians even against foreigners, with that of Constantius, whom he repeatedly accuses of having co-operated with barbarians against suspected rivals within the empire. There is no reason to suppose that Libanius had thought seriously about problems of defence or recruitment in the way Synesius was to do. His constructive thought is concerned only with such aspects of imperial administration as affected Antioch or at most the cities of the East.[1]

Libanius' educational views were closely related to his political attitude. He had nothing but scorn for Latin, the language in which much of the higher administrative work even in the East was still carried on. He resented that young men should desire to study Roman Law, even though this was the Law binding on every citizen of the empire. All Libanius' educational ideals derived from his passionate faith in 'logoi', in the power of the classical literature of Greece to inculcate in its reader both the practical and the moral qualities required for life. He felt that rhetorical education made men better morally, also that it made them more self-confident, more understanding, and more effective in every sphere of life in which a man of education might be expected to act. Finally, he believed that it was the common possession of 'logoi' that gave social relations, and indeed public life, the form and contents that made them worth while.[2] This faith was all the stronger for not being based on reason and analysis. Libanius gives no indication that he ever examined the relationship between his 'logoi' and the benefits they might bring.

Libanius assures us that the well-being of 'logoi' and of the pagan religion were necessarily linked. This proposition would not have been self-evident for an educated Christian, but follows from the close relationship that existed between religious feeling and love of 'logoi' in Libanius' own mind. It is not at all easy to get at his deepest views on either of these topics. Unlike Julian, he does not display his soul in his writings, and among the many references to gods and religious practices it is not at all obvious

[1] Letters to generals of barbarian origin: see below, p. 114. Praise of Julian: xviii. 169; Julian's Gothic contingent: Amm. xxiii. 27; Constantius' use of barbarians: *Or.* xviii. 33, 70, 92, 113; xii. 62.

[2] *Or.* xlix. 33; cf. A. J. Festugière, *Antioche païenne et chrétienne* (Paris, 1959), 217–25.

which represent his own feelings and which are literary reminiscences or rhetorical commonplaces.[1]

Libanius was certainly moved by religious art and ceremony,[2] but he also seems to have believed that gods really existed and answered prayer,[3] were in general concerned for the maintenance of morality,[4] and protected the old and the weak.[5] But in his deeper feelings he was perhaps more concerned with the gods as patrons of cities[6] or individuals, and so endowed with some of the arbitrariness of patrons, than he was with their role as embodiments of ideals of morality.[7] He felt some personal emotion towards the healing god, Asclepius.[8] His devotion to the patron gods of literature, Apollo and Hermes, seems more literary and conventional.[9] It is difficult to establish what Libanius thought about paganism as a whole or how he pictured the relationship of the multitude of gods to the physical world or to each other.[10] In the writings of Libanius the individual gods appear in extremely traditional roles. Dionysus will help the vines of his worshippers.[11] Artemis is thanked for saving the lives of his pupils by making them insist that her festival should be a holiday.[12]

References to the city gods of Antioch and indeed to those of other cities are relatively numerous.[13] Many of these references are in contexts which make them traditionally appropriate.[14] But there is more to it than that. It is surely not a coincidence that Julian combined the revival of paganism with a considerable effort to strengthen civic autonomy and to reduce the establishment of the central administration.[15] Belief in the city as the essential form of social organization, and in the value of the

[1] J. Misson, *Recherches sur le paganisme de Libanius* (Louvain, 1914).

[2] *Or.* lx. 6; cf. A. D. Nock, 'Sapor I and the Apollo of Bryaxis', *A.J.A.* lxvi (1962), 307–10.

[3] *Ep.* 616, 813, 822, 900.

[4] *Or.* xlii. 50, liii. 29, *Ep.* 390, 500.   [5] *Or.* xxx. 20.

[6] Refs. in Petit, *Libanius*, 192–3; Misson, op. cit. 74 n. 5; Chr. Lacombrade. 'L'Empereur Julien et la tradition romaine', *Pallas* ix (1960), 155–64.

[7] See the vague but unmistakable religiosity of *Or.* i. τύχη is a real divinity, though never associated with a specific cult.

[8] *Or.* i. 143, *Ep.* 706–8; 1303, 1534.

[9] *Or.* xv. 79, xxxi. 43; λόγιοι θεοί: *Or.* i. 234–5, 238; 274, *Ep.* 907, 1051, 1085, 1089; Norman, *Libanius' Autobiography*, xix.

[10] *Or.* xxx. 34 is a rhetorical argument, not a personal philosophy.

[11] *Ep.* 1212.   [12] *Or.* v.

[13] Petit, *Libanius*, 192–3; Misson, *Paganisme*, 74 n. 5.

[14] e.g. in *Or.* xi and in speeches on behalf of Antioch, such as *Or.* xix or xx.

[15] S. Mazzarino, *Aspetti sociali del quarto secolo* (Rome, 1951), 186.

cults of the city are different aspects of the same attitude of cultural conservatism.

In the fourth century there entered into men of even the highest social class and education a readiness to explain catastrophical or even merely striking events in terms of direct intervention by a deity.[1] In spite of the classical sobriety of his general attitude[2] Libanius was touched by this aspect of the spirit of the age. In the section of the *Antiochicus* concerned with the early history of Antioch he relates a significant number of miraculous signs. He wishes to show that Antioch had always been a pious city and one that was particularly dear to the pagan gods.[3] Many years later he was to ascribe the defeat of Adrianople to the anger of the gods at the failure to avenge the murder of Julian.[4] In 387 Libanius addressed the Emperor Theodosius, pleading for his city after the Riot of the Statues, and like John Chrysostomus he placed responsibility for the riot on demons.[5] He concludes the *Autobiography* with the announcement that famine was afflicting Constantinople: the insults he had suffered in the person of his son were being punished in a manner recalling the way Apollo had avenged the wrong done to his priest's daughter in Book I of the *Iliad*. 'That plague lasted for nine days: this famine has been wasting the city for four months now. If the punishment of one man is a great consolation to his victim think what it must mean for a city to be punished—and so large a city too.'[6]

But perhaps these and similar passages owe more to rhetoric, and to the exploitation of beliefs of contemporaries, than to profound conviction. Libanius could continue to include in his threnodies the commonplace of criticism of the gods for allowing the calamity to happen, without taking up the theological issues

---

[1] Notably the treatment of the Great Persecution by Lactantius in *De mortibus persecutorum*, and by Eusebius in the *Ecclesiastical History*; also of the fall of Rome by Augustine in *De Civitate Dei* and by Orosius in his *Historiae adversus paganos*; cf. S. Mazzarino, *The End of the Ancient World* (1966), 58–76.

[2] *Or.* xviii shows that for all his admiration of Julian, the emperor's Neoplatonic mysticism was quite strange to Libanius.

[3] *Or.* xi. 85–6, 95–8, 108, 113–18; Petit, *Libanius*, 206.

[4] *Or.* xxiv; I. Hahn, *Klio* xxxviii (1960), 225–32.

[5] *Or.* xix. 7, 30, 31, 34; cf. i. 252. The demons do not figure in speeches written in 387 *after* the pardon. They are a scapegoat rather than a firmly believed explanation; cf. Joh. Chrys. *Hom. ad pop. Ant.* 15. 1, 21. 1, 3.

[6] *Or.* i. 283–5; Norman, *Libanius' Autobiography*, 234–5.

which would certainly have been raised by Christian writers.[1] He could describe how Nicomedia had been destroyed in spite of the fact that the gods had co-operated in its foundation, without feeling challenged to explain that this disaster did not invalidate pagan worship.[2] He could point out that the temple of Apollo at Daphne was burnt at a time when sacrifices had been revived,[3] without answering the obvious Christian conclusion that the conflagration had proved the futility of the sacrifices. This behaviour suggests that Libanius was not inclined to look for divine judgements in history unless it helped his argument of the moment to do so.

On the other hand, Libanius shared the widespread contemporary belief in the efficacy of magic.[4] A dream, combined with an unusually sustained and disabling attack of gout, was sufficient to convince him that he was the victim of magic practices. This conviction was confirmed when there was found in his classroom a chameleon mutilated in such a manner as to produce by sympathetic magic precisely Libanius' symptoms.[5]

Again, like many of his contemporaries Libanius had in his character a strong element of puritanism. He reveals this in the early chapters of his autobiography, in which he insists on the sobriety of his childhood and student days. 'In my presence everyone expected everybody to behave decently, for I never so much as touched a ball all the time I was at Athens and I kept myself well away from the carousals and company of those who visited the houses in the meaner quarters at night and I made it quite clear . . . that the singing girls who have stripped many a man bare sang to me in vain.' Puritanism also finds expression in his concern for morals and his disapproval of the theatre and chariot racing.[6]

---

[1] *Or.* lxi. 3 ff., 11, 14, lx. 5, 13–14. The same τόπος in xvii. 4, xviii. 284; only the last takes up the theological challenge; ibid. 296.

[2] *Or.* lxi. 3 ff.   [3] *Or.* lx. 5.

[4] Libanius was accused of magic practices five times: *Or.* i. 43, 62 ff., 98, 194, 239.

[5] *Or.* i. 245–50; *Or.* xxxvi; Campbell Bonner, 'Witchcraft in the lecture room of Libanius', *T.A.P.A.* (1932) 32–44; Festugière, *Antioche*, 453–8.

[6] Quotation of i. 23 based on Norman's translation. The text is doubtful. Other examples: *Or.* i. 5. 7, 12, ii. 12. Concern for morals: *Or.* liii. 6, lxii. 24 ff. Theatre: *Or.* lxiv, *Pro saltatoribus*, of 361 is surely a rhetorical display, not a development of Libanius' opinion. In 384, *Or.* xxvi. 25 Libanius wished dancers would leave Antioch; *Or.* xlii. 8 Thalassius praised for not attending theatre; chariot-racing an unworthy interest: *Or.* xxxv. 13–14.

Libanius' paganism was certainly not superficial. All indications point in the same direction. He omitted all Christian topics from his panegyric of Constantius and Constans.[1] He enthusiastically supported Julian both during and after his short reign. He tactfully but unmistakably asserted a pagan point of view under the strongly Christian Emperor Theodosius.[2] In short, through all his life Libanius demonstrated his rejection of Christianity and his adherence to the old religion.

What was the root of such partisanship? Various causes might be suggested—conservatism, a delight in pagan ritual, a revulsion from the Greek of the Bible, the lack of logic shown by men who taught Homer while believing that the gods of Homer were demons. But these factors would move a theological mind like Julian's[3] more than they would Libanius' matter-of-fact and pragmatic outlook. Christian intolerance and Christian sectarian rivalries he must have disliked, but the writings do not give the impression that these were the real cause of his opposition. Monks he certainly loathed,[4] but Libanius' attitude to Christianity, which is already reflected in his earliest writings, would appear to have been formed before the monastic movement had become really prominent.[5]

It is more likely that Libanius saw the Christian religion as a dangerous rival of his beloved 'logoi'. Since the Hellenistic age the rhetorical education had come to be considered the central and essential element of civilization—the gods' greatest gift to man. Thus it had become closely associated with religion, in addition to being something of a religion in itself. Preoccupation with the arts of the Muses was considered not only an aesthetic and practical but also a moral training. The benefits of education could even be thought of as freeing the soul from earthly passion and fitting it for everlasting life.[6]

Libanius' writings suggest that he regarded rhetorical education in this light. True, in accordance with a personal outlook on

---

[1] *Or.* lix; P. Petit, 'Libanius et la "Vita Constantini" ', *Historia* i (1956), 562–82.

[2] Not only the famous *Pro templis* (*Or.* xxx) but also *Or.* vii. 8–12, xx. 48 ff.

[3] Cf. the rescript forbidding Christians to teach rhetoric: J. Bidez et F. Cumont, *Juliani epistulae et leges*, 61c.

[4] *Or.* xxx, lii. 10, ii. 32, xlv. 26, *Ep.* 1367; Festugière, *Antioche*, 239.

[5] See below, p. 234.

[6] H. I. Marrou, *Histoire de l'éducation dans l'antiquité* (2nd edn., Paris, 1950), 147.

life which allowed little expectation of life after death[1] he could only offer the worshipper of the Muses hope of everlasting fame.[2] Nevertheless, he too could talk of 'logoi' as 'not least of the sacred rites',[3] and was unshakeable in the belief that the classical Greek literature was the most precious possession of man, and its study the most effective means of achieving a finer humanity.

A recent aspect of the religion of the Muses was the conception of 'the Hellenes' which Julian made the designation for the adherents of his reformed paganism, but which Libanius and his friends are seen to have held a few years earlier. It is the idea of a community of men educated in the rhetorical tradition, a community not of birth nor of wealth but of education. Associated with it are the moral virtues of humanity and pity,[4] and the duty of mutual help between members. When a prominent Hellene is sick this is of concern to all. When young Jamblichus of a great philosophical family travels to Constantinople he is worthy of τιμή from all young Hellenes.[5] For Libanius the fact that a man was a rhetor and possessed of 'logoi' was in itself a reason why he should receive assistance. Thus the Hellenes formed an ideal community which bore some resemblance to the Christian church.

For a Christian it was impossible to accept the 'religion of the Muses'. However he might admire literature, preoccupation with it would only be the preparation for a more important study, the study of the Scriptures and of the Christian doctrines.[6] The community in which he sought to be a member was not a communion of education but of faith. Thus the acceptance of Christianity brought with it the deposition of 'logoi' from the supreme place among human possessions, and it is reasonable to suppose that of all the innovations produced by the Christian religion this was the one which Libanius felt most deeply.[7]

---

[1] Survival after death: *Ep.* 959, 963, 1068, 1396. Except in consolatory contexts survival has no importance for Libanius.

[2] *Or.* xxiii. 21.   [3] *Or.* xiii. 1; cf. lxii. 8.

[4] *Or.* xix. 13, xv. 25, xliii. 18, *Ep.* 278 (361), 1120 (363), *Or.* xiv. 12.

[5] *Ep.* 316 (357), 572 (357); cf. 982 (390).

[6] Marrou, *Histoire de l'éducation*, 421–6.

[7] See also Petit, *Libanius*, 197–216; Festugière, *Antioche*, 229–40; Piganiol, *L'Empire chrétien*, 239. To my mind, Piganiol's 'une religion de professeur' comes nearest to the emotional centre of Libanius' attitude.

2. THE LETTERS OF LIBANIUS

The network of personal relationships that centred on Libanius is vividly illustrated by his surviving correspondence.[1] The letters comprise the business correspondence of a man who was both an active schoolmaster and a prominent citizen, linked by ties of kin, friendship, or professional activities to many leading families in cities of the Roman East, from Alexandria to Constantinople.

His school figures most prominently in Libanius' correspondence.[2] Parents have to be reassured that their sons, living away from home at Antioch, are not succumbing to the temptations of the town, not mixing with the wrong people, but doing well at their studies.[3] Rumours have to be refuted.[4] Former students have to be helped in their careers. Many are commended to a provincial governor. Sometimes the recommendation is vague.[5] Sometimes it contains a request for a specific appointment.[6] To help ex-pupils was to advance the school. Well-placed old pupils were a good recommendation. Besides they further increased Libanius' influence and his ability to help present pupils.

Libanius' connections made him useful to many. Travelling, for instance, was a laborious business, but it could be made easier if a traveller was able to arrange for private hospitality in places along his route. Many of Libanius' letters were written to obtain for their bearer the hospitality of the addressee. When Hyperechius at Ancyra complained that many travellers from Antioch passed through Ancyra but none had brought him a letter, Libanius explained that if he had given these men letters they would have expected hospitality: 'All of them, I was well aware, wanted to stay with you and to have a good time and you would have seemed rude if you refused to put them up. But to entertain guests more numerous than the leaves would have been burdensome—not so much on account of the expense but because you

[1] On epistolography: Sykutris s.v. Epistolographie, P.W. suppl. 5, cols. 185–220; H. Peter, Der Brief in der römischen Literatur (Leipzig, 1901); O. Seeck s.v. Symmachus, P.W. 2, Reihe iv. 1, cols. 1155–8; B. R. Rees s.v. Epistolography, O.C.D., 2nd ed.; O. Seeck, Die Briefe des Libanius zeitlich geordnet is still essential for the understanding of the letters of Libanius.
[2] P. Petit, Les Étudiants de Libanius (Paris, 1957), passim.
[3] 'Report' letters: Ep. 141, 190, 139, 324, 1165, 681, 345, and others.
[4] Ep. 248, 449, 129, 419, 373, 428, 475.
[5] e.g. Ep. 743.　　　　　　　　　　[6] Ep. 154, 161–2, 807.

would have been obliged to neglect the business of your estate. And I knew that these men enjoy their food but are incapable of gratitude for hospitality, and think it a mark of manliness to speak ill of their host.'[1]

Furthermore, if a man had business in a strange town, it was useful to have support from local residents and if possible from an imperial official.[2] For such a man Libanius was a godsend. As soon as it was known that a friend of his had obtained a post Libanius was overwhelmed by demands for letters of recommendation.[3] Help was not sought by private travellers only; even a newly appointed governor might seek letters of commendation to leading men of his province.[4]

The fourth century was an age of close government control modified by influence. Influence and money could in general achieve anything, and here was another use for Libanius' connections. He might merely ask an official to help a traveller, but he might also seek to influence a judge in favour of the accused.[5] Official aid might be sought to help a man in private business[6] or to obtain his appointment to a public post[7]—often a post from which he was legally disqualified.[8] Libanius very frequently sent such letters to provincial governors. Occasionally he even wrote to Constantinople to obtain a favourable decision at court.[9] Libanius made requests to the officials at Antioch too, and a considerable part of his time was occupied with the making of them.[10] But detailed information on these activities of Libanius is only available for the requests he made by correspondence to officials elsewhere.

The letters throw light not only on the social relations of Libanius and his circle but also on their culture. The sending of a letter was more than an act of conveying information; it was an expression of civilized living. Letter-writing was an art, not only for Libanius, but for all educated people of his time. It gave men a chance to use in everyday life the knowledge of classical literature, and rules of rhetoric, the sensitivity in matters of style

---

[1] *Ep.* 704; request for use of public post; *Ep.* 268. D. Gorce, *Les Voyages, l'Hospitalité et le Port des Lettres dans le Monde chrétien des IVᵉ et Vᵉ siècles* (Paris, 1925).

[2] *Ep.* 595–6.   [3] *Ep.* 291.   [4] *Ep.* 394, 397, 396.

[5] *Ep.* 56, 83, 105, 110, 151, 163, 394, 400.

[6] *Ep.* 108, 1438.   [7] *Ep.* 1449, 545, 1260, 1224, 841.

[8] See below, pp. 178–9.   [9] *Ep.* 864–8, 850–2, 904–9, 922–30.

[10] *Or.* i. 108–9, *Ep.* 351, 589, 1437.

which they had acquired at school, together with inborn wit and
inventiveness.

. . . and the woman accepted the invitation and there she was inside the house or rather inside the net. For the savage and arrogant
fellow shut her up in a bedroom and told her that she ought to
thank Fortune seeing that she who lived by the work of her hands
had an opportunity of sleeping with a man who could afford to be
generous. But when he found her nobly shielded by modesty, and
not to be persuaded with promises or terrified with threats, he laid
hands on her and used force. Purity of character gave her extra
strength. Then Lucianus bared his sword, oh gods! . . .

This narrative forms part of a business letter in which Libanius
asks the provincial governor to punish a rape committed by
Lucianus, a minor official. It is nevertheless a short ἔκφρασις.[1]
Marrou has well observed that men educated in rhetoric never
ceased to be students, but continued all their lives to write the
exercises they had written at school.[2]

Gregory of Nazianzus praised as merits of letter-writing:
clarity, moderation in the use of rhetorical figures, and moderate
length.[3] He rejected the use of official titles as bad style. Libanius
seems to have agreed. He adheres quite rigidly to the practice of
not dealing with more than one principal topic in a letter. Many
of his letters are composed in three sections; first, compliments or
expressions of friendship for the addressee, then a passage in
praise of the bearer, and finally the main business. Sometimes
one or two sections are left out. Very rarely does Libanius go on
to some subject quite unconnected with the purpose of the letter.
Mere news and information were left to the bearer to tell[4]—
sometimes for reasons of security as well as style.[5]

The convention of omitting all that did not appertain to the
strict business of the letter often makes the letter-writers appear
unconcerned about the events of their time. In fact it is not fair to
blame, for instance, Symmachus on the evidence of letters for
being indifferent to the struggle for survival of the empire. Letters
were not the place for reflections on public affairs.[6]

---

[1] *Ep.* 636.
[2] Marrou, S. *Augustin*, 89 ff. Praise of letter style: *Ep.* 233, 606, 716, 1034.
Letters used as school models: *Ep.* 128, 695.
[3] Greg. Naz. *Ep.* 51 (*P.G.* xxxvii. 105–8).   [4] *Ep.* 753, 1429.
[5] *Ep.* 207 (vol. x, 190, l. 6); 402 (vol. x, 397, l. 3).
[6] On contraction of subject-matter of letters: Peter, op. cit. 101–77.

A letter was highly valued because it was personal.[1] Yet the letters reveal very little of the personality of their author, except in as much as his style of Greek is individual and recognizable. Personal feelings, except formal and conventional ones, of longing, friendship, jealousy at having the friendship of another preferred, consolation for a bereavement and so on, had no place in letters. Nor had descriptions of personal experiences, or expressions of private ideas, wishes, or opinions.

A letter of Libanius may express more clearly the personality of the man to whom it was written than that of the writer. In all circumstances Libanius was adept at assimilating his manner to that of the man he was dealing with. He is not normally obsequious but there are among his letters a few written in tones of extreme flattery. Outstanding among these are letters to Modestus[2] and to the praetorian prefect Tatian.[3] Both men were very powerful, and Modestus, at any rate, rather a rough character. Obviously Libanius found it necessary to flatter them rather crudely. To another very powerful person, the praetorian prefect Anatolius, Libanius wrote letters of astonishing insolence, but not, as Piganiol suggests, because he wished to flatter a rival of Anatolius.[4] Anatolius was a family friend, a friend of Libanius' uncle Phasganius, who enjoyed the rhetorical insults of the letters and very probably provoked them in his letters to Libanius.[5]

When written to people who shared a love of ancient Greek tradition, the letters express a friendship as conventional as their form. This tradition implies passionate devotion,[6] sympathy in good or bad fortune, and regular attentions paid by means of letters or more definite favours. Not to write when there was a chance, when an acquaintance was travelling between the towns of the two correspondents, was to do one's friend an

---

[1] *Ep.* 412 (vol. x, 408, l. 13).

[2] e.g. *Ep.* 389, 163. 6; 232, 1216; Modestus' character: Amm. xxix. 1. 10, xxx. 4.
2: 'subagreste ingenium'.

[3] e.g. *Ep.* 899.

[4] *L'Empire chrétien*, 99. On Anatolius: A. F. Norman, *Rh. M.* c (1957), 253–9.

[5] *Ep.* 492 (vol. x, 468, ll. 10 ff.); *Ep.* 578 (vol. x, 542, ll. 20 ff.); cf. *Ep.* 1397, adapted to character of severe and fanatically pagan governor of Syria, Alexander. *Ep.* 1368 and 1367 were written to Nicocles and Modestus about the same riot at Constantinople, but with regard to the addressees' susceptibilities. Also note the more pronounced literary character of letters written to educated orators, particularly to the sophist Demetrius of Tarsus.

[6] *Ep.* 435, 644, 1515.

njury.[1] On the other hand, it was bad manners to write a letter to a stranger. The opening of a friendship required special justification.[2] There was good reason for this. A relationship begun with a letter might easily lead to demands for favours, which it would be the friend's duty to grant.[3] Here the bonds of literary friendship, which united the educated men of the empire, were at variance with the requirements of impartial administration.

Nevertheless, these concrete expressions of friendship belong to the heart of the institution. It is there that the business and ideal sides of a correspondence such as that of Libanius meet. The needs of life called for relations between men of different cities, and the literary tradition gave such relations form and beauty, making them a means by which the literary learning, even of a man who was not a professional artist, could be employed creatively.[4]

The ideal function of the letter, uniting men of education by expressing admiration for the forms and traditions of the classical past, was developed and expanded when the literary letter came to be used by officials of the Christian Church. The letters of Christian bishops of the fourth and fifth centuries, of Theodoret,[5] of Augustine, of Basil, of Gregory of Nyssa, follow the same conventions as the letters of Libanius.[6]

It is in the content that we must look for differences. If the idea which united the correspondents of Libanius was love of the literary tradition, the letters of the bishops were an expression of common faith and practice, and a means of maintaining them. There was of course a long Christian tradition of letter-writing

---

[1] *Ep.* 212, 326, 410.   [2] *Ep.* 448, 95, 645, 836.
[3] See below, pp. 192 ff.
[4] Ed. Schwartz, *Die Ethik der Griechen* (Stuttgart, 1951), 191. 'Sie schufen sich so einen stillen Hort der Gemeinsamkeit, in dem sie hausten und die alte griechische Vorstellung bewahrten von einer übersichtlichen Umgebung mit klaren Grenzen, fester Geschlossenheit und natürlicher Harmonie. So haben sie einen Hafen angelegt in dem die feiner veranlagten Naturen sich aus dem Sturm und Getöse der Zeit des allgemeinen Zusammenbruches retten mochten.' This description of Epicurean friendship cannot be bettered as a summing-up of the friendship of literary letters.
[5] Theodoret, *Ep.* 7, 8, 13, 10; with Theod. *Ep.* 48 cf. Lib. *Ep.* 46 or 387; with Theod. *Ep.* 50 cf. Lib. *Ep.* 556.
[6] Cf. A. Puech, *Histoire de la littérature grecque chrétienne* (Paris, 1930), 304–13; R. R. Ruether, *Gregory of Nazianzus* (Oxford, 1969), 124–8. Letter as instrument of church unity: Basil, *Ep.* 204.

going back to the epistles of St. Paul. But when the bishops were educated men they adopted the conventions of literary letters, and the forms which had been used to express literary friendship were now used to express and to achieve religious communion. The literary letter gained a new function, a purposefulness it had never possessed before. The collections of letters of Basil or Augustine represent an important example of the adaptation of the classical tradition to Christian use—a process in which Libanius, to judge by his writings, was not in the least interested.

Fear of offending against literary propriety was not the only fear of fourth-century letter-writers. At the trials which the Emperor Valens held at Antioch, thousands of letters were used to incriminate people, and Libanius was thankful that none of his were produced.[1] We must remember too that Libanius usually anticipated some kind of public reading for his letters. As he read aloud fine specimens of letter-writing which he had received,[2] so he expected correspondents to read his letters to friends and acquaintances. Moreover Libanius wrote with posterity in mind. He intended to publish his copy-book[3] of letters, and the recipient of a letter might hope to be himself remembered for as long as the letters were read.[4] Libanius therefore tried to give his letters a timeless quality and this meant the omission of merely topical information. Neither he nor his contemporaries thought that the ability to provide a vivid and truthful picture of contemporary life was what made a good letter-writer.

When we consider the letters as historical documents, we must not overlook the possibility that, like some other letter collections, they have been edited for publication.[5] We know of one case. When a correspondent had been offended by some well-meant banter Libanius changed the address on the file-copy of his letter. Thus there would be no need for the friend to worry that his name would go down to posterity attached to this 'rude' letter.[6]

---

[1] *Or.* i. 175, *Ep.* 1264.   [2] *Ep.* 315.

[3] On Libanius' copy-books: Seeck, *Briefe*, 14 ff. Corrected by Silomon, *De Libanii Libris I–VI* (Göttingen, 1909). I have not seen this; but it is summarized s.v. Libanius, *P.W.* xii. 2, cols. 2523–6 (Foerster and Münscher). Libanius mentions his copy-book in *Ep.* 88, 1218, 1307. Silomon and Foerster–Münscher reject Seeck's view that Libanius published the books himself.

[4] Seeck, *Briefe*, 18 on Lib. *Ep.* 773.

[5] Cf. C. E. Stevens, *Sidonius Apollinaris* (Oxford, 1933), 60; Peter, op. cit. 150–8.

[6] Seeck, *Briefe*, 18–19 on *Ep.* 933, 915.

Libanius' correspondence has not been completely preserved.[1] One thin patch within the correspondence includes the last year of Constantius' reign and the period of Julian's stay at Antioch. We would scarcely guess that Constantius spent the winter 360–1 and part of the year 361 at or near the city. But even over the remaining portions of the ten-year period covered by our letter collection, the number of letters preserved varies from year to year, and it is likely that a greater proportion has been preserved for some periods than for others. There are relatively few letters for the years 354 and 355, the first years of Libanius' correspondence. This may be chance, but in any case these gaps must be taken into consideration by the historian.[2]

The features I have just described combine to limit the amount of historical information to be gained from a study of Libanius' letters. They make it particularly hazardous to draw conclusions from Libanius' silence. Libanius scarcely mentions Christians, but it would be absurd to conclude that they were not extremely important at Antioch. He scarcely mentions trading journeys either, but it is again a questionable deduction that such journeys were few.

3. THE ORATIONS OF LIBANIUS

For the historian the value of the speeches that fill the first four volumes of Foerster's edition of Libanius is that they enable him to observe public life at Antioch from close quarters in a way that is not possible for any other provincial city of the empire. No other such set of speeches exists. The nearest contemporary parallels are found in the writings of Synesius. Synesius was born into the same social class as Libanius and was filled with the same love of the Hellenic tradition.[3] But Synesius wrote from a provincial rather than a city point of view—perhaps an indication that city patriotism was weaker in Cyrenaica than in Syria.

---

[1] Preservation was not complete. *Ep.* 46 mentions five letters sent to Modestus, of which only two survive, *Ep.* 37 and 38. *Ep.* 387 mentions three letters sent to Thalassius; only one, *Ep.* 879, survives. On this cf. Seeck, *Briefe*, 21.

[2] Seeck's arrangement, ibid., 316–471, provides the best demonstration of the chronological order of the letters.

[3] Syn. *Catastasis* (*P.G.* lxvi. 1565–78); Lacombrade, *Synesios de Cyrène*, 231–6; *Ep.* 57–8, against Andronicus; on these Lacombrade, op. cit. 237– 3.

To get a comparable view of public life in cities we must go back about two hundred years to the cities of Bithynia, as they figure in Pliny's letters to Trajan, and in the speeches of Dio Chrysostomus, at a time when city councils were still able to take significant initiatives in the government of their cities.[1] A comparison of the Bithynia of Pliny and Dio with Libanius' Antioch provides a clear illustration of the changed condition of cities under the Late Empire.

Some of the speeches show Libanius in the role of festival orator in a tradition ultimately going back to Isocrates.[2] Such are the panegyrics of the Emperors Constantius and Constans,[3] and of Julian,[4] and the *Antiochicus*.[5] The three threnodies[6] belong to a related genre and are more formal still. But even the most formal and elaborate orations of Libanius are simpler and more factual than those of his predecessors, Aristides or Dio Chrysostomus. Libanius liked even his panegyrics to be based on authentic information.[7] We know that for *Oration* xviii he collected material from eyewitnesses about Julian's Persian campaign,[8] and the detail of the speech, for instance the account of how Julian arranged for a corn fleet from Britain to bring aid to devastated areas of Gaul,[9] shows that Libanius had taken similar trouble to gather information about the Gallic campaign.

But the bulk of the orations does not belong to this formal type. The less formal orations deal with topical issues of public life. They reflect the fact that a famous sophist was still a great public figure and by virtue of his position played a part in the public life of the city. He was obliged to defend himself, to support his

[1] Especially Dio Chrys. *Or.* xlvi–xlviii, l, li, political speeches delivered at Prusa; H. von Arnim, *Dio von Prusa*, 309–12.

[2] Menander in *Rhetores Graeci*, ed. L. Spengel, iii. 422–3 prescribes rules for display speeches.

[3] *Or.* lix.

[4] *Or.* xii spoken before the emperor: i. 127, *Ep.* 785; *Or.* xiii spoken before the emperor: *Ep.* 736.

[5] *Or.* xi spoken in part at Olympic games of 356, if *Ep.* 36 refers to it; cf. Petit, *Libanius*, 126. Translation and commentary by G. Downey in *P.A.P.S.* ciii (1959), 652–85.

[6] *Or.* lxi spoken to four: *Ep.* 33; *Or.* lx distributed only: *Ep.* 785; *Or.* xvii not spoken: *Ep.* 1264.

[7] *Ep.* 1322, 610, 436, 491, 867, 1111, 1106.

[8] *Ep.* 1220, 1434; cf. 1508.

[9] *Or.* xviii. 83 ff.; cf. also description of cities, ibid. 35; perhaps based on Julian's lost συγγραφή (Lib. *Ep.* 35. 6; Eunapius, frg. 14. 7).

clients, to participate in the numerous intrigues that constituted the relationship between citizens and the imperial administration. Form and language of the speeches often recall Demosthenes, but the contents reflect their own times. Important decisions are no longer made after public debate in assembly, council, or law court, but by decisions of a few individuals at Antioch or at Constantinople. Accordingly, the speeches do not read as if they were addressed to public meetings. The style[1] calls for an attentive listener. Libanius' classical learning is displayed by means of allusion rather than paraded in full. As Norman has shown,[2] Libanius is a master in the use of allusions to the language or situation of classical authors and employs these classical reminiscences with great effect to enhance the liveliness and to vary the mood of his compositions. But the allusiveness also extends to Libanius' treatment of facts. There are numerous passages which only a few definite persons would be in a position to understand. All this suggests that the speeches were aimed at very small groups of listeners or readers; in fact, that they are of the nature of pamphlets. The traditional form obscures an up-to-date purpose.

It follows that the setting suggested by the introduction and form of a particular speech is likely to be different from the circumstances in which the speech was actually given to the public. This is confirmed by the known case histories of certain of the speeches. *Oration* xiv for instance, a plea on behalf of the disgraced Aristophanes, would seem to have been spoken by Libanius in the presence of the Emperor Julian. But we know that when he had written the speech Libanius merely notified the emperor of the fact and gave the speech to Priscus, a philosopher in Julian's following, to hand on to the emperor. Priscus evidently did not do so, for some time later Julian asked Libanius for the speech. Eventually, the speech reached Julian. He read it and praised it in a letter to Libanius. When Libanius published the speech he published the letter with it. It is clear from this account that Libanius never spoke this oration before the emperor.[3]

Again, the introduction of *Oration* xv suggests that Libanius had been chosen to go as ambassador in order to effect a

[1] Strongly influenced by Aristides, cf. Boulanger, *Aristide*, 446.
[2] Norman, *Libanius' Autobiography*, xvi and notes *passim*.
[3] *Or.* xiv, *Ep.* 760; Julian, *Ep.* 53 (Wright) = 97 (Bidez–Cumont); Lib. *Ep.* 758.

reconciliation between his native city and Julian. In fact he had not been chosen as an ambassador, and there never was any prospect of his going to address Julian. If he meant the speech to reach Julian, as he probably did, it could only have done so through a messenger. The circumstances of the introduction are quite imaginary. As it turned out, Julian was killed before this speech was ready, and it was eventually delivered before a small, presumably hand-picked, audience.[1]

The Monody on Nicomedia (*Or.* lxi), and the lost threnody in which Libanius bewailed the death of his friend Aristaenetus, were spoken to an audience of four. Afterwards Libanius lent his hearers the manuscript and allowed them to read it to interested persons. When Libanius composed a funeral speech for his uncle Phasganius he thought it necessary to include material which might conceivably have offended the Caesar Julian. So he divided the speech into three parts. Two parts he spoke to large audiences. Only confirmed friends could be trusted to hear the third part. 'After I had accommodated these on a few seats, I shut the doors and read the oration, requesting the hearers to admire in silence any part of the speech that might seem fine, and not to draw the attention of a crowd by loud applause. And so far—may Nemesis remain kind—no frightening consequence has resulted.' Naturally Libanius withheld this part of the speech from publication altogether.[2] But normally delivery was followed by publication, that is, by the distribution to friends or interested persons of copies of the speech.[3]

The fact that the introductions of orations are often misleading[4] sets the historian a particularly tantalizing problem in the case of the interesting speeches of social criticism purporting to be addressed to the Emperor Theodosius in the last decade of Libanius' life.[5] Were these speeches addressed to the emperor only in Libanius' imagination? Or were some of the speeches sent as pamphlets to influential men at Constantinople? Were

---

[1] *Or.* xvii. 37; Socrates, *H.E.* iii. 17.   [2] *Ep.* 33, 283.

[3] *Ep.* 36, 263, 744, 785, 1217, *Or.* i. 113; A. F. Norman, 'The book trade in fourth-century Antioch', *J.H.S.* lxxx (1960), 122–6. Civic library and book copying at Teos in the Early Empire: *S.E.G.* ii. 584.

[4] Cf. the writings of John Chrysostomus, which have the shape of sermons, although they form part of a continuous treatise designed to be read; see Baur, *Johannes Chrysostomus*, 183–4.

[5] *Or.* xxiv, xxviii, l, xxx, xxxiii, xlv, xix, xx, li, lii, xlvii, xlix, xlvi.

certain of them perhaps even sent to the emperor himself? On the answer to these questions will depend not only our view of Libanius' place in the society of his time but also of the relation between the central government and the provinces and of the prestige of the traditional education.

Unfortunately there is only circumstantial evidence. First there is the fact that during these years Libanius was held in high esteem by leading officials of the central government. He was awarded the honorary rank of praetorian prefect.[1] When the praetorian prefect Cynegius visited the city, he paid Libanius the unprecedented honour of descending from his carriage to greet him.[2] After the Riot of the Statues, Libanius was allowed to plead for the city with the emperor's envoy, Caesarius, and later the military governor, Ellebichus, asked him to arrange which councillors were to go as ambassadors to Constantinople.[3]

After the fanatical Christian Cynegius had been succeeded as praetorian prefect by the pagan Tatian, Libanius' position at the centre of power improved further. Both Tatian and his son, the new *praefectus urbi*, Proculus, had become acquainted with Libanius when they had ruled over Syria.[4] The relationship had its vicissitudes,[5] but it was firmly established when Tatian became prefect,[6] and was maintained, at least as far as outward appearances were concerned, until he fell from power.[7]

At this time Libanius could also expect sympathetic support for his requests from Eusebius XXVIII,[8] possibly the *magister officiorum*, from Mardonius II, perhaps *praepositus sacri cubiculi* of Arcadius,[9] from the general Richomer, consul of 384, from

[1] P. Petit, 'Sur la date du *Pro Templis* de Libanius', *Byzantion* xxi (1951), 285–310.

[2] *Or.* lii. 40; cf. i. 231.   [3] *Or.* xxi. 8, xxxii. 5.

[4] Their biographies: Seeck, *Briefe*, 285–9, 248–50; on Tatian also J. Lallemand, *L'Administration civile de l'Égypte* (Brussels, 1964), 247–8.

[5] Libanius attacks Proculus: *Or.* xxvi. 30, xxvii. 13, 30, 39, 41, *Or.* xxix. 10; all c. A.D. 385. At this time neither Proculus nor Tatian held public office. Perhaps Libanius thought that Tatian's career was finished. But Proculus had honoured Libanius, *Or.* xlii. 43–4, and allowed him to make speeches of criticism: i. 223, *Or.* x is one of these.

[6] *Ep.* 840 (388), *Ep.* 1021 (391).

[7] The hostile speeches xlii of 390 (Petit, op. cit. 297) and xlvi of 392 (Seeck, *Rh.M.* lxxiii (1920), 84 ff., reflect Libanius' bitterness at Proculus' unwillingness to and support Cimon and Thalassius, but were probably published only after Tatian Proculus had been disgraced. The attacks on Proculus in *Or.* i. 212 of 383–4 and 221 of 385, were never published at all (Norman, *Libanius' Autobiography*, xiii–xiv).

[8] Seeck, *Briefe*, 145.   [9] Ibid. 203.

Ellebichus,[1] and from yet others. Thus Libanius had good reason to suppose that suggestions of his would be favourably received in high quarters.

Moreover there is evidence that writings of Libanius did reach Constantinople. The prefect Tatian sent Libanius a specimen of his own literary work.[2] It is highly probable that in return Libanius sent him writings of his own. We can go further. Since we know that Libanius brought the unfortunate condition of the Council of Antioch to Tatian's attention in a letter, it is likely that he would have sent him a copy of any speech bearing on that topic as well.[3]

That some controversial speeches of Libanius had reached Constantinople is suggested by a letter of late summer 388. Libanius advises his correspondent not to publicize his writings with a view to converting such men as did not yet admire them. By displaying the speeches he would not win Libanius new friends, but only create trouble for them both. It was better to live in peace.[4]

We have no explicit evidence that Libanius ever sent a speech to the emperor himself. But the Emperor Theodosius was very cordially disposed towards Libanius.[5] Certainly that emperor distinguished him. He allowed Libanius' bastard son, Cimon, to inherit.[6] He conferred on Libanius an honorary praetorian prefecture,[7] and sent him letters on at least two occasions.[8] It would have been in accord with Libanius' character, if he had used the emperor's manifest benevolence to send him writings.

That he did, in fact, do so, is strongly suggested by a letter Libanius wrote to the general Sapor. This man had been tried and convicted, and his property confiscated some time earlier, but the conviction had been reversed. When Sapor complained that Libanius had sent neither speech nor letter to the emperor on his behalf, Libanius replied that this had been a greater matter than he might ask from the emperor.[9] The general evidently believed that Libanius was in literary communication

---

[1] Seeck, *Briefe*, 167; also the general Saturninus, consul of 383, ibid. 264.

[2] *Ep.* 990 (390).

[3] *Ep.* 851–3 (388) but *Or.* xlix, *Ad Theodosium pro curiis*, seems to be later than 388. See Appendix II, below, pp. 270 ff.

[4] *Ep.* 867 (388).   [5] *Or.* i. 220.   [6] Ibid. 195.

[7] See p. 27, n. 1 above.   [8] *Or.* i. 219 (384), 258 (387).

[9] *Ep.* 977 (390).

with the emperor. An incident recorded in Libanius' *Autobiography* has the same implication. At a time when a *comes orientis* was threatening to cut the cypresses of the famous grove at Daphne, Libanius remarked to a companion of the official that he would ask the emperor to show some consideration for Daphne. The *comes* heard of Libanius' remark, took it at its face value, and proceeded to undermine Libanius' repute by encouraging a charge of treason against him.[1] Thus there is good reason to suppose that during the last decade[2] of his life Libanius did send speeches to Constantinople, and indeed to the emperor himself.

We may take it therefore that at least some of the speeches, together with Synesius' 'Discourse on Kingship',[3] and perhaps some of the speeches of Themistius, provide evidence that in the Later Empire leading exponents of culture were allowed a special freedom of speech in order to represent the grievances of the governed to the highest authorities.

If his position gave Libanius certain privileges he nevertheless required moral courage to exercise them. In spite of his well-known tactfulness[4] he had plenty of this. His lifelong championship of paganism in a strongly Christian city,[5] his protection of shopkeepers when they were most unpopular during famine, his efforts on behalf of Christians under Julian,[6] on behalf of Manichaeans[7] under Christian emperors prove that he was prepared to face limited risks, and very considerable dislike, in doing what he considered his duty.

Libanius possessed moral courage but also tact, adaptability, and discretion, and he needed them. Personal experience had taught him how dangerous it was to be on bad terms with the imperial governors. Even if they were unable to find anything against Libanius himself, there were many people both within

---

[1] *Or.* i. 262–3 (387–8).

[2] Before 381 he could only hope that his views about the city councils might reach the emperor through intermediaries. To this end he had talked to the praetorian prefect (perhaps Modestus, prefect 370–7) : *Or.* ii. 70.

[3] C. Lacombrade, *Le Discours sur la royauté de Synesios de Cyrène* (Paris, 1951), text, translation, and commentary.

[4] Eunap. *V. Soph.* 495.

[5] Even in his panegyric of Constantius and Constans, *Or.* lix, he shows by omissions that he does not share the emperor's religion; Petit, *Historia* i (1956), 562–82. There was some risk in his correspondence with Julian in Gaul: *Or.* i. 120.

[6] *Ep.* 763, 819 (362).   [7] *Ep.* 1253 (364).

and without the walls of the city whom they might attack.[1] Libanius had relatives, pupils, tenants, servants, all under his patronage, and all vulnerable.

We have several examples of Libanius' caution. He refrained from attacking the detractors of Julian soon after Julian's death, when they were most vocal and most dangerous. As we know, he defended the emperor a year or two later. At the same time, he refused to send his friend Aristophanes the whole of his correspondence with Julian, and withheld certain letters for reasons of security.[2] On another occasion a law had been made by a high official, probably the praetorian prefect Tatian, and Libanius at once wrote a speech opposing it. Yet, as long as the law was in force, Libanius did not publish the speech. Only after the official had again rescinded the law, did Libanius allow the speech to reach the public, for now it was no longer an act of criticism but of praise.[3]

Many of the speeches are likely to have had a similar history. This means that not every speech purporting to be addressed to the emperor in these years was sent, and that not every speech was published immediately after its composition, regardless of the political situation at that moment. Thus I cannot believe that the *Pro Thalassio* was sent at all,[4] or that the *Pro templis*, with its attack on Cynegius, was sent while that man was still praetorian prefect.[5] But we can be confident that some speeches were sent even to the emperor himself.

The problem of the publication of speeches addressed to an Antiochene audience is similar. But in trying to assess the likely audience of any particular speech it is necessary to remember that in these late years Libanius' position at home was weaker than at court, and his need for caution greater. In these circumstances he is likely to have read the more controversial speeches before small and invited audiences, if he read them at all, and

---

[1] *Or.* lii. 42.   [2] *Ep.* 1264 (364).
[3] *Ep.* 916 (390); cf. 283 (359–60).
[4] It insults men who could have reversed the decision about Thalassius. Libanius wrote the speech to relieve his feelings.
[5] Petit, *Byzantion* xxi (1951), 285–310, dates the speech in 386. Neither Libanius nor anybody else in the empire could afford to antagonize the praetorian prefect. I would suggest that Libanius sent it in 388 or later when Tatian was prefect. It was still relevant. The ravages of the monks continued. They could be prevented —if at all—only by positive measures such as Theodosius tried 390–2 (*C.T.* xvi. 3. 1–2).

did not just distribute them as pamphlets—or keep them locked up at home.

To sum up, the purpose and intended audience of any speech cannot be taken for granted but must be deduced from the way the subject-matter of the speech is treated. It is, however, reasonable to assume that Libanius took greater pains over his language when he was addressing men who were either of particularly high rank or unusually discriminating taste. Petit has shown that conclusions about the intended audience of a speech can be drawn from the density of its rhetorical ornament, and that in general conclusions so based agree very well with those drawn from the factual contents of the speech.[1]

If we are going to use the orations as sources, there are certain facts which we must bear in mind. First of all, that we are dealing with works of rhetoric. This means that the vocabulary is selected and Attic, the sentence construction careful, though much less embellished with figures of speech than that of some contemporary writers. There are hints and reminiscences of the classics scattered over the text and the parts of the speech are organized according to a traditional scheme.[2] Of these features, the select vocabulary provides most difficulty to the historian, as indeed it does to any reader. Libanius will not use terms that do not occur in Demosthenes, and this leads him to avoid the titles and technical terms in common use at the time. Instead he employs the nearest Attic equivalent.[3] Libanius also uses as few proper names as possible. He avoids the names of towns, countries, or individuals. If he must use them, he uses them only once or twice in the course of a speech. Evidently it was felt that the use of names gave to a piece of rhetoric too much of the occasional and individual, whereas great rhetoric should transcend place and personalities.

Another consequence of Libanius' predilection for the general statement is that he often makes it difficult, sometimes impossible, for the reader to establish whether he is generalizing from a single

---

[1] P. Petit, 'Recherches sur la publication et la diffusion des discours de Libanius', *Historia* v (1956), 479–509. Petit uses the analysis of C. Rother, 'De Libanii arte rhetorica quaestiones selectae' (Diss. Breslau, 1915), 104, to discuss audience and distribution of each oration in turn.

[2] The speeches usually follow the arrangement taught in schools: introduction, narration, statement of case, refutation of opponent, peroration. See R. Volkmann, *Die Rhetorik der Griechen und Römer* (Leipzig, 1885, repr. Hildesheim, 1963), 123 ff.

[3] Petit, *Libanius*, 'index de mots grecs' refers to helpful discussions of Libanius' consistent use of certain classical words in substitution for technical terms.

incident or referring to a common practice.[1] The only sure check
is to compare any single general statement with other information from the writings.

Of course, the speeches are completely one-sided. This is
particularly true of character drawing. There is scarcely any
limit to the abuse Libanius might employ. He tells us that
Optatus, a senator who prevented Libanius' friend and assistant,
Thalassius, from entering the Senate at Constantinople, as a boy
hated learning and fled from home. When he was brought back,
his parents thought this such a disaster that they did not reward
the man responsible. Next, he made an unsuccessful attempt to
kill his elder brother with the help of magicians. He made a
career by shamelessly attacking older men: while governing
Egypt, he was a bloodthirsty tyrant and persecutor of philosophers. He was arrested and narrowly escaped execution for
his crimes. The motive for his blackballing of Thalassius was
that Thalassius warned away from Libanius' school a pimp to
whom Optatus was indebted for professional services.[2]

Later in the same speech Libanius attacks Proculus, the *praefectus
urbi*. Libanius says of him that he knew no Latin, no Greek, no
Law; that in his adolescence he could not be taught to regard
incorrect speech as reprehensible; he was wanton and drunken.
'What pestilence removed so many Phoenicians as he when he
was governor? What plague devastated Palestine more than he?
How many wars would it have taken to equal the destructiveness
of his tenure as *comes orientis*? How much blood stained the earth?
How many swords ran through throats? How many new tombs
were dug?' This theme is elaborated at considerable length.[3]

One Silvanus had made unfriendly remarks about Libanius
and had taken his son away from Libanius' school to a Latin
teacher, whereupon Libanius wrote a speech against him, urging
that he should be inscribed in the council. He describes Silvanus
as having been bad at school and ungrateful for his free education,
conniving at the activities of his corrupted and corrupting son.
Silvanus wished his own father dead and hastened this event by
callous treatment.[4]

---

[1] *Or.* ii. 34 is a general statement, which xlix. 31 shows to be about a particular
man in a particular city.

[2] *Or.* xlii. 7–9, 28–9.   [3] Ibid. 40–1.

[4] *Or.* xxxviii; another piece of abuse: lxii. 63–71.

There is a certain sameness about these invectives. Again and again, a man, or even a group of men, is charged with lack of education, gross immorality, licentiousness. Charges of murder, complotting the death of relatives, and the use of magic towards these ends, might be lightly flung,[1] and if at all possible a man's low birth and the vices of his parents will be used against him. Of course, if a man had held public office the scope for charges was enormous, as we have seen in the case of Proculus.

The device of blackening one's opponents beyond recognition is not a peculiarity of Libanius. These inhuman monsters without redeeming feature appear again and again in the literature of the time. In Ammianus there are the Caesar Gallus, and the prefect Maximinus;[2] in Synesius there is the governor Andronicus.[3] Gregory of Nazianzus in his first invective against Julian suggests that he was responsible for the death of Constantius, and that he committed the ritual murder of children.[4]

Groups may be treated similarly. The monks, for instance, are dressed in black, eat more than elephants, pass the drinks around singing hymns, and cover up these activities with craftily acquired pallor.[5] Libanius surely knew that this was not generally true, but while attacking their campaign against the temples he sought to discredit them all round. The *agentes in rebus*, the spying and interfering agents of the central government, are attacked in the same way. They are men who have deserted their city councils for imperial office, they extort money when announcing victories, and blackmail shopkeepers, they pretend to have unmasked conspiracies against the emperor for extortion's sake, yet ignore genuine conspirators. They introduce young men and women of loose morals into the houses of respectable men and afterwards blackmail them. They extort money by threatening innocent people with charges of magic practice, they sell safety to forgers of coins, and they use their control of the *cursus publicus* to their own profit, feasting so shamelessly out of the proceeds of the

---

[1] Charges of magic were often brought to court. Libanius was accused no less than five times, see above, p. 14 n. 4.

[2] See E. A. Thompson, *Ammianus Marcellinus*, 56–71, 87–107.

[3] See above, p. 23 n. 3.

[4] *Contra Julianum* i. 92 and 47 (*P.G.* xxxv. 624 and 572); cf. also Lactantius, *De morte persecutorum* (ed. J. Moreau in *Sources chrétiennes*), vol. 2, commentary on viii. 15 and xxxviii. 1.

[5] *Or.* xxx. 8; cf. 31, 41, ii. 32. See Pack, *Studies*, 44.

fodder and of permits to travel as to ruin the beasts and to break down the service.[1] In spite of the villainous character Libanius ascribed to the *agentes in rebus* as a whole, he was nevertheless content to have the friendship of members of this corps, to accept assistance from some and to give it to others.[2] Libanius condemns the group entirely and in every way, only because the context of his speech demands that they should be presented in the most unfavourable light.

It goes without saying that the claque supporting the actors at the theatre was showered with coarse abuse. Libanius describes its members as foreigners expelled from their home towns for crimes; they ill-treat their fathers and beat their mothers, and flee from the craft of their ancestors. They make a living out of their youth while it lasts, and afterwards turn to the theatre, as the only place where they can make a living in idleness. There they become the obsequious servants of the actors, ready to do everything shameful both by day and night.[3]

Such abuse was not peculiar to Libanius but is an aspect of the whole rhetorical literature of the time. John Chrysostomus wanted to dissuade his Christian congregation from observing Jewish practices, and in sermons on this topic roundly abused the Jews. Christians must not share in the Jewish fasts, for the Jews fast from 'strife and contention' as is witnessed by the Bible;[4] and for insolence and licentiousness, since in the course of their fast they dance with naked feet in the market place.[5] For them fasting is a pretext for drunkenness. 'After gathering together troops of effeminate men and a mob of hardened prostitutes, and everyone concerned with the theatre and stage, they drag all this company into the synagogue, for there is no difference between synagogue and theatre.' Some will charge John Chrysostomus with effrontery in making this assertion, but he would answer that it was not he who made it but the prophets in the Bible. He argues from Jeremiah 3, 3 that a synagogue is a

---

[1] *Or.* xviii. 135–45; cf. xiv. 14.

[2] See Pack, *Studies*, 20; two 'good' *agentes in rebus*: Aristophanes XIV, 12–14, and Clematius II; cf. Seeck, *Briefe*, 110.

[3] *Or.* xli. 6 ff., lvi. 15; cf. below, pp. 212 ff.; cf. G. L. Kurbatov, 'Le terme δῆμος dans les œuvres de Libanius et la question des δῆμοι byzantins', *XXVe Congrès international des orientalistes* (Moscow, 1962), 504–10.

[4] Joh. Chrys. *Adv. Iudaeos* I (*P.G.* xlviii. 846), citing Isaiah 58: 4–5.

[5] *P.G.* xlviii. 846, 849.

brothel, Jeremiah 7 : 11 that it is a den of robbers, while further passages show that the Jews do not worship God, and that the synagogue is the home of a demon.[1] In another passage he contrasts the Christians' Easter fast, when the congregation is at peace in contemplating the possibility of eternal punishment, with the fast of the Jews, who are concerned only with the present. And apart from the fast day they are no better than pigs or goats in respect of extreme gluttony. All they live for is eating and to be cut up on behalf of the actors, to be wounded on behalf of the charioteers.[2] The resemblance between what John Chrysostomus says about the Jews and what Libanius says about the claque is striking.

The conclusion to be drawn from this resemblance is surely not that the claque was composed of Jews, but that all this violent abuse should be taken with a grain of salt. We should consider that these invectives are just the obverse of the rhetorical panegyric. At school the student learned both how to praise and how to abuse.[3] Afterwards, as a rhetorician, he was not likely to let any potential opportunity of employing his skill and knowledge pass unused.

Socrates, the ecclesiastical historian, replying to Libanius' criticisms of Christianity, argues that rhetoricians will attack either side equally competently. If Libanius had not been a pagan, he would have magnified the grounds of censure against Julian. While Constantius lived Libanius had praised him, but after his death he slandered his name. Socrates goes on to Julian's refutation of Christianity which Libanius had described with the verb 'attack' (ἐπιθέσθαι). Socrates claims that this word means 'to prepare a confutation' (ψόγος) of the kind prepared by sophists for their pupils. A man who makes such an attack on another person, at times tries to pervert the truth, and at others to conceal it, and he will falsify by every means the position of his antagonist. Thus criticism by Julian and Libanius could be rejected with little argument as the work of sophists displaying their art.[4]

It is probable that educated men would have inclined towards Socrates' attitude and would have been prepared to discount

---

[1] Ibid. 846, 847. [2] Ibid. 848.
[3] See model *laudationes* and *vituperationes* of Libanius, Foerster (ed.), vol. viii. 216–360. [4] Soc. *H.E.* iii. 23 (*P.G.* lxvii. 438D–439C).

a certain amount of abuse. What effect such speeches had on those who had not had the benefit of a rhetorical education is another matter. The attacks of a bishop made before a congregation of all classes might well be taken by some at their face value and so bring about ugly scenes of violence.

What then is a reader to believe? Libanius once declares that when composing a speech of praise he praises virtues a man has and passes over his failings but does not praise him for virtues he does not possess.[1] So it may be with his abuse. If we take careful note of Libanius' 'rogues' gallery' we see that the portraits have individual features. Lucianus is brutal and allows no favours.[2] Eustathius is brutal but allows too many and to the wrong people.[3] Tissamenes lets prisoners perish because he neglects their trials and goes to the theatre.[4] The principal charge, in Libanius' eye at least, may therefore contain elements of truth, but anything justifying or extenuating in the circumstances would be left out. The minor and more stereotyped charges are the small change of rhetorical abuse, and these would be applied to a greater or lesser degree whenever the main charges were not thought sufficiently damning or provable.

I have already mentioned the one-sidedness of his presentation of facts. Since the purpose of his speeches is to present an argument, he never refers to a fact or happening with sufficient detail to allow his hearers to judge for themselves whether it will bear the interpretation he gives it.

Moreover, he might use one and the same example in different speeches to prove contradictory points. So he once refers to a councillor who performed most of the liturgies in the city personally, even acting as bath attendant himself. Here Libanius is seeking to show to what a wretched state the councils had been reduced, in that there were no others left to share these duties. Yet in another speech he cites this man as one of those who were reluctant to let new members into the council but preferred to keep its profits to himself. I do not think it necessary to suppose that Libanius had changed his opinions on the causes of the decline of the councils in the interval between the writing of the

---

[1] *Ep.* 19, 578.   [2] *Or.* lvi.   [3] *Or.* liv.

[4] *Or.* xxxiii, xlv. He has scruples about capital punishment, xlv. 27; so has Eutropius, iv. 36 and perhaps Florentius, xlvi. 9; they are Christians. Jones, *L.R.E.* 983 quotes Ambrose, *Ep.* 25; Innocent I, *Ep.* 6, 3 on the uncertainty of the Church's teaching for a Christian governor in the field of capital punishment.

two speeches.[1] When he wrote the earlier one he was sixty-seven years old, and we must suppose that by then he knew all he would ever know about the way a council was run. The cause of the different interpretation is to be found in the contexts in which he uses the example.

The technique of rhetoric included a certain virtuosity in evaluating facts according to the context in which they were to be used. For example, the custom of the governor giving favours is viewed by Libanius from opposite standpoints in different speeches. In two speeches Libanius argues vehemently that the favours given to *honorati* who come to audiences with the governor undermine justice, and that these audiences should be stopped.[2] But in another speech Libanius complains that a governor has not honoured him with audiences,[3] and on yet another occasion he holds it against a governor that he has limited the audiences of the *honorati*, describing this action as hybris.[4] Libanius' writings abound in such contradictions. It must be emphasized that this is not a question of insincerity but of technique. When Libanius is writing a particular speech he is concerned with one point of view only and all facts in it are used to strengthen the one argument.

Just as Libanius interprets the facts comprised in a speech to make them serve his argument, so he simplifies his conclusions to make them more striking and effective. The speeches on the εἴσοδοι conclude in favour of the complete abolition of that practice. Now we need not for a moment believe that Libanius, who had been in and out of the official and private quarters of the highest officials all his life, had the slightest illusion that the cutting-off of the governor from his most prominent citizens[5] was possible or even desirable. His real aim must have been to point out the abuse of the system as strikingly as possible, so as to obtain legislation which would modify it.

Further, it would seem that many of the comparisons and moral maxims used in the argumentative section of the speeches are prefabricated. The orations on the Riot of the Statues provide an example of this. It has been noted that arguments used by Libanius also appear in sermons of John Chrysostomus. Goebel concluded that Libanius had imitated the rhetoric of his brilliant

---

[1] See above, p. 32 n. 1.   [2] *Or.* li and lii.   [3] *Or.* liv. 5–6, 61.
[4] *Or.* lvi. 3.   [5] *Or.* li. 22–5.

young pupil.[1] This is not very likely, since, apart from these shared arguments, the speeches are of a totally different character. John Chrysostomus is passionate and moral, and addresses Theodosius as a Christian soul. Libanius is cool, and addresses him as a ruler, arguing on the basis of examples from earthly government. The similarity arises from the fact that both had drawn on the store of argument which was acquired with their rhetorical education, and which included a portfolio of arguments that might be used by a speaker asking a monarch to forgive erring subjects. A few of the arguments which occur in the riot speeches of both Libanius and John Chrysostomus also appear in similar contexts elsewhere in Libanius. Others can be found in the writings of Julian, and it would not be hard to find them elsewhere, used in similar situations.[2]

Another feature which hinders the historian in his task of accurate reconstruction is Libanius' technique of dividing his account of the deed which he is making the basis of his indictment into several sections, and dispersing these without connecting links among his narrative. Thus, in the speech against Eustathius, Libanius describes the vindictive treatment of the councillor Julian in two parts, without indicating that there was a connection between them. He did the same with the case of the sycophant, Romulus, and with that of his friend and assistant, Thalassius.[3] This device breaks the unity of a narrative which might otherwise not bear the interpretation Libanius is suggesting, and on the careless listener might even produce the impression of several acts of arbitrary behaviour instead of one.

The total effect of rhetorical presentation is to make it very difficult for the historian to establish the truth about the situations which Libanius has described in so one-sided a way. This is a situation which frequently arises in our study of ancient authors. We may feel certain that Tacitus has grossly distorted the accounts of the treason trials under Tiberius, but in spite of our disbelief of Tacitus we have not the facts to put together and

---

[1] R. Goebel, 'De Joannis Chrysostomi et Libanii orationibus quae sunt de seditione Antiochensium' (Diss. Göttingen, 1910); accepted by Baur, *Johannes Chrysostomus*, and Foerster–Münscher in *P.W.* s.v. Libanius.

[2] This is briefly but convincingly shown by P. Petit in *Libanius*, 238 n. 3, and *Histroia* v (1956), 498.

[3] *Or.* liv. 22–5 and 45, Julianus; ibid. 39–44, 62, 78, Romulus; ibid. 47, 66, Thalassius. On the device cf. M. L. Clarke, *Rhetoric at Rome*, 26.

firmly establish an alternative system. It is always difficult to establish the truth of a case from the speeches made on behalf of only one of the two parties concerned in it. On the other hand, if we read Libanius' speeches to obtain information not on the situation Libanius was concerned to distort, but on wider historical problems, the rhetorical presentation will present fewer difficulties.

How valuable are Libanius' speeches to the historian? The answer to this depends on how much we trust his judgement in public affairs. This is shown to the best advantage in the *Pro templis*.[1] He is defending the temple from the activities of the monks and criticizing the attitude of the praetorian prefect in a speech addressed to the strongly Christian Emperor Theodosius. We must admire the skill with which Libanius approaches the problem. He does not write a passionate plea for paganism, like Symmachus' speech on the Altar of Victory. Theodosius' religious convictions were not to be shaken and such an address was likely to offend. Libanius approaches the matter from the angle of government. There is no imperial law ordering that the temples should be destroyed. That the monks should take on themselves this work of destruction, with all its incidental devastation and hardship, without imperial authorization, is intolerable in a peacefully ordered state. This argument is nicely calculated to appeal to Theodosius. It is the argument of a man of real political ability. We may conclude from this, and other examples of Libanius' political sense, that the opinions he expresses on public life, when they are not distorted by a close personal involvement or merely stated to support a particular case, are sound and worth considering.

---

[1] On the *Pro templis*, see Van Loy, 'Le *Pro Templis* de Libanius', *Byzantion* viii (1933), 7–39, 389–404; P. Petit, *Byzantion* xxi (1951), 285–310.

II

THE LIVELIHOOD OF THE PEOPLE OF ANTIOCH

I. THE TERRITORY OF ANTIOCH

THERE is some ambiguity about the name Antioch. The territory of Antioch comprised the city but also a large rural area administered from it, for as far as we know all land in the north of Syria was attributed to one or other of the cities for purposes of administration.[1] To the east of Antioch about fifty-five and fifty miles away (as the crow flies) lay the cities of Beroea and Chalcis. Due south about sixty miles from Antioch was the large city of Apamea with a large territory of its own. Twenty miles to the west of Antioch the seaport of Seleucia had a small territory only. Further south along the coast about sixty miles from Antioch was the city of Laodicea. In the course of the fourth century Antioch absorbed the small city of Gindarus about thirty-five miles to the north-east, which at the council of Nicaea was still represented by a bishop of its own.[1]

The boundaries of the territory of Antioch can be defined more closely. Certain tombstones of villagers who had emigrated to the West record the name both of the deceased man's village of origin and of the city to which the village belonged.[2] More importantly, the distribution of inscriptions dated with the era of Antioch seems to coincide with the extent of the Antiochene territory. H. Seyrig's map of the distribution shows that the impressive village ruins of the Ğebel Sim'ān, Ğebel Halaqa, and Ğebel Barīša areas belonged to the territory of Antioch, while Tērib, the ancient Litarba, belonged to the territory of Chalcis.[3] Of the villages along the Ğebel Zāwiye perhaps a third were attached to Antioch, the rest to Apamea. There is no evidence

---

[1] A. H. M. Jones, *C.E.R.P.* 270 n. 55.
[2] References in R. Dussaud, *Topographie historique de la Syrie antique et médiévale* (Paris, 1927).
[3] Julian, *Ep.* 58 (Wright) = 98 (Bidez–Cumont).

for the boundary to the south-west, west, or north-west of Antioch. Due north, the village of Qāra Mugara, below Mount Amanus, is situated within the territory of Antioch, but on this side too the boundary cannot be delineated exactly.[1]

On the basis of Seyrig's map one might perhaps estimate the total area of the territory at something like six hundred thousand or seven hundred thousand hectares—say, two thousand five hundred square miles. There is no direct evidence on the rural population, but if we assume a density of one hundred and fifty-nine persons per square mile, which was the population density of the province of Latakia, the most densely populated Syrian province in 1938, we get a total of nearly four hundred thousand.

Elsewhere in this work it is argued that the city itself had a population of around one hundred and fifty thousand.[2] According to a statement of John Chrysostomus, the very rich and the very poor each comprised about a tenth of the total population.[3] Unfortunately we lack the statistical material to confirm and develop this estimate. We can only gather the evidence about the sources of livelihood of a small number of persons from each class or profession. We cannot deduce from that evidence how large each group was or what proportion it formed of the whole.

2. THE UPPER CLASS

Before the Riot of the Statues the governor read an imperial demand for higher taxes to the notables of the city. These included ex-officials, councillors, lawyers, and veterans. These were the men, other than active employees of the state, who counted in the city. To these might be added the more prominent teachers and doctors, the bishop and clergy. Together, these comprised the upper class. Libanius' circle was almost entirely civilian. We therefore hear little about soldiers or veterans. He never

[1] G. Tchalenko, *Villages antiques de la Syrie du Nord* (Paris, 1953), vol. 3, 11–14 (by H. Seyrig) and map, ibid. 57.

[2] *B.R.* 513 *Geographical Handbook Series: Syria* (Admiralty, London, 1943), 190–8. The average density of 159 to the square mile may seem excessively high because the territory must have contained some *very* thinly inhabited areas. On the other hand, Syria as a whole was in a better condition in A.D. 400 than in A.D. 1938 when (acc. to *B.R. Syria*, 251) only half the cultivable area was cultivated. D. Oates, *Studies in Ancient History of Northern Iraq* (London, 1968), 16–17 cites much lower densities for N. Mesopotamia. On city population—see below, pp. 92 ff.

[3] Joh. Chrys. *Hom. in Matth.* 66 (*P.G.* lviii. 630).

mentions the affairs of the Church of Antioch. Otherwise we are well informed about the upper class of Antioch and other cities of the East. Out of it came the bulk of Libanius' pupils, friends, and correspondents.

The wealthiest Antiochene family mentioned in the writings of Libanius was that of the deceased praetorian prefect, Thalassius I. It appears to have been of curial origin but its members had almost cut their connections with the council.[1] Their estates and connections were scattered over a wide area.[2] A daughter of Thalassius I was married to a wealthy landowner of Cyrrhus in the province of Euphratensis.[3] A son, Bassianus, was an imperial notary and lived wealthy and powerful at Constantinople.[4] Another son, Thalassius, lived at Antioch.[5] The family also had property in Phoenicia[6] and near the Euphrates.[7] Bassianus and his grandmother Bassiana, an aunt of Libanius, had interests in Egypt. Megistus, an agent whom she sent to supervise these interests, appears to have been an Egyptian decurion, for an official tried to compel him to remain in Egypt. Presumably he had entered the service of a powerful family to escape curial service and the official was trying to bring him back to his duties. Libanius pleads with the official that Megistus should be allowed to return to his employers; alternatively he is to enrol him 'among the men who export corn from Egypt' which may well mean to inscribe him among the *navicularii*.[8] In the same year another agent was sent to inspect the family property in the province of

---

[1] Pedigree: Appendix II of Petit, *Libanius*.

[2] Cf. scattered estates of Jamblichus in Syria: *Ep.* 360; cf. 571; in Palestine: *Ep.* 982. Estates of wife of Euanthius: at Antioch and near Cyrrhus: *Ep.* 1335. Family of Letoius: home, bath, gardens, estate: *Ep.* 877. Land in Euphratensis where Letoius I spends a year: *Ep.* 1175, 1190, 1202, 1328; they are near Cyrrhus: Theodoret, *H.R.* 14 (*P.G.* lxxxii. 1413). Antiochus II, councillor of Antioch with estates in Phoenicia: *Ep.* 544, 1355; Quirinus I, resident at Antioch but with estates in Cilicia: Seeck, *Briefe*, 250–1, *Ep.* 1242; Parthenius, citizen of Antioch with estates in Phoenicia: Seeck, op. cit. 232; *Ep.* 236; Alexander IX, councillor of Antioch with estates near Cyrrhus: Seeck, op. cit. 55; *Ep.* 1291. On absence of great continuous complexes of estate see P. Lemerle, *Actes du XIIᵉ Congrès international d'études byzantines* (Belgrade, 1963), 278.

[3] *Ep.* 1150.

[4] *Ep.* 1490 (365); cf. Seeck, *Briefe*, 95.

[5] *Ep.* 620 (361); earlier he too had a court post, *Ep.* 377; Amm. xxii. 9. 16; cf. Seeck, *Briefe*, 290.

[6] *Ep.* 1364 (364).   [7] *Ep.* 1404.

[8] *Ep.* 626 (361), 705 (362); Petit, *Libanius*, 340 and 402; Liebeschuetz, *Rh. M.* civ (1961), 245–7.

Asia. Conveniently, the vicar of Asia had married a daughter of the house.[1]

But so powerful a family had enemies who were only waiting for an opportunity to harm it. The chance came when Julian became emperor. Thalassius and his family were Christians. In Phoenicia they were in possession of a temple which they had turned into a house. Now the house was seized and the family compelled to rebuild the temple.[2] At the same time Thalassius II was forced into the council of Antioch and ruinous demands were made on his property.[3] Bassianus, his brother, had married the daughter of Constantius' praetorian prefect, Helpidius. Included in her dowry was an estate which a certain man of Dolichene had given her in order to obtain the powerful assistance of her father.[4] When Julian became emperor and Helpidius lost his office, the man from Dolichene tried to reclaim his present.

The information about Libanius' own property shows that it was of the same kind as that of Thalassius, even if there was less of it. Libanius' family had long been rich and prominent,[5] many members of it had given the Olympic Games.[6] But his grandfather had lost his life and property after the Eugenius affair.[7] Also Libanius' mother sold property while he was at Athens to enable him to spend four more years at his studies.[8] The purchaser called on Libanius and asked him to confirm the sale with his signature. This Libanius did willingly and in so doing renounced any possibility of disputing the sale when he came home. A passage from a different speech describes how a would-be purchaser made use of Libanius' absence to harass his widowed mother. She did not, however, send for Libanius, nor did he come home uncalled. As a result, much land worked by many men was lost.[9] It is not clear whether this is the same transaction as that described in the *Autobiography*. At any rate it illustrates the precariousness of ownership of those unable to defend themselves. Libanius never recovered the lost family property.[10] But after 359,

---

[1] *Ep.* 642; Seeck, *Briefe*, 187–8 s.v. Italicianus.
[2] *Ep.* 1364 (363).   [3] See above, p. 42 n. 5.
[4] *Ep.* 1380.
[5] *Or.* i. 2 ff.; Petit, *Libanius*, Appendix III: property.
[6] *Or.* liii. 4.
[7] *Or.* xxxvi. 12, i. 3, li. 30; on the Eugenius affair: xi. 159–63.
[8] *Or.* i. 26, 58.   [9] *Or.* lv. 15.
[10] *Ep.* 1154 (364), *Or.* i. 125, li. 30.

when he had inherited the estates of his uncle Phasganius, he must have been by curial standards a very rich man.[1] He also received two salaries. As in his earlier appointment at Constantinople, he was paid separately by the city and by the emperor. His civic salary at Antioch was probably small,[2] but his imperial salary is likely to have been considerable.[3] In addition, he received fees and presents from pupils and their parents.[4] Even if fees came in as irregularly as Libanius sometimes insists,[5] his total income must have been ample.[6] His frequently paraded indifference to money[7] is the attitude of a man who would never conceivably be short of it.

In the matter of landed property we find him in possession of the Ζήζους χωρίον which had been purchased by Phasganius[8] and of another property, worked by Jewish peasants, that had belonged to the family for four generations.[9] He was obviously in a position where he could reflect on whether to buy or to sell

[1] *Ep.* 115, 126, 141, 186.

[2] Civic salaries. 1. Antioch: he held a civic appointment (Norman, *Libanius' Autobiography* on *Or.* i. 102–5), therefore must have received a salary. But the σύνταξις of *Or.* xxxi. 19 was his under-teachers'. 2. Constantinople: he had received a municipal salary in kind, *Or.* i. 80, *Ep.* 454 (355–6), 463–4; the letters refer to an attempt to make him repay part of it in gold.

[3] Imperial salary, at Antioch: *Ep.* 28, 140, 258, 800; at Constantinople: *Or.* i. 80, *Ep.* 572 (357). The Imperial Rhetor at Trier received 30 *annonae*: *C.T.* xiii. 3. 11 (376); the sophists at Carthage under Justinian 10 *annonae* and 5 *capita* totalling 70 *solidi*: *C.J.* i. 27. 42; cf. S. Bonner, 'Gratian's edict on the salaries of teachers', *A.J.P.* lxxxvi (1965), 113–17; Jones, *L.R.E.* 1001–2.

[4] Fees of sophist: *Ed. Diocl.* vii. 71. 250 *denarii* per pupil per month, about 4 *solidi* per year (50,000 *denarii* = 1 lb. of gold); grammarian: *Anth. Pal.* ix. 174 (Palladas) 1 *solidus* per pupil per year, see A. Cameron, *Cl. Rev.* xv (1965), 257–8; Petit, *Étudiants*, 144–6.

[5] *Or.* iii. 6, lxii. 20, xliii. 6–7.

[6] Libanius saved—and lost—at least 1500 *solidi* in 5 years at Nicomedia: *Or.* i. 61–2.

[7] e.g. *Or.* i. 58; also renunciation of rewards of patronage, ibid. 109, *Ep.* 1329; also of civic estate, *Or.* xxxi. 46.

[8] *Ep.* 126 (359–60).

[9] *Or.* xlvii, 13. Harmand shows that Libanius' Jewish tenants need not have lived in Palestine, and suggests that the estate lay in the valley of the Orontes (*Discours sur les patronages*, 73–87). When Harmand reproduces the plan of the remains of the great fortified farm at El Touba to suggest the appearance of Libanius' estate centre, he is mistaken (see op. cit. 142). This is a structure that belongs to the fringe of the desert and to the neighbourhood of Arab tribesmen, not to the settled Orontes Valley. The owner of this farm was the protector of his peasants in a military sense. Libanius was not a semi-feudal desert-fringe magnate, as in a different province Synesius was. See Lacombrade, *Synesios de Cyrène*, 76, 199–201, and Synesius, *Ep.* 125, 132–3.

land 'with the pleasant indecision of one who was forced to do neither'.[1] Even the men who administered his property were of some standing. Boethus belonged to a leading family of Elusa and was related to the powerful house of Argyrius at Antioch.[2] Another agent, Heraclitus, may well have belonged to a curial family of Tyre.[3] Sometimes Libanius had trouble with his peasants. After he had inherited the Ζήζους χωρίον from his uncle Phasganius, the peasants refused to recognize his ownership, claiming 'that they might be punished for wronging the imperial house if they did so'.[4] Pack may well be right that they had come, whether voluntarily or by force, under the patronage of one of the administrators of the imperial property. About thirty years later we again read of peasants who relied on patronage to protect them when they disobeyed Libanius' instructions.[5]

Land-ownership on a considerable scale involved Libanius in various commercial transactions. Early in 360 he sent Mocimus, a man who had previously worked for his uncle, to sell some farm produce at Apamea in Syria. The task of this servant was 'to turn straw into gold', and prominent citizens in Apamea were asked to facilitate the sale and not to stand by and let Libanius' products be spoilt. In view of the great cost of land transport at the time we cannot help wondering how Libanius got this bulky load to Apamea. Probably it had been shipped up the river Orontes, but it is just possible that Libanius owned an estate near Apamea.[6] In 362 we hear that Libanius was sending some peasants to sell wine in Cilicia. Part of the consignment was spoilt.[7]

In 357 Libanius sent slaves to purchase timber in Cilicia.[8] In 361 we hear that an official in whose temporary custody some

---

[1] *Ep.* 654 (361); Pack, *Studies*, 33.

[2] *Ep.* 118 (357), 166 (359–60). His father was for a time *eirenarch* at Elusa: *Ep.* 532 (356), cf. 119 (357); so was another relative, Zenobius II: *Ep.* 101–2 (359–60). On the powerful relatives at Antioch: A. F. Norman, 'The Family of Argyrius', *J.H.S.* lxxiv (1954), 44–8. Boethus lived at Antioch: *Ep.* 420 (355). The property he managed was therefore not at Elusa; otherwise Petit, *Libanius*, 408.

[3] *Ep.* 225, recalled to council?   [4] *Ep.* 121; Pack, *Studies*, 51.

[5] See below, 203.

[6] *Ep.* 133–6; Seeck, *Briefe*, 365; on the navigability of the Orontes: *P.W.* s.v. Orontes (vol. xviii, col. 1163); cf. *B.R. Syria*, 47. There are numerous letters to Apameans but no further hints at financial interests in the city.

[7] *Ep.* 709; cf. Petit, *Libanius*, 305 n. 5.

[8] *Ep.* 568.

timber had been left was holding on to it and had been doing so for no less than three years.¹ In 364 Libanius arranged with Severus V that he should send timber from his forests in Lycia. Clearly there was no specialized timber-trade. A wealthy man who needed it would have to import it himself.²

Some light on the way such overseas transactions were organized comes from a letter of 360. The sons, or more likely slaves, of Lollianus are sailing to Sinope κατ᾽ ἐμπορίαν. On the way they are to call at Constantinople and sell Libanius' house there. Themistius is asked to supervise them so that they are not cheated and do not in turn cheat Libanius. Libanius also tries to obtain local help for the business at Sinope. He writes to two leading citizens. But for his confidence in them he would never have sent a ship and a servant (οἰκέτην) to Sinope.³ It is just possible that the ship was Libanius' own, but perhaps more likely that he hired it. In any case the example shows that men like Libanius, even though their wealth was in land, were not entirely unconnected with sea trading. This is also suggested by the existence of a liturgy at Antioch that involved transport of corn for the government by sea—a liturgy from which Libanius was extremely anxious to free his own son.⁴

Such business activities, which perhaps also included some money-lending,⁵ must have occupied a significant amount of Libanius' time and thought. It is all the more remarkable how rarely they are mentioned in his letters. We are here faced with

¹ *Ep.* 649.
² *Ep.* 1191; cf. 1383. There was still much wood in Syria. See *P.W.* 2. Reihe, vol. iv, 2, col. 1559, s.v. Syria. Amm. xxii. 14. 4, wood even on Mount Casius. Much wood was used for the roofing of churches and houses in the hill villages. Libanius presumably required timber of a special kind.
³ *Ep.* 177–8. Libanius rarely uses παῖς in the sense of slave—see G. L. Kurbatov, 'Les esclaves et l'esclavage dans les œuvres de Libanius', *V.D.I.* lxxxviii (1964), 92–100, but it is so used in a comparable context in *Ep.* 568, l. 3 τοὺς οἰκέτας, l. 8 ὁ παῖς. Also the οἰκέτης of *Ep.* 177 should be one of the 'boys' of Lollianus. Perhaps the 'boys' were slave agents of a shipowner Lollianus, from whom Libanius had hired the ship. Cf. Rougé, *L'Organisation du commerce maritime*, 284–7 on πραγματευταί.
⁴ *Ep.* 959. The liturgy may often have been purely financial but in *Or.* liv. 47, the threatened man owns a ship—and so, we are told, do many others—and there is no shortage of ships. So ship-ownership was relevant. On the liturgy, see my 'Money Economy and Taxation in Kind', *Rh. M.* civ (1961), 242–54. *Or.* vii. 9 and viii. 1, ibid. 3 suggest that shipowning was not unusual among the rich.
⁵ *Ep.* 213 (360?), to Helpidius III, a Palestinian. *Ep.* 1423 (363), gold to Diodotus, a distant friend (*Ep.* 1429). Perhaps both loans were acts of friendship rather than business transactions.

a literary convention. Private business affairs were not a proper subject for a literary letter. In his correspondence Libanius the business-man is completely eclipsed by Libanius the sophist.

Libanius owned a considerable number of slaves. As appears to have been usual at Antioch and elsewhere at this time, most of the slaves were employed in various kinds of domestic service.[1] They attended him personally,[2] safeguarded his manuscripts,[3] helped him at school.[4] He was followed about by a 'boy' who carried his books.[5] When his horse was not available he was carried in a litter.[6] Incidentally he had only one horse at his disposal in the city, and the same was true of his friend, Olympius, a member of the senate of Constantinople.[7] Once he was given a present of at least three slaves.[8] This was a generous present, certainly, but not it seems exceptionally so, and the lady who then sent the slaves had on earlier occasions sent him 'many' others, including the tutor of his son. We recall that Libanius had described as poverty the condition of his under-teachers, compelled to live attended by three slaves or less.[9] Libanius felt sympathy for his slaves. He blames a Cilician for keeping in Cilicia a servant who had been living with a slave woman of Libanius. Whether the servant stayed away voluntarily or under compulsion, his master was doing wrong. If necessary, he should force him to come back.[10] While Libanius clearly had a large household, it is impossible to gauge its size. Libanius approves the frugal manner of life of the general who married his great-aunt. That man had one estate, eleven slaves, twelve mules,

---

[1] Slaves common: Joh. Chrys. *Hom. in Ep. ad Ephes.* 22 (*P.G.* lxii. 158), even a 'poor' man has slaves. Lib. *Or.* xxxix. 8, li. 6, l. 20, slaves of the rich. xxxi. 11, 'poor' under-teachers have 2–3 slaves. Joh. Chrys. *Hom. in Matth.* 63. 4 (*P.G.* lviii. 608), men own 10–20 villas and 1,000–2,000 slaves, *highly* rhetorical. Other references: Baur, *Johannes Chrysostomus*, 316–19; V. Schulze, *Antiocheia* (Gütersloh, 1930), 191, 264–7; A. Puech, *Saint Jean Chrysostome et les mœurs de son temps* (Paris, 1891), 143–51. The bulk of the evidence is concerned with *domestic* slavery. Slaves in sword workshop, *Or.* xlii. 21; female slave in corn mills, liii. 19; slavery on the land, only xiv. 45 (Greece). M. Hombert and C. Préaux, *Recherches sur le recensement dans l'Égypte romaine* (Brussels, 1952), 170 (based on census returns of Early Empire) find that of 351 urban dwellers 49 (13·7 per cent) were slaves. Out of 98 families only 21 had slaves, 85 in all. Some houses had 9, one had 16 slaves. These were all much smaller people than Libanius.

[2] *Ep.* 1446, *Or.* xxix. 5.
[3] *Ep.* 744.
[4] *Or.* iii. 11.
[5] *Or.* i. 148.
[6] *Or.* xxix. 5, or in a mule carriage, *Ep.* 1446.
[7] Libanius: *Or.* xxix. 5; Olympius: *Ep.* 1446.
[8] *Ep.* 734.
[9] *Or.* xxxi. 11.
[10] *Ep.* 567.

three horses, and four dogs.[1] Probably Libanius had more servants than he. He evidently did not have an adequate number of scribes to keep up with the demand for copies of his speeches— but then scribes may have been a very scarce commodity.[2]

The fortune of the house of Thalassius provides an example of the wealth which the new senatorial aristocracy of office was beginning to accumulate in the East, though it still fell far short of the wealth of the great senatorial houses of the West.[3] The property of Libanius, on the other hand, might be thought to represent the wealth of a rich Antiochene *curialis*.[4] Magnitude apart, the two properties had much in common. While our definition of the 'upper class' was political and professional, the whole group shares one fundamental economic characteristic: the status of all its members found expression in the ownership of land. The majority of the upper class owed their status to the inherited landed wealth of their families. Some were self-made men. These too would consolidate their position by investing in land. The upper class of Antioch was a landowning aristocracy. Its characteristic economic activities were landowning, corn-selling, and money-lending.[5] But the corn-selling and money-lending arose out of landowning. None of these men could justly be described as a banker or a corn-merchant.[6]

Nevertheless, it is likely that the commercial activities of the owner of a large estate were not restricted to trading in his own produce. The account of the famine of 362–3 shows that councillors dealt in corn that they had not themselves grown.[7] Similarly, the ship which sailed to Sinope for Libanius may well have engaged in more general trading. Perhaps it is unwise to insist too much on the mere absence of information. There is

---

[1] *Or.* xlvii. 28.

[2] A. F. Norman, 'The book trade in fourth-century Antioch', *J.H.S.* lxxx (1960), 122–6.

[3] Jones, *L.R.E.* 554–7.

[4] *Pace* Petit (*Libanius*, 410–11), the heir of Phasganius must have had a large fortune by curial standards.

[5] *Or.* lii. 15, i. 175, lxii. 64–5; also p. 46 n. 5 above. On loans to peasants see below, p. 64. Joh. Chrys. violently attacks usury, e.g. *Hom. in Matth.* 56 (*P.G.* lviii. 596–8); *Hom. in Ep. I ad Cor.* 43 (*P.G.* lxi. 374).

[6] On 'bankers' see below, p. 87. There is no evidence that specialized corn-merchants existed at all; in contrast σιτοπῶλαι had existed in fifth-century Athens: V. Ehrenberg, *The People of Aristophanes*, 132.

[7] See below, p. 130; cf. rich man with store of corn at unexpected end of drought, Joh. Chrys. *Hom. in Ep. I ad Cor.* 39 (*P.G.* lxi. 343).

good reason to suppose that there was a considerable amount of trading across Syria. Must we conclude that the men of Libanius' acquaintance were quite unconnected with it?[1] The absence of information on trade and merchants is partly a consequence of the character of our sources. From very early times the part played by trading or manufacturing activities in writings which follow classical literary conventions was a very small one. Independence of this convention is found only among some of the Christian writers. Thus the biographer of John the Almsgiver, Patriarch of Alexandria, includes, among the good deeds of his hero, also those he performed in the capacity of shipowner, money-lender, or landlord.[2] So too Bishop Gregory of Tours included stories of traders in his 'History of the Franks'.[3] But we must not therefore conclude that trade was more important in the Gaul of his day than it was in the times of Ausonius or Sidonius Apollinaris, in whose writings the classical tradition is followed strictly, and traders and their activities only very briefly mentioned.

Nevertheless, when all has been said that can be said in favour of the participation of the Antiochene upper class in trade and manufacture, the fact remains that the aristocracy of Antioch was not a commercial aristocracy as the aristocracy of Palmyra is said to have been,[4] but rather a class whose chief wealth came from the estates that its members owned and from the functions of government that they performed. It had little in common with the trading aristocracies of the medieval cities in Italy or Flanders.

The literary convention which deprives us of evidence about the commercial activities of members of the Antiochene upper class, also obscures our view of how great fortunes were originally built up. There is for instance no evidence at all about the economics of farming. The sermons of John Chrysostomus contain some violent attacks on usury,[5] but I know only a single case of a man who is said to have actually gained his wealth through usury.[6] Money-lending was probably the activity of a successful landowner rather than of one who was still making his fortune.

---

[1] Fuller discussion, pp. 76 ff. below.

[2] *V. Joh. Eleem.* in *Anal. Boll.* xlv (1927), 19–73, translation in E. Dawes and N. H. Baynes, *Three Byzantine Saints* (Oxford, 1948).

[3] Greg. Tur. *H.F.* v. 5, iv. 43, vi. 6, x. 26, vii. 31, vi. 16, iv. 94, viii. 1.

[4] Rostovtzeff, *Caravan Cities* (Oxford, 1932), 91–150.

[5] See above, p. 48 n. 5,   [6] *Or.* lxii. 64–5.

Advocacy was a profession chosen by many of Libanius' school-leavers who wished to make money[1] and the choice was often proved right. The career of the consular of Syria, Severus, had been built on the earnings of advocacy,[2] so had the position of the man Libanius calls Mixidemus, who earned his wealth and obtained a governorship through practice as an advocate. There are other less striking examples.[3] What made the profession profitable was perhaps not so much the fees received for services in court as the regular contributions made by clients to their habitual defender.[4] Advocacy bordered on patronage. Advocacy also had the advantage of bringing the man who practised it to the notice of the governor, and thus within reach of his favours.[5]

Of all the sources of wealth the most lucrative was undoubtedly the imperial service. It is true that salaries, though still considerable, were lower than in the Early Empire, but apart from the salary, very much profit could be obtained from the perquisites of power, particularly by the holders of *dignitates*.[6] For the humbler officials too there were the various *sportulae*, according to a tariff fixed by law.[7] Money could also be made through a wide range of abuses, such as the sale of admission to the presence of the governor,[8] or extortion by prison officials from prisoners.[9] Men in official positions could expect presents sent by favour-seekers. Such was the estate given as a present to the daughter of the praetorian prefect Helpidius, mentioned earlier. Officials were in an even better position than advocates to make profits, in income or estate, from patronage. It is no coincidence that the wealthiest men at Antioch were men who, like the praetorian prefect Thalassius, had made a splendid career in the imperial service. Two men known to have continued the tradition of private munificence in public building were Datian, the

---

[1] Wolf, *Schulwesen*, 76.

[2] *Or.* lvii. 3 ff.; also lxii. 46. Heliodorus, trader in fish sauce, rose to wealth through law.

[3] *Or.* xxxix. 12; cf. xxxviii. 3 (Silvanus) and lii. 15.

[4] *Or.* lii. 14.   [5] *Or.* xxxix. 10–14; cf. p. 197 below.

[6] On salaries of governors: A. H. M. Jones, *Ec. H. Rev.* v (1935), 305; *L.R.E.* 396–401. Salaries of office staff, ibid. 591, 593–4, 598–9. Before Justinian's raising of salaries the Augustal prefect of Egypt and his staff received 733 *solidi* (400 *solidi* for the prefect).

[7] Authorized *sportulae*: Bruns, *Fontes iuris romani* (ed. 7), no. 103 (A.D. 361–3) = *C.I.L.* viii. 17896. Commentary: Th. Mommsen, *Ges. Schriften* viii. 478 ff.; also Jones, *L.R.E.* 496–9, 591. *Sportulae* paid in gold: *Or.* xlvi. 42.

[8] *C.T.* i. 16. 7.   [9] *Or.* xlv. 10.

leading adviser of Constantius, and Ellebichus, the *magister militum*.[1] We can watch the enrichment of Modestus, who became praetorian prefect under Valens. In a letter of 358 Libanius describes him as poor. But in 364 Modestus, then prefect of Constantinople, was given much land by the emperor and later in the year was negotiating the purchase of further land near Antioch.[2] In the panic after the Riot of the Statues members of this group, men who had governed provinces and won high honours, could be seen carting their silver to safety, each using several carts drawn by many mules.[3]

But if these men invariably invested their wealth in land, they nevertheless remained in every sense city men. Even if we ought not to expect to find details on the administration of estates in the literary letters of Libanius, we might nevertheless look for references to the pleasures of country life, to the absence of bustle, the excitements of the chase, the entertainment of guests in a country villa.[4] We do not read about anything of the kind. The members of the circle of Libanius occasionally lived on their estates,[5] and might even have an eye for the beauties of landscape, though they perhaps preferred it man-made,[6] but their social life took place in the city of Antioch. It is characteristic that Libanius' friend, the senator Olympius, had a luxurious villa at Daphne.[7] Excavations have revealed that Daphne had many such fine villas.[8] When the wealthy citizens of Antioch grew tired of the summer heat and dust of Antioch, they retired, not to their estates, but to the fashionable suburb of Daphne.[9] The friends of Libanius were thus quite different in their tastes from the landowners of Gaul, whom we meet in the letters and poems of Ausonius and Sidonius Apollinaris.[10]

---

[1] Biographies in Seeck, *Briefe*, 113–16, 167–8.   [2] *Ep.* 55 (359), 1316, 1216.
[3] *Or.* xxiii. 19.   [4] Sid. Ap. *Ep.* ii. 2, 9, i. 3. Aus. *Idyl.* iii. 30; *Ep.* x. 18.
[5] Libanius spent his childhood there, *Or.* i. 4–5. It is mere supposition on the part of Harmand (*Discours sur les patronages*, 141) that Libanius wrote speeches or letters while living on his estates. Nothing in his writings indicates this.
[6] *Ep.* 1189, 419; Julian, *Ep.* 25 (ed. W. C. Wright) = 4 ed. Bidez–Cumont; Lib. *Or.* xi. 234 ff., lxi. 8.   [7] *Ep.* 660.
[8] J. Lassus, *Sanctuaires chrétiens de Syrie* (Paris, 1944), 303, based on finds of the Princeton Expedition of the 1930s; Doro Levi, *Antioch Mosaic Pavements* (Princeton, 1945).
[9] Students retire to Daphne in summer: *Ep.* 419 (355).
[10] C. E. Stevens, *Sidonius Apollinaris*, 68–74; S. Dill, *Roman Society in the last Century of the Western Empire* (London, 1905), 167–223; N. K. Chadwick, *Poetry and Letters in Early Christian Gaul*, 47–62.

3. THE SHOPKEEPERS

In the Antioch of Libanius, shopkeepers and craftsmen formed
a single class. Even if some tradesmen, such as greengrocers or
sellers of wood or of fish, from the nature of their trade did not
engage in manufacture, it was the general rule that the people
who made goods also sold them to the public.[1] In view of the
long hours during which shops were open, Libanius could wonder
when the shopkeepers found time to make their goods.[2] The
shopkeeper class included a wide diversity of trades. We hear of
bakers, greengrocers, silversmiths, goldsmiths, tavern-keepers,
barbers, stone masons, perfumers, metal-workers, cobblers, wea-
vers, sellers of cheese, of vinegar, of figs, and of wood.[3] Trades
were of varying degrees of respectability. Bakers and silversmiths
were relatively respected, cobblers much less so.[4] But there was
a great social gulf between the tradesmen as a whole and the
upper classes.

All tradesmen alike were liable to pay the oppressive Traders'
Tax, the *collatio lustralis*. All alike were included in the legally
underprivileged section of the population, the *humiliores*.[5] As such
they could be flogged and tortured and were liable to the more
painful forms of the death penalty. They might be thrown to the
beasts or burnt alive or they might be condemned to work in the
mines. The bakers were also liable to suffer the humiliation of
being driven round the city after a whipping to have their torn
backs displayed to the public.[6]

Libanius would always include the shopkeepers among the
sound and reputable citizens as opposed to the riff-raff,[7] and he

---

[1] ἐργαστήριον = shop as well as workshop: *Or.* xi. 254, xxxi. 25. Combination of
selling and manufacture: *Or.* xxviii. 18 (a silversmith). The combination usual:
Jones, *L.R.E.* 864; R. Meiggs, *Roman Ostia* (Oxford, 1960), 272.

[2] *Or.* xi. 255-7.

[3] Bakers, see below, p. 53; greengrocers: *Or.* liv. 42; tavern-keepers, xlvi. 10;
stone masons, *Ep.* 1176; silversmiths, *Or.* xxviii. 18; bronzesmiths, *Ep.* 197;
barber's shop, perfumery: *Or.* li. 10; sellers of cheese, vinegar, figs; cobblers:
Or. xxix. 30; sellers of fish, oil, and wood: *Or.* iv. 26; goldsmith, tanner, weaver,
builder: *Or.* lviii. 4. See A. F. Norman, 'Gradations in Later Municipal Society',
J.R.S. xlviii (1958), 79-85. A great range of trades is revealed in tombstones of
Corycus in Cilicia: J. Keil and A. Wilhelm, *Mon. Asiae Min. Ant.* iii (1931),
index 234-5.

[4] *Or.* xxix. 30.   [5] Jones, *L.R.E.* 519.

[6] *Or.* i. 228, xxix. 11; the θρίαμβος of the *Book of the Prefect*, xviii. 5-9.

[7] *Or.* xli. 11, lvi. 23.

took note of what was said among them, for instance on the question of the payment of teachers.[1] But his attitude is that of a helpful and considerate patron, not that of a man having dealings with his social equals. It is also quite clear that the tradesmen needed protection. They were not only liable to suffer as scapegoats in times of famine but they had to put up with outrageous behaviour on the part of anyone in an official position. Even students considered them fair game, for ragging and insult. As we will see, the trades were all organized into guilds. But at this period the guilds, with the partial exception of the bakers' organization, were evidently not strong enough to protect their members. This could only be done by an influential upper-class patron.

Detailed evidence about the shops and their owners is scanty and disjointed. We learn that Libanius' protégé, the baker Antiochus, had a mill, and both baked and sold his bread. He lived in rented accommodation.[2] Some mills were driven by water power.[3] We do not know whether there existed at Antioch any large public bakeries[4] distinct from such establishments as that of Antiochus. The fact that Antioch, like Rome and Constantinople, came to have a public distribution of bread[5] makes it likely that public bakeries were set up too. Perhaps certain mills which employed a large force of slave labour were attached to public bakeries.[6]

As has been mentioned earlier, the shopkeepers were liable to pay the Traders' Tax, the *collatio lustralis*.[7] This tax was assessed on the capital involved in a business and collected every fifth year to furnish gold for the donations made by the emperor to the army. It fell equally on the sea traders, who might use the sea to avoid it, and on the poorest of the shopkeepers, for instance on a cobbler who employed no other capital than his shoemaker's knife.[8] The formula used to assess the tax imposed a crushing

[1] *Or.* xxxi. 25, xlviii. 13 (on fugitive councillor). Libanius as patron: xxxvi. 4; warns students: lviii. 4.   [2] *Or.* xxix. 10, 27.

[3] *Or.* iv. 29. On water mills, see Jones, *L.R.E.* 699 n. 26, 1047–8 n. 27. L. A. Moritz, *Grain-Mills and Flour in Classical Antiquity* (Oxford, 1958), 131–9.

[4] On public bakeries at Rome and Constantinople, Jones, *L.R.E.* 699–701. At Constantinople private bakeries were very large. Ostia too had large private bakeries: R. Meiggs, *Roman Ostia*, 274.

[5] See below, p. 129.   [6] *Or.* liii. 19; cf. lvii. 54.

[7] *C.T.* 13. 1. 1 ff.; Zosimus, ii. 38; *P.W.* s.v. *collatio lustralis*.

[8] *Or.* xlvi. 22.

burden on the small trader, who might even be forced to sell his children into slavery to satisfy the collectors.[1]

An imperial law informs us that collection of the tax was normally organized by the traders' organizations.[2] Libanius recalls that he assisted some shopkeepers when the tax was being collected, he prevented the stronger from beating the weaker and the men who had hired workers from showing no consideration for the men they had hired.[3] A few years later Libanius described the collectors of the tax as 'the men who assault and bark and all but bite'.[4] These passages suggest that the collection was in the hands of some of the better-off tradesmen, and that they exerted pressure on their poorer fellows. The passage about the behaviour of 'men who had hired workers' also throws light on the organization of larger concerns. It suggests that men employed by the owners of larger undertakings often engaged in trade in a small way on their own account. Unless this was so, the employees would not themselves have been liable to pay the tax, and the whole weight of it would have fallen on the employer. As it was, when the tax had to be paid, the employer tried to reduce his own liability by insisting that his employees in their capacity as private traders should pay their share.

This situation might arise under a system of home industry. It could be imagined that the employees worked in their homes, that they were supplied with materials and tools by their employers, and received a fixed wage in return for a fixed quota of work.[5] Anything they made and sold above their quota would benefit themselves. When the time came to pay the tax the employer would be assessed for his employees and for the tools they used. Naturally he would attempt to shift part of the burden.[6]

---

[1] *Or.* xlvi. 23, full treatment in Jones, *L.R.E.* 431–2; the selling of children was a commonplace of sermons, see J. R. Palanque and P. de Labriolle, *The Church in the Christian Roman Empire* (trans. E. C. Messenger, London, 1952), ii. 561; and a fact of everyday life, Jones, *L.R.E.* 853–4.

[2] *C.T.* xiii. 1. 17 (399).   [3] *Or.* xxxvi. 4.

[4] *Or.* xlvi. 22.

[5] Cf. *C.T.* xvi. 20. 10, which assumes that dependants of clerics trade independently.

[6] All this is, of course, conjecture, but an organization of this kind existed in the cloth trade of medieval Europe. The merchant provided materials and the various small craftsmen each turned his share of raw material into a finished product. See H. Pirenne, *Histoire économique de l'Occident médiéval* (1951), 327–8, on the export industry of Flanders; also the *Cambridge Economic History* (Cambridge, 1952), vol. 2, 381–3 (E. Carus-Wilson); also on the archaic organization of the

Such an organization might also be concentrated within a single building. This is suggested by a passage of John Chrysostomus: ἐργαστήριον ἐν οἰκοῦντες ἄνθρωποι διαφόρως μὲν ἐμπορεύονται, πάντα δὲ εἰς τὸ κοινὸν ἀποτίθενται.[1] The men work in the same workshop, each of them earns some money from trading, but they all put their earnings in the same till. What are they doing? Are they co-operating or are they employed? In any case, each man seems to be doing a complete piece of work, including the selling. This would not suggest a high degree of specialization or division of labour.

Libanius tells us that goods could be bought at Antioch all over the city. As a result, he claims, no single part of the city is called 'agora'.[2] Now we know from several sources, including Libanius' *Autobiography*, that Antioch had an 'agora' in the normal sense; a large square, suitable for public meetings or markets and surrounded by public buildings. This was where Libanius' school in the council-house was situated. So when Libanius writes that no single part of the city was called 'agora' he cannot be using the word in a purely topographical sense. He must mean that there was no single area which could be described as *the* market of the city. In other words, Antioch did not have a single shopping centre as some other cities of the East evidently had. Facilities for shopping were provided in every part of the city.[3]

The lay-out of the shops is described rather vaguely: 'The cities that we know to pride themselves most on their wealth display only a single range of merchandise, that which is set out

silk industry in contemporary Syria, D. Chevallier, 'De la production lente à l'économie dynamique en Syrie', *Annales* xxi (1966), 59–70.

[1] Joh. Chrys. *Hom. ad pop. Ant.* 16 (*P.G.* xlix. 173). In return they would be paid in money or in money and kind by their employer: *Hom. in Ep. I ad Cor.* 43 (*P.G.* lxi. 372).

[2] *Or.* xi. 251 : τῆς δ' αὖ τῶν ὠνίων περιουσίας τί μὲν ἀφθονώτερον, τί δὲ διαρκέστερον, ἃ διὰ πάσης μὲν οὕτω κέχυται τῆς πόλεως, ὡς μὴ μέρος τι τῆς πόλεως ἐν ἀγορὰν κεκλῆσθαι μηδὲ δεῖν εἰς ἕν τι συνελθεῖν ὠνησομένους, ἀλλὰ πᾶσιν ἐν ποσὶν εἶναι καὶ πρὸ θυρῶν . . . Commentary by R. Martin in Festugière, *Antioche*, 56–7.

[3] The Agora, *Or.* i. 102: τῶν ἀγοραίων δέ τινα μεταστήσας ἄλλοσε τῆς συνοικίας καταβὰς αὐτὸς ἐκεῖσε ἐκαθήμην ψαύων τῆς ἀγορᾶς. Cf. Downey, *Antioch*, 621–4. Shopping centres: Rostovtzeff, *Excavations at Dura Europos: Preliminary report of 9th season, 1935–6* (Yale, 1944), 28, describes how a 'bazaar quarter' was formed by the irregular filling in of the agora with shops and houses. R. Martin, *L'Urbanisme dans la Grèce antique* (1956), 97, on markets of Miletus and Priene. D. Claude, *Die byzantinische Stadt* (Munich, 1969), 167–8, cites evidence for business areas of the period of the Later Empire; from Justiniana Prima, Sardis, Istrus, Berytus; ibid. 60 ff., a list of cities with colonnaded streets.

in front of the buildings, but nobody works between the pillars. With us these too are places of sale, so that there is a workshop opposite almost each one of the buildings.'[1] I take it that the 'single range of merchandise' describes goods laid out for sale on tables in front of the houses or inside open shop-fronts as at Ostia or Pompeii. On the other hand, the places of sale between the pillars represent cabins built into the great colonnades that crossed Antioch from north to south and from east to west. The cabins were very slightly built and had brushwood roofs. In spite of their primitive construction they served both as places of business and as homes for their occupants. Moreover, sites in the colonnade were in great demand. Any vacant space was quickly filled up and the occupiers are said to have clung to their pitch as to a rope, or as Odysseus clung to the wild fig-tree above the cave of Charybdis. The comparison conveys a vivid impression of the intense struggle for survival among the inhabitants of the teeming city.

Libanius suggests that no citizen of Antioch had to go far from home to buy the necessities of life. Perhaps we can deduce from this that the various trades of Antioch were not concentrated in specialized areas. Followers of each trade were found all over the city, or if there was some concentration it was neither complete nor obligatory.[2] Although the evidence is so unsatis-

---

[1] *Or.* xi. 254: ἕνα στοῖχον τῶν ὠνίων . . . τὸν τῶν οἰκημάτων προκείμενον, ἐν δὲ τοῖς μέσοις τῶν κιόνων ἐργάζεται οὐδείς, παρ' ἡμῖν δὲ καὶ ταῦτα πωλητήρια, ὥστε ἑκάστου μικροῦ τῶν οἰκημάτων ἀντιπρόσωπον ἐργαστήριον. I think Libanius means that there are almost as many shops between the pillars as behind them. In later years as municipal control relaxed the shops between the pillars of the colonnades in several cities encroached on the central roadway until this was blocked and the colonnade became a 'Soukh'. See J. Sauvaget, *Mémorial Sauvaget* i. 101–20 (Laodicea); *Syria* xxvi (1949), 314–18 (Damascus); *Rev. biblique* lxiv (1957), 22, (Petra); Claude, *Die byzantinische Stadt*, 58–9.

[2] Dispersal of trades, *Or.* xi. 252: οὐ γάρ ἐστιν ἀγυιὰν οὕτως εὑρεῖν ὠλιγωρημένην οὐδ' ἐν ὑστάτοις, ἣ τοὺς ἐνοικοῦντας ἑτέρωσε πέμπει ληψομένους τι τῶν ἀναγκαίων, ἀλλ' ὁμοίως ἀκμάζει τά τε μέσα τοῦ ἄστεος καὶ τὰ ἔσχατα. But note that the victuallers, σαλδαμάριοι, were obliged to sell their goods all over the city at Constantinople even when other trades were compulsorily localized: *Book of the Prefect*, xiii. 1. References to localized trades, see below, p. 57, n. 1. Concentration of trades may or may not be implied by the naming of streets after trades. At Antioch: a Mariners' Street, ῥύμη τῶν θαλασσίων (Malalas 397). A comprehensive assembly of references to streets named after craftsmen especially from Egypt: Stöckle, *Spätrömische und byzantinische Zünfte, Klio*, Beiheft ix (1911), 148–52. See also R. Mac-Mullen, *Enemies of the Roman Order* (London, 1967), 174 n. 14. Claude, *Byzantinische Stadt*, 178, Localization of trades at Constantinople: R. Janin, *Constantinople byzantine* (Paris, 1950), 96–106.

factory, the problem is of general interest. In the *Book of the Prefect* of Constantinople, location of some trades is controlled as part of the general supervision of trades and prices.[1] The free dispersal of trades over the built-up area of Antioch would agree very well with the unregulated condition of retailing at Antioch in the first half of the century.

About the appearance and interior arrangements of the more substantial shops, Libanius tells us nothing. We depend on the small-scale pictures of the 'topographical mosaic'[2]—and on analogy. The standard practice was perhaps not very different from that followed at Pompeii, where uncovered workshops and wall-paintings in the houses of the owners enable us to visualize the shops as they once were, full of craftsmen, salesmen, and customers. These shops show both the extent and the limits of the development of ancient workshop technique. There are shops which employed several dozen workmen. A tannery is thought to have been large enough to supply all the leather required by the whole city. On the other hand, even the largest of the workshops of Pompeii finds room within a private dwelling-house. Private apartments may be converted to workshop use, but the workshop is never situated in premises specially designed to be a workshop; there are no factory buildings in Pompeii.[3]

The situation would seem to have been similar in the Later Empire. Even the largest concerns, the imperial factories, appear to have been associations of individual craftsmen. At any rate Sozomen's description of the imperial clothing factory and mint at Cyzicus suggests that these consisted of a large number of craftsmen and their families settled in the city on the condition that they would produce a stated quantity of military tunics or coins. No doubt they received tools, materials, and remuneration

---

[1] *Book of the Prefect* ii. 11, goldsmiths, χρυσοχόοι; v. 2, dealers in Syrian silk, πρανδιοπρᾶται; vi. 13, dealers in raw silk, μεταξοπρᾶται; x. 1; perfume dealers, μυρεψοί; xv. 1, xvi. 3, xxi. 3, the wholesale purchase of meat for slaughter; xvii. 1, fishmongers, ἰχθυοπρᾶται. Bakers were not concentrated but a square was known as τὸ ἀρτοπώλιον (Stöckle, op. cit. 49–50).

[2] Doro Levi, *Antioch Mosaic Pavements*, i. 323–45, ii, Pls. 75–80. Cf. G. Downey, 'An illustrated commentary on Libanius' *Antiochicus*', *Miscellanea Critica*, i. 79–88.

[3] Rostovtzeff, *S.E.H.R.E.* 513 n. 19, also Pls. 14–15; T. Frank, *E.S.A.R.* v. 259 ff.; cf. Meiggs, *Roman Ostia*, 271–4; I. Richmond, 'Industry in Roman Britain', 77–86, in *The Civitas Capitals of Roman Britain*, ed. J. S. Wacher (Leicester, 1966).

from the imperial government.[1] At Antioch there were three
state factories, a mint, an arms factory, and a factory for making
the decorated bronze armour worn by officers. We hear nothing
about their organization, though we may wonder through what
private business some *monetarii* had gained their indisputably
curial fortunes.[2] Like their colleagues in state factories elsewhere,[3]
these workers occasionally made their presence felt. When the
Caesar Gallus threw blame for a shortage of food on the consular
Theophilus some five men from the arms works lynched him.[4]
A little later Gallus claimed to have discovered a conspiracy
against himself for which a *tribunus fabicarum* had promised
arms.[5]

The *fabricenses*, ranking as soldiers,[6] were a privileged group.
Ordinary shopkeepers and craftsmen had to submit to numerous
abuses. The tavern-keepers suffered from the officials of the three
high dignitaries who had their headquarters in Antioch, and
from other persons of power such as *agentes in rebus*. All exploited
their rank to obtain goods, particularly drinks, without paying for them. Even local, or semi-local officials, the *curator* and
defensor, abused their very limited power to the loss of the shopkeepers.[7] The garrison, the ἐγκαθήμενος λόχος, joined in the exploitation. These soldiers carried off everything there was in the
shops, and if there was no meat, nor anything else that appealed
to them, they took money.[8] This suggests that the soldiers were

---

[1] Soz. v. 15 (*P.G.* lxvii. 1256–7). ἔτους ἑκάστου ῥητὴν ἀποφορὰν τῷ δημοσίῳ κατα-
τιθέντες οἱ μὲν στρατιωτικῶν χλαμύδων οἱ δὲ νεουργῶν νομισμάτων. The workers supply
a fixed quota of manufactured articles to the state. They may well be working at home
and selling for their own profit cloaks in excess of the quota. Substituting a private
employer for the state, we get something like my reconstruction of the condition
of the workers in Libanius' *Or.* xxxvi. 4. Persson, *Staat und Manufaktur in dem
Römischen Reich* (Lund, 1923), 86, from which I have taken this interpretation of
the Sozomen passage, refers 'Linyfii Scythopolitani publico canoni obnoxii'
(*C.T.* x. 20. 8 (374) at Antioch) to the same form of organization. Each linen
weaver weaves a fixed quota (canon) of cloth for the government. Cf. Jones,
L.R.E. 834–7, also 'Die Bekleidigungsindustrie in der Zeit des Römischen Imperium', 156–67, in *Sozialökonomische Verhältnisse im alten Orient und im klassischen
Altertum*, eds. R. Günther and G. Schrot (Berlin, 1961).

[2] Malalas 307. 21 ff., 308. 1–4; *Not. Dig. Or.* 11, 18 (p. 32 ed. Seeck); *barbari-
carii: C.T.* x. 22. 1 (374); Julian, *Misop.* 368.

[3] Greg. Naz. *V. Bas.* i. 57.

[4] *Or.* xix. 47; cf. i. 103, assuming that χαλκεῖς = *fabri*. But in *Ep.* 197 (360) a
councillor (Petit, *Libanius*, 398) is appointed to supervise the χαλκεῖς. Could the
supervision of *fabri* be a curial *munus*? See also ii. 58.

[5] Amm. xiv. 7. 18; ibid. 9. 4.　　　　　　　　　　　　[6] Jones, *L.R.E.* 835–6.

[7] *Or.* xlvi. 11–13, 24.　　　　　　　　　　　　　　　[8] Ibid. 13.

exploiting an obligation on the part of the shops to supply the soldiers' rations.[1]

Such abuses, no less than the harsh penalties frequently inflicted after proper legal process,[2] were merely an expression of the fact that the shopkeepers as a whole had little political influence and that very few of them were men of standing. Among the many important and well-to-do citizens of Antioch mentioned by Libanius only Thalassius IV[3] and perhaps Alexander X[4] seem to have had any connection with trade or manufacture.

The explanation of the humble standing of the shopkeeper class is partly economic. Most of the shopkeepers were poor.[5] Their business and earnings were on a very small scale.[6] An order to maintain three lights outside the shop at night[7] or even to have the shop signs repainted could be expected to cause widespread hardship.[8]

But it must have been possible to make money at Antioch. In so important a centre of government there was considerable purchasing power. The count of the East had a staff of six hundred.[9] The consular had fewer officials, but the staff of the master of the soldiers was perhaps even larger than that of the count. Not all these men were stationed at Antioch, but many surely were, and their salaries must have been spent in the city. In addition many litigants and petitioners flocked to the courts of the three dignitaries. Moreover, the emperor and court, and the praetorian prefect of the East with his staff resided at Antioch for varying periods during the century.[10] The presence of officials was certainly no unmixed blessing; it might mean high prices[11] for everybody. But these provided profit for shopkeepers. The benefit derived

---

[1] Cf. *C.T.* vii. 5. 1 (399).

[2] Also destructive raids by the police: *Or.* xlvi. 18.

[3] Seeck, *Briefe*, 291.

[4] Ibid. 56; *Or.* xl. 10 ff. reading Ἀλέξανδρον not Ἀλεξάνδρου 285, l. 15; *Or.* lxii. 63 ff.

[5] *Or.* xx. 36–7, 'fear of starvation is our master'.

[6] The bulk of ancient manufacture came from small units. See Rostovtzeff, *S.E.H.H.W.* 1222 for metal work and ibid. 1228 for textiles in the Hellenistic world; also *E.S.A.R.* 5. 223, evidence for small-scale production at Rome.

[7] *Or.* xxxiii. 35.   [8] Ibid. 33; cf. xxvii. 31.

[9] *C.T.* i. 13. 1 (394).

[10] Under Constantius the praetorian prefect might be at Antioch even when the emperor was not; Strategius, 355–8: see Seeck, *Briefe*, 282–4; Hermogenes, 358–60: ibid. 173–4.

[11] Julian, *Misop.* 307B. Socrates, *H.E.* iii. 17 (*P.G.* lxvii. 424b).

by a city through being a centre of government was most strikingly shown when the province of Cappadocia was divided into
two, and the old capital, Caesarea, lost half its territory to the
capital of the new province: the effect on Caesarea was disastrous.[1] In addition to being a centre of imperial administration
Antioch had a lot of well-to-do local residents, and linen clothing
manufactured in the city was sold as far away as Rome.[2] The
city must have enabled some tradesmen to become prosperous.[3]
The fact that Libanius mentions so few cannot be due to economic
reasons only.

The case of Thalassius IV is very enlightening. The father of
Thalassius had owned a workshop for the manufacture of arms,
employing slaves. When the son tried to enter the senate of
Constantinople, incidentally an indication of great wealth, the
existence of this workshop was held to make him unworthy. To
this Libanius replied that Thalassius had never made any swords,
and had not even learned the craft, and that already his father
had been in the same position. He merely owned slaves who were
skilled, just as the father of Demosthenes had done.[4] So Libanius
believes that he has vindicated the gentility of Thalassius' father
and of Thalassius himself by showing that neither had done
manual work, nor had ever learnt a manual skill. In this atmosphere a successful craftsman-shopkeeper would soon retire from
direct participation in the business of his workshop. It is surely
significant that Thalassius, the son, possessed[5] landed estate and
was enrolled as a decurion of Antioch.[6] It is not clear whether
he still owned the sword workshop. If so, he made his participation as inconspicuous as possible in order to obtain the councillor's privilege of immunity from the Traders' Tax.[7] He certainly
continued to own a ship, and in about 380 took over the task of
supervising the copying of Libanius' writings, being even willing
to lose some money on the job.[8] The implications of the life of
Thalassius IV are confirmed elsewhere. In his sermons John
Chrysostomus frequently criticized the social stigma attached to

---

[1] Basil, *Ep.* 75–6. At Ptolemais in Cyrenaica decay follows transfer of provincial
government and of military headquarters: C. Kraeling, *Ptolemais, City of the
Libyan Pentapolis* (Chicago, 1962), 27.

[2] *V. Mel.* 8; cf. *P. Fouad*, 74.

[3] At least one tradesman in the council under Julian: *Misop.* 368B.

[4] *Or.* xlii. 21.   [5] Ibid. 4 and 37.   [6] *Or.* liv. 47.

[7] *C.T.* xiii. 1. 4.   [8] *Or.* xlii. 4.

the tradesmen class. Some wealthy members of his congregation have been known to abuse and even manhandle shopkeepers,[1] others merely feel ashamed to be found in their company.[2] John Chrysostomus imagines two cities, one inhabited entirely by rich, the other by poor men. The craftsmen would only be found in the city of the poor, for had any of them become wealthy they would have given up their trades.[3]

But if successful shopkeepers tended to sever their connections with trade or manufacture this does not mean that they necessarily ceased to be financially interested in their former trade. Members of the upper classes might well continue to profit from making or selling through agents. Julian tells us that the councillors of Antioch strongly resented his attempts to control prices because they were affected by two sets of control, those imposed on landowners and those on shopkeepers.[4] It is clear therefore that the curial class had a very strong financial interest in food shops at any rate, just as at Constantinople in Justinian's reign very many workshops could be said to belong to the church or to members of the senatorial nobility or civil service.[5] This was inevitable. Rents enabled members of the landowning class to accumulate capital. As possessors of capital they were in a position to build shops, markets, or storage facilities and to make loans. These activities provided investment for their money and naturally led to tradesmen becoming their tenants[6] or debtors.

4. THE WORKERS OF THE LAND

There was a sharp separation of city and country dwellers. Peasants came into town only occasionally to sell their products. Libanius comments on the remarkable self-sufficiency of life in certain large villages.[7] That a large number of peasants came

---

[1] *Hom. in Ep. I ad Cor.* 20 (*P.G.* lxi. 168). Libanius too tried to protect the tradesmen from arbitrary wrongs and warns his pupils against 'ragging' them. *Or.* xxix. 27–30, xxxvi. 4, lviii. 4.

[2] *Hom. in Prisc. et Aquill.* 1 (*P.G.* li. 192d), cf. Lib. *Or.* ii. 6, i. 87.

[3] *Hom. in Ep. I ad Cor.* 34 (*P.G.* lxi. 292e).

[4] *Misop.* 350B: οἱ δὲ ἐν τέλει τῆς πόλεως ἀμφοῖν μετέχοντες ταῖν ζημίαιν, ὥσπερ οἶμαι πρότερον ἔχαιρον διχόθεν καρπούμενοι τὰς ὠφελείας, καὶ ὡς κεκτημένοι καὶ ὡς καπηλεύοντες, τὰ νῦν εἰκότως λυποῦνται δι' ἀμφοτέρων ἀφῃρημένοι τὰς ἐπικερδείας.

[5] Justinian, *Nov.* xliii. 1. 1.   [6] *Or.* xlvi. 44.

[7] Ibid. 230. Nevertheless a considerable proportion of city dwellers are likely to have worked on the land if only at harvest time, as at Thessalonica (*Miracula*

into the city on Easter Day was sufficiently noteworthy to furnish John Chrysostomus with the occasion for a moral lesson on the simple life.[1] The fact that the animals of peasants coming to town to sell their produce might be commandeered to carry rubble must have deterred peasants from making inessential visits.[2]

City and country dwellers were also separated by a difference of language. While the city is likely to have had a Syriac-speaking population we do not hear about it. The upper class was Greek-speaking. But there is no doubt that many of the peasants spoke nothing but Syriac. The villages even in the environment of Antioch had Syriac names. Peasants coming into the city on Easter Day could be heard speaking a strange tongue.[3] Many of the famous hermits spoke only Syriac.[4] Further east, at Edessa, a Christian Syriac literature was coming into existence at about this time.[5] Libanius takes no interest at all in this non-Greek culture, not even to the extent of wishing to bring the benefits of Greek literary education to the Syriac-speaking population.[6]

There must have been a good deal of more or less shamefaced bilingualism. Theodoret, bishop of Cyrrhus, displays in all his writings the marks of a fully absorbed rhetorical education, but he came from a Syriac-speaking background. His parents lived at Antioch. His mother regularly visited the hermit Macedonius who knew no Greek. His father too was able to talk to Macedonius. Young Theodoret studied Greek rhetoric but then went into a monastery near Apamea where most of the monks spoke Syriac. It is clearly not chance that a man with this background should have chosen to write the *Historia religiosa*, to inform Greek readers of the ascetic feats of the hermits of Syria.[7]

Despite the language barrier landlords must have been able to make themselves understood by their peasants, because they not

---

S. Demetrii i. 13, 116) or at Edessa (Josh. Styl. 52). On this see Claude, *Byzantinische Stadt*, 179–80.

[1] Joh. Chrys., *Hom. ad pop. Ant.* 19. 1 (*P.G.* xlix. 188).

[2] *Or.* l.   [3] Joh. Chrys., op. cit.

[4] Macedonius: Theodoret, *Hist. Rel.* xiii (*P.G.* 1401d); Aphraates: ibid. viii (*P.G.* 1368b–c); Abraham: ibid. xvii (*P.G.* 1424c); Thalalaeus' knowledge of Greek requires explanation; he was a Cilician: ibid. xxviii (*P.G.* 1488a); cf. Festugière, *Antioche païenne et chrétienne* (Paris, 1959), 291–2.

[5] J.-B. Chabot, *Littérature syriaque* (Paris, 1934).

[6] Syriac-speaking tinkers: *Or.* xlii. 31, the only reference to Syriac.

[7] P. Peeters, *Le Tréfonds orientale de l'hagiographie byzantine*, (Subsidia Hagiographica xxvi, Brussels, 1950), 71–92.

only drew rents but also gave orders. This follows from a description of the work of a landlord's agent and also from the way tenants would rely on the protection afforded by a patron to reject their landlords' orders and to work only when it pleased themselves.[1]

What was the relation between landlord and peasant, and what were the orders the peasants refused? The peasants were not mere hired labourers.[2] If they had been, their employer could just have sacked them or at least stopped their pay. In fact he had to take them to court. A possible relationship is suggested by surviving Greek tenancy agreements. 'The tenant will divide the land into two portions which will be cultivated and left fallow alternatively. He will work on the vines twice a year in the month of Anthesterion (eighth month after the summer solstice) and in the month of Apatourion (fifth month after the summer solstice) . . .'[3] It is conceivable that the disputes arose over the landlords' efforts to keep their tenants to the terms of a contract of this kind.

The place and time of the inscription just cited are rather distant from the rural troubles related by Libanius. The regulations of the Talmud concerning Jewish tenancies in Mesopotamia are nearer. Here the tenancy agreement laid down the crops which a tenant paying a fixed rent was allowed to grow. Even the time of the harvest appears to have been at the discretion of the owner.[4] Since it was in the interest of the landlord to get in his rent in kind early, when corn prices were still high, and in the interest of the tenant to reap the corn later, when the yield would be greatest, the determination of harvest-time could give rise to disputes.

But the most probable solution is that the 'orders' were given in connection with work the peasants were required to do on the

---

[1] An agent's work, *Ep.* 1386: τούς τε ἄλλους ἐπὶ τὰ ἔργα κινῶν καὶ αὐτὸς οὐκ ὀλίγα συμπονῶν. Use of patron, *Or.* xlvii. 11: πρὸς τοὺς αὐτῶν κυρίους ⟨ἐπισπέρχοντας⟩ τοῦτο τῆς γῆς βουλομένης, ἄγριον ἔστησαν ὀφθαλμόν, ὡς ἀνάγκης μὲν ὄντες ἔξω, γνώμῃ δὲ ἐργαζόμενοι καὶ οὐχ ἁψόμενοι τῆς γῆς εἰ μὴ πείθοιεν αὐτούς. Ibid. 13: ἐπεθύμησαν μὴ ὅπερ ἦσαν εἶναι, καὶ τὸν παλαιὸν ἀποσεισάμενοι ζυγὸν ἠξίουν ὁρισταὶ τοῦ πῶς ἡμῖν αὐτοῖς χρηστέον εἶναι.

[2] This was rare on a permanent basis, see Jones, *L.R.E.* 792–3.

[3] P. Guiraud, *La Propriété foncière en Grèce jusqu'à la conquête romaine* (Paris, 1893), 436.

[4] J. Newman, *The Agricultural Life of the Jews in Babylonia* (London, 1932), 49–61, 79.

'home farm'.[1] John Chrysostomus tells us that on some estates peasants were not only required to pay a heavy fixed rent[2] irrespective of the quality of their harvest but also to perform certain labour services.[3] The continuation of the passage throws further light on the labour service. Chrysostomus upbraids landlords for charging an interest rate of fifty per cent, a rate of usury not sanctioned even by the customs of pagans—for loans made to the men who fill their threshing floors and wine presses.[4] In Egypt fifty per cent interest was commonly charged on loans of wheat made to peasants before the harvest, to be repaid after it.[5] It is likely that the loans in Syria were made under the same conditions, and that the men who filled the landowners' threshing floors and wine presses were free peasants or tenants with a harvest of their own who did additional work for the landowners. A similar arrangement is likely to have been required to furnish seasonal labour for olive plantations.[6] We can see that landowners had a strong motive for asking labour services. It would be cheaper to have the work done by tenants for nothing than to hire free peasants or seasonal labourers. It is also obvious that demands for labour services, whether in home farm, vineyard, or olive plantation would be resented, and provide a constant source of disputes.

The use of labour services would obviate the use of slave labour, and I have seen no evidence for the use of slaves for agricultural work in Syria.[7] The only passage to suggest that the use of slave labour was important is the statement of John Chrysostomus that some rich men owned one thousand to two thousand slaves. This is a scale of employment one would expect to find only in agriculture. Of all the provinces of the empire, only Italy and Spain provide evidence for the extensive use of

[1] Jones, *L.R.E.*, 805.

[2] Joh. Chrys. *Hom. in Matth.* 61 (*P.G.* lviii. 591) τελέσματα διηνεκῆ καὶ ἀφόρητα ἐπιτιθέασι . . . καὶ παρεχούσης τῆς γῆς καὶ μὴ παρεχούσης ὁμοίως αὐτοὺς κατατείνουσι.

[3] Ibid.: διακονίας ἐπιπόνους; Ibid. 592: ἀπὸ μὲν τῶν πόνων αὐτῶν . . . ληνοὺς καὶ ὑπολήνια πληροῦντες αὐτοῖς δὲ οἴκαδε οὐδὲ ὀλίγον εἰσαγαγεῖν ἐπιτρέποντες μέτρον . . . καὶ ὀλίγον αὐτοῖς ὑπὲρ τούτου προσπιπτοῦντες ἀργύριον.

[4] Ibid.: καὶ τοῖς οἰκείοις πόνοις καὶ τὴν ἅλω καὶ τὴν ληνὸν πληροῦντος . . .

[5] A. C. Johnson and L. C. West, *Byzantine Egypt: Economic Studies* (Princeton, 1949), 170. G. Mickwitz, *Geld und Wirtschaft im römischen Reich* (Leipzig, 1932), 183.

[6] G. Tchalenko, *Villages antiques de la Syrie du Nord* (Paris, 1953), 373.

[7] *Or.* xiv. 45 refers to Greece. Only two slave inscriptions are known from the hill villages: *I.G.L.S.* 650 and 1409–11, see Tchalenko, op. cit. 410.

slave labour on the land.[1] Moreover the passage of John Chrysostomus is highly rhetorical. In the absence of corroboration I
prefer to conclude that slaves were not exploited in agriculture
on a significant scale in Syria.[2]

But in many parts of the empire the condition of free tenant
farmers was beginning to resemble slavery in that certain classes
of *coloni* were becoming tied to the land.[3] This tendency had not
gone equally far in all parts of the empire. The papyri of Egypt,
for instance, provide no trace of the tied colonate in the fourth
century. Libanius' evidence on this aspect of the condition of the
peasantry is ambiguous and has given rise to considerable discussion. Libanius shows that it was neither usual nor thought
reputable for peasants to leave their land. His own Jewish
tenants had worked the land of his family for four generations.[4]
He exploits for purposes of abuse the fact that the father of the
consular Eutropius had been a peasant: 'Your father was born
in a village. But he shirked the toil of farm-work and in this way
sinned against the soil and against the gods who watch over
crops. For he became gate-keeper to a governor who was a
profligate . . .' Nevertheless the abandonment of farming is seen
as a wrong done to the gods of fertility, not as a breach of imperial legislation.[5] In the same way, Libanius mocks the monks
of Syria, 'who have run away from farm-work and claim to be
holding converse with the creator of the universe in the mountains', but he does not charge them—as it would have served
his purpose to do—with a breach of the law.[6] We might conclude
from this that Syrian tenancies were stable by custom and convenience, but not legally tied.[7]

Yet this is not the whole story. Libanius also tells us that
certain tenants abandoned their farms, and their families, to
seek refuge with a patron whose influence frustrated any attempt

[1] Jones, *L.R.E.* 793–4. On very limited use of slaves on the land in Aegean islands:
Jones, 'Census Records of the Later Roman Empire', *J.R.S.* xliii (1953), 49–64.

[2] Further light on the agricultural system may be thrown by study of the contexts in which the terms for agricultural workers cited by Heichelheim in *E.S.A.R.*
iv. 147, are used in the Talmud. See also G. Rouillard, *La Vie rurale dans l'Empire
byzantin*, 25 ff.; but these estates of sixth-century Egypt were probably larger and
more complicated in their organization than the fourth-century estates in Syria.

[3] On the colonate see the very clear and convincing account in Jones, *L.R.E.*
796–803.

[4] *Or.* xlvii. 13.   [5] *Or.* iv. 25.   [6] *Or.* xxx. 48.

[7] Cf. also *Or.* xxv. 38: the peasant free, but for the gods and the climate.

to bring them back by legal process.[1] I do not see how peasants could be driven to so desperate an act if they had the right to give up their tenancies and move elsewhere. The conclusion is unavoidable: that at least such tenants as had no land of their own, and were registered for purposes of taxation under the estates of their landlords, were not allowed to leave the estates under which they were registered.[2] How near to slavery their condition had sunk it is difficult to decide. No doubt the condition of the dependent peasantry varied from region to region and estate to estate. John Chrysostomus in the passage already discussed expresses the view that the peasants were cruelly exploited. The landlords' agents were tyrants whose pressure might include physical violence or dragging of peasants before the governor.[3] Libanius confirms both the tyranny and the fact that when no patron was involved the governor would be only too ready to support the landlord.[4] Yet if the peasant retained a patron the tables were turned.

Surprisingly, there is no evidence that tenants used patrons to protect themselves from the landlords' demands for rent. In fact rents as such are not mentioned at all in the *De patrociniis*. We might, however, deduce from Libanius' statement that peasants gave presents to their patron 'at the expense of their owner', that the landlord's rent was not fixed but varied with the farm's output, in other words it consisted of a certain proportion of the crop. On the other hand, John Chrysostomus mentions rents that remain the same irrespective of the harvest.[5] We might conclude that tenants paying fixed rents and sharecroppers existed side by side in the Syrian countryside.[6]

---

[1] *Or.* xlvii. 17.

[2] Jones, *L.R.E.* 796–7, (on *C.T.* xi. 1. 14; ibid. 26), shows that (*a*) the tied colonate resulted from registration under the landowner's estate; (*b*) tenants who also owned land of their own were registered under their own name and paid their tax to the collectors themselves. They were not usually tied.

[3] Joh. Chrys. *Hom. in Matth.* 61: καὶ τοῦ λιμοῦ τούτου καὶ τοῦ ναυαγίου τὰς τῶν ἐπιτρόπων βασάνους καὶ τοὺς ἑλκυσμοὺς καὶ τὰς ἀπαιτήσεις καὶ τὰς ἀπαγωγὰς καὶ τὰς ἀπαραιτήτους λειτουργίας μᾶλλον δεδοικότες . . .

[4] Peasants treated like slaves, 'soldiers' prompt to support landlord: *Or.* xlv. 5; cf. also xlvii. 13 before intervention of patron.

[5] Ibid. 11: διδόντες ἐξ ὧν ἀποστεροῦσι . . .; but *Dig.* vii, 4. 13 like Joh. Chrys., op. cit., n. 3, above, suggests fixed rents.

[6] Sharecroppers and tenants paying fixed rents co-existed on land owned by Jews in Mesopotamia, sharecropping being by far the commonest tenure; see Newman, op. cit., p. 63 n. 4 above.

It may or may not be significant that today sharecropping is the main form of tenure in the Near East. Normally the relationship between landlord and peasant is customary. It is not based on any legal contract and offers no legal protection to the worker of the land. The proportion of the crop claimed by the landlord varies. It is highest in the neighbourhood of towns, low on the edge of the desert.[1]

It is well known that the condition of the later Roman Empire favoured the absorption of the land of independent peasants into great estates.[2] But the speed of this process varied very greatly in different parts of the empire. Libanius provides evidence for the survival in Syria of an independent peasantry on a considerable scale. Libanius knows villages[3] of two kinds, those that had many masters,[4] and those that had only one. The former kind seem to be villages of peasant proprietors. For the decurions collected the taxes from the peasants directly.[5] Had the peasants been tenants, their tax would probably have been paid by the owners and collected by them together with the rent.[6] We also hear that villages of this type, protected by the power of a patron, would attack other villages and inflict severe damage on them; trees were cut, water-courses diverted, and even land seized. Nothing is said about the losses suffered by owners of the attacked villages.[7] It is therefore likely that the attacked villages, like their attackers, were occupied by peasant proprietors.

[1] D. Warriner, *Land Reform and Development in the Middle East* (London, 1948), 59.

[2] Jones, *L.R.E.* 774–81. L. Ruggini, *Economia e società nell'*'*Italia annonaria*' (Milan, 1961), 23 ff. Loss of land to creditor: G. Rouillard, 'Prêt de grains, A.D. 497', *Mémoires publiés par les membres de l'Institut français du Caire* lxvii (1934), 177–84.

[3] κῶμαι or ἀγροί. *Or.* xlvii. 4 and 11 show the two words used in the same sense, also xlvii. 11, ll. 13 and 18.

[4] δεσπότης.   [5] *Or.* xlvii. 7.

[6] *C.T.* xi. 1. 14 to Modestus, *P.P.O.* This makes landlords responsible for the tax payments of their tenants. But if tenants have land of their own in addition, they themselves pay the taxes due on that to the tax-gatherers. *C.T.* xi. 1. 7 of 361 implies the same principle: senators must not be held responsible for the taxes that should have been paid by fugitive *coloni* of other estates than their own. If a landlord is held liable for the taxes on the lands of his tenants, it is reasonable to assume that he was careful to collect them himself so as to have them complete for the tax-collectors. Hardy, 'Large Estates', 50–4, cites evidence from Egypt; the tax was collected with the rent, sometimes as a separate unit, sometimes not. But according to *C.J.* xi. 48. 20, it was customary in some places for landlords to collect the taxes with the rent, in others for the tenants to pay the collectors directly. On this see Jones, *L.R.E.* 805.

[7] *Or.* xlvii. 4–6.

Some areas of independent peasants can be located. In the *Antiochicus* Libanius remarks on the large size, population, and self-sufficiency of villages in the territory of Antioch. He states that at local fairs the villages make good each other's deficiencies and as a result of this mutual exchange have little need of the city of Antioch.[1] The description implies, even if it does not state, that the villages' independence of the city also included independence of city-dwelling landowners. Libanius does not specify where these villages were situated, but the remains of large and well-built villages on the hills to the east of Antioch would fit his description very well. In this area olive plantations were expanding over previously waste ground from the fourth to the early sixth century and Tchalenko has concluded from the large number of small-scale villas, each with its own oil press, that this expansion was accompanied by the growth of an independent peasantry.[2]

The location of another area of independent peasants is suggested by the *Pro templis*. Libanius discredits the monks' campaign against rural temples with the argument that these attacks are extremely damaging to the peasants. The victims are owners of the land they farm, yet they are country folk and of no consequence. There is no suggestion that the interests of city-dwelling landowners are involved. Apart from peasants only the emperor is said to suffer loss, for these attacks reduce the revenue from taxation.[3] It looks as if the affected peasants were predominantly peasant proprietors. The proximity of early monastic settlements and prominent rural temples[4] suggests that the region concerned was the neighbourhood of the plain of Dana on the edge of the hill region, facing Chalcis. It would follow that this too was an area of free peasants. On the other hand, boundary stones put up in connection with the great census of Diocletian on the Gebel Sim'ān, not far away to the north, reveal the coexistence of presumably free villages (κῶμαι) with great estates (ἐποικίαι).[5]

---

[1] *Or.* xi. 230.   [2] Tchalenko, *Villages*, 408 ff.

[3] Loss borne by peasants and emperor: *Or.* xxx. 10. The victims—no reference to owners—complain to bishop; ibid. 11; they are not councillors: ibid. 15.

[4] Tchalenko, op. cit. 145 ff.; vol. ii, Pls. vii, xlv, liv; Festugière, *Antioche*, 312–13.

[5] Tchalenko, op. cit., vol. iii. 6–11; *Ep.* 1041, slave of a free farmer accidentally burns the house of a neighbouring tenant.

That peasant proprietors could even be found in the neighbour-hood of Antioch is suggested by the *De angariis*. Animals of peasants who had come to the city to sell their produce were re-quisitioned to dispose of building rubble.[1] The animals of *honorati* were not requisitioned; other notables managed to get their animals excused even if with some difficulty.[2] Again all the suffer-ing was that of peasants. There is not a word about losses of landowners.[3] The victims of the requisitions were evidently poor men, farming on a small scale, but sufficiently numerous to be a significant factor in the feeding of the city.[4] Unlike the peasants on the limestone plateau, these men grew corn,[5] and on land sufficiently close to the city to be able to market their produce and return home on the same day.

Some of these men had their lands in the immediate environ-ment of Antioch and could hope to be back home at noon.[6] Others would have been obliged to spend a very long day with their donkey on the road. These are likely to have been the majority, for in the neighbourhood of the city pressure on the free peasant must have been very great. It has been observed in a study of the geography of modern Antioch that the purchasing power of rich city folk, the indebtedness of the peasant, and the covetous-ness of his patron, combine to deprive the independent peasant of ownership of the land.[7] All these factors were at work in antiquity and their effect must have been similar. Thus, much of the plain of Antioch is likely to have come into the possession of the Antiochene upper class. The absence of substantial archaeo-logical remains in the area might suggest that the working population lived in reed huts or other semi-permanent structures while the owners lived away from their estates at Antioch.[8] It is worth noting that in the present century the peasants of the plain of Antioch have been counted among the poorest and most ignorant in Syria.[9]

---

[1] *Or.* l. 26.
[2] Ibid. l. 9.
[3] Such losses would have been worth mentioning.
[4] *Or.* l. 31.
[5] Ibid. 28.
[6] Ibid. 26.

[7] J. Weulersse, 'Antioche, essai de géographie urbaine', *Bulletin d'études orien-tales* iv (1934), 27–79; relevant here: 30–1.

[8] R. J. Braidwood, *Mounds in the plain of Antioch* (University of Chicago, Oriental Institute publications xlviii, 1937).

[9] Weulersse, op. cit. 33; cf. also *B.R. Syria*, 171: 'The peasant and the town-dweller live, economically, in different worlds. For the former, life is truly Spartan. The fellah lives in a mud hut of one or two rooms, usually with no windows, four

Other estates are known from further afield. The estate of Jerome's patron and Libanius' acquaintance Euagrius lay thirty miles to the east of Antioch on the road to Cyrrhus, that is on the eastern edge of the plain near the ancient Imma.[1] Other rich citizens of Antioch owned estates near Cyrrhus.

What do we know about the living and working conditions of individual peasants? Déléage argues, from the fact that the government chose a small unit in which to assess the taxes of Syria, that the land there was worked in small units.[2] It may also be significant that when Libanius had difficulties with his Jewish peasants he was not concerned with individual tenants but with a group. This could simply be the result of solidarity among the peasants. But in modern Syria there is found a form of communal collective land-ownership known as *masha*. The land of a village is divided into three or four fields and distributed in strips among villagers each of whom receives a strip in each field. The land is redistributed at regular intervals. This form of cultivation would produce a strong sense of communal solidarity.

persons or more to a room, and two or three, often five or six, to a bed. His house has no conveniences whatsoever, the yard is the midden and sometimes the closet too; his living-room is bedroom, dining-room, and stable. He lives with his animals in order to protect them from theft or neighbourly malice. Pits or bored latrines are unknown. Water fetched by the women from often distant wells is too scarce for much washing: a mud-bath provides an occasional substitute. Wood fuel in many areas does not exist; dried dung, tediously collected, is used in its place. There is no artificial light, not even a rush dip: the peasant goes to bed and rises with the sun. When he is sick he lies in his corner till he is well again or dead; very occasionally the medical officer of the kaza or county may visit him, but more probably not. Distractions and pastimes he has none. An Alawite elder once said, "We are poor people. Only the landlords have amusements and good food. For us there is nothing to enjoy in life but to lie with our wives. It is the one pleasure that neither poverty nor the government can take away from us." Poverty is the rule, poverty such that the villagers often cannot afford the slightest improvements, such as the walling of a well. As for the women—the baking of bread, the fetching of water, and the collection of dung-fuel, itself often a two hours' task, occupy the greater part of the day.' *B.R. Syria*, 172: 'The peasant eats, mostly, what he grows himself. In the greater part of Syria—the plains and plateaux east of the coastal mountains—diet is very simple. Cereals are the staple food, eaten either as bread or pancakes or *borgul*, a kind of rough paste or porridge. Fat is supplied by olive oil or sheep's butter, called *semen* (*samne*) or *ghi*, and milk is consumed either boiled or as *leben*, a sort of cheese. Vegetables are very rare except in spring, and non-existent in winter, apart from onions, which with bread may then be the sole diet of the fellahin. Eggs and dried fruit, or grapes and melons in summer, are occasional variants. Meat is a rare luxury, reserved for festivals.'

[1] Tchalenko, *Villages*, 152; *P.W.* xiv. 2, col. 1914. On estates near Cyrrhus, see above, p. 42 n. 2.

[2] Déléage, *La Capitation du Bas-Empire*, 157–61.

It has been suggested that this form of cultivation goes back to ancient times.[1]

By modern Western European standards the lot of the peasant in many parts of Syria is likely to have been extremely harsh and crude. Nevertheless even at a low level of amenity it is possible to discern trends of change, for the better or for the worse. Libanius writing in the 380s suggests that the condition of the peasant was deteriorating. He is oppressed by heavy taxes and even more by the activities of the monks. 'I have said that the peasants used to have full chests and good clothing and gold coins and that dowries were given at their weddings. Now you can walk through many a deserted village, emptied by the pressure of taxation. And there is a greater evil still: the men who throng the caves, who display self-control only in their dress. Such peasants as are left in the villages have no need to shut their doors. He who has nothing does not fear robbers.'[2] Peasants protect themselves by retaining a patron or even by fleeing on to the patron's property.[3] The impression left by this evidence is similar to that gained by reading the Codes. It is a story of heavy exactions, patronage, flight, and deserted lands.

Nevertheless on a long-term view this picture of decline is misleading. It is contradicted by the evidence of the remains of certain villages on the limestone plateau to the east and southwest of Antioch. The remains are remarkably well preserved because many of the villages were abandoned by their inhabitants in the seventh or eighth century. The buildings remained undisturbed, except by natural forces, until modern times. Their remains provide a unique view of Syrian country life during the centuries of the Later Empire.[4]

On the basis of a survey of the village sites Tchalenko has concluded that starting from the second century the region experienced

---

[1] Libanius' Jewish tenants, *Or.* xlvii. 13. 'Masha' open field system: *B.R. Syria*, 265–6. B. H. Slicher van Bath, *Agrarian History of Europe* (London, 1963), 55: open fields were found in Netherlands, France north of the Loire, Germany, England, Ireland, Wales, and in Syria and in the Punjab. That the Jewish tenants worked an open field is suggested by S. Applebaum in *Israel and her vicinity in the Roman and Byzantine Periods* (notes for the delegates of the VIIth Int. Cong. R. Frontier Studies 1967), 18.   [2] *Or.* ii. 33.   [3] *Or.* xlvii. 17.

[4] H. C. Butler and H. K. Prentice, *Publications of the Princeton Archaeological Expedition to Syria 1904–5 and 1909* (Division II: Architecture, section B: Northern Syria); also the two splendid works: Tchalenko, *Villages*, and J. Lassus, *Sanctuaires chrétiens de Syrie*.

a steady growth of population and development by means of olive plantations. The trend continued through the fourth century, reached a climax in the fifth and early sixth centuries, and only came to an end at the time of the great Persian invasions of A.D. 603–30.[1]

The survival of a large number of houses of substantial character shows that a considerable section of the villagers must have been comfortably off. Tchalenko suggests that these were the homes of peasant proprietors who made their living from the olive plantations. He suggests that their forefathers were tenants of the estates that existed in the region earlier, and that they had brought new areas under olive plantation in return for ownership of the newly planted land.[2]

It might be thought that the prosperity of the olive-growing region was exceptional. In antiquity olives had always been thought the most profitable crop.[3] But archaeological remains in the wheat-growing areas to the East show a comparable building activity from the fourth to the sixth century, and, it would seem, a comparable increase in population.[4] So expansion was not limited to the limestone areas. But if some of the increasing population achieved a measure of prosperity, others seem not to have found a living at home, for many people emigrated to Italy and beyond.[5]

[1] Tchalenko, *Villages*, 377–438.

[2] Ibid. 404–17, cf. C. Courtois, L. Leschi, C. Perrat, C. Saumagne, *Tablettes Albertini* (Paris, 1952), 97–140 on Mancian tenure. Tenants who planted trees on uncultivated land were allowed to start paying rent after ten years and at one-third the usual rate. They could also sell their holding. Cf. also the *mugharasa* found in Syria today: the land remains the owners', but the trees are divided between owner and tenant. On this: *B.R. Syria*, 267. Joh. Chrys. *Hom. in Act. Ap.* 19 (*P.G.* lx. 146–50), which urges landowners to build churches on these estates, is not relevant to Syria, as these homilies were written at Constantinople: Baur, *Johannes Chrysostomus*, 2. 84.

[3] In Syria, for taxation, a little over one *iugerum* of mature olive trees was held equivalent to 5 *iugera* of vineyard or 20 *iugera* of arable. Jones, *L.R.E.* 768, on *Leges Saeculares*, 121 (*F.I.R.* ii². 795–6). On the economics of olive growing in fifth-century N. Africa: C. Courtois *et al.*, *Tablettes Albertini*, 203–5.

[4] R. Mouterde and A. Poidebard, *Le 'Limes' de Chalcis* (Paris, 1945); J. Lassus, *Inventaire archéologique de la région au nord-est de Ḥamā* (Damascus, 1935). According to Tchalenko, op. cit. 425, development in the Chalcis area lagged 200–300 years behind that of the hill region. There also is evidence for considerable building activity in the 4th century from the districts of Batanaea, Trachonitis, and Auranitis of southern Syria: G. M. Harper, 'Village administration in the Roman province of Syria', *T. Cl. St.* i (1928), 103–68.

[5] Evidence in the important study by L. Ruggini, 'Ebrei e orientali nell'Italia Settentrionale fra il IV e il VI secolo a. Cr.', *Studi et documenta historiae et iuris* xxv (1959), 186–308; 265 ff. See also below, pp. 81–2.

The ruins enable us to see the economic condition of Northern Syria of the fourth century in a wider perspective. The reader of Libanius is left under the impression that Syria was becoming poorer and more disorganized. The evidence of the ruins shows that in such important respects as wealth, population, and the area of land under cultivation, if one forms one's judgement over a longer number of years, Northern Syria was not declining at all but expanding. Many persons were actually becoming increasingly prosperous.

I do not think that we should conclude that Libanius is simply wrong, or indeed that he is deliberately misleading. The gloomy passages about the peasants almost all come from speeches written between 380 and 393. In these years following the battle of Adrianople the future of the empire hung in the balance. Syria is likely to have felt the strain. Taxation was certainly heavy, and abuses might grow unchecked, while the government was mainly concerned to ensure the empire's survival. But, thanks to the evidence provided by the ruined villages, we learn that, in the countryside at least, the decline did not last. With the return of more settled conditions, prosperity returned too, and the following period was one of expansion.

5. TRADE AND TRADERS

In the days following the Riot of the Statues fear of the punishment which the emperor might decree induced many citizens to flee from Antioch. The majority, we are told, did not have anywhere to go. We can deduce that the citizens of Antioch were true city dwellers, lacking close relations, whether of kinship or of occupation, with the countryside. It follows that for their livelihood most of the population for most of the year depended not on their own produce but on the food they could buy.[1]

The topography of the region facilitated the provision of food for the people of Antioch. The city had a fertile hinterland. A lake and the navigable river Orontes enabled the produce of a comparatively large area to be transported cheaply by water.[2] We know that an area in the limestone hills to the east of the city

---

[1] *Or.* xxiii. 3–9; cf. Petit, *Libanius*, 309, n. 1. Probably many worked on the land at harvest time, see above, p. 61 n. 7.

[2] *Or.* xi. 260–2; cf. Weulersse, *Antioche*, 30 ff.

produced only olive oil and some wine,[1] so that it cannot have been self-sufficient and must have depended on a market economy.

Libanius' statement that certain large villages in the territory of Antioch mutually satisfied each other's needs at fairs and had little need of the great city[2] does not necessarily contradict the rule of production for an urban market. It need only imply that these villagers never came into the city themselves but merely sold their produce in local centres where the fairs were held. Thence middlemen would transport the oil or wine to Antioch or wherever else it was sold. Tchalenko has observed that a number of sites on the periphery of the hill area, or in the plain immediately below it, with ruined colonnades, storehouses, oil presses, shops, and hostels, look like the remains of market centres.[3] Here the villagers would have sold their produce and here they would have bought the necessities which are not available on the hills, such as meat, vegetables, timber, or roof tiles.[4]

Peasants who lived closer to the city brought in farm produce on their own animals. No doubt the single load was small but together many small loads made an essential contribution to the feeding of the city.[5] We do not know how they sold the produce. The city had a very large number of small shops.[6] Presumably a peasant would sell his produce directly to a shopkeeper; peasants might also join the street-sellers who thronged the streets of Antioch.[7]

Great landowners must have had elaborate transport and storage facilities. Indeed we are told about the large number of camels, donkeys, horses, and oxen at their disposal.[8] These were presumably used to collect the rents of scattered estates, and in the case of the animals of councillors also to carry the tax to the public storehouses. Great landowners were thus in a position to buy up corn in the countryside and to sell it at a profit in the city.[9]

---

[1] Tchalenko, *Villages*, 68–75; ibid., vol. iii, Pl. xxxi.

[2] *Or.* xi. 230, referred to the hill villages by Festugière, *Antioche*, 52; Petit, *Libanius*, 307.

[3] Tchalenko, op. cit. 390–2.   [4] Ibid. 74–5.

[5] *Or.* l, *passim*; an essential contribution: ibid. 31.

[6] See above, pp. 55–9.

[7] See the topographical mosaic referred to above, p. 57 n. 2. Hawkers of fish: *Or.* xi. 258.

[8] *Or.* l. 32.   [9] See below, p. 130.

Some of the produce of the hinterland of Antioch was brought to the city in ships. These tied up in front of people's front doors so that women and children could unload them.[1] The skippers appear to have combined transport with retailing. But waterborne traffic was not limited to the produce of the hinterland. Other products—Libanius mentions timber[2] and fish[3]—came up river[4] from the seaport of Seleucia.

Some, perhaps most, of the water-borne trade was organized by landowners for their own needs. We have seen that Libanius on occasion sent farm produce up river to Apamea, and overseas to Cilicia, and as far away as Sinope on the Black Sea, and also that he imported timber from Cilicia and Lycia.[5] There was nothing unusual about this. Theodosius, the founder of a famous monastery near Rhosus, eventually built a ship with which to market the goods produced by the labour of the monks and to procure necessities for the monastery.[6] Secular landowners would do the same. Libanius includes ships with land and gold and silver among typical possessions of a rich man.[7] We also know that the public services required of councillors of Antioch included the transport of corn by sea.[8] It is likely that this duty sometimes involved nothing more than paying for the transport. But in one case it is certain that the councillor was required to transport corn in a ship of his own, and the passage shows that this was by no means exceptional.[9]

Libanius' information on trade is framed in the vaguest and most general terms. All harbours receive the produce of Egypt.[10] Ships sail from Seleucia to Constantinople but most travellers prefer the land route.[11] From Seleucia ships also sail to Italy.[12]

---

[1] *Or.* xi. 261. [2] Ibid. 262. [3] Ibid. 258.

[4] River navigable: ibid. 262; confirmed by Festugière, *Antioche*, 59; one day's voyage from the sea: Strabo xvi. 2. 7; cf. Pausanias viii. 29. 3; *P.W.* s.v. Orontes (vol. xviii, col. 1163). *B.R. Syria*, 47, has a graph of rate of flow during different months.

[5] *Ep.* 135–6, 177–8, 709, 568, 649, 1191; on these, see above, p. 46.

[6] Theod. *Hist. Rel.* (*P.G.* lxxxii, 1389 B9), cf. corn fleet of monastery of the Metanoia near Alexandria: *P. Cairo* iii. 67286; *P. Lond.* iii. 1152, 996, 995, pp. 248, 249.

[7] *Or.* vii. 9, viii. 1, 3, i. 54.

[8] *Ep.* 959; on the liturgy, cf. below, p. 165. [10] *Ep.* 1274.

[9] *Or.* liv. 47.

[11] This follows from the number of letters delivered by men travelling to Constantinople to inhabitants of cities on the way; see Seeck, *Briefe*, 316–466.

[12] e.g. *Or.* xlviii. 28, *Ep.* 1214, merchants sail to Greece; iv. 38, theft by shipwrecked sailors.

Sea-travelling and trading furnish Libanius with some rhetorical illustrations, but these hardly read like appeals to the experience of the audience.[1]

Much that Libanius says about Seleucia, the port on the mouth of the Orontes, consists of commonplaces about trade, such as were commonly found in panegyrics of cities. But it is a fact that the Emperor Diocletian incurred great expense in cutting the harbour of Seleucia.[2] Libanius claims that this was done on behalf of the people of Antioch, but other objectives are likely to have weighed at least as heavily in the mind of the emperor. We know that a large army operating in Mesopotamia might have to receive part of its supplies from Egypt.[3] We also know that corn raised as tax in Syria was sometimes carried overseas to wherever the emperor needed it.[4] Thus the need of the government is likely to have been the primary motive for the building of the new harbour at Seleucia. But the harbour existed and was frequented by corn ships. It must have provided great encouragement for trade.

Our written sources tell us remarkably little about trade. Nevertheless the volume of trade passing through Antioch must by the standards of the ancient world have been considerable. Far Eastern goods[5] could only enter the Roman Empire by one of two routes: either across Northern Syria or up the Red Sea. According to Chinese sources, even goods that had reached Ctesiphon in Mesopotamia by the over-land route continued their voyage by water, being shipped down the Tigris to the head of the Persian Gulf and then carried round Arabia to a Red Sea port.[6] It is nevertheless likely that at least some of the Far Eastern trade reached the Mediterranean via Antioch and the

---

[1] e.g. *Or.* viii. 3, xlvi. 33.

[2] *Or.* xi. 263–4; cf. *P.W.* s.v. Seleukeia (Pieria); rhetorical commonplaces: Themistius, *Or.* iv. 52c–d.

[3] Josh. Styl., 70.   [4] See below, p. 90.

[5] On eastern trade: E. H. Warmington, *The Commerce between the Roman Empire and India* (Cambridge, 1928); M. P. Charlesworth, *Trade Routes and Commerce of the Roman Empire* (Cambridge, 1936). On the recovery of the Indian trade in the fourth century: Charlesworth in *Studies in Roman Economic and Social History*, ed. P. R. Coleman-Norton, 131–43.

[6] J. I. Miller, *The Spice Trade of the Roman Empire* (Oxford, 1969), 119–20, 133–6. The Red Sea ports Clysma (Suez) and Aila (Aquaba) were only modest places: *Antonini Placentini Itinerarium* (*C.S.E.L.* 41, p. 187; 39, p. 185); cf. Claude, *Byzantinische Stadt*, 171, n. 88. The Chinese were informed about Antioch: F. Hirth, *China and the Roman Orient* (Leipzig, 1855), 49–50, 77–9, 207.

valley of the Orontes.[1] The network of roads linking Mesopotamia and the Mediterranean converges on Antioch.[2] Batnae
in Mesopotamia, on the Antioch–Edessa road, had an annual
fair, thronged with merchants, to which goods came from as far
as China.[3] Indian, Scythian, and Persian merchants are also
mentioned at Hierapolis, further west along the same route.[4]
Then, the location of the silk industry on the coast at Tyre and
Berytus is explicable on the assumption that the silk had come
there through Syria.[5] *The Book of the Prefect*, which was compiled
in the ninth century, still assumed that silk goods reached
Constantinople via Seleucia.[6] At Antioch itself the hostelries
outside the city gate, which could be described as 'a complete
quarter of the town',[7] evidently catered for large numbers of
travellers.

[1] Route for travellers *to* the Far East: Philost. *Vit. Ap. Ty.* i. 18, 19, 20 (to
India by land); Ptol. i. 12. 5 (to China). In the early Middle Ages, Jewish mer-
chants still reached the Far East either via Egypt and the Red Sea or Syria and the
Persian Gulf. Evidence from the Arab geographer Ibn Khurradhbah cited by
Lopez and Raymond, *Medieval Trade in the Mediterranean World* (Oxford, 1955),
29–33.
   The existence of a great 'free-trade' fair at Aegae on the Cilician coast east of
Tarsus (Theod. *Ep.* 70; *Itin. Hier.* 32) might suggest that there was an important
route bypassing Syria. But there is, as far as I know, no evidence that Far Eastern
trade passed this way. The Roman road system centres on Antioch, and it is
reasonable to assume that trade used the best roads, even if the roads were built
for military rather than economic purposes. I would suggest that the fair at Aegae
developed not because this was the end of the caravan route, but because the
temple of Asclepius attracted crowds of potential customers. When the temple
was destroyed, the fair had become firmly established. Temple demolished by
Constantine: Eus. *V. Const.* iii. 56; Soz. *H.E.* ii. 5; Zon. xiii. 12c–d; Lib. *Ep.* 695,
Or. xxx. 39.
[2] K. Miller, *Die peutingersche Tafel* (Stuttgart, 1962), Pl. x; *Itineraria Romana*
(Stuttgart, 1916), 751; Tchalenko, *Villages*, vol. 2, Pl. xxxix.
[3] Amm. xiv. 3. 3. According to U. Monneret de Villard, 'La fiera di Batnae e la
traslazione di S Tommaso a Edessa', *Accademia dei Lincei*, Cl. sc. morali, ser.
viii, vi fasc. 3–4 (1951), 96, *one* large caravan from the East arrived annually.
[4] Amm. xiv. 3. 3; at Hierapolis: Procop. Gaz. *Pan. Anast.* 18; G. Goossens,
Hierapolis de Syrie (Louvain, 1943).
[5] On the Phoenician silk industry: Procop. *H.A.* xxv. 13–26; Jones, *Ec. H. Rev.*
xiii (1960), 191–2.
[6] *Book of the Prefect*, v.
[7] *Or.* xi. 231; at Beroea (Aleppo) too the caravan halt was outside the gates:
J. Sauvaget, *Alep* (Paris, 1941), 62–4. Claude, *Byzantinische Stadt*, 171, deduces
from the fact that the caravan halt and surrounding suburbs lie on the route to
Antioch that it served communications between the two Syrian cities rather than
long-distance trade. Joh. Chrys. *Hom. ad Stagirium*, 2, 6 (*P.G.* xlvii, col. 458), defence of road to Mesopotamia against bandits.

Only one piece of evidence about this trade allows quantitative deductions. Edessa, a city situated on the northern fork of the trade route leading into Persia via Nisibis,[1] paid one hundred and forty pounds of gold in Traders' Tax every four years.[2] This is no more than one-twentieth of the land tax that a city of the importance of Edessa is likely to have paid.[3] It may well have been difficult to tax caravan traders. But if, in the absence of evidence to the contrary, we assume that they were taxed, and that their contribution was included in the quota of Edessa, we must conclude that even in trading centres like Edessa the economic significance of trade was very small, compared with that of agriculture.

But if transit trade contributed relatively little to the income of the imperial government, it left its mark on the life of the empire. In the third century Palmyra had become a great and splendid city, able for a short time to overrun the whole of the Roman East with hardly any other resources than the income derived from the caravan trade.[4] In the fourth and following centuries, less sensationally, silk clothing was the major status symbol. The senators wore it, lesser men emulated them.[5] Alaric, King of the Goths, was able to extort three thousand pounds of pepper and four thousand robes of silk from the city of Rome.[6] When the manufacture of silk materials was made into a government monopoly by Justinian, we are told perhaps with some exaggeration, that most of the population of the cities where the manufacture had been carried on, presumably Tyre and Beirut, were reduced to beggary. The silk industry clearly provided employment on a considerable scale. Moreover the fact that the government took over manufacture proves that the profit cannot have been insignificant.[7]

---

[1] A 'free-trade' fair: Greg. Tur. *Glor. Mart.* 32. A centre of exchanges with Persia: *Exp. tot. orbis*, 22.

[2] Josh. Styl. 31.   [3] Jones, *L.R.E.* 465 on *P. Oxy.* 1909.

[4] Rostovtzeff, *Caravan Cities* (Oxford, 1932), 91–150. J. G. Février, *Essai sur l'histoire politique et économique de Palmyre* (Paris, 1931); I. A. Richmond, 'Palmyra under the Romans', *J.R.S.* liii (1963), esp. 43–54.

[5] Amm. xxiii. 6. 67, xxii. 4. 5; cf. also Hier. *Ep.* 19.

[6] Zos. v. 41. Such articles found their way to Italy and Gaul through the fifth and sixth centuries and beyond: P. Lambrecht, 'Le commerce des Syriens en Gaule', *A.C.* vi (1937), 35–61; Bréhier, 'Les colonies d'orientaux en Occident au Ve–VIIIe siècle', *B.Z.* xii (1903), 1–39.

[7] Procop. *H.A.* 25.

In addition to the transit trade in goods of the east, Syria is known to have exported textiles.[1] When Melania at Rome wanted to buy her husband clothes which were both comfortable and suitably austere, she bought him 'natural coloured Antiochenes'.[2] So it would seem that cheap clothing in wool or linen was exported from Syria to Italy. In addition Libanius tells us that, while the wine produced in the territory of Antioch was sold in neighbouring areas, the olive oil was carried overseas.[3]

In fact wine was exported from Syria too,[4] but export of oil is likely to have been on a larger scale. Export may explain why in the hill region east of Antioch the area planted with olive trees continued to expand and the villages to grow throughout the fourth, fifth, and sixth centuries.

Where did this area find its expanding market? Antioch was certainly growing in the time of Libanius, but did the purchasing power of the city grow proportionally? And could it ever have consumed the produce of a hill area of about three thousand square kilometres[5] in addition to the unknown, but surely not inconsiderable, production of the plain of Antioch? In any case, the expansion of the hill villages continued even after Antioch had begun to decline, as a result of a terrible series of disasters in the early part of the sixth century.[6]

It is clear that the prosperity of the area depended in some way on the fact that Syria was part of the empire. When Syria had

---

[1] *Totius Orbis Descr.* 31.

[2] Jones, *L.R.E.* 850 on *V. Mel.* 8; also *P. Fouad.* 74.

[3] *Or.* xi. 20; the *Periplus, Georg. Graec. Min.* i. 293, of the first century shows that wine from the Laodicea area was exported to India (cf. Strabo xvi. 752). Syrian wine exported to Cappadocia, Joh. Eph. *V. SS. Or.* (*Pat. Or.* xvii. 129).

[4] F. M. Heichelheim in *E.S.A.R.* iv. 136.

[5] The area of hill region: Tchalenko, *Villages*, 423. Assuming that a soldier consumed ⅛ of a pint of oil per day or 37 pints per year (*P. Oxy.* 2046, 1920; Jones, *L.R.E.* 629 n. 44), that the yield of oil was about 10 gallons per acre (A. French, *The Growth of the Athenian Economy* (London, 1964), 27; 176 based on *F.A.O. Commodity Studies*, No. 9, 1965), and that about half the area, 370,000 acres, were planted with olive trees, the oil production of *c.* 30,000,000 pints would be sufficient for the needs of about 800,000 soldiers—and significantly more ordinary civilians whose consumption was less. The Talmud (M. Ketub v. 8); *E.S.A.R.* iv. 179, prescribes 0·07 pint a day as a minimum ration for a wife, while Cato (*Agr.* 58) advised that a mere 1¾ gallon a year (12 *sext.*) be given to a slave. Production of oil varies very greatly over the years. Oil was used for lighting: Augustine could work at night in oil-producing Africa. He could not in Italy (Brown, *Augustine of Hippo*, 20, on *C. Acad.* i. 3, 6).

[6] Tchalenko, *Villages*, 429–31.

been separated from the empire, first by the Persians, and later by the Arabs, decline set in, and it was rapid and catastrophic. In many cases land and villages were simply abandoned.[1] Since the remains show no signs of violence,[2] it could be that the disaster was caused simply by a cessation of demand for the olive oil of this area.

An important effect of the Arab conquest of Syria was the disappearance of the Roman army from the eastern frontier. This by itself might explain the ruin of the zone, if it now became possible for nomads to cross the old frontier and to graze their camels indiscriminately.[3] At the same time the departure of the army must have greatly reduced the market for olive oil. On the other hand, the oil-growing region cannot have been entirely dependent on the army. It is inconceivable that the steady development of the hill region over centuries was paralleled by a corresponding growth of the military establishment. It is, however, possible that large-scale expenditure of taxes on soldiers, officers, and, during the earlier period, on veterans[4] of the frontier army provided a starting-point for the economic development of the whole frontier region.[5]

The area of the *limes* of Chalcis, as well as the whole of Mesopotamia, is unsuitable for the growth of olives and must have depended on olive oil produced elsewhere.[6]

But the way the prosperity of the hill area continued to grow through the sixth century in spite of the damage done to Syria by Persian invasions and earthquakes suggests that its produce found markets further afield,[7] and that the oil exported in ships formed a significant proportion of the total production. The

[1] Tchalenko, *Villages*, 431–8. The latest dated building of the limestone hills is from 609 to 610: ibid. 433 n. 4.

[2] Ibid. 431.

[3] See for instance R. O. Whyte in *A History of Land Use in Arid Regions*, ed. L. D. Stamp (Unesco, 1961), 100.

[4] Tax-free allotments of land: Jones, *L.R.E.* 636 n. 63; in frontier provinces: Anon., *De rebus bell.* v. 4.

[5] Cf. the development of an oasis around a fort: *I.G.L.S.* 2704; public works carried out by the army: G. R. Watson, *The Roman Army* (London, 1969), 144–5. On the economic role of the army, but rather disappointing, E. Gren, *Kleinasien und der Ostbalkan in der wirtschaftlichen Entwicklung der römischen Kaiserzeit* (Uppsala, 1941), 89 ff.

[6] Tchalenko, op. cit. 425; Iraq grows no olives today: *F.A.O. Production Yearbook* xviii (1964), 118.

[7] Tchalenko, op. cit. 426–31.

population of Constantinople will have provided one growing market, and some oil could have been sold in Italy or further west.[1] But caution is needed. It cannot be assumed without question that destruction and dislocation caused by the barbarian invasions made the Western provinces to any significant extent dependent on olive oil from the East. The West was traditionally supplied from North Africa. The Vandal invasions may have interrupted the export of oil but they are very unlikely to have prevented it permanently. Certainly oil continued to fetch high prices in North Africa. There is no evidence that crops remained unsold.[2]

It is tempting to connect the export of Syrian oil with the fact that natives of oil-producing villages in the territories of Apamea and Antioch form a relatively high proportion of the Syrians who are found living in the western provinces of the empire in the fifth and especially the sixth century.[3] In northern Italy their tombs have been found at Aquileia and Grado and places on the roads leading from these ports into Rhaetia, Noricum, and Pannonia; and in Gaul along the Rhone and as far north as Trier.[4] But these Syrians were emigrants, not long-distance traders, and indeed during the fifth and early sixth centuries the majority do not appear to have been traders at all.[5] Clusters of oriental tomb inscriptions generally occur at places where there is also evidence of the presence of an oriental unit of the army.[6] It would seem that many of the orientals, or at least their ancestors, had originally left Syria as recruits. Perhaps the wide dispersion of the villagers of Antioch and Apamea is not so much

[1] Ibid. 424; oil exported in ships, *Or.* xi. 20.

[2] Tchalenko, op. cit. 424, refers to reduced Western competition. But according to C. Courtois, *Les Vandales et l'Afrique* (Paris, 1955), 317 ff., esp. 320, the cultivation of olive trees and the prosperity of N. Africa were undiminished. H. Pirenne, *Mahomet et Charlemagne* (Paris, 1937), 75, on Cass. *Var.* iii. 7, shows that oil continued to reach Gaul; also Greg. Tur. *H.F.* v. 5.

[3] 'Colonies d'orientaux en Occident,' *Dictionnaire d'archéologie chrétienne* (H. Leclercq and Cabrol); P. Lambrechts, 'Le commerce des Syriens en Gaule', *Ant. Cl.* vi (1937), 35–61; E. Salin, *La civilisation mérovingienne* i. 142 ff., 554; above all, L. Ruggini, 'Ebrei e orientali nell'Italia Settentrionale'. On the high proportion of Syrians, especially of villagers of Apamea or Antioch: Ruggini, op. cit., 266. V. Velkov, 'Schicksal einer frühbyzantinischen Stadt', in *Akten des XI. Internationalen Byzantinisten Kongresses* (Munich, 1960), 656, mentions an ἔμπορος from Ταρουτία in the territory of Apamea who died at Odessus on the Black Sea in 557.

[4] Ruggini, op. cit. 265.   [5] Ibid. 269–70.   [6] Ibid. 271.

evidence for the existence of intense trade connection as for the use by the imperial government of this densely populated region of independent farmers as a recruiting area.

Whatever the scale of long-distance trade, it is clear that the professional merchants played a very small role in the society of Antioch. The anonymous merchants who are occasionally mentioned in the writings of Libanius[1] and elsewhere appear to be humble landless men who are trying to make a living out of such resources as they have. This might consist of a particular skill, or possession of enough capital to buy a small quantity of stock-in-trade and some means of transporting it.[2] Such traders might include dependants of the powerful,[3] or veterans employing their retirement benefice,[4] or even clergy.[5] Presumably only the wealthiest or at least the most powerfully supported would be able to become shipowners.[6]

Overland long-distance trade was partly carried by camels.[7] Until quite recently camel transport in the Middle East was in the hands of nomads or semi-nomads, who conducted caravans carrying their own goods or goods belonging to traders over great distances comparatively cheaply.[8] If the nomads already performed this function in antiquity this might provide part of the explanation of why long-distance trade seems to have been so inconspicuous in city life.

On the other hand, a high proportion of trade is likely to have been directly or indirectly in the hands of landowners. The

---

[1] *Ep.* 1161–2, 988; trade an occupation reserved for the poor, *C.J.* iv. 63. 3.

[2] The Traders' Tax does not distinguish between merchants and shopkeeper-craftsmen: *Or.* xlvi. 22. *N. Val.* 15. 1. If army supplies failed, soldiers would have to maintain themselves by trade (*negotiatio*); some clergy did so too: *C.T.* xvi. 2. 8 = *C.J.* i. 3. 1.

[3] *C.T.* xiii. 1. 5, 7, 15, 21.   [4] *C.T.* vii. 20. 2, 3.

[5] *C.T.* xvi. 2. 8; 10; 14. 1.

[6] On ship-owning in this period: Rougé, *Recherches sur l'organisation du commerce maritime sous l'Empire romain* (Paris, 1966); Jones, *L.R.E.* 866. On 'traditional' ship-owning in modern Arabia (Kuwait): C. Coon, *Caravan* (New York, 1966), 326.

[7] *Or.* li. 8; on the camel in the Ancient World: C. H. Coster, *Late Roman Studies* (Harvard, 1968), 134ff.; E. Demouget, 'Le chameau et l'Afrique du Nord romain', *Annales* xv (1960), 209–47; R. Paret, 'Les villes de Syrie du Sud et les routes commerciales d'Arabie à la fin du VIᵉ siècle', *Akten des XI. Internationalen Byzantinisten Kongresses 1958* (Munich, 1960), 438–44.

[8] In *Problems of the Arid Zone* (Unesco, 1962), essays by R. Capot Rey, Mohammed Awa; J. Weulersse, *Antioche*, 66, on caravans distributing soap from Antioch in the nineteenth and early twentieth centuries. Local transport was until recently supplied by camel nomads: *U.S. Army Handbook for Syria* (1965), 334.

requirements of estate management and of tax collecting made it necessary for landowners to maintain facilities for transporting produce on a large scale. It is *a priori* likely that some landowners used their facilities to engage in a wider range of trading, in other men's produce, or in manufactured articles. Strictly speaking, a landowner became liable to pay the Traders' Tax as soon as he dealt in another man's produce. But one may wonder how closely such trading could be supervised.[1] It was this aspect of land-owning that the imperial government exploited by means of the institution of the *navicularii*. These were landowners who had been conscripted into ship-owning by imperial regulation,[2] so that they might make a specified number of shipments for the feeding of Rome and Constantinople. The number of duty voyages was very limited[3] and *navicularii* also engaged in trading on their own account,[4] assisted by the privilege of exemption from the Traders' Tax.[5]

It is an indication of the low development of trade under the Later Empire that the provisioning of the capital cities could not be imposed on a professional merchant class. The professional traders, among whom even the wealthiest, the rich merchants of Alexandria, were men of comparatively small means,[6] would have been able to ensure neither the regularity nor the volume of transportation necessary for the provisioning of the capital cities. The task had to be undertaken by men who were ostensibly not traders at all, but landed magnates.

6. PAYMENTS IN MONEY AND PAYMENTS IN FARM PRODUCE

It is impossible to reconstruct even the simplest and most schematic picture of the working of the Antiochene economy as a whole. We can, however, make valid statements about particular aspects of the economy. Thus, we can be sure that money was

---

[1] Only homegrown produce exempt: *C.T.* xiii. 1. 3, 6, 13; ibid. 17 shows that *curiales* did not normally pay.

[2] Ibid. 5. 14 (371); J. Rougé, *Recherches*, 245 ff.

[3] Only one voyage every 2 years?: *C.T.* xiii. 5. 21, 26. But if this was so, the 27,000,000 *modii* of corn transported annually to Constantinople in the time of Justinian (Jones, *L.R.E.* 698) would have required an enormous number of ships of the normal capacity of between 10,000 and 20,000 *modii* (ibid. 843).

[4] *C.T.* xiii. 5. 25.   [5] Ibid. 4, 24.   [6] Jones, *L.R.E.* 869–70.

used as a medium of exchange in most transactions in the city. Civic, as opposed to imperial, salaries were paid in money.[1] It was used in shops.[2] Peasants sold their products for money.[3] Decurions spent large sums on liturgies.[4] Much of their wealth must have been earned from the sale of farm produce to retailers.[5] Teachers were as a rule paid by the parents of their pupils in gold or silver coin.[6] Admittedly Libanius was frequently rewarded with presents. But this was not because the parent concerned had no coin available, or because he feared that money would lose its value, but because a present was felt to be a more dignified and personal reward than mere payment.[7] Parents would also use money to pay boarding charges for children receiving education away from home.[8] For a pupil to receive his maintenance allowance in kind was exceptional.[9] In a late oration Libanius tells us that men who had formerly rewarded their patrons with presents had now changed to paying them in gold and silver.[10] This has been taken as an indication that gold coins were more plentiful towards the end of the century,[11] but Libanius is only arguing that patrons have become greedier.

Libanius uses four terms to describe the medium of exchange: χρυσίον, χρυσός, ἀργύριον, ἄργυρος. The terms in -ιον clearly refer to coined money. χρυσίον no doubt refers to gold coins.[12] Libanius normally seems to use στατήρ to describe the *solidus*.[13] In one

---

[1] Teachers: *Or.* xxxi. 19; 'old-age pensioners' and 'club-bearers': *Or.* xlviii. 9; subvention for actors: *Or.* xxvi. 20 ff.

[2] *Or.* xxix. 2, xlvi. 12.

[3] *Or.* l. 28; ibid. 30. They evidently buy the products of the city for they return home with little money: ibid. 25–6.

[4] *Or.* xxxi. 17; *Ep.* 218.   [5] Julian, *Misop.* 350.

[6] *Or.* xxxi. 25, *Or.* iii. 6, *Ep.* 1539 (365), 833 (363), 446 (355–6), 540 (356–7).

[7] *Ep.* 273 (358?) a horse; 305 (361?) clothing; 1394 (363) a donkey; 1416 (363) wine, a cloak, a book; 837 (363) a horse; 1332 (365) a horse, Libanius replies with dogs; 911 (388) clothing; 1034 (392) wine; *Or.* liv. 17–18, oil and wine an alternative to gold and silver, cf. Petit, *Étudiants*, 144–5: 'Sa fierté y voit plutôt le présent de l'amitié que le salaire du professeur.'

[8] *Ep.* 23–4 (358–9), 80 (359) 100 'staters' from the prefect Anatolius are not enough! 428 (355).

[9] *Ep.* 319 (357).   [10] *Or.* li. 9 (*c.* 389).

[11] Piganiol, *L'Empire chrétien*, 294.

[12] Petit, *Libanius*, 302, nn. 3–5; salaries: *Or.* liv. 12, 17, *Ep.* 140, 466, *Or.* xiv. 2, i. 15; money-lending: xiv. 3, ibid. 54, lii. 14–15; extortion: *Or.* xiv. 15; ibid. 58, xxix. 26, xxxiii. 30, iv. 28–9.

[13] The 'stater' is consistently a gold coin, e.g. *Or.* liv. 18, i. 61, *Ep.* 80. 371. This could hardly be anything other than the *solidus*. But *Or.* xviii. 193 τὸν στέφανον ἀπὸ στατήρων ἑβδομήκοντα φοιτᾶν must refer to a larger unit. A tax of 70 *solidi* per city

passage he refers to amounts of half and a third of a στατήρ,[1] and may mean the *semis* and *tremis*, coined in gold to the value of a half and a third of a *solidus* respectively.[2] But he is writing very loosely. In another passage of the same speech he describes the same exaction as collection 'to the last drachma and obol'.[3] Yet 'obol' can stand for a very small coin; less than the price of a loaf of bread.[4] ἀργύριον of course just means 'money'. But Libanius as a rule uses it in contexts involving smaller sums than those in which χρυσίον is used.[5] It would seem therefore that Libanius usually, but not always,[6] employs the term for currency other than gold, that is, for the whole range of silver and copper coins. Libanius does not mention specific coins within this range. If the imperial government in the reigns of Valens and Valentinian began to run down the silver coinage,[7] this process has left no trace in the writings of Libanius.

It has been argued that Libanius uses the words χρυσός and ἄργυρος fairly consistently to describe the use of uncoined metal, whether in the form of ingots or of plate or jewellery.[8] But I do not think that this is true. Obviously these words must be used to describe the precious metals in an uncoined state,[9] but they are also found in contexts, such as debt or military pay, in which coin was unquestionably employed.[10] When Libanius uses the terms in a description of the piling-up of wealth, usually ill-gotten, silver and gold surely include both coined and uncoined precious metal, as well as gold and silver plate or jewellery.[11] The distinction between coined and uncoined metal was of course reduced by the government's habit of specifying levies by weight,

would not be worth raising. It is probably a measure of weight, since the crown gold was not paid, or at least not entirely paid, in coined gold: *C.T.* xii. 13. 4; cf. *Amm.* xxviii. 6. 7 (crowns and statues). Before Julian's edict some cities had offered 1,000–2,000 'staters'.

[1] *Or.* xxxiii. 14.
[2] J. W. E. Pearce, *Roman Imperial Coinage*, vol. ix (London, 1962), xxvi, 205.
[3] *Or.* lii. 13.   [4] *Or.* vii. 2.
[5] *Or.* liv. 42, l. 26–7, xxix. 2, xlv. 10, xxvi. 22.
[6] The χρυσίον of *Or.* xxxiii. 30 and the ἀργύριον of xlv. 10 are interchangeable.
[7] Jones, *L.R.E.* 148, 440.   [8] Petit, *Libanius*, 301, nn. 7–12.
[9] *Or.* xviii. 206 (gold from mines), ibid. 193 (crown gold), xxiii. 18 (silver (plate?) of fugitives after the Riot of the Statues).
[10] *Or.* i. 275 (outstanding debts); xlvii. 32, cf. ii. 37 (soldiers' pay); i. 113 (bribing of a copyist); *Ep.* 163 (fine exacted by *sacra largitio*); 454 (repayment of a salary drawn in kind).
[11] *Or.* xii. 31, lii. 14, xlvii. 29, lvii. 50; *Ep.* 300. But in xlvii. 4 χρυσός and χρυσίου τιμή are distinguished.

sometimes even those in gold. The government feared that it would be cheated of its dues through the use of contaminated or mutilated coins and therefore insisted that *solidi* received from tax-payers should be smelted down and weighed. Payments in uncoined gold were equally acceptable.[1] Unfortunately Libanius' word-usage is not sufficiently precise to enable us to define the respective areas in which coined or uncoined precious metals were used; or even to assert confidently that uncoined precious metal was used to any significant extent in economic transactions, as it was used in Western Europe during the early Middle Ages.[2]

Libanius gives us no information on prices and thus throws no direct light on the fantastic inflation of the *denarius* which the papyri show to have taken place in Egypt.[3] He is silent about prices even when a reference to the rising cost of living would be relevant to his argument. He describes the poverty of his under-teachers with a view to obtaining an increase in their remuneration, but he does not argue that their present income is steadily losing its purchasing power.[4] This suggests that for men who received their income in gold or silver coin, as the teachers are likely to have done, the inflation did no real damage. It could well be that inflation was felt more severely by craftsmen or shopkeepers who lived on the proceeds of numerous small transactions which would necessarily be carried out in *denarii*. Nevertheless there is nothing in Libanius to suggest that this was so.[5] There is no trace of any inconvenience in the use of the coinage. In this respect conditions at Antioch need not have been typical of the East in general. The inconvenience of the imperial currency of the fourth century lay in the fact that as a rule there were no intermediate denominations between the very valuable gold

[1] Tax *solidi* to be melted down: *C.T.* xii. 6. 12 (366); payment in bullion possible: ibid. 13; cash rents of *res privata* accepted in *solidi* only at a premium: *C.T.* xii. 7. 1. See J. P. C. Kent in *Essays in Roman coinage presented to Harold Mattingley* (eds. R. A. G. Carson, C. H. V. Sutherland), 190–204, esp. 199–200; Jones, *L.R.E.* 439 ff.

[2] M. Bloch, *Land and Work in Medieval Europe* (London, 1966), 197–8. R. Mac-mullen, 'The Emperor's Largesses', *Latomus* xxi (1962), 159–66, gives evidence for distribution by the emperor of rings, bracelets, *fibulae*, medallions, gold and silver dishes, ornamented armour, etc. Rich clothing part of accumulated wealth: Lib. *Or.* lii. 14, l. 20. Private individuals not to have their gold coined in the public mints: *C.T.* ix. 21. 7 (369).

[3] Mickwitz, *Geld und Wirtschaft*, 114; Jones, *L.R.E.* 440.

[4] *Or.* xxxi. 11 ff.

[5] Cf. L. C. West and A. C. Johnson, *Currency in Roman and Byzantine Egypt* (Princeton, 1944), 166 ff.

coins and the almost valueless debased *denarius*. Since Antioch
was sometimes an imperial residence it is conceivable that silver
coins were minted there even when they were not produced
elsewhere.[1] This would have greatly assisted the use of money
by private individuals.

Banking and money-lending provide a valuable index of the
development of an economy. The evidence for Antioch in our
period is scanty, but, such as it is, it suggests that the forms of
banking and money-lending were not highly developed. Money-
lending was a normal activity of landowners.[2] There existed also
professional money-lenders (τραπεζῖται). If one can judge by
a single passage these were men of humble standing with a
reputation for elusiveness.[3] Elsewhere we read that a banker's
wife used one of these men to make a payment to an official.[4]
Cases of payments made to third persons from a bank account
are known from Egypt.[5] John Chrysostomus describes men
depositing money with a bank.[6] Business was on a small scale.
A spectator might see the sum he had just deposited lent out
immediately afterwards.[7]

The loans mentioned in the writings of Libanius are made, as
far as one can see, to men in need, rather than to men about to
engage in business. A decurion who has borne heavy taxes or
liturgies might take up a loan and get into debt.[8] Shopkeepers
pressed by the theatre claque for money might take up a loan
for this purpose,[9] but there is no reference in Libanius to loans
taken up for production.[10] Loans made by landlords to peasants
have been mentioned in § 4, 'The Workers of the Land'.[11] There

---

[1] On lack of intermediate denominations: Jones, *L.R.E.* 443; issues of mint of
Antioch: J. W. E. Pearce, op. cit., pp. 85 n. 2, 273, 279–80. D. B. Waagé,
Antioch on the Orontes, vol. iv. 2, *Greek, Roman, Byzantine and Crusaders' coins* (Princeton,
1952).

[2] *Or.* i. 275, lii. 15. See also above, pp. 46 n. 5; 48 n. 5; 49 nn. 5–6; 64
n. 5.

[3] *Or.* xlii. 8.　　　　　　　　　　　　　　[4] *Or.* xxix. 33.

[5] Rostovtzeff, *S.E.H.H.W.* 1278 ff.; on scanty evidence from the Later Empire:
Johnson and West, *Economic Studies*, 172.

[6] Mickwitz, *Geld und Wirtschaft*, 156–7 cites Joh. Chrys. *Hom. in Ep. ad Rom.* 7. 7
(*P.G.* lx. 451); *Hom. in Ep. II ad Cor.* 16. 4 (*P.G.* lxi. 516).

[7] *Hom. in Princip. Act.* 4. 2 (*P.G.* li. 99).

[8] *Or.* xxxiii. 16.　　　　　　　　　　　　[9] *Or.* xlvi. 18.

[10] This was characteristic of the banking of antiquity: R. Bogaert, *Banques et
banquiers dans les cités grecques* (Leyden, 1968), 411–12; also by the same author,
'Banquiers, courtiers, et prêts maritimes à Athènes et à Alexandrie', *Chronique
d'Égypte* xl (1965), 140–56.　　　　　　[11] See above, p. 64.

is no evidence that bankers had branches in other cities. If you needed to pay elsewhere than at home, you either had to travel with the money or send a servant with it.[1] Scanty as the information is, it would seem that the financial transactions carried out by these professional financiers were on a very small scale compared with those involved in the administration of the estates of the city aristocracy,[2] and negligible compared with those of the imperial government. It is a very different picture from that found in the Middle Ages in Western Europe, where nobles and kings could not do without the loans of rich merchants or bankers.[3] The difference is likely to be due to the greater economic resources of the imperial government compared with those of the rulers of, say, medieval England or France. Not only did the Roman government find it vastly easier to raise levies from its subjects, but it also organized so large a part of the distribution of the products of the empire, that there was no scope beside it for the growth of large privately run enterprises, whether concerned with distribution of goods or the lending of money.

While private individuals, in the city at any rate, seem to have used money in most everyday transactions, the imperial administration was largely maintained by means of levies and expenditure of farm produce. The main tax, the φόρος, was in Libanius' lifetime normally paid in kind.[4] The councillors whose duty it was to collect the tax came to the villages to collect farm produce.[5] When the produce had been collected from the villagers, it had to be taken to a storehouse—a use to which Libanius suggests temples might be put.[6] There the corn was left in the charge of men whom Libanius calls ἀποδέκται.[7]

The accumulated produce was used to pay government employees, who were assigned rations rather than salaries, as is indicated by the words βασιλικὴ τροφή or τροφή or σῖτος, used by Libanius to describe a state salary, whether paid to the *comes orientis* or to a humble sophist of the little city of Elusa in

[1] Joh. Chrys. *Hom. in Ep. ad Rom.* 7. 8 (*P.G.* lx. 452); see *P.W.* s.v. Banken (suppl. vol. 4. 68–82 Laum).

[2] Cf. *Or.* lii. 15.

[3] H. Pirenne, *Medieval Cities* (Princeton, 1925), 221 ff. *Book of the Prefect* iii. 6 suggests that in ninth-century Constantinople τραπεζῖται still worked on a small scale.

[4] *Or.* xlvii. 8, xxv. 43, xxxiii. 19, lvii. 51.

[5] *Or.* xlvii. 7.

[6] *Or.* xxx. 42.

[7] *Or.* xxxi. 19, xxviii. 16, lvii. 51.

Palestine.[1] The fact that salaries were fixed in terms of rations of farm produce did not mean that they were also invariably drawn in farm produce. Thus we hear of a governor of Syria who would get money by forcing the storekeepers to buy his rations, no doubt at an advantageous price, and increased his profit further by using false measures.[2] An official might use force and deceit when he turned his rations into money, but the same matter could also be arranged in a more friendly way by men of less power. Thus in 359–60 Libanius wrote a letter to Eutocius, a leading councillor of Elusa in Palestine, that the local sophist wished his βασιλικὴ τροφή to be changed into money. Eutocius was to use his influence with the ἀποδέκται, to persuade them to buy the ration allowance of the sophist. If storekeeper and sophist came to an agreement on equal terms, both might benefit by it. The sophist would be saved the embarrassment of disposing of a quantity of corn larger than he required for food: the storekeeper would have procured for himself a stock of corn which he might sell when prices were favourable.[3]

Libanius does not enable us to estimate how frequently such arrangements were made on the occasion of the paying-out of government salaries. It seems likely that they were very common indeed. The inconvenience of drawing a high salary in produce was such that men will have used any opportunity of avoiding it. Since money was used in all transactions of everyday life, the opportunities must have been many.[4] All that was needed was that the civic liturgant in charge of the store of government corn should engage in some trade with the corn, to become to some extent a corn merchant.[5] Libanius himself received a salary in wheat and barley, part of which he drew in gold at a price fixed by the governor of Phoenicia. That a portion of the salary of a

---

[1] *Ep.* 132 (359–60) sophist of Elusa; 207 (360) imperial pension; 258 (361) sophist applies for σῖτος; 348 (358) salary of official; 345 (356–7), 356 (358) Libanius seeks σῖτος; 55 (359) *comes orientis* seeks increase of σῖτος; 28 (359–60), 207 (360), 740 (362) salaries of sophists at Antioch.

[2] *Or.* lvii. 51.   [3] *Ep.* 132 (359–60).

[4] On the whole topic: S. Mazzarino, *Aspetti sociali del quarto secolo* (Rome, 1951).

[5] One wonders whether the ἀποδέκται of the Later Empire acted as bankers and made credit transfers on the written order of private individuals in the manner of the σιτολόγοι of the Early Empire, e.g. *P. Oxy.* 2588–91; F. Preisigke, *Girowesen im griechischen Egypten* (Strasbourg, 1910), 119. I have seen no evidence. A. E. R. Boak cites a case of borrowing of wheat from Isidorus and the other σιτολόγοι of Karanis in 310: *Byzantina Metabyzantina* i (1946), 51 from Cairo. *Journal*, 57052 (unpublished).

man working at Antioch should have to come from Phoenicia and not from the environment of his city reveals a disadvantage of the policy of collecting taxes in kind. It was troublesome but not impossible to organize expenditure at a distance from collection. But this difficulty could be modified from the salary-earner's point of view, if he could sell the salary in kind in the place where he received it and transfer the proceeds. Some such arrangement must also have been assumed by the officials who compelled Libanius to repay in gold at Antioch a salary which he had drawn in kind at Constantinople.[1] I do not think that these local agreements by which various officials drew money instead of kind were even, strictly speaking, illegal. They were far too convenient for that. What was wrong with them was that they were so easily abused by powerful officials to the ruin of the storekeepers and of the territories whose taxation was in the stores.[2] Thus numerous laws were issued prohibiting *adaeratio* in various circumstances, but it is hard to believe that they were generally observed. The laws should be taken to indicate the prevalence rather than the rarity of the practice of turning wages in kind into cash.[3]

Not all the taxation of Syria was used to pay officials or soldiers stationed in the province. The surplus was transported out of the province to wherever it was needed. In the time of the Persian Wars of Constantius the councillors of Antioch were obliged to transport corn at their own expense to supply the armies in Mesopotamia.[4] When Julian was staying at Antioch with his court and army there was not enough corn in Syria to feed them all and further supplies had to be brought in by sea from Egypt.[5] Later, at the time of Emperor Theodosius' expedition against the usurper Maximus, decurions of Antioch had to pay for the sea transport of corn to the West to ensure 'the safety' of the emperor and of his soldiers and of the two capital cities'.[6]

The transport duties of the councillors of Antioch illustrate an important feature of the imperial system of taxation: the

---

[1] *Ep.* 454, *Or.* i. 80; cf. Petit, *Libanius*, 409.

[2] Mazzarino, op. cit. 136–68.

[3] Themistius took it for granted that the recipient of a large salary has to bargain in connection with its *adaeratio*. Them. *Or.* xxiii, ed. Dindorf 353D (winter 377–8).

[4] *Or.* xlix. 2; cf. *Ep.* 21 (358).

[5] Julian, *Misop.* 369B; cf. Lib. *Ep.* 1414.

[6] *Or.* liv. 47; cf. ibid. 40, *Ep.* 959. On the σιτηγία see my 'Money Economy and Taxation in Kind', *Rh. M.* 104 (1961), 242–56.

principle that the transport of the products collected in taxation is itself a tax.[1] At the same time, we can observe the advantages of the system. It ensured that the government would have supplies to maintain its armies wherever they happened to be operating. If the imperial government had paid its servants, or more important, its army in cash it would still have been obliged to ensure that there were supplies available for the men to buy. It had been the purpose of Diocletian's price edict to prevent prices from rising whenever troops came into a neighbourhood, so that the whole of a soldier's pay and donatives might not be absorbed by the purchase of a few necessities.[2] What the price edict failed to achieve, the system of taxation and payment in kind, once it was working smoothly, would achieve admirably. Food would be available wherever the soldiers or civil servants wanted it, and if there were changes in prices the profits were made by state employees, not by civilian profiteers.

The system was—at least during the first decades of its existence[3]—extremely flexible and adaptable to the needs of the moment. The taxes to be raised each year were announced in the *delegatio* issued annually at Constantinople. In the drawing-up of the *delegatio* the numbers of troops in each province were taken into account, so that in each area there was levied only that amount actually needed by the government.[4]

In perspective, the whole system can be seen to be an effective response to the military crises which confronted the empire so frequently and on so many frontiers from the third century onwards. By the combination of levies in kind with compulsory transport duties, the government was able to exploit the resources of the empire far more quickly, more effectively, and even more equitably, than would have been possible under a system based on money. The money-directed means of distribution which carried the 'trade' of the empire were too undeveloped to respond on an adequate scale to the rapidly changing circumstances.

On the other hand the system had far-reaching social consequences. It was devised to provide the resources for increased

---

[1] Jones, *L.R.E.* 458–9.

[2] Text of edict in T. Frank, *E.S.A.R.*, v. 314; *A.E.* (1947), 148–9; a new text is in preparation by S. Lauffer.

[3] On stabilization of the indiction by the early fifth century: Jones, *L.R.E.* 452–3; stereotyped returns of office establishments: ibid. 451.

[4] Déléage, *Capitation*, esp. 39–40, 69–71; Jones, *L.R.E.* 450–6.

military expenditure. Moreover it provided means by which the rate of taxation could easily be raised, and the imperial government did not fail to exploit this possibility. Eventually the burden of taxation became crushing, with disastrous consequences to the peasants farming marginal land in some areas.[1]

But from the point of view of the present study another effect is more important. As a result of heavy taxation the imperial administration came to dispose of a very considerable proportion of the produce of the empire. At the same time the Diocletianic tax system required a much more closely meshed net of provincial administration than had been needed to administer the Early Empire. The eventual result was a great shift in the relative importance of the imperial administration and self-governing institutions of the cities, to the disadvantage of the latter.

7. POPULATION AND PROSPERITY

Antioch was certainly a very large city. Ausonius wrote of it as the fourth largest city in the empire, smaller than Rome or Constantinople but comparable to Alexandria.[2] As usual the total population is difficult to assess. The circuit of walls extended for about ten kilometres[3] and surrounded an area of 1,750–2,100 hectares.[4] A considerable part of the area is, however, unsuitable for building and the actual extent of the built-up area is unknown.[5] Housing is also known to have spread beyond the walls, but again we do not know how far.[6] The built-up area was densely inhabited.[7] But the city does not appear to have possessed high blocks of tenements. At any rate Libanius recalls that the three-storeyed houses of the rich did not keep the refreshing zephyr from the houses of the poor.[8] Thus Antioch is likely

[1] Jones, *L.R.E.* 468–9, 819–23.

[2] Aus. *Ord. urb. nob.* ii. 22 (388–9). Acc. to Strabo xvi. 2. 5 (Augustan period) Antioch was a little smaller than Alexandria.

[3] Plan: Pl. 11 in Downey, *Antioch*.

[4] Estimate of J. C. Russell in 'Ancient and medieval populations', *Trans. Am. Phil. Soc.* xlviii. 3 (1958), 82. F. Stählin, E. Mayer, A. Heidner, *Pagasai und Demetrias* (Berlin–Leipzig, 1934), 191 gives total area within the walls as 1,924 hectares.

[5] Russell, op. cit., from maps in *D.A.C.L.*, *Enci. Ital.*, *P.W.*, estimates the built-up area as 900–1,200 hectares.

[6] G. Downey in a letter to the writer.   [7] *Or.* xi. 169–73.

[8] Ibid. 225; Libanius lived 'upstairs': i. 103, cf. *Ep.* 1043. The topographical mosaic (Doro Levi, *Antioch Mosaic Pavements*, vol. i. 323–45) shows only low—

to have had a lower density of population than Ostia, where high blocks were numerous. The street plan and the character of the housing of Ostia are unusually well known. In a recent study they have been made the basis of a calculation of the population of the city. From this it would appear that Ostia had about three hundred and ninety inhabitants per hectare of built-up area.[1] Assuming the same density for Antioch, and also making the somewhat arbitrary assumption that the built-up area of Antioch extended over one thousand hectares,[2] we reach a total population for Antioch of three hundred and ninety thousand. But if the population of Antioch did not live in high tenements its density must have been very much lower, perhaps only half as great.[3] This would imply a total around two hundred thousand.

An alternative approach is furnished by literary evidence. As usual this is very difficult to assess.[4] When in 363 a prominent citizen of Antioch had tried to persuade the emperor to take measures against pagans, Libanius commented that among one hundred and fifty thousand 'men' not all could be good.[5] Libanius appears to intend to state the total population of the city.

In one sermon John Chrysostomus says that the city contained one hundred thousand Christians.[6] In another he puts the population ($\delta\hat{\eta}\mu\sigma\varsigma$) of the city, professedly in the time of St. Ignatius (A.D. 115), at two hundred thousand.[7] In yet another

one- and two-storey—buildings. Theophanes (A.M. 6018) mentions five-storeyed houses in the sixth century; *P. Oxy.* xxxiv. 2719 a seven-storeyed house at Oxyrhynchus. A three- or four-storeyed house at Karanis, Rostovtzeff, *S.E.H.R.E.*, 2nd edn., 288–91.

[1] J. E. Packer, 'Housing Population in Imperial Ostia and Rome', *J.R.S.* lvii (1967).

[2] Cf. p. 92 n. 4 above.

[3] Population densities per hectare estimated by Russell, op. cit., 64–5, 79–80: Dura Europos 125; Pompeii 160; Augustan Rome 250–350; Oxyrhynchus 183; Karanis 169. The estimates, reached by different criteria, are obviously very approximate. For comparison, medieval Venice—after the plague—had a density of population of 240 per hectare, but some areas were very much more densely populated (ibid. 60). According to R. Mols, *Introduction à la démographie historique des villes d'Europe* (Louvain, 1954–6), ii. 93, in the sixteenth to eighteenth centuries Venice had a population density of 320–70 persons per hectare, but in some parishes the density surpassed 1,000 per hectare.

[4] See G. Downey, 'The size of the population of Antioch', *T.A.P.A.* lxxxix (1958), 84–91, summarized in *Antioch*, 582–3.

[5] *Ep.* 1119; Seeck, *Briefe*, 414.

[6] Joh. Chrys. *Hom. in Matth.* 85. 4 (*P.G.* lviii. 762).

[7] Id. *Hom. in Ign.* 4 (*P.G.* l. 59).

sermon he informs us that the poor in need of support comprised a tenth of the people of Antioch, that the Church looked after three thousand persons and that these amounted to a mere fifth of those in need.[1] It would follow from this estimate of the poor that the total population of the city lay between one hundred and fifty thousand and three hundred thousand.

Are the figures of Libanius and of John Chrysostomus more than guesses? Libanius' own statement that the population of Antioch could only be numbered by the Pythian oracle[2] would seem to cast strong doubts on the validity of any estimate. Nevertheless it was not beyond the power of the bureaucracy of the Roman Empire to establish and maintain lists containing the names of a very large number of persons. Thus Rome and Constantinople and, at a later date, Antioch itself[3] possessed lists of the very large numbers of persons entitled to a share in the public distribution of food.

Unfortunately there does not appear to have been a public food distribution at Antioch in 363, so the existence of a list of persons entitled to public food cannot have served as a basis of Libanius' estimate. On the other hand it is likely that under the Early Empire as well as during the later years of Diocletian the urban population was subject to a poll tax. This again would require the drawing-up of lists from which the total population could be calculated. Even if the lists were not kept up to date after the end of the poll tax, the fact that the total of the population had once been known would prevent estimates of the population from being entirely unrealistic.

---

[1] *Hom. in Matth.* 66. 3 (*P.G.* lviii. 630). In addition there are huge figures for the number of earthquake victims in 526: 250,000 (Malalas 420. 5 ff.), 300,000 (Procop. *B.P.* ii. 14. 6). Estimates made after catastrophes are usually wildly exaggerated, but for the earthquake of 528 the casualties are reported 'as about 5,000' (Malalas 443. 3) or 4,870 (Theophanes A.M. 6021). The city in which Chosroes settled his Antiochene captives (Procop. *B.P.* ii. 14. 1–4) is said to have had 30,000 inhabitants (Joh. Eph. *H.E.* vi. 19).

[2] *Or.* xi. 169.

[3] A list mentioned in model law of the Tabula Heracleensis (the so-called *lex Iulia municipalis*), *I.L.S.* 6085 = Bruns, edn. 7, no. 18, l. 15. The system of individual rations regulated in *C.T.* xiv. 17 would be unenforceable without a list. Evagr. *H.E.* vi. 8 derives the number of victims of the earthquake at Antioch of 588 from the fall in the consumption of bread. This suggests that there was a list of the persons entitled to rations. The poll tax: Jones, *L.R.E.* 10, 63. Early Empire urban census returns from Egypt: M. Hombert, C. Préaux, *Recherches sur le recensement dans l'Égypte romaine* (Brussels, 1952).

That the figures given by the literary sources are of the right order of magnitude is confirmed by evidence for the population of Alexandria. Alexandria was provisioned, at least partly, by an imperially provided supply of corn whose total in the time of Justinian is known to have been two million *medimni*. This would have fed something like three hundred thousand persons. On the basis of this A. H. M. Jones has estimated the total population at between two hundred and fifty thousand and three hundred and seventy-five thousand.[1] Of course the calculation could not be made without certain unprovable assumptions, notably that military rations of three pounds a day[2] represent the average ration of a citizen of Alexandria, and that the subsidy amounted to a very large proportion of the total corn supply of the city.[3] But these assumptions are not unreasonable and the calculation based on them provides an acceptable order of magnitude for the total population of the city.

Another approach has been adopted by Russell, who has based his calculation on the information about the buildings of the city contained in the Syriac *notitia* of Alexandria.[4] He concluded that under the Early Empire, before the calamities of the late third century the city had 215,377 citizens. This estimate is of the same order of magnitude as the statement of Diodorus that Alexandria had three hundred thousand 'free' citizens.[5]

Together the various figures for Alexandria suggests a population that ranged between two hundred thousand and four hundred thousand inhabitants compared with a range of between one hundred and fifty thousand and three hundred thousand for Antioch. That Alexandria emerges as the larger city is in itself

[1] Jones, *L.R.E.* 698 and 1040 on Procop. *H.A.* xxvi. 41–3.

[2] *P. Oxy.* 1920, 2046.

[3] On great difficulties of such calculations: F. G. Maier, 'Römische Bevölkerungsgeschichte und Inschriftenstatistik', *Historia* ii (1953), 323 ff.; also D. Jacoby, 'La population de Constantinople', *Byzantion* xxxi (1961), 81–109; A. Krisis, 'Über den Wohnhaustyp des frühen Konstantinopels', *B.Z.* liii (1960), 322–7; P. Charanis, 'Observations on the demography of the Byzantine Empire', *Proceedings of the 13th Congress of Byzantine Studies* (Oxford, 1967), 445–63. R. Duncan Jones, 'Human numbers in towns and town organisation of the Roman Empire', *Historia* xiii (1964), 199–208.

[4] Russell, op. cit. 66–7 on basis of P. M. Frazer, 'A Syriac *Notitia Urbis Alexandrinae*', *J.E.A.* xxxvii (1951), 103–7.

[5] Frazer, loc. cit. calculates reduced population at 121,948; on reduction: Eusebius, *H.E.* vii. 21. We do not know how fast the population recovered— clearly it had done so in Justinian's time. Early Empire figure: Diod. xvii. 52. 6.

reasonable. After all it was a great port as well as a centre of civil and ecclesiastical government, and the Nile enabled the production of all Egypt to be transported cheaply to the city. But both cities appear to have been extraordinarily large. Venice, by far the largest city of medieval Europe, had only seventy-seven thousand inhabitants.[1]

The suggested size of Antioch raises the problem of food supply. It has been estimated that in medieval Europe one hectare of arable land was required to feed one city dweller and that the arable had to be supplemented by one and a half to one and three-quarters as great an area of pasture. Antioch appears to have been fed mainly from its own neighbourhood. We know neither the productivity of ancient agriculture in Syria nor the area of wheat-growing land available within economic transporting distance of Antioch. Thus we cannot calculate the maximum population of Antioch possible on the basis of the available food production. But it is obvious that the problem of food supply—at least as long as there was no large-scale imperial provision—would set strict limits to the size of the city. For this reason it is probable that the population was closer to the lower than to the higher limit of the suggested range, that is, nearer to one hundred and fifty thousand than to three hundred thousand.[2]

This is still a large population. One would like to know how the classes described earlier fitted into this great mass. Obviously the 'upper classes' provided only a very thin top layer. Even the shopkeepers may well have contributed only a small proportion of the total. Unfortunately we are quite unable to reconstruct the social and economic structure of the population of Antioch— or indeed of any other great city of antiquity. The ancient evidence is quite inadequate. If the problem can be solved at all it can only be done with the aid of comparative material provided by the sociologist.

The population of Antioch was growing. In the *Antiochicus*, written in the middle of the century, Libanius emphasizes that

---

[1] Population of Venice: Russell, op. cit. 60, gives 77,700 in A.D. 1363.

[2] Land required to feed city population: B. H. Slicher van Bath, *The Agrarian History of Europe* (London, 1963), 15, 22. W. Abel, *Die Wüstungen des ausgehenden Mittelalters* (Stuttgart, 1955), 131. Food supply of Antioch: *Or.* xi. 250, greater part of city's corn brought through eastern part of city. Julian, *Misop.* 368 implies that corn was not normally brought from Chalcis (75 km. away) or Hierapolis (190 km.).

the city was receiving a steady flow of immigrants.[1] The influx continued throughout the rest of the century.[2] It may be that the rapid growth of population had in it an element of recovery from the disasters of the third century,[3] but early in the fifth century an extension was made to the ring of city walls.[4] The newcomers evidently included a shiftless element, but there was nothing discreditable about the motives of the majority of the immigrants. In the famine of 383 strangers flocked into the city because the consular had been distributing grain. The hopes of these men were disappointed,[5] but we can see that a city which could be expected to contain large stocks of government grain even in time of famine would attract immigration. It was also easier to make a living at Antioch than at other places through buying or selling or the exercise of a trade.[6] In addition there were various openings at different levels in the imperial administration.[7]

The growth of population set up some strains within the city. According to the *Antiochicus* every member of the δῆμος had a wife and household.[8] A panegyric is likely to exaggerate the respectability of the inhabitants of the city praised but perhaps not to the extent of falsifying the facts entirely. In the last quarter of the century the city was certainly more restless. In his later speeches Libanius frequently blames rootless immigrant elements for public disturbances. Food crises too appear to have become more frequent. Nevertheless the greatest disturbance of all, the Riot of the Statues, was put down very easily. We do not have the impression that the city housed a huge shiftless and discontented population.[9]

This is not contradicted by the sermons of John Chrysostomus, written during the last decades of the century. It is true that he tells us much about the horrors of poverty that could be seen at Antioch. The homeless sleep on straw in the colonnades of baths and temples. Beggars throng the entrances of churches and the

[1] *Or.* xi. 163–9.
[2] *Or.* x. 25, ii. 66, xix. 53, xxvi. 5–6, xli. 6, xxi. 25.
[3] Downey, *Antioch*, 356–61, 268. Reconstruction: *Or.* xi. 228–9.
[4] Malalas 346; G. Downey, 'The Wall of Theodosius', *A.J.P.* lxii (1941), 207–13.
[5] *Or.* xxvii. 6–7; cf. x. 25. [6] *Or.* xi. 164.
[7] *Or.* ii. 66–7; cf. 35–6 on the most successful immigrants.
[8] *Or.* xi. 151.
[9] On disturbances and food crises, see below, p. 128.

banquets of the rich. Parents are known to have blinded their children in order to arouse the pity of passers-by. The need of the poor was at its greatest in winter. Work was not to be had and the cold was too great for men to be able to spend the night in the open.[1] On the other hand he estimates the totally destitute as one-tenth of the population of the city. One suspects that by the standards of antiquity this proportion is not a high one.[2]

A rather vague indication that the city was prosperous is provided by the evidence on building.[3] Building activity was intense at the time of the *Antiochicus*. Building and rebuilding were going on all the time. Contemporary houses are more elaborate than older ones.[4] Of course we do not know to what extent, if any, the mass of the population benefited from this. Perhaps excavations will one day enable us to assess the character of the building activity more exactly.

It is certainly significant that building did not cease during the later years of the century and even continued through the 380s, a crisis period for the empire as a whole. We hear of public-prestige building by governors and members of the new nobility and of domestic building by private individuals, also of the rebuilding of a bridge[5] and of new fortifications.[6] Libanius' evidence on building at Antioch might be taken to signify little more than that in the government service men might still amass wealth to display on conspicuous building schemes. Yet even this reveals a state of affairs very different from that obtaining in cities in the West, where the new nobility spent their money on country villas rather than town houses.

Since the new citizens came both from other cities and from the countryside,[7] the question arises whether the growth of Antioch

---

[1] Sleeping in colonnades: *Hom. de Lazar.* 1. 8 (*P.G.* xlviii. 973); *Hom. de diabol. tent.* 3. 5 (xlix. 270–1). Beggars: *Hom. in Gen.* 5. 3–4 (liv. 602–3); *Hom. de Lazar.* 1. 8 (xlviii. 973); *Hom. in Matth.* 48. 5–6 (lviii. 492 ff.). Blinding of children: *Hom. in Ep. I ad Cor.* 21. 5 (lxi. 176–9). Winter: *sermo de eleemosyna* (li. 261–72). Also on poverty: *Hom. in Ep. I ad Cor.* 30. 4 (lxi. 251); *Hom. in Ep. I ad Thess.* 11. 3 (lxii. 465).

[2] Joh. Chrys. *Hom. in Matth.* 66. 3 (*P.G.* lviii. 630). Only some of the immigrants rootless paupers: *Or.* lvi. 23.

[3] Petit, *Libanius*, 314–20.   [4] *Or.* xi. 195, 227; ibid. 221–2.

[5] *Or.* l, *passim*; xxvii. 3.

[6] *Or.* xxx. 14. If this work was carried out at Antioch it is separate from the extension of the walls carried out under Theodosius II; see Downey, *Antioch*, 452–3.

[7] Petit, *Libanius*, 312.

was at the expense of other areas of Syria. It is true that the flourishing condition of villages and small towns to the east of Antioch, as revealed by their still visible remains, strongly suggests that city and country flourished together. But some evidence might seem to point in a contrary direction. Libanius tells us of the drastic decline of Cyrrhus[1] and of Emesa. Now in both cases he was thinking principally of the decline in numbers of councillors, and this was a phenomenon which affected all cities to a greater or lesser degree. But at Emesa the men who purchased the councillors' land did not settle in the city; they pulled down the houses of the former owners and thus disfigured the city.[2] It is impossible to decide whether Libanius exaggerates or how typical this kind of behaviour was. Libanius tells us that the councils of two small cities of Syria, Paltus and Balanea, were in a bad state,[3] but also implies that there remained in those cities well-to-do men who could perform curial duties if they were made to. On the other hand, Gindarus actually lost its independence and was incorporated into Antioch in the middle of the century.[4]

That the prosperity of Antioch and its hinterland was not shared by the whole of Syria is suggested by the distribution of dated inscriptions.[5] The number of inscribed stones derived from the regions of Antioch, Apamea, and Chalcis grows steadily through the fourth and fifth centuries and in the case of the regions of Apamea and Chalcis only reaches its climax in the sixth century.[6] On the other hand, the regions of Laodicea and Seleucia are not represented in this index by any inscriptions of the fourth century or later. This evidence is too incomplete and its selection too arbitrary to provide the basis for anything but a provisional hypothesis. But such as it is, it suggests that the

---

[1] *Ep.* 1071–4 (393).

[2] *Or.* xxvii. 42; *Ep.* 846 (388); ironically Emesa (Homs) was to flourish under the Arabs.

[3] *Or.* xlix. 12; cf. *Ep.* 696 (362) on Alexandria ad Issum.

[4] Jones, *C.E.R.P.* 270 n. 55.

[5] *I.G.L.S.* iv (1955), index of dated inscriptions.

[6]

	B.C.	1st c. A.D.	2nd c.	3rd c.	4th c.	5th c.	6th c.	7th c.
Antioch	9	2	22	11	43	54	40	2
Apamea	0	0	11	11	25	62	97	4
Chalcis	0	0	0	4	3	4	13	2
Laodicea	9	4	7	6	0	0	0	0
Seleucia	11	2	4	3				

prosperity of the Late Empire was restricted to the inland areas of Syria.[1] The prosperity of the olive-growing region has an earlier parallel in the development of Numidia in the third and fourth centuries.[2]

The index of dated inscriptions also provides striking evidence of the fragility of this prosperity. With the Persian occupation of Syria in 611 the Greek inscriptions come to a sudden complete stop. In the course of the same invasion the great city of Apamea was destroyed. It was never rebuilt. Antioch survived, but as a shadow of its former self.

[1] Prosperity extended to Palestine at least up to the time of Justinian; see M. Avi-Yonah, 'The Economics of Byzantine Palestine', *Israel Exploration Journal* viii (1958), 39–51. S. A. M. Gichon, 'Roman Frontier Cities in the Negev', *6th International Congress of Limes Studies* (Zagreb, 1961), 195–207. Gerasa saw church building on a considerable scale, if of bad workmanship, in the age of Justinian. C. M. Kraeling, *Gerasa, City of the Decapolis* (New Haven, 1938),171–294. R. Paret, 'Les villes de Syrie du Sud et les routes commerciales d'Arabie à la fin du VIᵉ siècle', in *Akten des XI. Internationalen Byzantinisten Kongresses* (Munich, 1960), 438–44.

[2] Development of olive-growing areas in Numidia: W. H. C. Frend, *The Donatist Church* (Oxford, 1952), 42–8. The extent of the decline of the cities of *Africa proconsularis*—if indeed there was a decline before the fifth century—is by no means clear. See B. H. Warmington, *The North African Provinces from Diocletian to the Vandal Conquest* (Cambridge, 1954), 27–54; H.-J. Diesner, *Der Untergang der Römischen Herrschaft in Nordafrika* (Weimar, 1964), 119–25. C. Courtois, *Les Vandales*, 149–50, 313–16.

III

THE AUTHORITIES AT ANTIOCH

I. THE COUNCIL: THEORY AND PRACTICE; IDEAL AND REALITY

THE Roman Empire had once been a confederation of self-governing cities controlled by a thin and widely meshed net of imperial administrators. The imperial governors were in a position to decide any civic matter with which they concerned themselves. Even so-called 'free' cities, of which Antioch was one, had the terms of their freedom defined by the Roman government.[1] Nevertheless under the Early Empire the interventions of the imperial representatives in city affairs was intermittent. The speeches of Dio of Prusa show that in the early second century the cities of Bithynia retained the possibility of pursuing a vestigial foreign policy in the field of inter-city relations.[2] In internal affairs there remained considerable scope for initiatives by individual local politicians,[3] provided these did not provoke public disturbances.[4] Dio proposed to improve the resources of his native city by public works and enlargement of the city territory and population,[5] and there is no reason to suppose that this scheme was unique.

In the fourth century the net of imperial administration had become stronger and more closely meshed and civic self-government had declined into the rule of small hereditary oligarchies, the *curiales*.[6] Nevertheless civic self-government was still an essential element in the imperial structure, and the city council, the βουλή or *curia*, the instrument of the local oligarchy, was now

---

[1] Plutarch, *Praecept. ger. rep.* 824E–F; D. Nörr, *Imperium und Polis in der hohen Prinzipatszeit* (München, 1966), 122. The 'freedom' of Antioch: Downey, *Antioch*, 145, 153, 165. The significance of the status: A. H. M. Jones, '*Civitates liberae et immunes* in the East', in *Anatolian Studies presented to W. M. Buckler* (Manchester, 1939), 103–17.

[2] Dio Chrys. *Or.* xxxviii, xlv. 13. Nörr, op. cit. 48–52.

[3] Subject to the governor's permission: Dio Chrys. *Or.* xlv. 15; sometimes requiring the governor's coercive power: ibid. xlvi. 19.

[4] Ibid. xlv. 14.   [5] Ibid. 13.   [6] See Jones, *G.C.* 179–92.

the only institution through which self-government could be carried on. The city council is described in the *Antiochicus*: 'The whole structure of the city is founded upon the council as a tree upon its root . . . Councillors can reckon up fathers, grandfathers, great-grandfathers, and ancestors even more remote, who have held the same rank. They have their forebears to teach them civic patriotism, and as each man receives his inheritance, he understands that he must hold it for the common benefit.'

The relationship of council to people is paternalistic. 'In relation to the people the council imitates the role of a father. It does not permit want to fall upon the commons. In return the commons pay to the council the wages of nurture in goodwill, grieving at the council's distress, rejoicing to the utmost at its good fortune.' Councillors are filled with competitive zeal to spend their fortunes on behalf of their city. They provide food for their fellow citizens in times of famine. They maintain the city's baths and amuse the populace with spectacles.[1] Moreover, as men of intelligence and education, they are in a position to express their views effectively to the governors. They advise good governors and restrain lawless ones.[2]

Libanius sees the role of the councillors as one of service to an ideal: the maintenance of Greek civilization. Their liturgies make possible the survival at Antioch of the essential features of Greek city life. Moreover their position enables councillors to fulfil in their lives the traditional ideal of civilized personality. Competitive public spirit can find expression in civic munificence,[3] while wisdom, moral authority, and ability to communicate find full scope in public life, particularly in dealings with the governors.[4] It was this ideal aspect of the council's role that Libanius had in mind many years later, when he called on the Emperor Theodosius to restore the councils to their former flourishing condition.

The councils are no less worthy of your zeal than your armed forces. The latter do indeed keep safe the cities, but it is owing to the former that there is anything worthy of preservation. While the councils are in the condition I have described, there is nothing fine for which to fight . . .
. . . I wish your reign to be celebrated not only for campaigns, battles, trophies and victories, but also for the education and literary

---

[1] Quotations: *Or.* xi. 133, 152; duties: ibid. 134–8.
[2] Ibid. 139–43.   [3] Ibid. 134.   [4] Ibid. 139, 146.

art of which Greece is the mother . . . therefore, in order to help at one stroke the councils and the now discarded books, punish the men who are too little concerned with what is right and reveal both institutions restored to their former strength, the council-chambers and the schools.[1]

Libanius' view of the function of the council is clearly idealized. It is all the more striking that even the *Antiochicus*, his account of the functions of the governing body of Antioch, does not include that essential role of any true government, leadership. The councillors spend money and give advice,[2] but there is no pretext that they govern the city. They advise the governors, but the governors make the decisions.

The imperial government was no less concerned for the preservation of the councils than Libanius himself.[3] But its point of view was different. In the first place it was concerned to ensure the availability of men who would perform a multitude of duties for the empire, notably the collection of taxes. Over and above this, the imperial government regularly acted on the assumption that in its council a city possessed a government which could be held responsible in two related fields, the maintenance of civic services and of public order.

Thus in 303 the citizens of Antioch fought and defeated a unit of the Roman army that had mutinied while constructing a new port at Seleucia. Surprisingly, the Emperor Diocletian's reaction to what might seem a meritorious action was to execute a number of leading councillors. Libanius did not think that the mutiny had been provoked by any specific act or omission on the part of the councillors, or even that any specific charge was made against them by the imperial authorities. He informs us that the executions had not been preceded by a trial. The councillors had been executed κατ' αὐτὸ τὸ πολιτεύεσθαι.[4] It would seem therefore that when the emperor heard of the clash between soldiers and civilians he immediately ordered the execution of leading councillors of the cities concerned. In other words the councillors were held jointly responsible for the maintenance of civilian peace and order. When this broke down, regardless of cause, the emperor punished the responsible group of men.

[1] *Or.* xlix. 32.   [2] *Or.* xxxv. 6 ff.
[3] *C.T.* xii. 1, *De decurionibus, passim*; Jones, *L.R.E.* 740–54.
[4] *Or.* xix. 45; cf. xi. 159–62.

These events happened when the more centralized administration of Diocletian was still new. But the policy of treating the council as a real and responsible government survived throughout the fourth century. When the Caesar Gallus in 354 proposed to establish price control at Antioch, and his proposal met with outspoken opposition from the council, Gallus had the principal councillors imprisoned under threat of execution.[1] Evidently he felt that price-control measures could only be put into force through the agency of the councillors. Eight years later, Julian in a similar situation waited several months for the council to take measures needed to deal with a famine. Only when the council had failed did he allow the initiative to pass to imperial officials.[2]

After the death of Julian certain men attacked the property which the great courtier Datian owned near Antioch. Judging from the language of a letter of Libanius, the council was held responsible for the outrage and anticipated the powerful man's revenge.[3] Presumably the local police force should have prevented the disturbance. But of course the police force was feeble, and one may wonder whether it could have done so. We are here faced with a fundamental weakness of the principle of curial responsibility. The councillors' ability to maintain order depended on their wealth and generosity, and on their prestige in local society. They lacked real coercive power. For this they depended on the imperial administration.

In 387 the Riot of the Statues was to reveal dramatically both the extent of the council's theoretical responsibility and its actual helplessness. The famous riot was caused by a heavy increase in taxation. The letter announcing the additional exactions was read in the governor's court to the assembled and graded notables of the city: ex-governors, decurions, barristers, veterans. These men responded with an emotional plea of the city's inability to pay. Finally all broke into a prayer to God to help the city. The protest was then taken up by the crowd which had gathered outside the governor's residence and this demonstration rapidly developed into a riot. The behaviour of the crowd threatened the security of the governors, and the houses of the rich were endangered. Eventually the mob overturned and disfigured

---

[1] Amm. xiv. 7. 2.   [2] See below, pp. 130–1.
[3] *Ep.* 1184; cf. 1259.

certain pictures and statues of the emperor and his family—an act which the imperial government inevitably construed as a symbol of rebellion.[1]

In this infinitely menacing situation order was restored without difficulty by the 'archers'. It would seem that the decision to intervene was a personal decision of their commander.[2] It certainly did not come from the council. The council had done nothing; in fact at the crucial moment it did not exist. Its members were scattered and in hiding and had no means of meeting or even communicating.[3] So complete an abnegation of responsibility is only explicable if the council had in fact already ceased to exercise real responsibility many years previously. But as far as the imperial government was concerned the council was still responsible for the city. While the councillors had been only one group among others in the assembly of notables that preceded the riot, and had shown that they completely lacked authority during the riot, they were nevertheless called to account for the fact that an act of rebellion had taken place in their city. There was a real danger that all or some councillors would be executed on the orders of the Emperor Theodosius, as some of their predecessors had been executed by Diocletian— and for the same reason.[4] Eventually the council was merely imprisoned until the emperor's general pardon arrived in the city. None of the councillors had actually received individual punishment, but the whole episode is a vivid demonstration of responsibility without power.

2. THE EMPEROR

The reason for the growing divergence between the theoretical responsibility of the council and its actual powers was of course the fact that the councils were subjected to control by the whole hierarchy of the post-Diocletianic administration, from the emperor downwards. The emperor himself—unless he happened to reside in the city—was a remote figure, but nevertheless an awe-inspiring one. His power, if he should choose to use it, was

---

[1] Downey, *Antioch*, 428 ff.; R. Browning, 'The Riot of A.D. 387 in Antioch', *J.R.S.* xlii (1952), 13–20.

[2] *Or.* xix. 34–5.   [3] Ibid. 32–3.

[4] *Or.* xxiii. 25, xix. 44–6. Another view: Browning, op. cit. 20.

almost unlimited. When in 387 representations of the imperial family had been disfigured, it was widely anticipated that the emperor would hand over the city to the army for plunder and destruction.[1] Whenever an imperial letter arrived in the city, the governor would summon the principal citizens, no matter what they were doing, to attend a public reading of the imperial commands. In the theatre, imperial letters would be listened to in silence by a standing audience.[2] All public building operations were carried out in the name of the emperor.[3] Whenever the civic authorities wished to institute a reform of any importance an embassy had to be sent to Constantinople to obtain imperial authorization.[4] A charge of treason, particularly if linked with one of magic, was a most fearsome threat.[5]

The unlimited power of the imperial office, and the fear it aroused in the minds of subjects, is reflected in the political theory of the time. The authors of panegyrics, who intended to civilize as well as praise the emperors whom they addressed, again and again praise the emperor for his humanity, his φιλ-ανθρωπία.[6] In other words, the ruler is encouraged to be clement and not to use his overwhelming power to oppress his subjects. The preaching was not without effect. The Emperor Theodosius, in spite of a violent temper not always under control, was eager to have a reputation for humanity.[7]

But while the idea of the emperor loomed powerfully and fearfully over Antioch, the reality was a long way away at

[1] *Or.* xix. 5, 7; xxiii. 14.

[2] *Or.* i. 157; cf. Dvornik, *Early Christian and Byzantine Political Philosophy* (Princeton, 1966), 694.

[3] G. Downey, 'Imperial Building Records in Malalas', *B.Z.* xxxviii (1938), 1–15, esp. 6–11.

[4] *Ep.* 870 (388), honours for a sophist; *Or.* xlviii. 19–21; ibid. 27, membership of council; lvi. 24, permission to expel foreigners; Julian, *Misop.* 367D, arrears of taxation.

[5] Cf. Amm. xxix. 5 ff.; Lib. *Or.* i. 171 ff. on 'Theodore' trials. Libanius was repeatedly in danger of the double charge: i. 98–9 (354); ibid. 239–41 (385); ibid. 264–5 (387); ibid. 273 (388).

[6] e.g. Themistius, *Or.* i on φιλανθρωπία of Constantius; *Or.* xix on that of Theodosius; cf. Pack, *Studies*, 70 ff.; Piganiol, *L'Empire chrétien*, 310; G. Downey, 'Personification in the Antioch Mosaics', *T.A.P.A.* lxix (1938), 349–63, also 'The Pagan Virtue of Megalopsychia', ibid. lxxvi (1945), 279–86. Libanius' use of μεγαλοψυχία as generosity in forgiving: *Ep.* 256, 200, *Or.* xiii. 17, xviii. 153, ibid. 202; lix. 85, *Ep.* 1259, *Or.* xv. 40; generosity in financial sense: lvii. 3, xii. 134, *Ep.* 731, *Or.* xxxv. 4, xxxi. 35. In a wider sense of moral excellence: *Ep.* 1513, 1425.

[7] *Or.* xix. 16 ff., xxiii. 13; cf. Joh. Chrys. *Hom. ad pop. Ant.* 21 (*P.G.* xlix. 215–16).

Constantinople. The emperor might send a letter conveying commands which were of absolutely overriding authority, but it would depend on the attitude of the governors whether the commands were obeyed.[1] We even hear of an edict, authorizing the council to take steps to restore its numbers, that was received at Antioch but never published.[2]

Again, while the panegyrics and the official theory suggest that the emperor was the person behind every act of government policy, the real author of policy was known to be the praetorian prefect of the East. It was he, for instance, who directed the measures aimed at restoring the strength of the council,[3] or who permitted the monks to wander across the land destroying pagan temples.[4] Further, while it was the emperor's name that gave edicts and rescripts their overriding authority, informed men knew that the words were not really his. So Libanius might have occasion to congratulate a friend on the high literary qualities of an imperial letter which had just been read out at Antioch.[5] Moreover the contents of a letter might express the policy of the emperor, or the praetorian prefect, or of one of the other heads of departments. They might, on the other hand, merely be the result of a successful intrigue, such as that by which the bishop of Gaza obtained imperial permission to destroy the pagan temples in that city.[6]

A direct channel of communication between cities and the emperor was provided by embassies.[7] These might be sent spontaneously by city councils or provincial assemblies, to complain of an official or to obtain authorization for some local initiative, or just to ask for indulgence in connection with arrears of taxation. But most of the embassies were compulsory. Embassies were required regularly to take the 'crown gold' to the emperor on the

---

[1] *Ep.* 1201 (364) emperor's letter needs local support. 958 (390) imperial letter signed but held up at court. *Ep.* 115 (359–60) imperial letter might be used to override the law. *Ep.* 144 (359–60) imperial letter needs support of governor. *Ep.* 169 (358–61), cf. 204, governor slow to obey imperial letter. 200 (359–60) *comes orientis* asked to carry out emperor's pardon. See also 214 (360?), 265 (361), 271 (361).

[2] *Or.* xlviii. 15.   [3] *Or.* xlix. 3, 31.

[4] *Or.* xxx. 46 ff.   [5] *Ep.* 559 (357).

[6] Marc le Diacre, *Vie de Porphyre*, ed. H. Grégoire and M.-A. Kugener (Paris, 1930), 26–7; 34–54; cf. Jones, *L.R.E.* 344–7.

[7] On embassies see C. Lacombrade, *Discours sur la royauté*, esp. 11–20, 139–40. Jones, *L.R.E.* 336–7, 362–3, 763–6.

occasion of an imperial anniversary.¹ Obligatory embassies also might carry petitions. Thus an embassy, sent by Ancyra in 363 to take crown gold to Jovian, had the special mission of countering anti-pagan sermons of certain Christians.² Again, we are told that the assembly of the province of Cyrenaica, which sent Synesius to carry the crown gold of the province to the Emperor Arcadius, had previously discussed such matters as the number of barbarian mercenaries in the army, and whether the province should continue as a separate military command or be united with Egypt. Clearly, the final resolution contained requests on these matters as well as the more customary ones for relief from taxation.³

There was of course a provincial assembly of Syria. It was attended by the representatives of seventeen cities and provided the occasion for the great show of the Syriarch.⁴ We also hear of it in an entirely different context. The bishop of Apamea was killed by angry pagans while watching the destruction of a pagan sanctuary. The identity of the killers became known and the sons of the bishop wanted to avenge their father. But they were prevented, so Sozomen informs us, by ἡ ἀνὰ τὸ ἔθνος σύνοδος.⁵ We are not told what the assembly did. Perhaps it refused to pass a resolution calling on the emperor to punish the men who had killed the bishop. Be that as it may, the incident shows that at this time the Assembly of Syria did concern itself with matters of general public interest.

An increase in the importance of the provincial assemblies at this period is not surprising. One factor alone must have made the assemblies more influential, relatively, than ever before. They represented all landowners, senators as well as councillors. As the influence of councillors and civic councils declined, the provincial assembly will have become the only effective corporation in a province.⁶

---

¹ See Appendix on embassies in Libanius.
² *Ep.* 1436 (363), they also praise the provincial governor: 1439.
³ Lacombrade, op. cit. 11–20.
⁴ *Ep.* 1399 (363); listed in Jones *C.E.R.P.* 531. Antioch, Seleucia, Laodicea, Gabala, Paltus, Beroea, Chalcis, Anasartha, Gabbula, Apamea, Epiphaneia, Arethusa, Larissa, Mariamne, Balaneae, Raphaneae, Seleucia ad Belum.
⁵ Sozomen vii. 15 (*P.G.* lxvii. 1457).
⁶ P. Guiraud, *Les Assemblées provinciales dans l'empire romain* (Paris, 1887), 219–85; J. A. O. Larsen, *Representative Government in Greek and Roman History* (U. of California, 1955), esp. 145–61; also 'The position of Provincial Assemblies in the Government and Society of the Late Roman Empire', *Cl. Phil.* xxix (1934), 209–20.

Embassies sometimes achieved their object. The codes contain a significant number of laws drafted in answer to the requests of ambassadors.[1] The diocesan assembly of Oriens (or the provincial assemblies of Oriens) gained the return of Ursicinus to the post of commander-in-chief in the East.[2] Ambassadors of the council of Antioch in 388 achieved the recall of the unpopular consular Lucianus.[3] But the purposes of the embassy might be frustrated. The praetorian prefect Probus made a habit of compelling embassies to carry resolutions expressing gratitude for his government.[4] Intrigue and corruption at court could also do much to foil an embassy. Ammianus describes how two embassies of the province of Tripolitania not only failed to achieve their object but resulted in the execution of one ambassador and very great danger to the others.[5]

For, in order to get grievances remedied, it was not sufficient for ambassadors to carry a suitably phrased resolution to Constantinople and to make a frank and tactful speech at the imperial reception.[6] Relief could only come through an imperial letter, and this could only be obtained after a lengthy period of intrigue, and the intelligent exploitation of 'presents' and of influence. But when such aids were available, almost any petition had a chance to receive the assent of an over-worked emperor. In the imperial codes not a few laws state that exemptions from the provisions of the law shall not be valid even though supported by a rescript of the emperor himself.[7] Of course the evil, that justice and administrative decisions could be perverted by corruption or influence, was not restricted to court but pervaded the entire administration. It is not surprising that Libanius at Antioch held a more sober view on kingship than Themistius could afford to proclaim at court. In the writings of Libanius we do not read about the 'living law'—admittedly even Themistius uses this concept mainly in contexts of imperial clemency.[8] We also read only little about the divine mission of kingship.

---

[1] Jones, *L.R.E.* 362, nn. 90–2.   [2] Amm. xviii. 6. 2.
[3] *Or.* lvi. 14, 21.   [4] Amm. xxx. 5. 8–9.
[5] Ibid. xxviii. 6. 7; cf. Lib. *Ep.* 1263 (364); unsuccessful ambassador on trial.
[6] Lacombrade, *Discours sur la royauté*, 80–7, argues that the speech was spoken at the imperial reception.
[7] See Jones, *L.R.E.* 410 on *C.T.* i. 2. 2, 3; *Nov. Th.* v. 2. 1, vi. 1. 4, viii. 1. pr. xvii. 1. 3, xvii. 2. 5.
[8] Them. *Or.* i, pp. 16 ff.; xi, p. 182; viii, p. 141; ix, p. 151; xix, p. 277.

Instead, Libanius insists that justice should be certain, and should be enforced, that the law is binding even on the emperor, and that if a law is bad it should be changed.[1]

3. THE *COMES ORIENTIS* AND THE *CONSULARIS SYRIAE*

The emperor was represented at Antioch by two officials: the *comes orientis* and the consular of Syria. While the consular's power was generally restricted to the province of Syria, the rule of the *comes orientis* extended over the whole diocese of Oriens. The origin of this office is obscure. According to Malalas the first *comes orientis* was appointed to organize supplies for the Persian campaign of 334–5. On the other hand, the composition of his staff suggests that the majority of his responsibilities were judicial rather than financial.[2] The letters provide us with some information about the activities of Modestus, *comes orientis* from 358–62. During these years Modestus engaged in a good deal of travel over the whole of his command from the Euphrates to Egypt.[3] This is compatible with the theory that he was organizing the food supply for the troops—but also with judicial work.[4] Further, when Modestus was in the province of Euphratensis, Libanius wrote to him in terms which suggest that he was conducting military operations.[5] This is rather surprising. The troops were under the command of the *magister militum*, and the division between civil and military commands was otherwise complete. There is no doubt that the *comes orientis* was a civil official. Nevertheless, the passage from Libanius does not stand alone, and Ammianus tells us of military operations against the Isaurians carried out by Modestus' predecessor, Honoratus Nebridius.[6]

---

[1] Lib. *Or.* li. 2, xxx. 55, xlvii. 36–7; l. 32. Bad law should be changed: xlviii. 26; cf. l. 12.

[2] Malalas 218–19; *Not. Dig. Or.* xxii. 17. 33, 40; *C.T.* i. 13 (394); Jones, *L.R.E.* 105, n. 61; a different view, G. Downey, *A Study of the 'Comites Orientis' and the 'Consulares Syriae'* (Princeton, 1939); cf. also Piganiol, *L'Empire chrétien*, 322; O. Seeck in *P.W.* iv. 659–61.

[3] References in Seeck, *Briefe*, 213–15. The date of the creation of a separate diocese of Egypt is still debated: A. H. M. Jones, 'The date of the *Apologia contra Arianos*', *J. Theol. S.*, N.S. v (1954), 224–7; J. Lallemand, *L'Administration civile de l'Égypte* (Brussels, 1964), 55–6. A *comes* active in Egypt in 386, *Or.* xxxiii. 27; meanwhile he orders the consular to buy corn in Euphratensis, ibid. 6–7.

[4] During Julian's Persian campaign the *comes* Rufinus V in Mesopotamia, *Ep.* 1341, 1398, 1400.

[5] *Ep.* 46 (358–9), 49 (359), 58 (359).   [6] Amm. xiv. 2. 20.

In his intervention in the internal affairs of Antioch the *comes* was backed by some military force. It was the *comes* who brought military units into the city after the Riot of the Statues and he who punished the offenders.[1] The consular, on the other hand, seems to have been without any military protection at all, for he watched the gathering of the riot helplessly.[2] As a rule it was the *comes* who was in charge in times of crisis.[3]

When writing about a consular, Libanius usually gives the impression that he was acting on his own responsibility and without prompting from a superior. But there is no doubt that the *comes orientis* was the consular's superior.[4] In precedence he ranked next to the two proconsuls and above all other governors and vicars.[5] Moreover the post of *comes orientis* was often given to a man who was going on to higher offices.[6] Consulars of Syria more often were content to retire to the immune leisure of an ex-governor, after holding a single qualifying office. The tenure of a consular of Syria often lasted less than a year. The terms of the counts tended to be longer.[7] Within the city the spheres of duty of the two officials coincided, but no doubt in case of conflict, the will of the *comes* prevailed.[8] In the present work the term 'governor' is used to describe consular and *comes* alike.

In comparison with provincial governors of the Early Empire the majority of officials were very inexperienced indeed. As a rule they were appointed by the praetorian prefect of the East

---

[1] *Or.* xix. 36. With Foerster (ad loc.), and unlike Seeck (*Briefe*, 107), I assume that Celsus III, who was in charge of the subsequent trial and punishment (xix. 55, xxxiii. 10), was the *comes*.

[2] *Or.* xx. 3.

[3] *Or.* i. 206 ff., 226 ff., xxix. 2 ff.; Malalas 389–90, 392–3, 395–8. Joh. Chrys. *S. Melet.* (*P.G.* l. 517), ὁ τῆς πόλεως ἄρχων is probably the *comes*.

[4] *Or.* xxvii. 6, xxxiii. 27, xl. 10.   [5] *Not. Dig. Or.* xxii. 17. 33.

[6] Some careers: Modestus, praetorian prefect under Valens (Seeck, *Briefe*, 213–18); Nebridius, praetorian prefect under Constantius and Valens (ibid. 219); Tatian, praetorian prefect 388–92 (ibid. 285–9; Lallemand, op. cit. 247–8). For a list of known office-holders, see Downey, op. cit., n. 1.

[7] Brief tenure of governorships was usual, Jones, *L.R.E.* 380 ff.

[8] Seeck in *P.W.* iv. 1, col. 660 attributes to the *comes orientis* in relation to Antioch the same position as was held by the *praefecti urbi* of Rome and Constantinople in relation to their cities. But in Libanius' speeches the *comites* do not really appear in that role except in time of crisis, as, e.g. Philagrius and Icarius in the famines of 382 and 384–5 respectively. Normally consulars like Tissamenes or Florentius appear to have been in charge of most aspects of civic life, cf. *Or.* xxxiii, xlvi, liv, iv; but *Or.* xxvii. 6 shows *comes* and consular adopting opposite policies during famine.

after being brought to his attention by some influential friends.[1]
The claims of influentially supported self-advertisement were
reinforced by money.[2] It was a consequence of this method of
appointment that governorships were only held for very short
periods. The entreaties of friends and the attractions of money
continued to be irresistible and no sooner had one man taken up
his governorship than a place had to be found for another. The
terms of governorships had become significantly shorter in
Libanius' lifetime.[3] In view of this, the real governors of the
province must have been the heads of the provincial office staffs.
Unfortunately, we hear very little of these officials, apart from
the fact of their venality.[4]

The governor's supervision extended to all aspects of civic life.
This involved a considerable amount of paper work, which was
normally completed in the afternoon,[5] but a conscientious governor might work deep into the night, to the annoyance of his
officials.[6] Two activities took up a great deal of a governor's
time: the supervision of tax-collecting and the dispensation of
justice. Taxation is treated in a later section. Judicial work
occupied so much of governors' time that the codes often refer
to them simply as judges. On at least one occasion a governor
got so far behind with his cases that the prison became overcrowded, with the result that many lost their lives while awaiting
trial.[7] Governors in their eagerness to get trials finished and to
be free to see to the taxes, were rationing the time available to
barristers and making impossible the delivery of speeches in the
grand manner of the rhetorical tradition.[8]

Ever since the early days of Roman administration governors
had drawn to themselves a large part of the legal business, and
the jurisdiction of municipal magistrates had correspondingly

---

[1] *Ep.* 1224 (364), 333 (357–8), 562 (357), 871 (388), 959 (390), 1474 and 1476
(365).

[2] *Or.* xlviii. 11, iv. 21, ii. 42, lii. 22, xviii. 130; cf. also *Ep.* 1441, 864, 655, 841,
86, 215, 435.

[3] *Or.* ii. 42. cf. p. 111 n. 7 above.

[4] *Or.* xlvi. 42; domineering *officiales*, *Ep.* 142, *Or.* xxxv. 8; Cf. also xxxiii. 31.

[5] *Or.* lii. 6.   [6] *Or.* xxvi. 33–4.

[7] Overcrowded prison, *Or.* xlv. 17–18 and *passim.* Cf. Pack, *Studies*, 111–12.
Much of the civil business trivial, xlv. 18; governor tries suits of powerful against
their inferiors or tenants, xlv. 3–6; murder, xxiv. 6, xlv. 6, 25–6; a variety of cases,
li. 6, lii. 8.

[8] *Or.* lxii. 43.

tended to wither away. This development had been accelerated by the reforms of Diocletian. In the fourth century it would seem that practically all cases were decided in the governor's court, or at least by delegates appointed by the governor.[1] Moreover we hear of only very few cases decided by a delegate. Two of these took place under Julian.[2] Libanius also mentions beatings inflicted on traders by order of the curial official in charge of the bakers' guild.[3] But he too had been specially authorized by the governor.[4] On other occasions traders are punished by the governor himself.[5] We never hear of any case of the independent exercise of jurisdiction by a civic official.[6]

A governor's power was almost unlimited. In *Oration* liv Libanius attacks the consular Eustathius for not treating him with sufficient respect. Among the honours Libanius claims for himself are the privilege of being summoned by edict, or better still, by herald, to the governor's presence,[7] help for Libanius' son in the exercise of his profession of advocate,[8] tokens of solicitude when Libanius was ill, preferably made visible to all by means of a visit.[9] Such a speech delivered today would embarrass its audience, but in fourth-century Antioch these τιμαί were not felt to be trivial. On such tokens of the governor's interest and goodwill depended the security of a man's property, if not indeed his personal security, as well as his ability to help friends and inferiors.[10] If the governor's favour was withdrawn, not only would a man like Libanius be exposed to prosecution

---

[1] Governor's jurisdiction: Jones, *G.C.* 121–3, 134; A. N. Sherwin-White, *Roman Society and Roman Law in the New Testament* (Oxford, 1963), 1–23. *O.G.I.S.* 515 (Ant. Pius) cases below 250 *denarii* heard by civic magistrates, cf. *O.G.I.S.* 527, trial of illegal money-changers. Effect of reforms of Diocletian: Lallemand, op. cit. 146–7; Jones, *L.R.E.* 479. Delegated jurisdiction: *C.J.* iii. 3, *De pedaneis iudicibus*; cf. C. Lécrivain, *Le Sénat romain depuis Dioclétien*, 101–3.

[2] *Ep.* 1353, 1361. Julian encouraged this. *C.T.* i. 16. 8 = *C.J.* iii. 3. 5; also *C.I.L.* iii. 459, 14198.

[3] *Or.* xxix. 10–11, xxvii. 26–7. On delegated jurisdiction exercised by local magistrates in Egypt see Lallemand, op. cit. 146–7, 109–11 (λογιστής), 116–17 (*defensor*), 121 (*strategos-exactor*), 129 (*prytanis*), 131–2 (*praepositus pagi*). See also P. Collinet, *Études historiques sur le droit de Justinien*, vol. iv (Paris, 1932), 64–6.

[4] *Or.* xxix. 22.   [5] *Or.* xlvi. 7, 10, iv. 26–7.

[6] Cf. G. Rouillard, *L'Administration civile de l'Égypte byzantine* (Paris, 1928), 153 ff. Eventually governors were relieved of some of the minor civil and criminal cases by the jurisdiction of the *defensor*: Jones, *L.R.E.* 480. Arbitration by the bishop (see below, p. 240) also lightened the load.

[7] *Or.* liv. 5–6.   [8] Ibid. 7–15.

[9] Ibid. 30–6.   [10] Cf. below, p. 196.

and his property endangered, but friends and clients would be similarly threatened.[1]

4. THE GENERAL

It is significant that the imperial officials who played a role in the government of Antioch were overwhelmingly civilians. Still, in addition to the two governors a very high-ranking general had his headquarters at Antioch. This was, no doubt, what enabled Libanius to make the acquaintance of the various generals with whom he exchanged letters during the later years of his life. None of these men was a citizen of Antioch; one, Richomer, was a Frank; another, Sapor, probably a Persian. Others may have been born subjects of the empire, but the letters reveal nothing about their origins. Generals were not expected to be men of education: Libanius praises the fact of their having written rather than the style of their writing.[2]

That officers did not normally come from the educated city aristocracies is confirmed by the prosopography of Libanius' pupils. A certain amount of ambiguity is caused by the fact that Libanius uses the word 'soldier' to describe members both of the military and of the civilian branch of the imperial service.[3] But Petit has found only two certain cases of pupils of Libanius who entered the fighting service.[4] Since the careers of a large number of pupils are known, this negative evidence is highly significant. It is true that some members of the civic aristocracy

---

[1] *Or.* lii. 41–2.

[2] *Ep.* 867 (388) Promotus; 2 (383 or 387), 868 (388), 884 (388) Ellebichus; 1060 (392) to Bacurius; 957 (390) Sapor; 1043 (392) for Bacurius; 857 and 897 (388) to Saturninus; 1054–5 (392) Demonicus; 1057 Moderatus; 1104 (393) Varanes; 1062 Addaius (392); 318 (357), 350 (358?), 520 (356), 596 (357) Sebastianus; 426 (355) a general, *comes Isauriae.* For details of lives and careers of these men, see prosopography in Seeck, *Briefe.* Bacurius had been king of a tribe in Northern Armenia, became an officer in the Roman army, Amm. xxxi. 12. 16. Libanius was also on good terms with Lupicinus, a general at Antioch in the 370s, *Or.* i. 165. Libanius' dislike for generals must not be exaggerated, cf. Pack, *Studies,* 16; Harmand, *Discours sur les patronages,* 108.

[3] 'Soldiers' who are civil servants: *Ep.* 821, 81; 'hoplites' who are civil servants: *Ep.* 301, the ἐν ὅπλοις βίος of *Or.* xliv. 2 is service with the *agentes in rebus,* cf. lxii. 14. Officially the civil service was a *militia,* Jones, *L.R.E.* 566.

[4] Petit, *Étudiants,* 166; Firminus II was a 'soldier' before becoming a sophist (*Ep.* 1048). A civil servant would be more likely to become a sophist than a member of the armed forces.

did join the army, as officers or *protectores*,[1] rather than as other ranks.[2] The outstanding example of a *curialis* of Antioch who served as a *protector* is the historian Ammianus Marcellinus.[3] But the evidence of Libanius suggests that this was exceptional. Thus most of the generals are likely to have come from an unliterary background. But it is evident that they did not like to be thought indifferent to culture, and, when duty had brought them to Antioch, they went out of their way to be polite to its famous citizen, the greatest living exponent of classical education. The prestige of rhetoric was still sufficiently high to induce high-ranking men without much learning to do homage to 'logoi'.

What command did these men hold at Antioch? In the last years of Libanius' life 'the general' was a powerful figure. He was able to exact some payment from the council.[4] He protected tenants against their landlord.[5] He helped the council to obtain the dismissal of the consular Lucianus.[6] His officials exploited the tavern-keepers.[7] When a general retired from office he regularly sold the stores of the hostel of the public post, which it was the shopkeepers' duty to replace.[8]

So powerful an officer must have been either the *magister militum per orientem* or the *dux Syriae et Euphratensis*. Since the *dux* was stationed at Barbalissos on the Euphrates,[9] it is probable

---

[1] On *protectores*, Jones, *L.R.E.* 636–40. *Or.* ii. 45 tells of successful advocates who joined the army to be able to marry a rich wife but had no intention of fighting in battle. They could have achieved this aim through service in the *protectores*, who had high prestige but were not attached to particular units.

[2] R. Grosse, *Römische Militärgeschichte* (Berlin, 1920), lists unpleasant features of life in the ranks: extortion from pay and selling of leave (247); heavy physical work (222–3; 225–9); savage discipline (236–7); legionary service was particularly severe and deterred volunteers (Vegetius ii. 3).

[3] E. A. Thompson, *The Historical Work of Ammianus Marcellinus* (Cambridge, 1947). Under Julian three officers were forced back into the council of Antioch: xlix. 19. An aunt of Libanius married a general, xlvii. 28.

[4] *Or.* xlvii. 33, following the interpretation of Reiske, ed., vol. 2. 522, n. 37, rather than Harmand, *Discours sur les patronages*, 42, 159, or Petit, *Libanius*, 190. For τιμή = salary, pay, cf. lvii. 51. A privilege like *C.T.* vii. 11. 1–2 might form the basis of the extortion.

[5] *Or.* xlvii. 13.

[6] *Or.* lvi. 21; cf. xxxix. 14, Mixidemus puts pressure on governors through general.

[7] *Or.* xlvi. 13.　　　　　　　　　　　　　　　　　　　[8] Ibid. 20.

[9] I assume that the *dux* of Coele Syria and Augusta Euphratensis (*Not. Dig.*, ed. Seeck, 69–71) still had his headquarters where the *dux* of Augusta Euphratensis had had them, i.e. at Barbalissos (*Martyrium SS. Sergii et Bacchi* in *Anal. Boll.* xiv (1895), 377, 384). On date of this: A. H. M. Jones, 'The Date and Value of the Verona List', *J.R.S.* xliv (1954), 21–9.

that the general at Antioch was the *magister militum per orientem*. This is confirmed by the fact that the *magister militum per orientem* is known to have been regularly in residence at Antioch in the fifth century.[1] He had permanent headquarters in the city.[2]

But if the *magister militum* had permanent headquarters in Antioch we are faced with the problem of why this extremely powerful man is mentioned in relatively few of Libanius' speeches. He is not mentioned in the speeches about the Riot of the Statues, nor in those against the governor Eustathius (388), against Tissamenes (386), Icarius (384), Severus (381). He does not figure in the correspondence. Why not? One would expect behaviour of the kind described in the *De patrociniis*, and witnessed also by much other evidence about military commanders in the fourth century,[3] to have been a constant source of dispute between the military and civil administrations and between soldiers and civilians.[4] The problems of army supplies must have provided ample occasion for conflict between governors and general. But evidently such conflicts were not a constant feature of public life at Antioch. Soldiers evidently had a bad reputation; they often behaved aggressively to civilians. We hear of disputes over the use of privately owned pastures by animals belonging to the army.[5] But if we take the evidence about Antioch as a whole such incidents are not prominent. One must conclude that as a rule the needs of the army were supplied without much trouble.

Part of the explanation is likely to be that there were not many soldiers stationed near Antioch. Military remains show that the eastern edge of Syria was full of military camps and posts situated on the main lines of communication.[6] It is likely that the greater

---

[1] Downey, *Antioch*, 454, 459, 471–2, 484 ff., 490, 530.

[2] Theophanes, A.M. 6018; Euagr. i. 18: τῶν στρατηγῶν τὰ καταγώγια. On this see Downey, *Antioch*, 626, n. 5. After the Riot of the Statues the commissioners stayed at the καταγωγή of the general (*Or.* xxii. 17) and also held their investigation there (xxi. 7). It had a courtyard from which the public could hear the trial. (Joh. Chrys. *Hom. ad pop. Ant.* 13. 2 ff. *Or.* ii. 8 and li. 4 show that Libanius uses καταγωγή to describe the residential quarters not only of the general but of any official.

[3] *Or.* xlvii; cf. *C.T.* xi. 24. 1, 3, 4.   [4] Jones, *L.R.E.* 631–2.

[5] Vices of soldiers: Joh. Chrys. *Hom. in Matth.* 61. 2 (*P.G.* lviii. 590–1); attacks on civilians: *Or.* xlvii. 33; soldiers are bad neighbours: *Or.* lii. 11; disputes over pastures: *C.T.* vii. 7. 3 (398).

[6] R. Mouterde and A. Poidebard, *Le 'Limes' de Chalcis* (Paris, 1945), summarized in map at end of vol. 2. The stations of the *limitanei* mentioned in the *Notitia* as far as they have been identified were to the east of Chalcis. The stations of *alae*, *cohortes*, and units under the *magister militum* are not recorded; see D. van Berchem,

part of the garrison of Syria was stationed in that area. Just outside Antioch there was a military training ground.[1] There must
also have been within short marching distance of the city the
camp of the unit that intervened so speedily in the Riot of the
Statues. But there is no evidence that the number of soldiers
involved was large. It is likely that the area around Antioch
and the city itself only became filled with troops when a campaign was being prepared against the Persians.[2]

In the 390s, but not before, we hear of a unit garrisoned permanently in the city itself, the ἐγκαθήμενος λόχος. We are told
that the men go into wine shops and refuse to pay for their drinks.
They enter food shops and take away food without paying for it
and extort money if there is nothing to take away.[3] Army entertainers follow the example of the soldiers.[4] Antioch did not find
the experience of having a garrison a pleasant one. But this was
after the Riot of the Statues.[5] Up to that rising it seems to have

L'Armée de Dioclétien et la réforme Constantinienne (Paris, 1952), 27. Harmand, *Discours
sur les patronages*, 85, supposes that the later fourth century saw a general retirement
of troops and peasants from the *limes* area of Chalcis. This is completely unjustified.
All that Mouterde and Poidebard (235–8) show is that a few posts which were no
longer occupied by troops became a refuge for monks, and that settlements and
some great farms were fortified. That the process of fortification is older than the
peace which ceded Nisibis to the Persians in 363, is shown by the great domains of
El Touba fortified between 326 and 353. See *Le 'Limes' de Chalcis*, 197–201. The process of fortification is also mentioned by Libanius, *Or.* xlix. 23. It may have gone
on through the century, perhaps against the Persians, perhaps against the Arabs
who were getting more adventurous, cf. the story of Princess Mavia, Soc. *H.E.* iv.
36 (*P.G.* lxvi. 556); Sozomen vi. 39 (*P.G.* lxvii. 1408); Theodoret *H.E.* (*P.G.*
lxxxii. 1181). She defeated the *magister militum* and the Duke of Phoenicia and
Palestine in 372–3, and finally married her daughter to the Roman general,
Victor. Nevertheless, to judge by the inscriptions, most of which seem to date from
the fourth, fifth, and sixth centuries, this period was one of very considerable building activity in the *limes* area of Chalcis. The region was certainly not becoming
depopulated and declining. By the end of the fifth century there may have been
a military withdrawal: Devreesse, *Le Patriarcat d'Antioche* (Paris, 1945), 249–51. His
view is based on the military history of that period and of the sixth century.

[1] *Or.* xv. 76; cf. xviii. 199, xx. 47. Theodoret *H.E.* iv. 22–6; *H. Rel.* 11 (*P.G.*
lxxxii. 1317). On drill, Veget. i. 26. 7, ii. 23; *I.L.S.* 2487, 9133, 9134; Grosse,
Römische Militärgeschichte, 221–2, 261.

[2] Antioch was a 'base' during Persian wars, *Or.* xix. 54, xx. 47. Full of troops
in 360 xli. 177–9; during Julian's stay at Antioch, Amm. xxii. 12. 6–7, 14. 3, xxv.
4. 7.

[3] *Or.* xlvi. 13.

[4] Ibid. 14; on army entertainers see *Excavations at Dura Europos, Preliminary Report
of 9th Season* (Yale U.P., 1944), pt. 1, 248 ff.

[5] *Or.* xix. 36, the troops came in under the civilian *comes orientis*, not under
a general. All was over by midday, *Or.* xxii. 9.

been deliberate policy not to use the army to control the population.[1] This policy was resumed in later years. In the great riots that took place towards the close of the fifth century the civilian officials were sometimes in great danger, to the point of having to flee the city.[2] On at least two occasions order was restored by the *comes orientis*, no doubt with the help of troops, but not under the command of a general.[3]

Libanius' *De patrociniis* and the correspondence of Abinnaeus show that in areas where troops were stationed there was intervention by military officers in civil administration on a considerable scale.[4] But elsewhere—at Rome and Alexandria no less than at Antioch—a real attempt seems to have been made to keep the civil administration civilian,[5] even though this policy reduced the coercive power of the authorities.[6]

---

[1] It was not used during any of the food shortages; not even in 354 when the consular was lynched and the house of Euboulus set on fire, cf. Petit, *Libanius*, 234–45.

[2] Malalas 389. 15 to 390. 3 (488); 392. 12 to 393. 8 (494–5); 395. 20 to 398. 4 (507).

[3] In 494–5 and 507, cf. Downey, *Antioch*, 504–7.

[4] *The Abinnaeus Papyri*, eds. H. I. Bell, V. Martin, E. G. Turner, D. van Berchem (Oxford, 1962). Soldiers take part in collection of *annona*: nos. 66 ff. Officer arrests suspected criminals for trial by *dux*: nos. 44, 49, 50, 51–3, 55, 56, 57. For the ordinary man an officer would represent the authorities as well as a civilian official, cf. Turner, *Greek Papyri*, 146. See also *I.G.L.S.* 2501.

[5] See account of civic disturbances in J. R. Martindale, 'Public Disorders in the Late Roman Empire' (unpublished Oxford B.Litt. thesis, 1960). On Rome and Constantinople see also Jones, *L.R.E.* 692–5. For the opposite view: R. MacMullen, *Soldier and civilian in the Later Roman Empire* (Harvard U.P., 1963).

[6] *C.J.* 1. 29. 1 (386–7): 'Viri illustres comites et magistri peditum et equitum in provinciales nullam penitus habeant potestatem, nec amplissima praefectura in militares viros.'

IV

THE INTERRELATION OF IMPERIAL
GOVERNORS AND CIVIC COUNCIL
IN THE GOVERNMENT OF ANTIOCH

I. SECURITY AND JUSTICE

As we have seen, Antioch was the centre of government of a considerable area. Within this area villages enjoyed a certain amount of autonomy.[1] In the *De patrociniis* we hear of ἄρχοντες[2] and φύλακες τῆς χώρας,[3] who seem to be filling the roles of village headmen and local police respectively. Presumably these would be the men who would arrest a suspected murderer and hand him over for trial to the city authorities. We know little about the working of village self-government in Northern Syria. Inscriptional evidence assembled by Harper comes mainly from the Hauran, where villages did not form part of a city-territory.[4] Nevertheless, institutions of some pretentiousness existed in Northern Syria too. The large settlement on the site of modern Sergilla, in the territory of Apamea, thanked a benefactor who had put up a bathing establishment, and did so in a hexameter verse with literary reminiscences.[5] A magistrate of another village in the territory of Apamea had the ambitious title of στρατηγός.[6] Some βουλευταί of Touron in the Orontes valley between Antioch and Apamea contributed to a restoration of the hill sanctuary of Zeus Koryphaios.[7]

---

[1] There is no evidence of *pagi*, supervised by curial *praepositi*. This does not preclude their existence. On Egyptian *pagi* see Lallemand, *L'Administration civile de l'Égypte*, 131–7.

[2] *Or.* xlvii. 7.

[3] Ibid. 6. On village police in Egypt see Lallemand, op. cit. 166; Johnson and West, *Byzantine Egypt*, 98.

[4] G. M. Harper, *Yale Cl. S.* i (1928), 105–68, from the North he cites a Komarch and a πραγματευτής of Abbossos, *P.A.E.S.* 881 = *I.G.L.S.* 1908; see also *I.G.L.S.* 657 νομογράφος.

[5] *I.G.L.S.* 1490.

[6] Ibid. 1538.

[7] Ibid. 652 (367–8) βουλευταὶ Τούρου suggests councillors of Touron rather than councillors of Antioch resident at Touron. But A. H. M. Jones, *C.E.R.P.* 288

We also hear of a village of Apamea that put up a building and met the expense out of its own funds.[1] The *dekaprotoi* of a village of the same area in 388–9 gave a mosaic to the church.[2] But on the whole there is surprisingly little evidence of communal action even from the large and well-built villages of the hill country.[3] Churches were built by individual donors. These were presumably wealthy landowners of the neighbourhood, laymen or clerics. They might act singly or, as in the case of the 'cathedral' of Brad, in combination, but always as private individuals not as representatives of the community. Village communities as such appear to have taken little part in building.[4]

The picture is quite different in the Hauran. Here communal building has been commemorated on numerous inscriptions.[5] Since Northern Syria is not otherwise poor in inscriptions the contrast must be significant. The villages of the large city-territories of Northern Syria must have had weaker communal organization than the villages of the Hauran, which were not included in the territory of a city.

Another feature of the North Syrian villages that might be a consequence of weak communal organization is irregularity of street plan.[6] While the craftsmanship and beauty of many of the buildings, profane or secular, is up to best city standards, no attempt was made to confine building within a geometrical grid, as in the cities.[7] The larger villages were more like the Arab cities of the future.[8]

There are few visible traces in the area of communal enterprises of any sort, whether by village authorities or by the governments of Antioch or Apamea in whose territory the villages lay.

---

has argued convincingly that the βουλευταί of *I.G.R.R.* iii. 1131, 1134, 1152, 1187, Waddington 2019, 2204, 2216 are city councillors who happen to live in a village.

[1] *I.G.L.S.* 1426.   [2] Tchalenko, *Villages*, vol. 3. 35, no. 39.

[3] But cf. *I.G.R.R.* iii. 1020, village that belonged to a temple.

[4] J. Lassus, *Sanctuaires chrétiens de Syrie*, 249 ff. But Lassus (ibid. 255) is not justified in deducing from Joh. Chrys. *Hom. in Act.* 18. 6–9 that the donors in the territory of Antioch were urban estate owners. This sermon was spoken at Constantinople. There is no evidence how work involving many donors was co-ordinated.

[5] Harper, loc. cit.   [6] Tchalenko, *Villages*, vol. 2, Pls. cxxi–cxli.

[7] Proved for Beroea, Dura-Europos, Damascus, Apamea, as well as Antioch; Downey, *Antioch*, 70, n. 70.

[8] Irregularly laid-out quarters were added to the street grid of Hellenistic Beroea (Aleppo), according to J. Sauvaget, *Alep* (Paris, 1941), 61, in the fourth and fifth centuries A.D.

There are no inscriptions for instance commemorating public works carried out by the city authorities for the benefit of their country folk. In fact the inscriptions from the villages provide very little evidence of intervention of any kind by city folk in the affairs of the country.[1] If, as is likely, some of the donors were wealthy residents of Antioch or Apamea, they do not (with one exception)[2] mention the fact on inscriptions.

When the countryside was converted to Christianity the villages came under the supervision of the bishop of Antioch or Apamea. This was exercised through περιοδευταί. These ecclesiastical inspectors appear on inscriptions and are mentioned among contributors to churches.[3] But, again to judge by inscriptions, the bishops themselves were directly responsible for little building in the countryside. There even are very few honorific references to them.[4]

Some areas were highly insecure. Robbers are mentioned frequently. They made their most disastrous appearance after the Riot of the Statues, when they killed many of the fugitives.[5] They exacted a regular tribute from the herdsmen looking after race horses,[6] and were thought to be in league with innkeepers.[7] An inscription commemorates Barsephones and his cousin Antiochus murdered in the inn of Theodorus near Laodicea.[8] On one occasion a whole village turned to brigandage and enjoyed a considerable period of daring and successful robbery, culminating in a raid in which the brigands masqueraded as government officials requisitioning their perquisites.[9]

But rural insecurity can be exaggerated. Watch-towers form a normal part of the landscape in this area. They are densest on the eastern side of the plateau facing the desert and its nomads.[10] But otherwise the villages are unfortified. Moreover travellers were rarely molested. Libanius appears to have been

---

[1] Tchalenko, *Villages*, 7–8, for a remarkably brief list of non-local influences in the limestone hill area.

[2] *I.G.L.S.* 586.

[3] Ibid. 1935, 130, 332, 389, 310, 421, 460, 634, 733, 1726, cf. Festugière, *Antioche*, 391; Tchalenko, *Villages*, vol. 3. 38, nn. 39 f.; *C. Laod.* can. 57.

[4] Lassus, *Sanctuaires*, 253.

[5] *Or.* xix. 57, xxiii. 18, xxxiv. 7.   [6] *Or.* xxvii. 4.

[7] *Or.* xxxiii. 40, cf. xlv. 6.

[8] Tchalenko, *Villages*, vol. 3. 31–2 (no. 34), cf. R. Mouterde, *Syria* vi (1925), 243.

[9] Amm. xxviii. 2. 13; Lib. *Or.* xlviii. 36; also about bandits: *Ep.* 1385.

[10] Tchalenko, *Villages*, vol. 1 30–3.

perfectly confident that his letters would reach their destination. We never hear that a letter had been intercepted by bandits. Perhaps the main roads were well policed,[1] or else brigandage was not universal but concentrated in the desert fringe within striking range of nomad raiders.[2]

We do not know what cases could be tried by village officials. Harmand has argued that Libanius' suit against his Jewish tenants was brought before a village court.[3] This is extremely unlikely. Justice was highly centralized.[4] In view of the regard for rank which characterized the age[5] it is improbable that a case brought by Libanius, an *honoratus*, probably even a *praefectorianus*, would be heard by a judge of lower rank than the provincial governor. Libanius tells us that precisely cases between landlord and tenants were commonly heard by the governor in the city.[6] Needless to say, a villager suspected of murder would be handed over to the city to be tried by the governor.[7] It had always been a principle of Roman administration that capital punishment should only be awarded by a Roman official.[8] But the jurisdiction of imperial governors had for a long time been increasing at the expense of that of local courts. In the writings of Libanius no local court is mentioned at all. It is therefore unlikely that local courts, whether at city or village level, exercised any but the simplest police jurisdiction.

In the pursuit and arrest of criminals governors were assisted by local institutions. Of the village police, the φύλακες τῆς χώρας, we know only that they were unable to deal with the lawlessness incited by military patrons.[9] In the city too the council was in control of a police force. Libanius mentions 'club-bearers' (κορυνηφόροι) and 'guardians of the peace' (εἰρηνοφύλακες), and he hints at some abuse as a result of which the pay of the former remains in the hands of the latter.[10] Elsewhere Libanius mentions an εἰρήνης φύλαξ at the Palestinian city of Elusa. This post was

---

[1] Joh. Chrys. *Hom. ad Stag.* 2. 6 (*P.G.* xlvii. 458), special bodies of local levies guard roads. Guard-houses every 1,000 paces for night watch.

[2] *I.G.L.S.* 1600 (fifth c.).   [3] Harmand, *Discours sur les patronages*, 192–3.

[4] Jones, *L.R.E.* 479.   [5] Piganiol, *L'Empire chrétien*, 410.

[6] *Or.* xlv. 5. On governor's jurisdiction cf. pp. 112–13 above.

[7] *Or.* xlv. 25.

[8] Sherwin-White, *Roman Society and Roman Law in the New Testament*, 37.

[9] See above, p. 67 n. 7.

[10] *Or.* xlviii. 9. With the 'club-bearers', cf. the 60 night-watchmen of Oxyrhynchus: *Chr.* i. 474 = *P. Oxy.* i. 43.

eagerly sought after, presumably because it was profitable.[1] Libanius' use of titles is always inexact, but curial police officers with the similar title of eirenarch are known elsewhere. They were appointed by the governor from a list of men proposed by a local council.[2] The main function of this officer was to seek out, arrest, interrogate, and finally accuse thieves and robbers, but the men he commanded for this purpose were only weakly armed. It is likely that the men whom Libanius describes as εἰρηνοφύλακες were officers of this type, and that the 'club-bearers' represent the police force under their command. The φύλακες who watched in the streets at night were probably drawn from them,[3] and it was presumably as holder of the office of 'Guardian of the Peace' that a councillor might find himself compelled to hunt bandits.[4]

The discovery of criminals was assisted by the ἐπιμεληταὶ τῶν φυλῶν. Whenever a body was found in the city it was the duty of these functionaries to inform the governor of all they knew about the circumstances.[5] At the trial following the Riot of the Statues the ἐπιμεληταί acted as accusers.[6] They would also knock up any shopkeeper who had failed to maintain the lights outside his shop.[7]

The ἐπιμεληταὶ τῶν φυλῶν were clearly connected with the eighteen tribes of Antioch.[8] It is not stated how they were appointed. Did the democratic procedure of election, which had long since disappeared from government at the level of the city, survive at the level of the tribe? The tribes of Antioch certainly reached some corporative decisions. Each tribe possessed a bathing establishment and each tribe strove to make its own baths the finest.[9] Each tribe entered a competitor for a boxing competition that formed part of the ancient festival of Artemis, for which prizes too were offered by tribes.[10] Tribes are also known to have put up statues to a public benefactor.[11] It is likely therefore that the tribes elected their own officers.[12]

[1] *Ep.* 101–2 (359–60), 532 (356).
[2] *P.W.* Suppl. 3, s.v. Eirenarcha, cols. 419–23 (Schulthess); vol. ix. 2, cols. 2032–5, s.v. Irenarcha (Pfaff); *D.S.*, vol. 3. 1, 572–3; *C.T.* xii. 14. 1 (409) abolishes the post.
[3] *Or.* xxxiii. 37.   [4] *Or.* xxv. 43.   [5] *Or.* xxiv. 26.
[6] *Or.* xxiii. 11.   [7] *Or.* xxx. 36.   [8] *Or.* xix. 62.
[9] *Or.* xi. 245; ibid. 231.   [10] *Or.* v. 43–4.
[11] *Or.* xxii. 40; xv. 76 public supplication begins on tribal level.
[12] Election of Egyptian φύλαρχος: *P. Oxy.* 1187; cf. Jones, *L.R.E.* 724 n. 25, also P. Mertens, *Les Services de l'état civil et le contrôle de la population à Oxyrhynchus*

Local police work was closely supervised by the governor. The
tribal officers reported to him and the curial chief of police was
probably appointed by him. In addition he commanded a force
of his own. We frequently read of police actions, arrests, beatings,
raids on shopkeepers suspected of charging too high prices,
searches carried out by 'soldiers'. This word might describe
officiales or real soldiers[1] but could hardly be used to describe the
civic 'club-bearers'. Men of this force might be used outside the
provincial capital. Thus security units of the consular of Palestine
($\pi o\lambda\iota\tau\iota\kappa\grave{\eta}$ $\chi\epsilon\acute{\iota}\rho$) formed part of the task force sent to suppress
paganism at Gaza.[2] Before being concentrated for this operation
the men had been stationed in some of the smaller towns of the
province.[3] When used in larger operations the governor's force
might be stiffened with units of the army.[4] But even without
such strengthening it was probably strong enough to enable a
governor to hunt bandits.[5]

The force immediately at the disposal of the consular was not
strong enough to suppress a full-scale riot, or even to guarantee
the safety of the governor himself in a massive popular disturbance. The Riot of the Statues was only checked by the 'archers'.
This appears to have been a body of men distinct from those
previously discussed. They were maintained precisely for occasions 'calling for arrows'. Their commander, 'a man experienced
in war', only intervened when he thought fit.[6] There is no
reference to orders from the consular.

The independent action of the commander of the 'archers'
can be explained if he was identical with the 'night-prefect'
($\nu\nu\kappa\tau\acute{\epsilon}\pi\alpha\rho\chi o\varsigma$) mentioned in sources of the fifth century. This
officer was not appointed either by the civic government or by

(Liège, 1958), 16–45, on the $\phi\acute{\nu}\lambda\alpha\rho\chi o\varsigma$ and $\sigma\nu\sigma\tau\acute{\alpha}\tau\eta\varsigma$ $\tau\hat{\eta}\varsigma$ $\phi\nu\lambda\hat{\eta}\varsigma$. Liturgants nominated by tribal officer: *P. Oxy.* xxxiv. 2715.

[1] *Or.* liv. 42, xlv. 5, xlvi. 18, xxvi. 30, xxix. 33, xxxiii. 32.

[2] Marc le Diacre, *Vie de Porphyre, évêque de Gaza*, eds. H. Grégoire and M.-A.
Kugener (Paris, 1930), 27, 63, 99.

[3] Ibid. 27 $\beta o\eta\theta o\grave{\nu}\varsigma$ $\pi o\lambda\lambda o\grave{\nu}\varsigma$ $\acute{\epsilon}\kappa$ $\tau\epsilon$ $\emph{A}\zeta\acute{\omega}\tau o\nu$ $\kappa\alpha\grave{\iota}$ $\emph{A}\sigma\kappa\acute{\alpha}\lambda\omega\nu o\varsigma$. No doubt there was
a link between these detachments and the *stationarii*, members of the provincial
officium, posted in each city whose duty was to report crime: Jones, *L.R.E.* 521
n. 114; 600 n. 89. The $\delta\eta\mu o\sigma\iota\epsilon\acute{\nu}o\nu\tau\epsilon\varsigma$ of the *Life of Porphyry*, 25 and 99, might be
stationarii. They might also be a local police force under the $\epsilon\grave{\iota}\rho\eta\nu\acute{\alpha}\rho\chi\eta\varsigma$ (24) who
only assisted the Christians when under pressure from imperial security forces.
A different view: Grégoire and Kugener, op. cit. 104.

[4] As *Life of Porphyry*, 27.   [5] *Ep.* 1385 (363).

[6] *Or.* xix. 34–5.

the governors, but by a diploma signed by the emperor himself.[1] We hear of the νυκτέπαρχος again in 507, when the Emperor Anastasius appointed a man of Constantinople to this position. The new chief of police proceeded to arrest some riot leaders of the Green Faction in a church which he entered with a force of Goths, and was later killed in a street battle with rioters.[2]

The νυκτέπαρχος of Antioch should probably be compared with the *praefectus vigilum* of Constantinople[3] rather than with the police officers of provincial towns.[4] The large population of the city made a special arrangement necessary. The 'archers' had no equivalent at Constantinople, since there the imperial guard was available for occasions 'requiring arrows'.

It is significant that the 'archers' did not form part of the regular army. In his account of the Riot of the Statues Libanius clearly distinguishes the 'archers' from the army units τὰ ἀπὸ τῶν λόχων brought into the city by the *comes orientis* after the rioters had already been dispersed.[5] At the time the city evidently was without a garrison of regular troops. After the riot we hear of a garrison, the ἐγκαθήμενος λόχος.[6] But this did not remain: the great riots of the second half of the fifth century once again found the city without soldiers, and this time the νυκτέπαρχος proved quite unable to deal with the trouble. The presence of regular army units in the city remained exceptional.[7]

This was so not only at Antioch. After the dissolution of the praetorian guard and the *vigiles*, Rome had no disciplined security forces at all and we hardly hear of troops being drafted into the city to deal with emergencies. At Alexandria troops were used more frequently than at Rome, but not so much to maintain order as to force the emperor's religious policy on a recalcitrant city.[8] It seems to have been a principle of administration that the authorities of great cities should not be able to rely on the instant availability of overwhelming force for the maintaining of public order. Alternatively the imperial government may have felt that the discipline of the army was not to be risked by involving soldiers closely with the life of a great city.

[1] Palladius, *Dialogus de vita S. Joannis Chrysostomi*, ed. P. R. Coleman-Norton (Cambridge, 1928), 97.   [2] Malalas 398. 9–10.   [3] Jones, *L.R.E.* 692.
[4] Jones, op. cit. 726 n. 29; Oertel, *Die Liturgie*, 281–3.
[5] *Or.* xix. 36.   [6] *Or.* xlvi. 13.   [7] See above, pp. 117–18.
[8] See J. R. Martindale, 'Public Disorders in the Late Roman Empire' (Oxford, unpublished B. Litt. thesis, 1960).

In these circumstances one would expect a city like Antioch to be exceedingly turbulent, and so it might, particularly when disturbed by religious controversies or famine. But in fact we know of only two occasions during the fourth century, in 354 and 387, when tension led to violence. The violence of 354 had been instigated by the Caesar Gallus,[1] while the Riot of the Statues of 387 was quelled very easily. In fourth-century Antioch, as already in second-century Prusa,[2] the fact that there was not enough force at the disposal of the authorities compelled the government to show some consideration for the governed.

The restraint which lack of crushing military power imposed was felt by the governors as well as the councillors. But it was felt by the councillors more, for a governor had enough 'soldiers' at his disposal to enforce an order, even if not to suppress large-scale public disorders. The council's force appears to have been completely ineffective. It could not be, or at least was not, used to reinforce the demands of the curial tax-collectors,[3] and the councillor set over the bakers' guild relied on 'soldiers' to inflict punishment.[4] When in 384 a food shortage produced a tense atmosphere in the city which demanded decisive action by the civic authorities, many councillors left the city, fearing that their houses might be attacked.[5]

2. THE FOOD SUPPLY OF THE CITY

It had been the experience of all the larger cities of the Graeco-Roman world that the corn supply could not be exposed to the very wide fluctuations of the market price. Under the Early Empire most cities had some civic machinery for buying corn and selling it below market price. The operation could be performed without financial loss if the corn was bought cheaply in large quantities just after the harvest and then released throughout the year at constant price. But in times of shortage, the civic officers working the scheme might be expected to make large contributions from their own property. In a large city this might be very expensive.[6]

---

[1] Amm. xiv. 7. 2, 5; Lib. *Or.* i. 103, xix. 47.
[2] Dio Chrys. *Or.* xlvi. 12, xlviii.
[3] Lib. *Or.* xlvii. 7–8.   [4] *Or.* xxix. 33.
[5] Ibid. 4; cf. i. 230.   [6] Jones, *G.C.* 217–18.

There is evidence that at this time Antioch too had an organization for providing subsidized food. In A.D. 181, according to Malalas, at the conclusion of the Olympic Games, Artabanes the Syriarch (or perhaps the first Alytarch) threw tokens (καλαμίων συντόμια) into the crowd which entitled the holders to bread. This was to be provided out of the revenue of estates set aside for that purpose for ever.[1] The bread was to be known as ἄρτοι πολιτικοί, recalling the *annonae civicae* of Constantinople.[2] This looks like the establishment through private munificence of a corn-buying fund, linked with a distribution of free, or at any rate cheap, bread. A later passage of Malalas informs us that the Emperor Probus (276–82) instituted a distribution of corn (σιτήσεις) at public expense.[3]

We do not know whether these institutions survived into the fourth century or whether they perished like so many other civic foundations of the Early Empire. But it may be significant that the sources for the best-documented episode in the history of the food supply of Antioch, the famine of 362–3, mention no standing organization either civic or imperial for supplying cheap food to the people of Antioch. On the contrary, Julian describes his measures as if they were quite exceptional. There is no suggestion that the imperial administration had been in the least concerned with the corn supply of Antioch before Julian ordered corn to be brought from Hierapolis and Chalcis.[4] Moreover the corn imported by Julian was not rationed but simply sold on the market at a fixed price.[5] It was this which frustrated the emperor's intentions, for it enabled speculators to buy up the corn.[6] It is difficult to imagine that a system of uncontrolled distribution would have been adopted if rations of bread or corn were already being distributed regularly in return for tokens, as described by Malalas.[7]

---

[1] Malalas 289–90; *Chron. Pasch.* 490.

[2] *C.T.* xiv. 17; Jones, *L.R.E.* 696; cf. also *Sardis* vii. 166.

[3] Malalas 302 of text as emended by A. Schenk von Stauffenberg, *Die Römische Kaisergeschichte bei Malalas* (Stuttgart, 1931), 392. Malalas' *Chronicle* combines valuable information, particularly about Antiochene history, with grotesque errors. On this see Stauffenberg, op. cit.; Downey, *Antioch*, 39–40; E. Bikerman, 'Les Maccabées de Malalas', *Byzantion* xxi (1951), 63–83.

[4] Julian *Misop.* 369, 370D. The uniqueness presumably lay in the fact that the corn came from the *res privata* of the emperor.

[5] Ibid. 369B.

[6] Ibid. 369D; cf. Lib. *Or.* xviii. 195.

[7] Malalas 289–90. At Rome the token bore the name of recipient and the amount of his ration: *C.T.* xiv. 17. 5 (369).

It would seem therefore that at this time Antioch lacked regular distributions of subsidized food.

Under conditions of normal food supply councillors of Antioch were not apparently required to purchase corn for the city. Libanius praises the readiness of councillors to feed the poor in time of famine. But unlike the heating of baths or the provision of public shows this was not part of the regular cycle of duties.[1] Even in times of food crisis we know of only one possible case of corn-buying by councillors.[2]

The conclusion must be that in the middle of the fourth century the food supply of Antioch was left largely to free enterprise and the working of the unregulated market. Judging by the *Antiochicus* this worked quite well. Food crises were not frequent. No doubt the provisioning of Antioch was assisted by the situation of the city. The Orontes valley was fertile and the river and its lake provided cheap water-borne transport.[3] Even so the price of wheat at Antioch was very much higher than it was in the Egyptian or Mesopotamian countryside.[4] There must have been considerable hardship—and scope for charity. Shopkeepers provided monthly assistance for beggars, at least nominally on a voluntary basis.[5] The church supported 3,000 poor.[6]

During the second half of the century, the food situation became more difficult and crises became more frequent.[7] We hear of difficulties in 354–5, while Gallus was Caesar of the East,[8] in 362–3, when Julian was at Antioch,[9] perhaps in 375, when there were riots with shouts directed against Valens,[10] in 382–3,[11] and 384–5.[12] In addition, the crowd shouted complaints against the

---

[1] *Or.* xi. 134.   [2] *Or.* i. 227—if indeed this expense was on corn.

[3] Favourable situation: *Or.* xi. 19–25; advantages of lake and river: ibid. 260–2; army easily fed: ibid. 178.

[4] Julian, *Misop.* 369B: 1 *solidus* (ἀργύριον) for 15 *modii*; twice the Egyptian or N. African rate, cf. Jones, *L.R.E.* 445–6.

[5] *Or.* xlvi. 21.   [6] See below, p. 239.

[7] On the topic as a whole Petit, *Libanius*, 105–22.

[8] Amm. xiv. 7. 2, 5; Lib. *Or.* i. 96–7, 103, xix. 47; cf. E. A. Thompson, *The Historical Work of Ammianus Marcellinus*, 60–3.

[9] G. Downey, 'The Economic crisis at Antioch under Julian the Apostate', *Stud. in Econ. and Soc. Hist. in honor of A. C. Johnson*, ed. Coleman-Norton (Princeton, 1951), 312–21; P. de Jonge, 'Scarcity of corn and corn prices in Ammianus Marcellinus', *Mnemosyne*, ser. iv, vol. i (1948), 238–45; Petit, *Libanius*, 109–18.

[10] Amm. xxxi. 1. 2; a religious cause is more likely.

[11] *Or.* i. 205 ff.

[12] Ibid. 227–8, 233, *Or.* xxix *passim*, *Or.* xxvii. 6–8, 11, 25–9.

shopkeepers in the theatre in 386,[1] 388–9, and in 392.[2] Evidently the food supply was not keeping up with the growth of population.[3] It would seem that some time within this period public food distributions were introduced.

When the emperor pardoned the city after the Riot of the Statues in 387 'the city again had its land and the poor man his nourishment'.[4] The emperor therefore *restored* a distribution of food, and this must mean that one had existed before, but had presumably been stopped as a punishment for the riot. It could be that distribution was financed out of the revenue of the estates returned to the city at the same time. Something like this appears to have happened at Carthage.[5] But we know that the civic estates of Antioch were mostly leased to civic councillors to compensate them for the expenses incurred for the city. An alternative source of finance is therefore more likely. A law of Justinian brackets the corn distribution of Antioch together with those of Alexandria and Constantinople. Constantinople and Alexandria received their cheap corn out of taxation.[6] Eventually the number of recipients of the distributed food became very large. Euagrius, a contemporary, tells us that according to a calculation made from the decline in consumption of bread the number of persons killed in the earthquake of 588 amounted to 60,000. The calculation is likely to have been made from the list of persons entitled to the civic food ration.[7] There is no evidence as to when the distribution of subsidized food was introduced. The most likely period is that of Valens' prolonged stay in the city (370–8), when Antioch for the last time filled the role of imperial residence.

In addition to the beginning of public distributions of food, the second half of the century saw a great increase in the control exercised by the imperial administration over all aspects of the food supply of the city. A comparison of the crises of 354–5[8]

---

[1] *Or.* xlv. 4.

[2] *Or.* liv. 42 (388–9); xlvi. 5 (392); also iv. 26–7 (389?—soon after defeat of Maximus).

[3] See above, p. 97.   [4] *Or.* xx. 7.

[5] *C.T.* xiv. 25. 1. On the civil estates cf. below, pp. 149 ff.

[6] *Nov. Just.* vii. 8. On the corn supply of Alexandria: V. Martin, D. van Berchen, 'Le panis aedium d'Alexandrie', *Rev. phil. litt. hist. anc.* lxix (1942), 5–21.

[7] Euagr. *H.E.* 6. 8. I assume that the food was distributed in the form of bread as at Rome and Constantinople, Jones, *L.R.E.* 696–7.

[8] See above, p. 104.

or 362–3 with those later in the century shows this quite clearly. Julian expected that all practical measures taken to remedy the situation would originate with the council. He was disappointed, but in the later crises the situation was taken out of the hands of the council altogether.

When Julian arrived at Antioch in July 362, he was greeted with complaints about the high price of food.[1] Food production was suffering from the effects of drought at a time when demand for food had been enormously increased by the arrival of court and army.[2] Julian summoned the leading councillors and these promised to solve the problem. In fact they achieved nothing. To some extent this failure may have been due to the fact that they found the high corn prices profitable, but of course the basic causes of the shortage, the presence of the army and the drought, were beyond the council's control. Julian allowed the council three months to deal with the situation. Only in October did Julian intervene directly in the management of the market. He introduced price control, with the effect that eatables disappeared from the market.[3] He also had corn brought, first from the Syrian cities of Chalcis and Hierapolis,[4] and later from Egypt, to be sold in Antioch at below market price.[5] This measure too failed to achieve the desired effect: some of the corn was bought up by speculators.[6] As the *comes* Icarius was to realize within Libanius' lifetime,[7] the cheap corn should have been rationed.

Even now supervision of price control seems to have remained with the council; councillors were certainly blamed for its failure.[8] After Julian had left the city[9] control was taken over by the imperial officials, the *comes orientis*,[10] and Alexander, consular of Syria. The latter exercised very close supervision over the shopkeepers. He compelled them to keep accounts and appointed auditors to examine them.[11] This is the last we hear

---

[1] Julian, *Misop.* 368D.

[2] Full references in works cited p. 128 n. 9. Importance of army stressed by Socrates, *H.E.* 17. 2–4; the poor harvest, *Ep.* 699 (winter 361–2); shortage of corn anticipated, *Ep.* 1351 (spring 363) ἡ (γῆ) πέρυσι διψῶσα οὐκ ἔπιεν; Julian, *Misop.* 369.

[3] Julian, *Misop.* 369D.   [4] Ibid. 368.   [5] Ibid. 369A–C.

[6] Ibid. 369D; Lib. *Or.* xviii. 195; landowners bought cheap corn for their use, and kept their own produce off the market to sell it at higher price later.

[7] At least he rationed peasants leaving the city to two loaves: *Or.* xxvii. 14.

[8] *Or.* xvi. 21–7, 40, xv. 23.

[9] *Ep.* 827.   [10] *Ep.* 1379.   [11] *Ep.* 1406.

of the famine. By now the situation must have been eased by the departure of Julian and his army.

The events of 362–3 vividly illustrate the weakness of curial government when faced by a food crisis. The economic interest of the councillors as landowners and producers of corn was at variance with the interest of the city as a whole, and under the conditions of the Roman Empire there could be no political pressure to counter this. Moreover the councillors lacked the power, economic or coercive, to initiate radical measures. They could not import corn on a large scale from areas which did not normally supply the city, and they could not enforce measures which would be resisted by the shopkeepers without the support of the forces at the disposal of the governors. It is not surprising therefore that in the ensuing years the council lost control over the market.

In the crises of the 380s, there is no longer any question of clashes between the council and imperial representatives over the management of the food situation. In 384 for instance, when the city could be compared to a ship labouring in a stormy sea, the council abdicated completely.[1] Action was taken by the governor alone.

In these years we hear that governors appoint or depose the magistrate in charge of markets,[2] appoint supervisors of guilds,[3] fix prices,[4] authorize the beating of a trader who has exceeded the fixed price,[5] supervise weights and measures,[6] bring in corn from outside and arrange for its distribution.[7] In 384–5 Icarius took a step which would have been beneficial in the crisis under Julian. He posted soldiers at the gates to prevent anyone taking more than two loaves out of the city.[8]

Control of the shopkeepers by governors remained. In the last years of Libanius' life, we hear that various groups of shopkeepers were disciplined in turn by the governors Eustathius,[9] Eutropius,[10]

---

[1] *Or.* xxix. 2–4; cf. i. 226.

[2] *Or.* xxvii. 18; cf. 11 (Pherenicus).

[3] Candidus: xxix. 9; deposed, i. 230; his successor Callippus: xxvii. 27; μέρος γε παρὰ σοῦ τὸ τῶν ἀρτοπόπων παρειλήφει shows that he took Candidus' place, but proceeded to exercise authority over other trades as well. On the supervisors of trades, see below, p. 187.

[4] *Or.* i. 226, xxvii. 27, xxix. 2, iv. 35.

[5] *Or.* i. 207, 226.

[6] *Or.* xxvii. 11, xlvi. 10.

[7] *Or.* xxvii. 6 ff., *Or.* i. 205.

[8] *Or.* xxvii. 14.

[9] *Or.* liv. 42.

[10] *Or.* iv. 27, 35.

and Florentius.[1] Tissamenes ordered the shopkeepers to renew the painted signs outside their shops and to maintain a triple light at night.[2] Price control seems to have become permanent.[3] Acceptance of this change of affairs entailed a radical change in outlook on the part of the curial class. Libanius and the historian Ammianus Marcellinus,[4] in spite of their great admiration for the Emperor Julian, agreed with his opponents in the council that the attempt to fix prices was unworkable. In his contemporary writings, Libanius praises Julian's intentions but not the regulations he made to carry them out.[5] He sincerely believed that the city would fare best if the market was left unregulated (αὐτόνομος).[6] If this was the view of a committed follower of Julian, we can only guess at the attitude of his opponents. Nevertheless, thirty years later all acquiesced willynilly in the reality of permanent control.

3. BUILDING

Imperial legislation suggests that in the fourth century the governors everywhere took the councils' place in the control of public works. In fifty-one out of fifty-three laws under the title *De operibus publicis* in the Theodosian Code the legislator assumes that the initiative in civil building is taken by a governor. This state of affairs is taken for granted even in Libanius' idealized description of Antioch, the *Antiochicus*. Among contributors to the fabric of the city Libanius mentions in the first place the provincial governors.[7] Buildings are also put up by courtiers or ex-officials.[8] He says nothing about building activity by council or councillors.

We hear of a number of building schemes carried out by governors. Proculus extended a theatre, and carried out work on roads,

---

[1] *Or.* xlvi. 7 ff.   [2] *Or.* xxxiii. 33–6.

[3] *Or.* iv. 35: τὴν ἀγορὰν ἐτάραττε οὐδαμοῦ στῆναι τὰς ἐφ' ἑκάστῳ τιμὰς ἐῶν ... τοῦτ' αὐτὸν ἐποίει κινεῖν τὰ τεταγμένα [καὶ] παρὰ τῶν εὖ φρονούντων καὶ νενομοθετημένα. Permanent price control elsewhere: *Nov. Val.* v. 1 (Rome). Cassiodorus, *Var.* vii. 11, 12; cf. x. 1, 12, iv. 5, xi. 11 (Ostrogothic Italy); A. Stöckle; *Spätrömische und Byzantinische Zünft* (*Klio*, Beiheft ix, 1911, repr. 1963), 100, on price regulation in Constantinople in *The Book of the Prefect.* L. M. Hartmann, *Urkunde einer römischen Gärtnergenossenschaft vom Jahre 1030* (Freiburg, 1892), 67.

[4] Amm. xx. 14. 1.

[5] *Or.* xvi. 15, 20–5, *Or.* xv. 20; cf. in 385 xxvii. 27.

[6] *Ep.* 1379 (363).

[7] *C.T.* xv. 1; *Or.* xi. 193. On building activity see Petit, *Libanius*, 314–30.

[8] Ibid. 194: οἱ τῆς περὶ τὸν βασιλέα γεγόνασιν ἑταιρίας, i.e. *comites*.

colonnades, and baths.¹ Other governors who engaged in public
works were Tissamenes and Florentius.² The most detailed
account of a building scheme is to be found in the letters about
Modestus' colonnade.³ The governor decided what work would
be done and assembled the necessary resources. Some men were
simply ordered to transport pillars from Seleucia to Antioch.
These were presumably councillors. Others, presumably *honorati*,
were allowed to choose whether they would contribute to the
building or not.⁴ The councillors obeyed without a word, but
some of the ex-governors voiced the fear that, as the work dragged
on, what was still voluntary would become compulsory. Some
time later Libanius reminded Modestus to make sure his stoa
would be well spoken of.⁵ Evidently Modestus had been exercising pressure to ensure completion of the work.

Public works, especially maintenance, required the compulsory
services of men below the rank of councillor. A shopkeeper might
be compelled to perform physical labour unless he could hire
a substitute. Duties mentioned are the transport of new pillars
to replace old ones, and the disagreeable and dangerous task of
keeping the inner channels of the aqueducts (or drains?) clear
of obstructions.⁶ The compulsory disposal of building rubble gave
rise to an abuse which Libanius attacked in a most effective
speech. Peasants who had come to town to sell their produce
were compelled to load their animals with rubble on the return
journey. At a price, this convenience was also made available to
honorati for private building.⁷ Significantly the arrangement was
made by the governor or his officials. The council had no say in
the matter.

The Codes suggest that public works absorbed a considerable
portion of the remaining civic revenue.⁸ The evidence of Libanius
confirms that at Antioch the forced contributions of councillors
and others were supplemented by civic money payments, and
public works could be profitable. Perhaps no conclusions should

¹ *Or.* x, *Ep.* 852.
² See below, p. 134 nn. 4–5. Building by governors elsewhere than in Syria:
Ep. 216 (Phoenicia), 1229 (Galatia).
³ *Ep.* 196 (358–9), 242 (358–9), 617 (361).
⁴ *Ep.* 196. 3. A building liturgy: *Ep.* 620 (361).
⁵ *Ep.* 617.   ⁶ *Or.* xlvi. 21.
⁷ *Or.* l, *passim*; granted to private builders, ibid. 16.
⁸ See below, p. 156.

be drawn from the fact that the rebuilding of a temple should be a desirable and rewarding duty for a councillor in the reign of Julian.[1] After all, that emperor was closely interested both in the rebuilding of temples and the restoration to cities of their revenues. But in 384, more than twenty years later, Libanius could strive to get a friend the job of rebuilding a bridge. Clearly he thought he was doing him a favour.[2] About the same time Libanius proposed that the disposal of building rubble should be paid for out of the same public funds as the building operation itself.[3] Evidently a considerable part of the cost of the building work was still borne by public funds.

Occasionally governors made use of their private fortunes for civic building. Florentius, who was consular of Syria about 392, built a stoa and widened a road in the process. The stoa would be a source of gold for the consular, as similar schemes had been to their builders on earlier occasions.[4] Libanius anticipates that Florentius will reimburse himself out of the rents of shopkeepers, who would open shops behind the pillars of the colonnade. Perhaps Tissamenes, who had a stoa painted and then rewarded the painters by forcing the shopkeepers to get their shop signs repainted, was similarly engaging in public works at his own expense—with the difference that he had found means of exploiting his power to reduce his costs.[5]

We have seen that in the *Antiochicus* Libanius follows his account of the building activities of governors with a reference to the buildings put up at their own expense by men who had been companions of the emperor.[6] These were the ex-governors and *honorati* who had made a great career in the state service and had then established a home, or at least one of their homes, at Antioch, where they became the real leaders of society. The characteristic contribution of a man of this class to the beauty of the city was a splendid private residence.[7] It is likely that many of the fourth-century mosaics excavated by the Princeton expedition decorated private houses of such men.[8] On the other

---

[1] *Ep.* 1392 (at Tarsus).   [2] *Or.* xxvii. 3.

[3] *Or.* l. 3.   [4] *Or.* xlvi. 44.

[5] *Or.* xxxiii. 34; cf. *Or.* xlviii. 38: ἐσμὸς κακῶν τέχναις.   [6] *Or.* xi. 194.

[7] Ibid. 195: ὁ μὲν οὐκ ἐγείρων οἰκίαν ἢ τῶν γε οὐσῶν ὠνούμενος . . . μάτην ἡγεῖται πλουτεῖν . . . διὰ ταῦτα τὸ μέτρον οὐχ ἵσταται τῇ πόλει. Cf. invitations to great men: xlviii. 38, xxi. 32. The splendid houses of the *honorati*: ii. 54–5.

[8] Doro Levi, *Antioch Mosaic Pavements*.

hand at least two of these great men, Datian, for many years close adviser to the Emperor Constantius,[1] and Ellebichus,[2] *magister militum utriusque militiae per orientem* in the 380s, presented public buildings to the city.

In one respect the building situation at Antioch was untypical: for a significant number of years Antioch was an imperial residence and this meant that the emperors took a special interest in the appearance and beauty of the city.[3] Constantine and Constantius built the Great Church.[4] Constantius developed the harbour at Seleucia and constructed colonnades and fountains at Antioch.[5] Valens rebuilt the market-place.[6] Even Theodosius, who never visited Antioch, built or at least altered a palace at Daphne.[7] The construction of buildings in the great cities of the empire may well have been a means of expressing the open-handed generosity expected of an emperor.[8] On the other hand the emperor was often given credit for building schemes for no other reason than that they were carried out in his reign.[9]

It will be noticed that in the evidence about public works at Antioch council and councillors play a very small part. Organization of public building was largely in the hands of the imperial authorities. Voluntary public building, on the initiative and out of the financial resources of councillors, was very rare. We only hear of the two enlargements of the 'plethron', one in 328 by Libanius' uncle, another in 332 by Argyrius.[10] Significantly a further enlargement, for the games of 384, was carried out by the *comes orientis* Proculus.[11] Leading councillors could still afford to follow the example of *honorati* in the building of splendid private residences—'the bitch imitates her mistress' is Libanius' unkind comment on the practice.[12] But even these, the wealthiest men of their order, were, as far as our information goes, no more

---

[1] *Ep.* 441 (355), in addition a house and garden: 114 (359–60).

[2] *Ep.* 898 (388).

[3] *Or.* xi. 194 οἷς ἔνι τούτου τυχεῖν ἐκ βασιλικῶν χρημάτων implies that at this time (under Constantius) governors received imperial subsidies for public works at Antioch.

[4] Malalas 325–6.   [5] *Or.* xi. 263; Julian, *Or.* i. 33.

[6] Malalas 338–9; Downey, *Antioch*, 403–10, 622–40.

[7] *Or.* xx. 44.   [8] Jones, *L.R.E.* 425.

[9] G. Downey, 'Imperial Building Records in Malalas', *B.Z.* xxxviii (1938), 1–15.

[10] *Or.* x. 10, 12.   [11] *Or.* x, *passim.*

[12] *Or.* xlviii. 38, *Ep.* 660 on villa of Olympius II, admittedly a *curialis* who entered the senate, cf. Seeck, *Briefe*, 223–4.

willing than their poorer colleagues to spend money on public building. There is a very great contrast with the age of the Younger Pliny and Dio Chrysostomus,[1] when competitive expenditure on public buildings had been one of the principal means of expressing civic pride and civic patriotism. The change at least partly reflects the financial weakening of the curial class. But some of the money that had formerly been spent on public works was now spent on religious building or charity. Economic and ideological developments were combining to transform traditional concepts of public duty.

4. THE OLYMPIC GAMES AND THE SYRIARCHY

In the lifetime of Libanius, the Olympic Games were still a great event at Antioch. They were held partly in the city itself, partly in the suburb of Daphne, in the months of July and August every leap year, following the same cycle as the original Games at Elis. The cycle of games can be followed through Libanius' life. The earliest Games mentioned in the writings of Libanius are the Games provided by Libanius' maternal uncle Panolbius in 328.[2] In 332 Argyrius gave the Games.[3] Argyrius had been placed in the Council of Antioch by Libanius' grandfather against some opposition. The relation between the two families remained close.[4] In 336 Libanius' younger uncle on the maternal side, Phasganius, provided the Games.[5] After this there is no information for some years, but in this time Libanius' cousin must have been 'agonothete', since his name is not recorded among later givers of the Games.[6] The Games of 352 were given by Letoius.[7] He

---

[1] See Jones, *G.C.* 236–8, on civic building under Early Empire.

[2] On the Olympic Games see G. Downey, 'The Olympic Games of Antioch in the Fourth Century A.D.', *T.A.P.A.* lxx (1939), 428–38; Petit, *Libanius*, 122–36. The features in which the following account differs from those of Downey and Petit are argued more fully in my 'The Syriarch in the Fourth Century', *Historia* viii (1959), 113–26. On the buildings used for the Games see the index of Downey, *Antioch*, s.vv. Olympic Games, Plethrion, Daphne, Xystos. The three buildings might be compared with the palaestra, stadium, and gymnasium at Olympia; on these *P.W.* xviii. 1, s.v. Olympia, cols. 139–42; plan, cols. 81–2. On the resemblance, Stauffenberg, *Kaisergeschichte*, 475.

[3] *Or.* liii. 4, x. 9 (Panolbius), x. 10 (Argyrius).

[4] *Or.* xlix. 13, x. 12.   [5] *Or.* i. 13, x. 12.

[6] Surely πάλαι in *Ep.* 544, l. 1 (356–7) refers to an earlier year, not simply to earlier in 356.

[7] *Ep.* 552 (517, l. 17); 551 (514, l. 14) show that when Letoius performed the Games, Libanius and Themistius were at Constantinople, and an ambassador to

too proved a firm supporter of Libanius when the latter wished to settle at Antioch. In 355 Antiochus II went on an embassy to the emperor, to obtain the customary subsidy for the Games of 356.[1] For the Games of that year Libanius delivered an oration.[2] Libanius does not mention the 'agonothete' of 360. Two men, Alexander and Candidus, are described as producing the Games of 364. Downey is probably right to conclude that the Olympic Games were now too expensive a burden for any one man.[3]

For the games of 380 Libanius wrote a speech but was unable to deliver it.[4] In preparation for the Games of 384, the count of the East, Proculus, ordered the 'plethron' to be enlarged.[5] In the year 384 Libanius wrote another speech for the Games, but was again prevented from speaking it.[6]

In 388 the Games were given by Letoius II on behalf of his son. This Letoius was the nephew of the liturgant of 352. He sent envoys to Egypt (Alexandria) to obtain athletes.[7] We do not know the name of the 'agonothete' of 392. In this year a pupil of Libanius, a sophist, came to Antioch for the Games and recited a speech in commemoration of Libanius' recently deceased son.[8] These were the last Olympic Games of Libanius' life.

Not only did the Olympic Games survive but they were popular. The wrestling contests held in the 'plethron' at Antioch were traditionally watched by only a small and select gallery of spectators. But in the fourth century the spectator area was enlarged no less than three times, and the audience took on more of a mass character.[9]

the emperor from Antioch would travel beyond Constantinople. This fits only 352. For another view see Downey, *T.A.P.A.* lxx (1939), 431.

[1] *Ep.* 440, 36, 439; I do not agree with Seeck, *Briefe*, 76 and 333, that Libanius' cousin shared in these games. The fact would be mentioned in the letter.

[2] *Ep.* 36 (358–9). This εὐφημία might well be the *Antiochicus. Ep.* 1243 of 364 shows that Libanius had then written only *one* Olympic Games speech. It is nevertheless remarkable how little there is in *Or.* xi about the Olympic Games. Perhaps our *Antiochicus* is a rewritten, and certainly a lengthened version of the speech spoken at the Games of 356. Foerster (edn. i. 2. 412) dates the speech in 360 with reference to pp. 498. 1 ff. and 531. 3, but neither reference excludes 356. Petit, *Libanius*, 206 sees in the speech a cautious pagan manifesto, inspired by Julian's appointment as Caesar in 355.

[3] *Ep.* 1167, 1179–83, 1189. Note that for reasons argued in *Historia* viii (1959), 113–26 I have not included Celsus, the Syriarch, among the givers of the Olympic Games.

[4] *Or.* i. 184.   [5] *Or.* x.   [6] *Or.* i. 222.
[7] *Ep.* 1017, 843.   [8] *Ep.* 1037–8.
[9] The traditional small audience: *Or.* x. 5–8; Libanius' fear for the future, ibid. 21–2, 36.

For the main games at Daphne the citizens thronged into the pleasant suburbs. In 404 this made it possible for a few men from Constantinople to consecrate one Porphyrius bishop of Antioch in spite of his unpopularity with a large section of citizens.[1]

Athletes came from all over the Greek world.[2] We hear little about individual events. A letter about the Olympic Games of Apamea mentions the 'pancration', wrestling and boxing.[3] It is reasonable to assume that competitions in these sports took place at Antioch too.[4] We also hear of a pupil of Libanius who was going to take part in the games as a runner.[5] There were competitions for rhetors[6] and poets.[7] Libanius might be expected to show excitement at a competition in which a number of gifted colleagues and potential rivals sought to display their abilities. In fact, he ignores the contests altogether. It is unlikely therefore that the Games brought to Antioch any orators of great standing. Libanius, as far as we know, never entered. There is no evidence that he spoke his festival oration of 356 in a competition.

Athletic contests, the traditional spectacle of the Olympic Games, still had popular appeal.[8] The sermons of John Chrysostomus are full of metaphors drawn from athletics and he and other Church Fathers warn their congregations against the moral dangers of watching the performances of athletes.[9] But the games also included chariot races[10] and these were a thoroughly 'contemporary' as well as a traditional entertainment. We do not know whether the games included performances by the enormously popular[11] Mimes and Pantomimes.[12]

---

[1] Pall. *Dial.* 16. 53 ff.

[2] *Ep.* 1179 (364) to vicar of Asia, 1180 (364) to proconsul of Asia, *Ep.* 1181 (364), 1182 (364) to consular of Bithynia, 1183 (364) to prefect of Egypt, 843 (388) to an Egyptian.   [3] *Ep.* 636 (361).

[4] *Ep.* 843 invites wrestlers.   [5] *Ep.* 843, 1017 (388).   [6] *Ep.* 1183 (364).

[7] *Or.* liv. 56, if ἑορτή means the Games of 388.   [8] *Ep.* 1182 (364).

[9] J. A. Sawhill, 'The use of athletic metaphors in the biblical homilies of St. John Chrysostom' (Diss. Princeton, 1928); C. Spicq, 'L'Image sportive de II *Cor.* IV, 7–9', *Ephemerides Theologicae Lovanienses* (1937), 209–29; 'Gymnastique et Morale', *Rev. Bibl.* (1947), 229–42, cf. p. 140 n. 5 below.

[10] The μαστιγοφόροι of *Or.* liv. 34 are the escort of the 'agonothete' at the Olympic Games, x. 4.

[11] Reference in Baur, *Johannes Chrysostomus*, vol. 1. 192–204. = 243 ff. trans. M. Gonzaga.

[12] Petit, *Libanius*, cites *Ep.* 1399, 1400; but these refer to the Syriarchy; on this see below, p. 141. Seeck, *Rh. M.* lxxiii (1920), 92, associates the favours given to the theatrical claque at the expense of the council in 388 (*Or.* lvi. 2) with the preparation of the Olympic Games. This is not necessary.

The Games concluded, as did the old Games at Olympia, with a great banquet,[1]—not one to which all and sundry were invited, but a select gathering of decurions and members of high society, invited by the 'agonothete'.[2] Adolescent sons were invited together with their fathers, even though it was usual for manners to become extremely relaxed, and this practice worried Libanius. He feared that the future leaders of the city would be corrupted, and acquire in early youth a bad reputation which would one day make it impossible for them to stand up to the governors.[3] His pamphlet against the practice recalls the fervour of Christian moralists.

It had become customary for the host to give presents to his guests. This custom became so expensive a burden as to threaten the continuance of the Games. Libanius campaigned against it and helped to achieve its abolition in 380.[4] The banquet and the present-giving appear to be, apart from the New Year gifts of gold,[5] the only examples in fourth-century Antioch of the provision of public banquets and distributions of money which formed so striking a feature of the competitive munificence of councillors under the Early Empire.[6]

The Olympic Games were already an anachronism. Even if to all but a few confirmed pagans the Games had become a purely secular festival,[7] it was inappropriate that the chief festival of a largely Christian city should be dedicated to Zeus. Moreover the Games celebrated an educational ideal in which physical and literary education each contributed to the formation of a balanced personality. This ideal had long been losing ground. The literary side of Greek education had prevailed over the physical side.[8] Fourth-century sources do not suggest that athletics played a significant role in the lives of young men. Of the one

---

[1] *Or.* liii, partially translated into French in Festugière, *Antioche*, 201–6.

[2] *Or.* liii. 3.

[3] Ibid. 27. Note the puritan emphasis on the unsullied reputation of public figures.

[4] *Or.* xxxviii. 5; cf. liii. 16. This was shortly before the accident to Libanius' foot (ibid. 3–4); according to *Or.* i. 183, just before the Olympic Games of 380.

[5] ἔκφρασις καλανδῶν, 7 and 8 (Foerster (ed.), vol. 8. 474–5).

[6] A. R. Hands, *Charities and Social Aid in Greece and Rome* (London, 1968), 89–94; R. Duncan Jones in *P.B.S.R.* (1963), 160–77; ibid. (1965), 202–21; *Historia* xiii (1964), 198–208.

[7] Libanius consistently affirms its religious nature.

[8] H. I. Marrou, *Histoire de l'éducation dans l'antiquité* (Paris, 1950), 185–6.

hundred and five students of Libanius known to us only three are stated to have engaged in athletics.[1]

At the same time institutions serving the athletic ideal were everywhere going out of existence. The last reference to the ephebic system of athletic and pre-military training occurs in A.D. 323.[2] We last hear of gymnasia around 370.[3] At Antioch the ephebate had been abolished before the middle of the third century,[4] and there is no evidence to suggest that a gymnasium was functioning in Libanius' lifetime.

It is significant that Christian writers attack athletics not as an instrument of education but as a spectator sport. They are worried about the moral effect of watching athletics, not of taking part in them. Indeed the training of an athlete furnishes Christian writers with effective metaphors to describe the disciplined Christian life and particularly the life of the ascetic.[5]

The great majority of athletic festivals had come to an end already. The early third-century monument of an athlete records victories won at Caesarea, Tyre, Tarsus, Laodicea, Ascalon, Scythopolis, Sidon, Tripolis, Hierapolis, Leucas (Balanea), Beroea, Zeugma, Apamea, Chalcis, Salamis, Cition, and Antioch.[6] Of all these cities of Syria, Palestine, or Cyprus, only Antioch and Apamea[7] are known to have had athletic games in the time of Libanius. The original Olympic Games at Elis in Greece were prohibited by imperial decree in 393.[8] That the Olympic Games of Antioch survived until 520[9] is a remarkable fact, and striking evidence of the relative strength and persistence of the Hellenic tradition in that city.

[1] *Ep.* 843, 1017; 1278–9, on Horus see A. Cameron, *J.R.S.* lvi (1966), 31.

[2] *P. Oxy.* 42.

[3] The latest known gymnasiarch: ibid. 2110; cf. P. J. Sijpesteijn, *Liste des gymnasiarques des métropoles de l'Égypte* (Amsterdam, 1967). In the third century one gymnasiarch is known for almost every year. Then the list thins out progressively to end in 370. The last reference to a gymnasium: Bas. *Ep.* 74.

[4] *Or.* xi. 157: τῆς τῶν ὁπλιτικῶν μελέτης presumably refers to the ephebate; ibid. 158–9 illustrates that the end of military training did not destroy courage. The Persian attacks took place in the middle of the third century, perhaps in 256 and 260 (Downey, *Antioch*, 256–7).

[5] Joh. Chrys. *De educ. liberis*, 19; *De Maccab.* 1. 1, 3. 2 (*P.G.* l. 619, 625). This metaphorical use is common to pagan and Christian writers: see M. L. W. Laistner, *Christianity and Pagan Culture in the Later Empire* (Cornell, 1951; paperback 1967), 136 n. 14, cf. p. 138 n. 9 above.

[6] *C.I.G.* 4472 (221) = *I.G.R.* iii. 1012 = *I.G.L.S.* 1265.

[7] *Ep.* 627, 663, 668 (all 361); 1172 (364).   [8] Cedren., *Hist. Compend.* 323D.

[9] Malalas 417; cf. G. Downey in *T.A.P.A.* lxviii (1937), 147–8.

Besides the Olympic Games, one other great liturgy can be followed through the whole of the period covered by Libanius' writings. This was the Syriarchate.[1] The Syriarch, who was normally a councillor of Antioch, was elected to produce shows. These were enormously expensive, even though the liturgant was aided by an imperial subsidy, which had to be requested anew by each new holder of the office.[2] While the Syriarch may have produced chariot races or theatrical entertainments at other times also, his greatest effort was the organization of a show for the seventeen cities of Syria. Of this show, wild beast chases formed the most spectacular part.[3] There is no evidence that gladiators figured in the programme, at least in the second half of the century.[4] The principal show of the Syriarch was held in summer or autumn.[5] Preparations, including the procuring of beasts from a province as distant as Bithynia or of hunters from Pamphylia,[6] might start a year before the show. The Syriarch might hold his office over a period of years.[7]

The frequency of the shows and the great expense of wild animals made this a very burdensome liturgy indeed. While some holders of the liturgy showed great enthusiasm, the Syriarchate was not always easy to fill. When Celsus produced his wild beast chase in 364, he gave the city a spectacle which it had not seen for some time.[8] It looks as if the sequence of shows had been interrupted, perhaps since 360. In the 380s a governor exercised severe pressure on decurions to compel them to undertake the liturgy. Evidently the city protested, for in 383 a law was issued stating that each and every person who undertook the

---

[1] The following is argued more fully in my article in *Historia* viii (1959), 113–26.

[2] *Ep.* 1459, 1147–8 (363–4), *Ep.* 545 (356–7), 970–1 (390).

[3] Various entertainments at different times: *Ep.* 1400; cf. 544; 17 cities: 1399 (363); 'for Syria': 1518 (365); Syriarch title: 1400, 1459 (363).

[4] Gladiators: last mention in Libanius, *Or.* i. 5. Nothing compels us to link the gladiators with the Olympic Games of 328. The show could have taken place in the following years. Panolbius might have been Syriarch shortly afterwards. Gladiators had been prohibited in 325 by *C.T.* xv. 12. 1, but this law was obviously not observed at once. Libanius' silence suggests that they did stop soon after. John Chrysostomus does not mention gladiators, Baur, *Johannes Chrysostomus*, 192. Gallus watched boxers not gladiators: *Amm.* xiv. 7. 2.

[5] On date of *Ep.* 218 (360): Seeck, *Briefe*, 372.

[6] *Ep.* 1509 (365), 586–8, 598–9 (357).

[7] Start of liturgy of Libanius' cousin: *Ep.* 544 (356–7); end: 217 (360). Malalas 285 suggests a full term of four years. Libanius' cousin served longer than he needed.

[8] *Ep.* 1399 (363).

Syriarchiate must do so of his own free will.[1] Three years later a governor who had failed to persuade a councillor of Antioch to undertake the beast show proceeded to disgrace the provincial capital by having the show produced by a citizen of Beroea.[2] Shortly after, the praetorian prefect Tatian tried to ease the burden by ordering senators who owned property in Syria to contribute to the expense of the show. But characteristically, these influential men got Tatian's regulation repealed by his successor.[3]

We last hear of the show in 390 when Argyrius was preparing for a show which his father had been promoting in his name as long ago as 359.[4] As we have observed in connection with the Olympic Games, the family tradition of giving was not yet dead.

This great liturgy, like the Olympic Games, was something of an anachronistic survival. The Syriarch performed his liturgy for the provincial assembly of Syria, and his office was a vestige of the provincial imperial cult. The spectacle which he provided was too popular, and too important as a means of fostering loyalty among provincials, to be abandoned when the emperor became Christian. It was considered sufficient to suppress features that might give offence to Christians.[5]

The objectionable features included the two kinds of spectacle which were peculiarly associated with the imperial cult: gladiator shows and wild beast hunts.[6] Constantine prohibited gladiator shows in 325. While this law was largely ineffective in the West, where gladiator shows continued into the reign of Valentinian III,[7] it seems to have prevailed in the East. There is no evidence that gladiator shows were given at Antioch later than the

---

[1] *C.T.* xii. 1. 103 (383).   [2] *Or.* xxxiii. 14–15. 21.
[3] *C.T.* vi. 3. 1 (393).   [4] *Ep.* 970–1 (390), 113 (359–60).
[5] See Hispellum inscription, *I.L.S.* 705. In the fifth century vestiges of the cult were abandoned. *C.T.* xii. 12. 12 is the only law referring to provincial assemblies taken into the Code of Justinian (*C.J.* x. 65. 5); cf. *P.W.* iv. 1, s.v. Concilium (Hülsen), 829; O. Hirschfeld, 'Zur Geschichte des römischen Kaiserkultes', *S.B. Berliner Akademie* xxxv (1888), 833–62. E. Kornemann, 'Zur Geschichte der antiken Herrscherkulte, *Klio* i (1901), 140–2. The latest law concerning a provincial priest is *Nov. Marc.* iv of 454. In reconquered Italy Justinian had provincial governors elected by the notables and bishops of a province: *C. Just. App.* vii. 12 (554). Justin II tried this in the East: *Nov.* cxlix (569).
[6] L. Robert, *Les Gladiateurs dans l'Orient grec* (Paris, 1940), 118, no. 63; 271; 309.
[7] A. Chastagnol, *Le Sénat romain sous le règne d'Odoacre* (Bonn, 1966), 21–2.

Olympic Games of 328.[1] On the other hand wild beast chases continued in East and West into the sixth century.[2]

It will be observed that these two great traditional festivals were maintained through the fourth century with some difficulty. Liturgants who would assume the burden were not always easy to find. On the other hand we hear of two families, those of Letoius and Argyrius,[3] who performed the liturgies for respectively two and three generations and with much of the traditional spirit of curial munificence. The story of the great liturgies confirms the view, put forward by Libanius and supported by much other evidence, that the decline of the curial class did not affect all *curiales* alike, but that a small group of the wealthiest families maintained and perhaps even increased their wealth and power, at the expense of the rest.

It is also worth noting that the governors came to take a very considerable part in the organization of these great liturgies. The Syriarchy would on some occasions have remained unfilled but for pressure by the governor. But governors concerned themselves with the Olympic Games too, as is witnessed by Proculus' enlargement of the 'plethron'. Indeed, even so trivial a matter as whether a particular poet was to be invited to give a recital depended on the governor.[4]

We might add that in 465 the function of the Alytarch, and the expenditure of the imperial funds assigned to him, were transferred to the *comes orientis*,[5] and the funds and office of the Syriarch were transferred to the consular of Syria. This measure was not

---

[1] See p. 141 n. 4 above. On the attitude of the Greek East to gladiator shows and wild beast hunts see L. Robert, op. cit. 240. Plutarch was exceptional in his outright condemnation, e.g. xxx. 822c. Robert is wrong to conclude from *Or.* i. 5 that Libanius had a taste for gladiator shows. He could scarcely bear to see a man whipped, *Or.* liv. 43–4. In *Ep.* 217 Libanius expresses the view—probably conventional—that beast chases provide a display of intelligence fighting brute force. It was suggested that they provided a harmless way of gratifying our bloodthirsty instincts, Robert, op. cit. 329–30. The popularity of wild beast chases among the wealthiest classes is shown by the large number of surviving hunter mosaics, including the famous Megalopsychia.

[2] Chastagnol, op. cit. 57–63; Jones, *L.R.E.* 977; Cass. *Var.* v. 12 (523).

[3] Letoius I: Olympic Games of 352 (p. 136 n. 7 above); Letoius II Games of 388 for his son (p. 137 n. 7 above). It is likely that he had earlier given the Games in his own name. Argyrius the elder: Olympic games of 332 (p. 136 n. 3 above); Obodianus, son of Agyrius, prepares show of Syriarch for his son, the younger Argyrius, in 359–60 (*Ep.* 113). The younger Argyrius prepares show of Syriarch in 390 (970–1).

[4] See p. 138 n. 7 above.   [5] *C.J.* i. 36. 1.

a response to a shortage of councillors wealthy enough to produce the shows, for it expressly forbids that any councillor should henceforth perform the duties. Wealthy councillors could still be found at Antioch, but the government did not want them to produce the shows. Perhaps it wanted councillors to spend their money on duties of greater advantage to the army or administration. Perhaps, too, it feared the popularity that a private individual might win through a splendid production, and the capacity to disturb the smooth run of administration that he might obtain in consequence. Whatever the reason for the law, it is significant that this traditional means of expressing civic patriotism was finally suppressed and transformed into a routine responsibility of the imperial administration.

5. ROUTINE ENTERTAINMENT

The entertainment of the people of Antioch reached its climax in the Olympic Games and the shows of the Syriarch. But a good deal of more ordinary entertainment was provided in the way of theatrical shows and chariot races, while numerous baths served the cleanliness no less than the recreation of the populace. These services were needed to keep the huge population of the city contented and orderly, and therefore they were subject to close supervision by the governors. Thus the consular Tissamenes intervened in the detailed arrangements of theatricals,[1] and the consular Florentius insisted that races should be provided even during the season when the horses were normally allowed to recover on their pastures.[2] The *comes* Icarius had a councillor beaten after complaints about the insufficient heating of the water in a bathing establishment for which he was responsible.[3] Always it was to the governor that councillors had to make their excuses for inadequate performance of duties.[4]

Of the entertainments, theatrical shows figure most prominently in the literature of the time. This was because the subject-matter of the performances was extremely offensive to moralists. Shows no longer included whole plays, though extracts of the classical plays might occasionally be recited. The staple theatrical fare was provided by the Mime, a kind of ballet based

[1] *Or.* xxxiii. 8.
[2] *Or.* xlvi. 41.
[3] *Or.* xxvi. 5–6, xxvii. 13, xxviii. 6.
[4] *Or.* xlix. 8–9.

on classical mythology but including sketches on contemporary themes.[1] John Chrysostomus and other Christian preachers were extremely hostile to the Mime because of its blatant presentation of erotic scenes.[2] Libanius could forgive the Mime much because of its literary origin,[3] but in his later years he too attacks actors and dancers as a source of demoralization and of public disturbance.[4]

Actors and dancers were of course extremely popular. At the same time, the profession was legally a disgraceful one and regulated by laws of incredible callousness.[5] As membership of the Church was not compatible with appearances on the stage, actors were only accepted into the Church on their deathbed. But in case actors should use the pretence of dying as a means of discharging themselves from their profession, it was laid down that the genuineness of their condition should be certified by the provincial governor or at least the *curator* of the city.[6]

Like other professional groups whose activities were subject to regulation by the government, stage artists would appear to have been organized in guilds. Evidence about their organization is inevitably scrappy. We are informed that Tissamenes, a young man of very good Antiochene family, who had been on close terms with the dancers and had written songs for them to dance to, suddenly became ἡγεμὼν ἔθνους.[7] ἔθνος here cannot have its common meaning of 'province', because Tissamenes became a provincial governor only some years later. As in some other passages, the word is likely to describe a group of men working at the same occupation. If so, the passage is evidence that the dancers of Antioch were supervised by a prominent citizen.[8]

Since the entertainers were in a position to retain a claque, though at a reduced wage, even when they were not performing,[9] it is likely that the stage artists, or at least their organization, received a salary all the year round. This is confirmed by another passage which suggests that the entertainers had made

---

[1] See *P.W.* xviii. 2, s.v. Pantomimus (E. Wüst), 847–9.

[2] Joh. Chrys. *Hom. de poenitentia* 6. 1 (*P.G.* xlix. 314–15), *Hom. in I Thess.* 5. 4 (*P.G.* lxii. 428), *Hom. de David et Saul* 3. 1–2 (*P.G.* liv. 695–7).

[3] *Or.* lxiv. 108 ff.   [4] *Or.* xxvi. 25–6, xli. 6–9.

[5] *C.T.* xv. 7. 1, 8.   [6] Jones, *L.R.E.* 1020–1.

[7] *Or.* xxxiii. 3–4.

[8] On other supervisors see below, p. 221; on use of ἔθνος see below, p. 222 n. 9.

[9] *Or.* xli. 7; the retaining fee at least partly from temple revenues? xxvi. 24: ἄξιον τῆς τούτων ἕνεκα ἡδονῆς ἱεροσυλεῖν.

a demand for higher wages and that these were conceded to them in case they might go elsewhere.[1] Since the claque was divided into the followers of the actors and those of the dancers, it may follow that actors and dancers formed separate organizations.[2]

The actors' pay increase was financed by means of a new tax levied on shopkeepers who were occupying stalls between pillars of the great colonnades.[3] It may well be that stage artists received all their basic wage out of public funds, and that the liturgical contribution of councillors was limited to the payment of fees, or of prizes for particular performances, and the provision of costumes and other stage properties.[4] Certainly theatrical entertainment is not included by Libanius when he lists the principal liturgical duties.[5]

Judging by the comparative frequency with which they are mentioned by Libanius, it would seem that most of the run-of-the-mill liturgies were concerned either with the heating of baths or the provision of chariot races. The horse races were immensely popular at Antioch, and famous all over the ancient world, at least while the Emperor Constantius was in residence.[6] Races were held on the days of the old festival of Poseidon,[7] of Calliope,[8] of the New Year,[9] and as part of the show of the Syriarch. They may well have been a good deal more frequent. At a meeting there might be as many as sixteen races.[10]

---

[1] *Or.* xxvi. 24; cf. lvi. 2: τιμαῖς ταῖς κατὰ τῆς βουλῆς τετιμημένοι.

[2] *Or.* xli. 7, members of the claque also reach agreements with individual actors, ibid. 9: οἱ μὲν τούτῳ συμπράττοντες οἱ δὲ ἐκείνῳ.

[3] *Or.* xxvi. 20 ff.

[4] Payment of a dancer for a particular performance: *Or.* xlviii. 40; payment for domestic performances: xxvi. 25. A ruinous theatrical liturgy: Joh. Chrys. *De ed. lib.* 4–8. The date of this treatise is uncertain, and hence also whether it was delivered at Constantinople or at Antioch (Laistner, *Christianity and Pagan Culture*, 78–84). The description of a liturgy which is performed only for popular applause (c. 10) suggests a civic liturgy of Antioch, rather than the praetorian games of Constantinople, which were a once-and-for-all burden balanced by the great privileges of senatorial rank (Jones, *L.R.E.*, 538–9).

[5] *Or.* xlix. 10, xxxv. 4.

[6] *Totius Orbis Descr.* 32 (mid fourth century). Chariot races were peculiarly associated with the emperor as is suggested by *Or.* xxxiii. 8, τὴν μὲν βασιλείαν τῇ παρουσίᾳ τιμῶντες, and by other evidence cited by Claude, *Byzantinische Stadt*, 77.

[7] *Or.* i. 230.   [8] *Ep.* 811 (363).

[9] ἑ. καλανδῶν 8 (Foerster (ed.), vol. 8. 474).

[10] *Or.* xvi. 41; cf. P. Friedländer, *Sittengeschichte*, vol. 2. 46–7 = *Roman Life and Manners*, vol. 2, 37–8. A varied programme including chariot races: *P. Oxy.* xxxiv. 2707 (sixth century).

The liturgies connected with chariot races were not all equally expensive. The men who produced races on New Year's Day, and had to throw gold to the people, surely spent more than councillors who gave races on lesser occasions. When Argyrius, son of Obodianus, was preparing chariot races, he was given two teams of horses by the emperor.[1] Again, these will not have been given for an ordinary race meeting. The chariot liturgy came early in the career of a young councillor. At the start of the liturgy a young man would buy race horses. At the end of the liturgy he would sell them again.[2] We do not hear of any organizations that furnished the stores required for racing; there is no reference to 'factions'. Charioteers could make a lot of money.[3] We do not know whether they were organized in a guild and paid a retaining fee like the actors and the dancers. A claque was employed in the hippodrome[4] as in the theatre. But there is no evidence that actors and charioteers were professionally applauded by the same men. The claque of four hundred which Libanius blames for so many troubles in the last decade of his life is never associated with the hippodrome. Until 360 at any rate, the chariot races were free from riots.[5]

The production of chariot races was undoubtedly expensive. The Emperor Julian granted the city three thousand 'lots' of uncultivated land to benefit the men obliged to keep race horses and to mitigate the expense of the liturgy.[6] We hear of two councillors of Antioch who were impoverished by the expense of providing races.[7] But this number is not large, and there is considerable evidence that the performance of horse racing liturgies was not unpopular. Chariot racing was the passion of all classes.[8] The young councillors who had acquitted themselves of the racing liturgy remained ardent supporters of the races. They would still consider that they had had a good or a

---

[1] *Ep.* 381 (385).　　　　　　　　　　　[2] *Or.* xxxv. 14.
[3] *Or.* ii. 57.　　　　　　　　　　　　　[4] *Or.* xxxv. 13.
[5] *Or.* xi. 268; use of magic on behalf of charioteers: xxxv. 13, xxxvi. 15; charioteers in magic trials: i. 162; cf. Amm. xxviii. 1. 27, 4. 5, xxvi. 3. 3 on magic trials at Rome.
[6] Julian, *Misop.* 370D; as an atticist he presumably avoids use of Latin technical term *iugum*. But Rostovtzeff, *S.E.H.H.W.* 481, argued that Julian meant 'lots' and that these went back to the original settlement of Greeks at Antioch.
[7] *Or.* liv. 22, cf. 45 (Julianus); xxvii. 13 (Hermeias).
[8] *Or.* xxxv. 18; Joh. Chrys. *Hom. de Lazar.* 7. 1 (*P.G.* xlviii. 1045 ff.); *Hom. in Gen.* 41. 1 (*P.G.* liv. 374); *Hom. de Anna* 4. 5 (*P.G.* liv. 660–1).

bad day according to whether their favourite charioteer had won or lost, and would spend evenings in argument with their servants about the merits of rival charioteers.[1] The liturgy had clearly not been a traumatic experience. Indeed, the chariot races could still arouse the old spirit of civic munificence. The *primates* of Antioch sent as far afield as Spain to get horses for racing.[2]

The maintenance of the many public baths of the city[3] provided the second group of regular liturgies. We can form no estimate of how many separate liturgies were involved. One man cannot have been required to maintain all the baths, and even within a single institution it is by no means necessary that the man who paid to heat the water also paid for the cleaning and maintenance of the building, or for the oil provided for the bathers, or for the staff employed at the bath.[4] But the water-heating duty is the only one mentioned by Libanius. The two references to it throw more light on the councillor's eagerness to escape from curial duties altogether than on the nature of the duties. Hermeias, a man of good family who had lost a considerable amount of property on the chariot liturgy, was obliged for a second time to perform the duty of heating 'the large furnaces' of the baths. When the public complained the *comes* had Hermeias beaten.[5] In the second case we only hear that a governor insisted that a certain man should heat the baths regardless of his poverty.[6]

Hermeias and the unnamed pupil of Libanius were unlucky but they were not necessarily typical. Once again two victims of the system out of the many councillors known is a small proportion. Moreover Libanius suggests that for the heating of baths too the leading councillors were ready to volunteer.[7]

But here caution is needed. The fact that certain councillors volunteered for liturgies connected with the baths or indeed with chariot racing might be taken as evidence that the liturgical

---

[1] *Or.* xxx. 14.   [2] Symm. *Ep.* iv. 62.

[3] Petit, *Libanius*, 126, map shows six baths found by excavation. It is uncertain which, if any, can be identified with baths named in literary sources. For these see s.v. Baths in index of Downey, *Antioch*.

[4] *Or.* xlix. 31, ii. 34 lists duties required in the baths. No doubt some of them were normally performed by paid men or slaves. *Ep.* 748 (362) liturgant closes the baths in the evening.

[5] *Or.* xxvi. 5–6, xxvii. 13, xxviii. 6.

[6] *Or.* i. 272, liv. 38.   [7] *Or.* xlix. 10.

system of Antioch was working well. But this was not the case. According to Libanius, these leading councillors were ready to take on duties quite unnecessarily in order to keep the council small, so that the profits of membership might be shared by as few men as possible. As a result, councillors who were trying to escape from their duties got away, the duties themselves were not properly performed, and the financial strength of the council sank steadily.[1]

That this was happening is confirmed by evidence other than that of Libanius. In the late 380s the praetorian prefect Tatian tried to compel senators to contribute to the heating of the baths and the expenses of the Syriarch.[2] The attempt failed. But in 409 a special grant was made, either by the emperor or by the praetorian prefect, to assist the finances of the councillors of Antioch which were in a chronic state of crisis.[3]

6. FINANCING THE CIVIC SERVICES

The survey of civic services has shown that in the fourth century the liturgies of the councillors provided a considerable number of civic services. But we have also come across civic expenses which were not met in this way. These include the payment of the police,[4] of Libanius himself and his under-teachers,[5] the retaining fee for actors and dancers,[6] and the cost of some building operations.[7] Clearly the city had revenues of its own, whether derived from local taxes or from the rents of landed estate.

Unfortunately we have only one certain piece of quantitative information about the estates. Julian granted the city three thousand 'lots', presumably *iuga*, of uncultivated land, free of tax, as an endowment to benefit the councillors who were obliged to maintain horses for chariot races.[8] The three thousand 'lots' were of course an addition to the older estates of the city. There is a passage which has been thought by some scholars to give

---

[1] Ibid. 8: κἂν τοῖς ἀμελουμένοις ἃ δικαίως ἂν ἐτύγχανε προνοίας ἐκ τοῦ μὴ πολλοὺς εἶναι τοὺς βουλεύοντας τοῖς οὖσιν ἡ παραίτησις.

[2] *C.T.* xii. 1. 131, vi. 3. 1.   [3] *C.T.* xii. 1. 169.

[4] *Or.* xlviii. 9; cf. *P. Oxy.* xii. 1499, payment of bath attendants by council of Oxyrhynchus.

[5] *Or.* xxxi. 19–20.   [6] See above, pp. 145–6.

[7] *Or.* xxvii. 3, l. 3; cf. *P. Oxy.* 1104; *P. Goth.* 7, public works at Oxyrhynchus.

[8] Julian, *Misop.* 370D, cf. p. 147 above.

the area of these older estates too. Julian told the council of Antioch that the city possessed ten thousand (or just very many?) 'lots' of land of its own.[1] This has been taken to refer to land which belonged peculiarly to the city rather than to the citizens, in other words, the civic estates. The sentence of which the statement is part is concerned with public not private sacrifices, and estate which would be relevant to such a sacrifice would be that belonging to the community.[2] But if this interpretation is the right one, the civic estates of Antioch were very large indeed, for if we assume that the 'lot' represents the standard fiscal measure, the *iugum*, ten thousand *iuga* would represent something like one hundred thousand hectares and perhaps a seventh of the total territory of Antioch.[3] This is a huge area if we bear in mind that the total area of the estates of all the cities of the province of Asia in the fourth century amounted to only 6,736½ *iuga*.[4] Moreover Asia comprised many cities, including the great cities of Smyrna, Ephesus, and Pergamum. But it is also worth remembering that the *iugum* of Asia appears to have been larger than that of Syria and that the walled area of Smyrna, Ephesus, and Pergamum combined was still smaller than that of Antioch.[5]

Even if this interpretation is uncertain it may be worth while to explore its financial consequences. The rents of such estates

[1] *Misop.* 362. Jones, *L.R.E.* 816 n. 108, understands μυρίους κλήρους γῆς ἰδίας κεκτημένη to mean that the territory of Antioch comprised *countless*, not *ten thousand*, *iuga*. He takes the γῆ to be privately owned land. Since the much smaller Cyrrhus had 50,000 *iuga* of privately owned land, Theod. *Ep.* (Azema), 42, Antioch must have had very much more than 10,000. But if ἰδίας is translated 'of its own' (as opposed to land in private ownership) and Julian is understood to refer to civic estates the comparison with Cyrrhus is irrelevant. On the other hand μυρίους still need not mean more than a 'large amount' which could be more—or considerably less—than 10,000 *iuga*.

[2] *Misop.* 362: ὑπὲρ αὐτῆς οὐ προσάγει . . . κατὰ φυλὰς βουθυτεῖν . . . ἕνα γε κοινῇ ὑπὲρ αὐτῆς προσφέρειν τῷ θεῷ ταῦρον.

[3] Assuming that the 10,000 *iuga* are the equivalent of 400,000 *iugera* of second-best arable land. If a high proportion of the land consisted of vineyards or olive plantations the area would be considerably less. On the Syrian *iugum*, equivalent to 20 *iugera* of best arable, 40 *iugera* of second-class arable, 60 *iugera* of third-class arable, or 5 *iugera* of vineyard, see Jones, *L.R.E.* 62; *F.I.R.* ii². 795–6; for total area of territory see above, pp. 40–1.

[4] *F.I.R.* i². 108.

[5] The *iugum* of Asia: A. H. M. Jones, *J.R.S.* xliii (1953), 49–50, interpreting *I.G.* xii. iii. 343, employs an equivalent of 100 *iugera* per *iugum* for arable land and of 24 *iugera* of vineyard. The areas of walled cities in hectares according to Russell, *Trans. Am. Phil. Soc.* xviii, pt. 3 (1958), 80–2: Smyrna 600, Ephesus 345, Pergamum 160, Antioch, 1,750–2,100 of which 900–1,200 inhabited.

calculated at an average Egyptian level[1] would amount to something like two hundred thousand *solidi*, a very large sum, which would have paid for about a quarter of the corn supplied annually by the government for the people of Constantinople in the reign of Justinian.[2] But productivity and hence rents are likely to have been very much lower than in Egypt—perhaps only one-seventh of the Egyptian level. Even so, the estates might bring in thirty thousand *solidi* of rents. If taxes were collected at the Numidian level there would be left a residue of about thirteen thousand *solidi*, of which the councillors to whom the estates were let would take a share, perhaps half.[3] But even six thousand five hundred *solidi* would have paid for a great part of the civic services—if these did not include a regular and general distribution of free corn.

Whether civic revenues were indeed as valuable as this, or whether they were in reality very much smaller, there is no doubt that in the middle of the fourth century all civic properties and revenues were taken over by the imperial government. The temple properties were confiscated by Constantine. The date of confiscation of civic estates and revenues is not known, but it is more likely to have taken place early than late in the reign of

[1] Rents: Jones, *L.R.E.* 807–8; $\frac{1}{2}$ *solidus* per *arura* of arable land (1 *arura* = 0·25 hectare; *iugerum* = 0·27 hectare). In sharecropping leases for arable land the division is half and half. Taxes are paid by the owner.

[2] Pricing the public corn of Constantinople, 8,000,000 *artabae* (ibid. 698), at 10 *artabae* per *solidus* (ibid. 446).

[3] Ibid. 464, cites a tax yield (including fees) of 58$\frac{1}{2}$ *solidi* per *centuria* (200 *iugera*) from Egypt. From Numidia the corresponding yield is 8$\frac{2}{3}$ *solidi*. The Egyptian figure is about a century later and taxes may well have increased in the interval. But most of the difference is surely due to the fertility of Egypt. In Egypt good soil on the average produced a tenfold yield (ibid. 767). This is probably a high yield by ancient standards. In medieval Europe before 1250 the average yield of corn was less than fourfold: B. H. Slicher van Bath, *Yield Ratios: 810–1820* (Wageningen, 1936), 16. Columella (iii. 3. 4) informs us that in Italy under the Early Empire corn yielded fourfold crops. But higher yields are reported. According to *E.S.A.R.* iv. 128, citing Bab. Kethub. 112, a fivefold yield could be anticipated in Palestine. Cicero claims that Sicily (is he thinking of the volcanic soils around Mt. Aetna?) yielded eight- to tenfold crops (*II Verr.* 3. 112). Varro even claims ten- to fifteenfold crops for Italy (*R.R.* i. 44). In *Excavations at Nessana*, ed. H. Colt (London, 1962), vol. 1. 227–8, P. Mayerson concludes from *Nessana P.* 82 that in this area wheat yielded sevenfold and barley eightfold. He finds that this corresponds to an average Bedouin harvest today. He explains the high yield through flood-water irrigation. Egypt is likely to have been exceptionally productive because a very high proportion of the land cultivated at all was—and is— 'good land', and because the annual deposit of flood soil enabled the land to bear a crop every year instead of in alternate years only.

Constantius.¹ We have no evidence at all about the fate of local taxes at Antioch. We do not know what administrative changes accompanied confiscation of the estates. We only know that the emperor exploited his newly gained rights of ownership to make gifts of civic land to private individuals. It is also clear that the confiscation did not deprive the city of all responsibility for its old property. The *De rhetoribus,* written between 355 and 360, informs us that the Council of Antioch had at its disposal the leases of a number of estates of various size. It had leased most of the estates to councillors, but was in a position to lease farms to others as well, to teachers employed by the city for instance.²

It would not seem that the amount of money available for the city was radically reduced by the confiscation. Libanius does indeed praise Julian for restoring the estates to the city, but only briefly and only in *Oration* xiii,³ not in his full account of Julian's achievement, *Oration* xviii. Evidently he did not consider the restoration of the estates one of Julian's major acts.

On the other hand, the council would appear to have lost all control over its revenues. This is the implication of the *De rhetoribus.* The council is in a position to lease the teachers land. The simpler expedient of raising their salaries is not considered.⁴ The reason for this is clear. Even the existing salaries were not paid directly by the civic authorities. The recipient could only draw them after prolonged and humiliating pleading with governor, officials, and finally with the ἀποδέκται, the men in charge of the storehouse where the taxes in kind were kept.⁵ Civic salaries were therefore paid out through the same organiza-

---

¹ That estates were confiscated follows from the fact that Julian restored them: *C.T.* x. 3. 1, *C.J.* xi. 70. 1, Amm. xxv. 4. 15, Lib. *Or.* xiii. 45. The date may well have been *early* in Constantius' reign, for the house that was restored to the city of Tyre by Julian had been given to the father of its present owner by an emperor (*Ep.* 828). But Hermogenes, the father of this Herculianus (Amm. xiv. 10. 2 calls him Hercu*lanus,* cf. Seeck, *Briefe,* 173, s.v. Hermogenes II), was lynched in Constantinople in 342. Again, *C.T.* xv. 1. 9 (362) implies that since the confiscation a considerable period of time had elapsed. Otherwise it would not have been possible for 'very many persons' to build themselves houses above the civically owned shops. Temple properties had been confiscated by Constantine: *Or.* xxx. 6, 37, lxii. 8. So the sons of Thalassius had had plenty of time to turn a temple into a house (*Ep.* 1364). Perhaps the two acts of confiscations followed close upon each other. In favour of a Constantinian date also Julian, *Or.* i. 43.

² *Or.* xxxi. 16–17, 20.   ³ *Or.* xiii. 45.
⁴ *Or.* xxxi. 15 implies that they could not.   ⁵ Ibid. 19.

tion as imperial salaries.[1] Thus control by the administration over civic expenditure was complete. An application to increase the salary of teachers might well be refused under the terms of a law forbidding the payment of a salary out of civic resources except on the order of the emperor.[2]

Thus it is possible to see in the confiscation of the civic estates another chapter in the long history of the imperial government's attempts to control civic expenditure, a history which goes back to the Younger Pliny's mission in Bithynia and the *curatores* of the Early Empire.[3] After Constantius' act of confiscation the cities were no longer in physical control of their revenues, and it was therefore quite impossible for them to indulge in unauthorized expenditure.

Julian, in accordance with his policy of encouraging self-determination by the cities, restored the confiscated estates and taxes. He also, as we have seen, granted the council an additional three thousand 'lots' of waste land.[4] Even then the irresponsible way in which the councillors shared out the new land among themselves augured badly for the success of Julian's policy. But as it happened the policy was scarcely put to the test. Julian died and the Emperors Valens and Valentinian once again confiscated the civic estates.[5] This time the change of ownership was

---

[1] See above, pp. 88–9. It is not known whether there was a separate state treasury for imperial revenues in money comparable to the δημοσία τράπεζα known from early fourth-century Egypt (Lallemand, *L'Administration civile de l'Égypte*, 218–19). The organization of treasuries is likely to have been much more complicated than the account in the text suggests. I have rejected the two-treasury theory of Petit (*Libanius*, 96–104). Petit argues that the 10,000 κλῆροι of *Misop.* 362 are 'lots' going back to the period of first settlement, and that these had remained a separate category of civic land. Only these 'lots', he argues, were confiscated; land acquired by the city through legacies remained in the possession of the city. Revenue from the confiscated 'lots' was paid into the treasury of the ἀποδέκται, while revenue of the unconfiscated estates continued to pour into a separate civic treasury. But it is very unlikely that the atticist Julian, who in *Misop.* 370D used κλῆρος in place of the technical and Latin *iugum* (Déléage, *Capitation*, 160), should have used it in a different sense in 362c. Furthermore, even in the unlikely event that the 'lots' formed a separate category of land at Antioch, and perhaps a few other Hellenistic foundations, there is no reason at all to suppose that the bulk of the cities of the empire possessed land of a comparable category. Yet the confiscation of civic estates was universal.

[2] *C.T.* xii. 2 (349) = *C.J.* x. 37. The use of building material ἐκ τῶν πολειτικῶν προσόδων was fixed in the smallest detail for each year of the indiction by the proconsul of Achaea in 359 at Chalcis: *I.G.* xii. 9. 907.

[3] Jones, *G.C.* 136.　　　　　　　　　　[4] Julian, *Misop.* 370D.

[5] *C.T.* v. 13. 3 (364), x. 1. 8 (364) refer to temple lands; *C.T.* vii. 7. 2 shows that in September 365 city councils were hiring out the use of civic pastures to competitive bidders. Thus secular possessions of cities were probably confiscated later

permanent: the properties *iuris rei publicae* still formed a category of land under the imperial *res privata* in the reign of Justinian.

It is all the more surprising that the evidence of writings of the last decade of Libanius' life leaves no doubt that the council continued to administer landed estate bequeathed to the city by 'men of old'. The estates were farmed for the city, and their produce was, or should have been, the property of the city.[1] Thus argued Libanius in 385, urging that animals taken from these estates should carry the building rubble out of the city. After the Riot of the Statues, the city briefly lost its lands, τὴν αὐτῆς γῆν, but among other privileges the forgiving emperor soon restored its wealth to the city.[2] Between 388 and 390 we hear that a doctor, who farmed land belonging to the council, always paid his rents and sometimes exceeded them[3]. These civic lands had not been acquired after the confiscation of civic resources: men who had died within twenty years would hardly be described as 'men of old'.[4] The council was still administering at least part of the old civic estates. Petit has argued that the city estates fell into several categories and that only one of these categories was confiscated. This in itself would be perfectly possible, even though Petit's reconstruction of the set-up does not convince. Nevertheless the known facts can be explained without the hypothesis of the existence of several categories of civic land. Elsewhere[5] I have argued that, after a short period of direct administration by agents of the *res privata*, the government returned the administration of the lands to the civic councils against the payment of two-thirds of the so-called *canon*, a rent fixed once and for all, to the *res privata*. As a result of this arrangement the city would once again have a regular income. Moreover since the share allotted to the *res privata* was fixed, a council would be able to increase its income by raising the rents of the estates. Alternatively it would be in a position to subsidize its members in the traditional way by leasing lands to councillors on

---

than temple lands. Bruns, ed. 7, 97 = *F.I.R.* i². 108 (370 or 371) shows that confiscation of civic lands was complete.

[1] *Or.* l. 5.

[2] *Or.* xx. 7 records its restoration; cf. ibid. 38: τὰς οὐσίας.

[3] *Or.* lii. 33.

[4] *Or.* l. 5: παρὰ παλαιῶν ἀνδρῶν ἐν διαθήκαις δεδομένα τῇ πόλει.

[5] On Petit's view see p. 153 n. 1 above. For my explanation see 'The finances of Antioch in the 4th century A.D.', *B.Z.* lii (1959), 344–56.

favourable terms. The consequences of confiscation were thus softened considerably.[1]

Nevertheless one would expect the loss of two-thirds of the civic income to have had a significant effect on the services of the city. If estates really amounted to more than ten thousand *iuga* the effect of confiscations ought to have been dramatic, but even if the estates were much smaller it should have been noticeable. The surprising thing is that as far as Antioch is concerned we do not hear of any effects at all. In the speeches composed under the Emperor Theodosius, Libanius has much to say about the troubles of the council, but he never argues that loss of civic revenue owing to the confiscation of the estates had anything to do with it. Again, any significant economies on the major civic services would surely have provoked public disturbances. There is no evidence that any such disturbances took place.

A possible explanation is that part of the decline in civic revenue was made up out of imperial funds, drawn either from taxation or from the *res privata*. We know that the emperor did spend money on Antioch. As we have seen the Olympic Games[2] and the Syriarchy[3] received grants from the imperial treasury. The emperor gave horses for chariot races.[4] He spent money on great building schemes[5] and he paid a salary to Libanius and possibly other teachers in the city.[6] But the largest imperial contribution by far must have been absorbed by the food distribution, which is first mentioned in connection with the Riot of the Statues in 387.[7]

Thus the imperial government undoubtedly did accept responsibility for the well-being of the inhabitants of Antioch. This being so, it would be unlikely to adopt a measure which would inevitably result in a massive reduction of the amenities

---

[1] The estates of a particular city continued to be a unit of administration: *C.T.* xv. 1. 18 (374); cf. *Nov. Th.* 23, *Nov. Marc.* 3. They continued to be let largely to councillors: *C.J.* xi. 59. 5 (376 or 377), *C.T.* x. 3. 4 (384), ibid. 3. 5 (400). The councillors collected the whole rent before handing over two-thirds to the imperial authorities: *C.T.* xv. 1. 33 (395).

[2] *Ep.* 439 (355). *C.J.* i. 36, definite sums were set aside for the subsidy of Olympic Games and Syriarchy.

[3] See above, p. 141.   [4] *Ep.* 381 (358).   [5] See above, p. 135.

[6] See above, p. 44; Libanius' rival drew πυρός (*annona*), *Or.* i. 110; imperial salary of sophist of Elusa, *Ep.* 132.

[7] See above, p. 129. *Nov.* (Just. II) cxlix of 569 suggests that imperial subsidies for fortifications, heating of baths, and theatricals were not unusual.

of the city. I would therefore suggest that when the imperial government confiscated the civic estates it took over at the same time responsibility for some of the fixed and regularly recurring expenses that had been met out of their revenue. An example of this may be provided by the retaining fee paid to the actors, at least part of which was derived from the spoils of temples.[1] The simplest explanation is that the emperor had assigned the revenues of certain confiscated temple properties for this purpose. Another example of extended imperial responsibility may be provided by the food distributions, which as I have argued earlier, were not yet in existence during Julian's stay at Antioch. They could well have been introduced to compensate the city for any reduction in the corn-buying capacity of the civic authorities. If the preceding argument is correct, it would follow that the city felt the loss of revenue only when new or irregular expenses had to be met. This may be the reason why the laws forbidding cities the use of more than the third of the *canon* allotted to them envisage expenditure on buildings and fortifications,[2] not on corn nor on police, education, the theatre, nor any other form of entertainment except heating of the baths.[3]

Whether the suggested increase in imperial expenditure actually took place or not, it remains unlikely that any service which benefited the bulk of the population was reduced as a result of the confiscation of the estates. There is, however, evidence of economies in other fields. Expenditure on pagan cult in the largely Christian city had become minimal. Julian complained of this fact at the time when his pagan revival was at its height.[4] Libanius never mentions the gymnasium. It had no doubt ceased to function at Antioch as elsewhere. It cannot be chance that the evidence for the gymnasia and their officials fades out just in the years when the civic estates and taxes were finally confiscated.[5] The ephebate had already come to an end at Antioch before the beginning of the century.[6] The Museion too was decrepit, for at one time at least it served as the headquarters

---

[1] *Or.* xxvi. 24.

[2] *C.T.* xv. 1. 18 (374), v. 14. 35 (395), xv. 1. 32 (395), 33 (395).

[3] Ibid. xv. 1. 32 (395); but iv. 13. 7 (374) refers to *probabilibus expensis*.

[4] Julian, *Misop.* 362.

[5] See above, p. 140; cf. Claude, *Byzantinische Stadt*, 75–6, on evidence for end of odea, gymnasia, and palaestra.

[6] See above, p. 140.

of the *comes orientis*.[1] These were changes of the very greatest
cultural significance. 'The collapse of the gymnasia (the focal
point of Hellenism) . . . more than any other single event brought
in the Middle Ages.'[2] It is part of the same trend that we hear of
only few competitions in rhetoric or poetry for prizes awarded
by the city.[3] This is all the more significant since we are observing
Antioch through the eyes of a sophist who might be expected
to be interested in such occasions. But his writings leave the impression that patronage of great men, rather than festive competition, provided the rewards for artists.[4] But even in the sphere
of the cultural services the decline must not be exaggerated.
While there was a reduction in many activities characteristic of
Hellenic life, literary schooling for children was perhaps more
widespread and systematic than ever before.[5] But education, unlike the other activities, was subsidized, since a number of teachers
drew imperial salaries.

We have no statement of the total cost of the services provided
for the citizens of Antioch. But an estimate of the order of magnitude is possible. A law issued in 409 confirms a grant of six
hundred *solidi* by which the chronically unstable finances of the
magistrates (i.e. the holders of liturgies?) have been restored.[6]
Now for a grant of this kind to achieve its purpose it must have
been of the same order of magnitude as the expenses of the
magistrates of Antioch.

The significance of a sum of six hundred *solidi* can be seen by
comparing it with salaries of the period. It is a third larger than
the salary of the augustal prefect of Egypt,[7] of the same order
as the income of the bishop of a large city.[8] More to the point,
it would pay for twelve first-grade African lions for the public
spectacles.[9] On the other hand the purchase of corn in times of

[1] Malalas 317. But in 354 it was used for teaching: Norman, *Libanius, Auto-
biography*, note on i. 102. It was still standing in 438; Downey, *Antioch*, 450, *Chron.
Pasch.* 584–5. On 'museums' as centres of education see references in Marrou,
Histoire de l'éducation, 528, n. 14.

[2] E. G. Turner, *Greek Papyri* (Oxford, 1968), 84; cf. M. P. Nilsson, *Die Hellenistische Schule*, 84.

[3] Reduction in literary festivals and competitions, *Or.* xlviii. 32.

[4] A. Cameron, 'Wandering Poets', *Historia* xiv (1965), 470–509, esp. 484 ff.

[5] Marrou, op. cit. 406 ff.   [6] *C.T.* xii. 1. 169 (409).

[7] Jones, *L.R.E.* 397; Just. *Ed.* xiii. 3.

[8] *L.R.E.* 905–6; Just. *Nov.* cxxiii. 3.

[9] *S.E.G.* xiv. 386; *L.R.E.* 1017–18.

shortage would require expenditure of an enormously greater scale to be a significant contribution to the feeding of one hundred and fifty thousand people. It might be added that six hundred or even one thousand *solidi* would be only a small proportion of the income of ten thousand *iuga* of civic estate.[1]

Of course we have seen that liturgies did not pay for the whole of the civic services. Services not paid out of liturgies included some building work, the maintenance of dancers, and the salaries of teachers and doctors. Now it is quite impossible to estimate the expense of the first two items, but for the salaries of doctors and teachers we have Justinian's regulations for Carthage. The total wage bill comes to five hundred and ninety-nine *solidi*.[2] Antioch was a city of similar importance and her doctors and teachers are likely to have received a comparable wage. I would conclude that the cost of civic services not met out of liturgies is likely to have been of at least the same order of magnitude as that met out of liturgies—and this is leaving out of account the unknown but certainly large cost of the food distribution. If this is included in the reckoning, liturgies would only account for a small fraction of civic expenditure.

We are faced with a long-term trend. In the Early Empire councillors had far more money to spend. Six hundred *solidi* might be expended on a single festival of an ordinary Italian *municipium*. On the other hand in the reign of Justinian the councillors of Alexandria contributed a mere one hundred *solidi* out of a total civic budget of 1,889 *solidi*.[3] In contrast the *augustalis* provided three hundred and twenty *solidi*, presumably from taxation. We do not know the sources of the rest of the funds, but they were evidently not provided by liturgies.[4]

The importance of councillors for the financing of the civic services was declining, and the finances of Antioch towards the end of the fourth century were moving towards the condition of those of Alexandria in the reign of Justinian. But one important institution of the sixth-century city was still missing: the four

---

[1] Price of wheat: *L.R.E.* 445–7, a single soldier's annual ration of wheat might cost 1⅓ *solidi*. *Rents*: *L.R.E.* 807; a common rent was ⅓ *solidus* per *arura*.

[2] *C.J.* i. 27. 1. 41 (534).

[3] Just. *Ed.* xiii. 15; Johnson and West, *Byzantine Egypt*, 104–5.

[4] But *C.J.* i. 4. 26 (530) and x. 30. 40. 4 (530) show that money was still being provided for civic expenses by private individuals. Just. *Nov.* cxxviii. 116 (545) makes no reference to this.

factions. The Reds, Blues, Greens, and Whites, which had existed at Rome at least since the beginning of the empire, basically represented a rationalization of the entertainment liturgies. They were large semi-public corporations which furnished everything in the way of equipment or performers required for a theatrical show or a chariot race, and would relieve the liturgant of much of the trouble of organization and all capital outlay.[1] But the four factions did not yet exist at Antioch during the fourth century.

This dogmatic statement needs justification, for Malalas, who was, as we have seen, in many ways well informed about Antioch, mentions factions there as early as the reign of Caligula.[2] But the evidence of fourth-century sources suggests that Malalas is wrong, and as is his habit has transferred conditions of his own time to a much earlier period. The factions are mentioned by neither Libanius nor John Chrysostomus. Moreover, Libanius tells us explicitly that the councillors of Antioch owned race horses while they were obliged to produce races, and sold them when they had completed their duty.[3] If the factions had existed, they and not the councillors would have owned the horses and even horses purchased by a liturgant would have been given to one or more of the factions.[4] Finally, the pattern of public disturbances at Antioch in the fourth century is quite different from that of the faction-centred rioting of Constantinople. A faction was a permanent organization like a modern football club and tended to build up a great following of supporters whose rivalry with the supporters of other factions easily degenerated into rioting. Where chariots raced under the always-changing names of a succession of curial liturgants, permanent loyalties would not develop, and we do not hear of characteristic hippodrome disturbances. At Antioch race meetings were untroubled.[5] The theatre was the centre of disorder, and responsibility for this is

[1] Friedländer, *Sittengeschichte*, vol. 2. 32–40 (vol. 2. 27–33 in English edn.), on among others: Suet. *Nero* 22. 2, Dio. lxi. 6. 2, lvi. 27. 4; S.H.A. *Commod.* 16. 9.

[2] Malalas 244. 15; I would suggest that the reference to the Greens engaging in rioting against the Jews is an anachronistic reflection of later conditions when the Jews sat with the Blues. Otherwise Stauffenberg, *Kaisergeschichte*, 188–93.

[3] *Or.* xxxv. 14.

[4] Emperors presented horses to the factions with reservations as to their future use: *C.T.* xv. 7. 6 (381) (= *C.J.* xi. 41. 2); *C.T.* xv. 10. 1 (371), 2 (381).

[5] The psychology of a young faction supporter, Menander the Protector: *Suda*, 703. Untroubled race meetings at Antioch: *Or.* xi. 268.

assigned not to the factions but to the claque.[1] Conceivably, the claque could have been furnished by factions, but there is no suggestion at all that the claque was divided into rival groups.

In at least two other cities of the East the situation appears to have resembled that at Antioch. At Alexandria civic disturbances arose in the theatre rather than in the hippodrome,[2] and at Gaza race horses clearly were entered in the name of the liturgants not of the factions.[3] It looks as if at about 400 the factions were not yet organizing the civic entertainments in Greek cities other than Constantinople.

We do not know when the factions came to Antioch. The earliest reliably reported faction riot occurred in the last years of the emperor Zeno, about 490.[4] But we have hints, no more, that an important reorganization of the entertainments of the cities of the East had taken place many years earlier. Two laws of 426 mention officials described respectively as *cornicularii thymelae equorumque* and *actuarii thymelae et equorum currulium*, who are found at Constantinople and other cities, and whose appointment must be confirmed by the emperor.[5] The titles of the officials suggest that the theatre and the hippodrome were now under joint administration and formed a separate department from the other civic services. That one of the officials had the title *actuarius* suggests that he was concerned with the distribution of *annona*.[6] This may mean that horses and drivers and actors were at this time largely maintained out of taxation, in the same way that the evidence suggests that they were being maintained at Rome.[7]

---

[1] See below, pp. 212 ff. *Or*. xxxv. 13 mentions a claque of the hippodrome but this is not blamed for disturbances.

[2] Socrates, *H.E.* vii. 13.

[3] Jer. *V. Hil.* 20.

[4] Malalas 389–90; Downey, *Antioch*, 498 ff.

[5] *C.T.* viii. 7. 21 (426, *P.P.O.*): 'irenarchas quoque et cornicularios tam classium urbis Constantinopolitanae quam thymelae equorumque currulium civitatum diversarum non aliter nisi . . . manus sanxerit principalis praecipiat ordinari'; cf. ibid. 22 (426, *P.U. Cpl.*): 'actuarios quoque thymelae et equorum currulium, suarios etiam et optiones per omnes regiones urbis Constantinopolitanae'.

[6] *L.R.E.*, 706.

[7] The fourth-century Roman factions were semi-public institutions: 1. The horses did not pass into full ownership of the organization (*C.T.* xv. 10. 1 (371), 7. 6 (381)). 2. At least some of the fodder was publicly supplied. ibid. 10. 1: fodder for pensioned-off Palmatian and Hermogenian horses; ibid. 2: a levy of beans from Capua).

The factions might well have been introduced as part of a new organization, which would have had the purpose of remodelling the administration of theatrical shows and chariot races of the Eastern cities, in accordance with a pattern that was being followed at Constantinople, and at Rome and other cities of the Latin West.[1] Indeed, the factions of Constantinople could have been used to advise and equip branch organizations elsewhere.[2] This would explain the sense of solidarity which came to unite supporters of the same colour in widely separated cities.

7. IMPERIAL TAXATION

The duties the councillors performed for imperial taxation have no direct relevance to the civic services. But indirectly they are extremely relevant. The energy and finance that had to be devoted to imperial taxation was not available for the city. If the councillors of the fourth century had less money to spend on behalf of the city than councillors of the second century, this was at least partly because they were required both as taxpayers and as tax collectors to make a greater contribution to the empire. If the scope of the civic activities of the councillors contracted until they were little more than unpaid tax collectors, this can only have come about because the imperial government was ready to condone neglect of civic duties, but never ceased to insist that taxes must be collected.

Most of the duties performed by councillors for the imperial government were connected with the land tax, which was assessed and raised in kind on the basis of the *iugatio–capitatio*.[3] This tax comprised a great variety of levies of different types which satisfied all needs of the civil and military administration,

[1] There is evidence for the existence of factions in provincial cities of the Latin West under the Early Empire, e.g. *I.L.S.* 5308, 5307, 5278, 5312–13, 9348. Tert. *Apol.* 38. 2, uses *factio* generally, to describe associations of any kind. In the fourth century they were also at Constantinople, e.g. Greg. Naz. *P.G.* xxxvi. 301–4. But I have seen no reliable evidence that they existed at this time anywhere else in the Greek East. Malalas' story of the origin of the factions (Malalas 173 ff.), a fantastic piece of folk legend, treats them as something Roman.

[2] Malalas 507, charioteer Calliopas transferred to the Greens of Antioch from faction staff of Constantinople (ἀπὸ φακτιοναρίων Κωνσταντινοπόλεως); cf. A. D. Vasiliev, *Dumbarton Oaks Papers* iv (1948), 22–49.

[3] Déléage, *La Capitation du Bas-Empire* (Mâcon, 1945); Jones, *L.R.E.* 448–62.

ranging from recruits to wheat.[1] Assessment, distribution, collection, transport, and storage of levies was an extremely complicated operation, involving numerous compulsory duties by curial and village officials. The full complexity of the machinery is revealed by Egyptian papyrus documents.[2] Compared with these the evidence of Libanius is fragmentary and vague. It provides impressions rather than an objective description of the situation.

The evidence of Libanius suggests that the pressure of taxation was heavy in the years before the death of Constantius, that is in the years when the Persians resumed their attacks on Mesopotamia. In 359–60 Priscianus, governor of the province of Euphratensis, had to work hard to satisfy the demands of his superior. No doubt the problem was the raising of supplies for the army. In his letters, Priscianus complained of the poverty of his province and Libanius replied that there was poverty at Antioch also.[3] Among the one thousand five hundred and forty-four surviving letters of Libanius, very few mention taxation. It is surely no coincidence that a large proportion of the letters that do mention it was written at this time. One Herodianus was fined for some tax offence.[4] Libanius asked that the fine should be remitted and the tax not increased. The consular of Phoenicia is asked not to let one Sophronius suffer loss by reason of his ownership of horses. Presumably Sophronius was threatened with requisition or compulsory purchase.[5] Another letter is written for a man who has been subjected to an unjust exaction at the behest of Ursulus the *comes sacrarum largitionum*.[6] In 361 Libanius complains to Modestus, the *comes orientis*, that one Dulcitius, owning an estate near Beroea (Aleppo), has been forced to sell grain, evidently at a loss, to deceitful officials.[7]

---

[1] Déléage, op. cit. 23–33; 71–80.

[2] Lallemand, *L'Administration civile de l'Égypte*, 205–19. The duties were time-consuming: Aurelius Isodorus of Karanis held six posts largely concerned with tax-gathering between 300–1 and 313. Aurelius Sakaon of Theadelphia served seven or possibly ten years in such posts (307–42). Most duties involved personal liability for deficits. See A. E. R. Boak, 'An Egyptian Farmer of the Age of Diocletian and Constantine', *Byzantina Metabyzantina* i (1946), 40–53.

[3] *Ep.* 149, 160, 625.   [4] *Ep.* 307 (361).

[5] *Ep.* 313 (357); *C.T.* xi. 17. 1–4.

[6] *Ep.* 221 (360?); a similar exaction *Ep.* 163 (359–60), the agents of the *sacra largitio* invade the house of a recently deposed governor like brigands. On court-martial of Ursulus: Amm. xx. 2. 5, Lib. *Or.* xviii. 152.

[7] *Ep.* 276 (361); cf. Mazzarino, *Aspetti sociali*, 161–2.

Letters also show that there was tension among the councillors of Antioch.[1] Many years later, Libanius was to claim that the Persian wars had greatly weakened the council. Year after year, councillors had been sent to the Tigris and incurred huge expenses there which they could only meet by selling their ancestral estates.[2] A letter of 358 helps to explain how this happened. The fortress of Callinicum on the Euphrates was supplied from Syria and the supplies were transported part of the way by the Syrians.[3] It is likely that the cost of transport was imposed on the councillors, including those of Antioch. Callinicum was on the Euphrates, not the Tigris, but it is conceivable that at a time when large armies were fighting on the Tigris, the duty of the Antiochenes to send supplies to the Euphrates was extended to cover the zone of operations. A glance at a map will show that, even if we leave out of consideration the hazards of the desert,[4] the transport of corn from the neighbourhood of Antioch to the Tigris must have been very expensive indeed. Since the period of military crisis covered by the letters of Libanius was very short in comparison with the long succession of campaigns against the Persians, who invaded Mesopotamia almost every summer between 337 and 351, and then again in 359–61, it is easy to see that the needs of the army in Mesopotamia during these years must have placed a crushing burden on the council of Antioch. We can therefore accept Libanius' statement that the council grew weaker every year under the pressure.

Julian granted or remitted arrears of taxation to cities generally[5] and to Antioch in particular,[6] but his Persian campaign must have imposed some new burdens. There are few references to taxation in letters written under Julian, and in the years following his death, even though the letters of 364 are preserved very fully.

---

[1] *Ep.* 643 (361), attempt to enrol Miccalus, brother of senator Olympius, son of ex-governor Pompeianus into the council; 639, attempt to enrole Libanius' brother. 644, 661, 677 show Libanius worried.

[2] *Or.* xlix. 2.

[3] *Ep.* 21 (358), ἣν δεῖ τρέφεσθαι παρ' ἡμῶν οὐκ ἐκεῖσε κομιζόντων, ἀλλ' ἑτέρωσε τὴν τροφήν, ἐκεῖθεν δὲ εἰς Καλλίνικον ἄγειν νόμος τὸν ἄρχοντα τῶν περὶ τὸν Εὐφράτην.

[4] Josh. Styl. 82.

[5] Julian, *Misop.* 365, 366–7D; Amm. xxv. 4. 15; *Or.* xviii. 193; Julian, *Ep.* 73 (Bidez–Cumont) to Thracians; W. Ensslin, 'Kaiser Julians Gesetzgebungswerk und Reichsverwaltung', *Klio* xviii (1923), 127–44. Julian's campaign must have produced new burdens: *Ep.* 1351, 1392.

[6] G. Downey, *Studies in Econ. and Soc. Hist. in honor of A. C. Johnson* (Princeton, 1951), 314–15.

Peace with Persia is likely to have resulted in lower taxes. The Emperor Valens is praised by Themistius for first stabilizing and then halving the indiction.[1]

By 380, after the battle of Adrianople, taxes were heavy again. In a speech of 381 Libanius mentions deserted villages, villages deserted because of the combined depredations of monks and taxes. At the time he professes to consider the monks the worse evil.[2] That the taxes had forced Syrian land out of cultivation is asserted by Theodoret, bishop of Cyrrhus, about forty years later.[3] One wonders how far these statements refer to a trend, how far to special circumstances. After all, archaeological evidence suggests that on the whole, the fourth and fifth centuries were a period of prosperity and expansion in the villages of northern Syria. There is, however, other evidence that taxation was a heavy burden in the 380s. Tissamenes, the consular of 386, forced the taxpayers to pay the whole of the year's tax by the end of the fourth month. A number of persons, both councillors who were collecting the tax, and ordinary taxpayers, received beatings from the 'soldiers'[4] of the consular. In 387 the Riot of the Statues developed out of a demonstration against taxes demanded in a recently arrived imperial letter.[5] Since the whole landed upper class, *honorati*, councillors, advocates, and even veterans had taken part in the protest it would seem that the letters must have demanded a 'superindiction', a supplementary levy on the land tax.[6] The previous year had brought the extremely burdensome levy of the Traders' Tax,[7] and in the year after the riot one embassy, perhaps two, carried crown gold to the Emperor Theodosius.[8] Governors complained that the long hours devoted to the taxes left them insufficient time for their judicial duties.[9]

---

[1] Jones, *L.R.E.* 147.   [2] *Or.* ii. 32.

[3] Theodoret, *Ep.* 43 (*P.G.* lxxxiii. 1220–1); on taxation of Cyrrhus, id. *Ep.* 43, 44, 45, 47, Déléage, *Capitation*, 160–1.

[4] *Or.* xxxiii. 19–20, 32; Theod. *H.E.* iv. 5, a band normally employed to persuade unwilling tax-payers with sticks and clubs used to break up an orthodox crowd.

[5] *Or.* xix. 25; Theod. *H.E.* v. 19 (*P.G.* lxxxii. 1240–1), some taxpayers tortured. Joh. Chrys. *Hom. ad pop. Ant.* 8. 4 (*P.G.* xlix. 102), the greater part of the gold has been collected.

[6] *Or.* xix. 25; Petit, *Libanius*, 146; R. Browning, *J.R.S.* xlii (1952), 14–15.

[7] *Or.* xxxiii. 33, xxxvi. 4.

[8] See Petit, *Libanius*, Appendix V.   [9] *Or.* xlv. 24.

In this situation there was considerable pressure on the councillors. It is clear from several passages that as far as the government was concerned, the individual tax collector was personally responsible for the taxes which he was required to collect.[1] If he failed to collect the tax, he was beaten, unless he paid the deficit out of his own pocket, if necessary by selling his land. At this stage, there is no evidence that the responsibility of the council as a whole[2] came into play. All the official pressure was on the individual tax collector. The responsibility of the council was evidently invoked only when the individual tax collector's property had proved insufficient.[3] There was, of course, nothing to stop a wealthy councillor from volunteering to help a colleague in difficulties before he went bankrupt, but this, according to Libanius, was not usual—quite the contrary. Leading councillors exploited the difficulties of poorer colleagues to buy their land cheaply, or even to use it to win the support of the powerful.[4]

In these years the councillors were also heavily burdened by a maritime corn transport duty.[5] In 390, among the reasons given to explain why Libanius' son wished to avoid the council was that he feared ships and corn and the sea.[6] Evidently corn transport by sea was among the most expensive duties required of councillors at the time. In 388 torture was threatened to compel the councillor Romulus to 'send corn on ships' in spite of the fact that he had been previously released from this duty on the ground of poverty.[7] Under the same governorship, Libanius tried to have the ship of his assistant Thalassius exempted from the necessity of carrying corn. Such exemption had been granted to others as there was no shortage of ships. Nevertheless the request was turned down, 'just as if the safety of the emperor and of his soldiers and of the two capital cities depended on the one ship of Thalassius'.[8] No doubt the need for sea transport of corn arose from the campaign against the usurper Maximus.

---

[1] *Or.* xxxiii. 32, xlvii. 8, xlv. 24. [2] *C.T.* xii. 6. 20 (386).
[3] Jones, *L.R.E.* 457 on *P.S.I.* 684.

[4] *Or.* xlviii. 37; unlike Petit (*Libanius*, 152–3) I cannot see in this passage a reference to the collective responsibility of the council as a whole. The rich councillors deprive their poorer colleagues of land for personal profit or to gain powerful friends. There is no hint that they make up their colleagues' deficits.

[5] See my article in *Rh. M.* civ (1961), 242–56.

[6] *Ep.* 595 (390); Jones, *L.R.E.* 829, n. 11, thinks that *curia* and *navicularia functio* are alternatives.

[7] *Or.* liv. 40. [8] Ibid. 47.

The circumstances produced tension among the curial class. In 387 Libanius was very careful to establish in a speech that he had not helped anybody to avoid a particular liturgy.[1] This speech, and reforms attempted by the praetorian prefects Cynegius and Tatian,[2] suggest that the decline in numbers and wealth of the council had been considerable. It is a reasonable deduction that the years of heavy tax pressure had contributed to this weakening.

While there can be no doubt that at certain times the pressure on the council was felt to be heavy, it is quite impossible to make an objective assessment. We depend on general statements which cannot be checked against individual cases. Libanius only mentions one councillor who has actually been bankrupted by tax collecting.[3] It is possible that this means that bankruptcies were rare, and that as a rule the collectors were able to force the whole of the required tax, and more, out of the helpless peasants. On the other hand Libanius' information about taxation is so incomplete that any deductions from silence are hazardous. It could be that the making up of deficits out of the collector's own pocket was simply taken for granted. It is, however, likely that the greatest damage to the council was not caused by actual financial losses, but by fear and uncertainty aroused in the minds of councillors by the pressure of the government. Corporal punishment, with or without lashes weighted with lead, was the established punishment for men who did not collect the tax assigned to them, and fear of this punishment was a powerful motive to induce councillors to desert their councils.[4]

---

[1] *Or.* xxxii. 12.   [2] See below, pp. 271 ff.

[3] *Or.* xlvii. 7–10. A few others are said to have been impoverished, e.g. *Ep.* 1398 (363), fortune of Urbicius of Apamea greatly diminished; cf. *Ep.* 715. 6. A case of *cessio bonorum*: *Ep.* 1496 (365), a Galatian decurion.

[4] Jones, *L.R.E.* 750; *Or.* xxxiii. 32, xxviii. 7; ibid. 16 shows that the taxes were involved; xlvii. 8, xlv. 24; *C.T.* xii. 1. 126 (392): even *principales* must be *devoti nihil debentes* if they are to enjoy immunity from beatings. Beatings of councillors for various reasons: xxviii. 24 (Eustochius), xxviii. 24 (Hermeias beaten to death), liv. 51 (Monimus beaten to death), xxviii. 9 ff.(Lamachus), liv. 42–3 (supervisor of lentil-sellers), xxv. 43; beatings empty the councils, xxviii. 22–3.

V

THE TRANSFORMATION OF
CIVIC INSTITUTIONS

I. THE CHANGING CHARACTER OF THE COUNCIL[1]

OUR survey of the administration of Antioch has shown certain areas in which the council made decisions. It could pass resolutions to be carried by embassies to the emperor. It appointed and granted immunity to sophists. It administered the old civic estates and controlled the expenditure of part of the old revenues on civic services. Also, as will be discussed later, it was responsible for the maintenance of its own numbers. But none of these activities involved decisions of policy. It was the council's duty to ensure that the services of the city were kept running and that the duties required by the empire, notably the collection of taxes, were performed. But all its activities were carried out under the supervision of the governors, and in practice all initiatives came from the imperial officials.

Essentially the council was a body which appointed men to perform the duties which the governors required to be done. We have only one account of how such appointments were made but that is illuminating. After the Riot of the Statues, the temporary military governor, Ellebichus, invited several councillors to a dinner, at the end of which he informed them that it was now time to send to the emperor the embassy which had been postponed on account of the riot. Three men volunteered at once and proceeded to look for a fourth ambassador. They found Eusebius, the sophist, Libanius' assistant and deputy. But the next morning at the general's audience the whole issue was reopened. Each of the councillors gave reasons that made it impossible for him to go to Constantinople and Libanius was

[1] Apart from the relevant sections of Jones, *G.C.* and *L.R.E.*, a good account of councils in the fourth century is found in J. Declareuil, 'Quelques problèmes d'histoire et des institutions municipales au temps de l'empire romain', *Nouvelle rev. hist. droit fr. et étrang.* (1902, 1904, 1907, 1908, 1910; published as a single volume in Paris, 1911).

instructed to find other ambassadors. The matter was next discussed in the council: without any decision. Finally, Libanius called in the general. Ellebichus entered the council chamber in an angry mood and soon had everyone willing to go. He then simply nominated some men and named others who were to look after the property of the ambassadors during their absence.[1]

The council was also held responsible collectively for the way the men it had appointed carried out their functions. We have noted the working of collective responsibility in the sphere of public order. The same principle was applied even more frequently in the sphere of taxation: not only was the individual tax collector liable to pay out of his own property any tax which he had failed to collect, but the council as a whole was obliged to make up the deficit if the collector's property was insufficient.[2]

In a situation characterized by collective responsibility and by the absence of politics there was very little scope for the exercise of personal initiative or leadership by civic magistrates of the traditional types. One would therefore expect the old offices to become merely honorific or to disappear altogether. This or something like it appears to have happened. In Egypt references to the old civic offices fade out in the course of the fourth century.[3] At Antioch the magistrates had already become insignificant by the middle of the century. At any rate the writings of Libanius do not contain a single reference to them. There is no indication even that Libanius regretted the good old days when civic magistracies were positions of influence and respect. The decline of the magistracies must have taken place long before his time. Civic magistrates, *duumviri*, continue to figure in legislation, mainly in laws addressed to Western officials. There is conclusive evidence that in cities of the West civic magistrates continued to be appointed into the seventh century, but none that their duties were more than formal.[4]

At Antioch early in the fourth century, the *curator* appears to have acted as the leading citizen. Significantly this official owed

---

[1] *Or.* xxxii. 2–6; cf. *Ep.* 550 (356–7).   [2] See above, p. 165.

[3] Johnson and West, *Byzantine Egypt*, 322, on the disappearance of the *archon*, *exegete*, *cosmete*, *agoranomus*, *eutheniarch*, and *prytanis*; F. Oertel, *Die Liturgie* (Leipzig, 1917), under the respective titles.

[4] Jones, *L.R.E.* 761; E. Stein, 'Die Munizipalverfassung von Ravenna vom IV. Jahrhundert bis zum Ende der oströmischen Herrschaft (751)', *Klio* xvi (1919), 59–71 = *Opera Minora* (Amsterdam, 1968), 20–32.

his pre-eminence to the imperial government, for *curatores* had originally been appointed by the central administration to supervise civic finance, and in the fourth century—at least in the West—their appointment was still confirmed by an imperial letter.[1] Two *curatores* of Antioch left their mark in history. In 312 Theotecnus organized the pagan reaction for Maximinus Daia.[2] In 354 Luscus, a supporter of the Caesar Gallus, induced some soldiers to lynch the praetorian prefect Domitianus and the quaestor Montius.[3] On each occasion the *curator* would appear to have acted as the agent of an emperor rather than of the council or of the city.

In the second half of the fourth century the *curator* seems to have lost importance all over the empire.[4] One reason for this is that the imperial government had greatly reduced the need for supervision of civic finance by taking over a large part of the civic revenue. At the same time the *curator*'s status will have been closely assimilated to that of a civic official. At any rate no further *curator* is known to have played a prominent role at Antioch.[5]

The only local official mentioned at this time as performing more than a narrow liturgical or supervisory role is the *defensor*: this office too was an imperial creation. It owed its importance to the Emperors Valentinian and Valens. It was intended to champion the lower orders against the oppression of the powerful and to counter the growing extra-legal power of patrons by the establishment of an officially authorized patron.[6] We observe the *defensor* of Antioch acting in precisely this capacity. A baker's wife had suffered extortion on the part of an official. As was his habit in such cases, Libanius took her to the *defensor* (σύνδικος τῆς πόλεως). The extorted money was restituted.[7] But on another

---

[1] Jones, *G.C.* 136–8; *C.T.* xii. 1. 20 (331); Jones, *L.R.E.* 726.

[2] Eus. *H.E.* ix. 2; Downey, *Antioch*, 333–4.   [3] Amm. xiv. 7. 17.

[4] *C.T.* viii, 12. 3 (316) reversed by 8 (415) because of *vilitas* of *curator*.

[5] *Or.* xlvi. 13 is the only reference: the λογιστής and the σύνδικος, surely the *defensor*, exploit the tavern keepers. Libanius refers to them as δύ' ἄρχοντε, a title he reserves for imperial functionaries, cf. Petit, *Libanius*, 72 ff.

[6] B. R. Rees, 'The *Defensor Civitatis* in Egypt', *J. Jur. Pap.* vi (1952), 73–102; Jones, *L.R.E.* 726–7; also below, p. 205.

[7] *Or.* xxix. 12 identifying the σύνδικος τῆς πόλεως with the *defensor*. But the plain σύνδικοι of, e.g. *Or.* x. 4, xxviii. 3, xxiii. 25; xxxvi, 7 are simply advocates who have a semi-official position because they are registered with a court. Here σύνδικος is a synonym for ῥήτωρ; otherwise Petit, *Libanius*, 79.

occasion the *defensor*, far from protecting the tavern keepers from
wrong, joined his colleague, the *curator*, in exploiting them.[1]
Twice, the *defensor* appears to be exercising a wider authority.
We read that he invited the *comes orientis* Icarius to the theatre
on behalf of the city.[2] Another time he induced the notables of
the city to welcome their recently deposed governor Lucianus
outside the gates, under the mistaken impression that he had
regained office.[3] The *defensor* might thus occasionally act as if
he were the leader of the city, but he was not the representative
of the council. Membership of the council was a disqualification
for the office of *defensor*. The council might select a man for the
defensorship but the formal appointment was made by the praetorian prefect.[4] Even so, the importance of the *defensor* must not
be exaggerated. In the tense and anxious days after the Riot of
the Statues, the city was without a secular leader.

It has been argued that the apparent insignificance of *curator*
and *defensor* reflects the strength and influence of the leading
members of the council who overshadowed these agents of
imperial control.[5] But there is really no evidence for this. The
regular appointment by the central government of a supervisory
official in every city was a task beyond the capacity of ancient
bureaucracy. As a result the agents of control were sooner or
later absorbed into the system of local government, and came to
share its weakness in face of provincial governors. At Antioch,
the residence of three powerful imperial officials, the pressure
was exceptionally heavy.

While the old magistracies were dwindling into insignificance,
the organization of the council itself was changing and its traditional structure assimilated to the standard Late Empire pattern. In the *Antiochicus* Libanius gives a tantalizingly brief account
of the working of the council.[6] It is divided into three classes
(τέλη). The council appoints leaders for each class and the rank
and file follow where their hard-working 'generals' lead.

---

[1] *Or.* xlvi. 13.   [2] *Or.* xxvii. 32.   [3] *Or.* lvi. 9.

[4] *C.T.* i. 29. 1 (368); chosen by council: ibid. 6 (387); but the appointment
remained formally with the prefect: Just. *Nov.* viii, *notitia*, 37 (535); Jones, *L.R.E.*
727 n. 31.

[5] Petit, *Libanius*, 88; R. Ganghoffer, *L'Évolution des institutions municipales en
occident et en orient au bas-empire* (Paris, 1963), 173.

[6] *Or.* xi. 144, cf. *Ep.* 1393 (363), councillors of Tarsus filling up τὸν τέταρτον
χορόν of their council?

A letter of 364[1] may throw light on the function of the classes. Ariston, a man belonging to 'the second συμμορία', is performing a duty of tax collecting. Now some people want him to become 'supervisor of stonemasons'. Ariston's συμμορία protests. The current regulations require that the 'supervisor of stonemasons' should be furnished by another συμμορία, that led by Conon. The second συμμορία has therefore passed a resolution requesting the consular of Syria to free Ariston from the illegal threat.

If we are justified in identifying the τέλη of the *Antiochicus* with the συμμορίαι of the letter, it follows that each class of the council had specific duties assigned to it. The men who would undertake the duties assigned to a particular class would be selected by, and normally from among, the members of the class.[2]

But in the 380s this division of labour within the council had broken down. 'Do you observe us standing before you, easily counted, we who were 1,200 and are now 12? That is the council. ... By us are performed the duties in the city, the duties in the countryside, the greater duties and the lesser, the lighter and the heavier. On this account you hear the names of the same persons [again and again?].'[3] This situation is incompatible with the working of the class organization. As long as this was followed, a councillor would only perform the duties of his class and there would be no need for the same person to perform a lesser liturgy as well as a greater. In the 380s, it would seem, nominations to compulsory public services were made by and from the undivided council. This was the standard procedure in the cities of the empire.

At the same time a new leading class was developing within the council. In the two late orations on the subject of the council, Libanius is much concerned with the activities of a small group of powerful councillors who had taken over control of the council and were exploiting their power in their own interest. Especially, he claims, they sought by every means to keep the council small, because it was profitable to share with as few colleagues as possible the profits that could still be made out of membership.[4]

---

[1] *Ep.* 1176.
[2] The arrangement suggested here is unparalleled. A different explanation of the passages: Petit, *Libanius*, 85–6. See also A. F. Norman, *J.R.S.* xlviii (1958), 83.
[3] *Or.* xlix. 8.   [4] *Or.* xlviii. 4, 37–8, xlix. 8–11.

The existence of great inequalities of wealth within the council was certainly not new, and the richest councillors must always have exercised a disproportionate influence. Libanius' own family held a predominant position in the first half of the century.[1] But during the fourth century a powerful factor was strengthening the inherent tendency of a city council to fall under the control of its wealthiest members: the imperial policy towards the so-called *principales*.

In the imperial legislation of the fourth and fifth centuries the *principales* figure as a privileged group among the councillors. They were chosen by their colleagues[2] from the men who had performed the whole range of civic liturgies, and thus discharged all duties owed to their city.[3] As *principales* they would continue to sit in the council[4] and perform duties largely for the imperial government.[5] Individual *principales* might be given responsible missions. A *principalis* might supervise a guild,[6] or revise the census.[7] A *principalis* is likely to have taken the chair at a meeting of the council.[8] Collectively the *principales* acted as a kind of executive committee of the council. They had important financial duties. It was probably they who organized the distribution of various government levies and their collection.[9] *Principales* were

---

[1] His uncles Phasganius and Panolbius were leaders of the city. His cousin Marcus performed the Olympic Games and the Syriarchy (*Ep.* 544). His cousin Theodora was married to the Praetorian Prefect Thalassius. See above, p. 136, for the domination by Libanius' family and its allies of Olympic Games. On extreme concentration of wealth within the curial class in N. Africa see R. P. Duncan Jones, *P.B.S.R.* xxxi (1963), 165.

[2] On the still-obscure story of the *principales*: O. Seeck, 'Decemprimat und Dekaprotie', *Klio* i (1901), 147–87; Jones, *L.R.E.* 731 nn. 41–2. Election by council only stated *C.T.* xii. 1. 171 (412), *P.P. Gal.*; implied ibid. 75 (371), 'si . . . ab universo ordine comprobantur habeantur immunes'.

[3] *C.T.* xii. 1. 39 (350), 77 (372), 127 (392), *P.P.O.*

[4] Ibid. 127: 'a nexu propriae originis non recedat'; ibid. 189 (436) at Alexandria: 'nec senatoriis minime functionibus obstringatur, in curia tamen permaneat'. See also ibid. 171.

[5] Ibid. 39 (350), 150 (395), *P.P.O.*   [6] See below, p. 221.

[7] Basil, *Ep.* 281, but *peraequatores* might be chosen from ordinary councillors or *honorati*, Petit, *Libanius*, 149. *Principales* were excused the humbler and more personally inconvenient posts of ordinary councillors.

[8] Lallemand, *L'Administration civile de l'Égypte*, 126–7, on the προπολιτευόμενος in Egypt.

[9] *C.T.* xii. 1. 117 (387), *P.P.O.*; x. 25. 1 (406), *P.P.O.*; xii. 1. 173 (409), *P.P.O.* = *C.J.* x. 22. 1; the *potentes* among the *curiales* have been abusing the distribution of taxation to their own advantage and the disadvantage of their colleagues. *C.T.* xi. 16. 4 (328) = *C.J.* xi. 48. 1: the distribution of extraordinary levies is taken

also in charge of the register of the council; they inscribed new members—and allowed existing members to escape.[1] The *principales* were also made responsible for the enforcement of new laws, against pagans, for instance,[2] or against heretics.[3] They were instructed, together with the *curator* and *defensor*, to bring to justice men who abused the public post.[4] Tutors were ordered to declare the property of their wards before the *primates*, the *defensor*, and *officiales*.[5] In the law which granted immunity from taxation to the estates of the daughters of the Emperor Arcadius, it was ordered that these estates be registered as exempt in the presence of the *censuales* and of the *principales*, 'who undoubtedly are pressed by the burden resulting from this exemption'.[6]

In return for these duties and responsibilities *principales* were privileged above their colleagues in the council. While ordinary councillors were losing the privileges with regard to corporal punishment which they had once enjoyed, *principales* retained them.[7] In addition the status of *principalis* might be distinguished

away from *principales*. *C.T.* xii. 1. 126 (392), Praef. Aug.: *principales devoti et nihil debentes* are immune from corporal punishment, but evidently only after fulfilling considerable financial obligations. See also Lallemand, op. cit. 121.

[1] *C.T.* xii. 19. 3 (400), *P.P. Gal.*: *defensores* and *principales* responsible for taking action if decurions flee from council. ibid. xvi. 2. 39 (408), *P.P. Ital.*: unfrocked priests to be placed in *curia* or *collegia* by *decemprimi*. *Nov. Maj.* vii. 1. 18 (458), West: *principales* are guardians of rolls of *curiae* and *collegia*. *C.T.* xii. 1. 79 (375), *P.P.O.*; *principales* of Osroena, i.e. probably of city of Edessa, have obtained exemption for *curiales*.

[2] *C.T.* xvi. 10. 13 (395), *P.P.O.*

[3] *C.T.* xvi. 5. 40 (407) *P.U.R.* = *C.J.* i. 5. 4.

[4] *C.T.* viii. 5. 59 (400), *P.P. Ital. et Afr.* Also informed of law on deserters, *P.P. Ital. et Afr.*, *C.T.* vii. 18. 13 (403).

[5] *C.T.* iii. 30. 6 (396), *P.P.O.* = *C.J.* v. 37. 42.

[6] *C.T.* x. 25 (406).

[7] Legislation on the beating of councillors: *C.T.* xii. 1. 39 (after 349), *P.P. Illyr.*: all *curiales* and *primarii* exempt from corporal punishment. *C.T.* xii. 1. 75 (371) *P.P. Gal.*: chief priests of provinces and *principales* not to suffer corporal indignities unworthy of *honorati*. *C.T.* ix. 35. 2 (376), *P.P. Gal.*: all *curiales* exempt from torture except for treason and unspeakable practices; only *decemprimi* immune from lead scourges. *C.T.* xii. 1. 80 (380), Praef. Aegypt.: no decurions at all to be tortured or lead-whipped. Similar, *C.T.* xii. 1. 85 = *C.J.* x. 32. 33 (381), *P.P.O.*, to which Libanius appeals, *Or.* xxviii. 5, xxvii. 13. *C.T.* xii. 1. 126 (22 June 392), Praef. Aug.: *principales* who are loyal and *devoti* (have paid up) shall not suffer corporal indignities. *C.T.* xii. 1. 127 (30 June 392), *P.P.O.*: men who have performed all duties and reached first place in their city become count, class III, and immune from corporal indignities; the implication is that ordinary councillors were not immune. *C.T.* ix. 35. 6 (399), *P.P. Afr.* = *C.J.* ix. 41. 17, *principales* not to suffer corporal punishment. *C.T.* xii. 1. 190 (436), *P.P.O.* = *C.J.* x. 32. 57: the five *primates* of Alexandria immune from corporal indignities. The privileging of the

by honorary imperial rank.[1] The social rank of a *principalis* can be estimated from the fine laid down for members of this group in the anti-Donatist legislation: twenty pounds of gold. This places them at the same level as members of the senatorial order. Ordinary decurions are threatened with a fine of only five pounds.[2]

The government needed an executive committee to transmit its orders to local authorities and to watch over their enforcement. In consequence it privileged a number of councillors who carried out this service. For the actual fulfilment of its orders it needed men in innumerable liturgical posts. These were the ordinary councillors, and in their case there could be no question of privilege. The government was determined to exercise the utmost pressure on them through threats of punishment which had formerly not been applicable to councillors.

We are nearing the end of a long-term development of civic self-government. It began with government by elected magistrates, a council, and the people. At the end of the fourth century, magistrates and people have lost their political functions, and even in the council authority is restricted to a small group.[3]

2. THE FLIGHT OF THE COUNCILLORS

City councillors had once been the most highly respected inhabitants of their city, who might feel with some justification that they were the successors of the Athenian statesmen of classical

leading councillors made its way slowly and became definite only in 392. Libanius does not appear to have recognized it. Probably it is a case of practice gradually hardening into law.

[1] *C.T.* xii. 1. 75 (371), *P.P. Gal. C.T.* xii. 1. 109 (385), *P.P.O.*: grants rank of ex-count, *consessus*, and right of *osculum* to all councillors who, after performing all other duties, have been made to undertake the *agonothesia* (the provincial spectacle?). *C.T.* xii. 1. 127 (392), *P.P.O.*: gives right of count, class III, and immunity from corporal punishment, to whoever has performed all duties and reached *primum sequentibus ceteris locum*. *C.T.* xii. 1. 171 (412), *P.P. Gal.*: if the rank of count is what is meant by *splendoris et honoris ornamenta*.

[2] *C.T.* xvi. 5. 52 (412), cf. 54.

[3] At Gaza the three προτεύοντες together with the *defensor* constituted the civic authorities, *V. Porph.* (ed. Grégoire et Kugener), 25, 27, 95, and 104, note on 'les principaux'. In the nomination debate of 370 at Oxyrhynchus only ten councillors spoke. These may well have been the *principales* (*P. Oxy.* 2110; Jones, *L.R.E.* 729–31). At Antioch the younger (xxxv. 23) councillors perform the liturgies (ibid. 4, 8, 14), but as a rule (ibid. 20) leave speaking to the older men, i.e. the *principales* (ibid. 6–8) or to an *honoratus* like Libanius (ibid. 25).

literature. In the fourth century they lost their social pre-eminence and even their private affairs became subject to the arbitrary decisions of governors. In a world where everything depended on the favours of the powerful, the character and attitude of the governor of the moment would determine whether a councillor was crushed under a heavy load of liturgies, or whether he managed to keep free of them altogether. Even if a liturgy was well within a councillor's means, the fact that his property was in land and he had no ready money might cause him considerable embarrassment.[1] If a liturgy proved too heavy, he ran a real risk of a public beating, which was not only an indignity but might inflict grievous harm.[2] Bankruptcy might be rare but the insecurity of a councillor's position made his status a very undesirable one.[3]

At the same time the fourth century saw the growth of a new class which suffered from none of the disadvantages of the councillors. The government service was expanding steadily, and with it the number of privileged ex-officials, and the number of fortunes made in the imperial service. The most prominent members of the new class, the *honorati*, οἱ ἐν ἀρχαῖς γεγενημένοι, had gained senatorial rank on retirement from a post in the administration or by honorary codicil. These men not only enjoyed hereditary immunity from the duties of councillors but could claim the jurisdiction of the prefect of Constantinople rather than that of the provincial governor.[4] They were the new leaders of society.

By the second half of the fourth century entry into the official aristocracy had become a widespread social ambition. As recently as the first or second decade of the century, Argyrius, the founder of one of the great curial families of Antioch, had shouldered his way into the council, where he quickly rose to a position of wealth and leadership.[5] We know of no such career in the second half of the century. Julian was obliged to force into the council men who were clinging to immune posts in the imperial civil service. Thus, the interval of forty or so years between the entry of Argyrius and the reforms of Julian witnessed a striking change

---

[1] Jones, *L.R.E.* 756 n. 100. [2] See above, p. 166.

[3] Even at so great a city as Apamea the councillors might go into hiding on arrival of the governor: *Ep.* 1351, cf. 1392 (363). Fears of poor councillors: *Ep.* 374 (358), 1318 (364); Libanius' fear for Cimon: *Or.* xxxii. 8, *Ep.* 959 (390).

[4] Jones, *L.R.E.* 543–54 on the new aristocracy, 485–94 on *praescriptio fori*.

[5] *Or.* xlix. 18; A. F. Norman, *J.H.S.* lxxiv (1954), 44–8.

in the standing of the council. It had been the goal of ambitious young men: it became the bogy which such men did their best to flee.[1] Libanius, as we have seen, was an old-fashioned civic patriot. Nevertheless in his professional capacity he was as proud of old students who had obtained governorships as a modern headmaster is of old boys who have distinguished themselves in public life. He even felt obliged to defend his record as educator of officials against critics who claimed that he had not produced enough of them.[2]

In these circumstances it was inevitable that great efforts should be made by councillors to enter the new official aristocracy whenever opportunity offered. The government was enlarging the senate of Constantinople, and councillors from provincial cities, including Antioch, duly transferred. Except around 359 overall numbers will have been small, but in view of the heavy expenditure expected of a senator they must have come from among the wealthiest men in the council.[3] Diocletian had greatly increased the number of provinces and hence the number of governorships. It was imperial policy to appoint governors for very short periods and only a small proportion of governors would hold more than one governorship. As a result it was comparatively easy for the more powerful and well-connected councillors to work their way into governorship,[4] and perhaps even to

---

[1] (a) *Or.* lvii. 54: Severus, now consular of Syria; ibid. 3 ff., describe his rise through advocacy. (b) *Or.* lxii. 68 and 70; an unnamed imperial civil servant risen through usury. (c) *Or.* xl. 10: a fugitive *colonus*, Alexander, makes money under a shopkeeper and through usury. His sons study Latin and Law at Rome, ibid. 6. One of them becomes assessor to the praetorian prefect of the East, ibid. 7. (d) Julian, *Misop.* 368B: a trader of some sort *dragged* into the council. (e) *Or.* xlii, other references in Seeck, *Briefe*, under Thalassius IV: Libanius' friend and assistant, and son of a sword-maker, was evidently enrolled in the council, for he was threatened with a σιτηγία. Only a little later he tried to enter the senate of Constantinople, but was rejected because of the sword workshop. (f) *Or.* iv. 15–16: Eutropius, later consular of Syria, son of a fugitive *colonus*, who had made money as a member of the provincial *officium*, was enrolled in council by the prefect Cynegius, but strong enough to compel the council to release him (20). Shortly after he became consular. The implication of all passages is that the newly rich were not willing to enter the council. Contrast upward mobility into council of Early Empire: R. Meiggs, *Roman Ostia*, 204–6, 210–12.

[2] *Or.* lxii. 27–62.

[3] Evidence assembled by P. Petit, 'Les sénateurs de Constantinople dans l'œuvre de Libanius', *Ant. Class.* xxvi (1957), 347–82. About 359 Themistius enlarged the senate from 300 to 2,000. Them. *Or.* xxxiv. 13.

[4] Petit, *Libanius*, 345 lists: Calliopius V (Seeck, *Briefe*, 102–3); Olympius II (*Ep.* 70); Panolbius (*Or.* i. 3); Pannychius (*Ep.* 95); Olympius V (Seeck, *Briefe*,

achieve immunity from curial status for their children.[1] Others found places in the central departments of the imperial service and among the notaries[2] and *agentes in rebus*.[3] Of these posts, too, an increasing number came to confer hereditary immunity.

Not only a post in the imperial administration, but even a profession which was closely associated with the administration was used to escape from curial duties. While several laws expressly deny immunity from curial service to advocates, the very existence of these laws shows that there was a tendency for advocates to be treated as immune.[4] An advocate attached to the court of a governor travelled with him, and so might claim legitimate engagements in other cities to avoid being called to a liturgy.[5] In addition, advocacy was no longer a free profession. Advocates were registered with the courts in which they practised, and their fees were fixed in just the same way as those *officiales* might charge for their services. Thus the position of an advocate tended to be thought of as an official one. Finally, advocates, in the course of their work in court, acquired experience of the judicial business that took so much of a governor's time and so qualified themselves for a governorship. At the same time they established the close relations with their chief, which might afterwards be useful in securing official appointments.[6] As a result of all these factors the profession of advocate, in fact if not in law, came to provide protection from curial duties.[7] Since both education and tradition made advocacy the natural profession for a man of curial family,[8] and since it was inevitable that an advocate should come before the eyes of the authorities as a potential official, we can see that it was nearly impossible to prevent councillors from deserting in this way.

325; *Ep.* 1258, 1264); Antiochus II (*Ep.* 1387); Celsus I (*Ep.* 696, 1399); Aristophanes (Seeck, *Briefe*, 90); Hilarius VII (Zos. iv. 34); Eutropius V (*Or.* iv. 20–1); Pelagius (i. 211).

[1] Jones, *L.R.E.* 740 ff. on legislation to check the escape of councillors.

[2] e.g. Spectatus, cousin of Libanius (Seeck, *Briefe*, 281–2). Honoratus (*Ep.* 358–9, 365–6, 300).

[3] e.g. Olympius VI (*Ep.* 602–4; Seeck, *Briefe*, 225), Aristophanes (*Or.* xiv. 12); sons of Marcellus (*Ep.* 362); child enrolment of son of Marianus (*Ep.* 875–6).

[4] *C.T.* xii. 1. 46 (358); ibid. 87 (381), *P.P.O.*: Libanius never claims that advocacy carries immunity. *Ep.* 794, 834: a councillor acts as advocate.

[5] *Ep.* 293–4 (359–60).   [6] *Ep.* 838 (363), *Or.* liv. 7–9; *C.T.* xii. 1. 77 (372).

[7] *Ep.* 959 (390): council and bar alternatives.

[8] The prosopographical evidence on advocacy is evaluated by Petit, *Étudiants*, 179–83, and 169, table.

The government struggled hard to stem the exodus from the councils. A long series of laws bears witness to the efforts of successive emperors. At the same time their repetitiveness suggests that the struggle was only very partially successful.[1]

One can see why the imperial government might find it difficult to enforce its laws. The administration was riddled with favouritism—and corruption. There is, for instance, the case of Honoratus, the son of Quirinus, who was enrolled while still a child among the notaries. In 358 all absentee notaries were ordered to Constantinople. Libanius immediately wrote to leading notaries to ask that Honoratus should be allowed to stay at home on grounds of health without losing his place on the roll. He even asked that Honoratus should be given precedence over other similarly placed youths.[2] The letter achieved its object. Three years later, Honoratus occupied a good position at court. At the same time the praetorian prefect had recalled all *agentes in rebus*. Now Marcellus, a doctor and friend of Libanius, had enrolled two sons, scarcely weaned, in this *officium*, so that they might enjoy security for life. These boys, while still too young to go beyond the gates of Antioch, were ordered to report to the prefect at Sirmium in Dalmatia. Libanius, fearing that the boys might be struck off the roll, asked the prefect to use his authority to prevent this.[3] Of these child officials Honoratus was the son of a former governor and may have been immune from curial duties even without a position in the civil service. The sons of Marcellus were probably liable to serve in the council. In any case it is clear that a civil service which tolerated child members will also have tolerated other forms of illegal entry.

How influence could be used to frustrate the law, and how if one avenue failed another would open, is shown by the adventures of Dianius, a young Bithynian of curial family. Dianius, fearing that he would be enrolled in the council, compelled to perform a liturgy beyond his means, and beaten for not performing it adequately, fled to Antioch, where he was received as a guest and pupil by Libanius. Some time later, a kinsman of Dianius became vicar of the diocese within which his home town was situated. Dianius set out for home with letters to the vicar, who happened to be a friend of Libanius, and to a leading

---

[1] Jones, *L.R.E.* 740 ff.   [2] *Ep.* 358–9, 365–6, 300.
[3] *Ep.* 362, 875–6.

councillor of Nicomedia. They were to make sure that Dianius was not subjected to the 'slavery' of curial service. He also carried letters for Themistius, the famous philosopher, and for the praetorian prefect of the East asking that Dianius might be registered as a barrister at the court of the prefect. If the Bithynians could not provide Dianius with the security he required, he was evidently going to try his luck at Constantinople. In the event he stayed in Bithynia, but shortly afterwards the vicar was killed in the disastrous earthquake of Nicomedia. Dianius' situation might have become an extremely disagreeable one, but luckily the governorship of Bithynia fell to another friend of Libanius, Alexander III, who was to govern Syria under Julian. So Libanius advised Dianius not to try to obtain a governorship for himself but to cultivate the friendship of Alexander. He was sure to make a career and Dianius would rise with him. At the same time Libanius wrote a letter of recommendation for Dianius to Alexander. This is the last we hear of Dianius, but we may be certain that, while Alexander governed Bithynia, Dianius was free from vexation.[1]

In these circumstances, the flow of councillors into immune positions of the imperial service was slowed down[2] but not stopped. Pack has assembled case histories of men whose attempts to evade curial duties were supported by letters of recommendation from Libanius.[3] On the basis of this material I would conclude that eleven men out of a total of twenty-two succeeded in reaching the security of an immunity-giving position.[4] This means that a man who asked Libanius' help to get an immune position would have an even chance of success. Pack concluded that Libanius had been successful six times in eighteen attempts. Even this would show that the law was not being enforced very successfully. After all an unsuccessful candidate could always try again. There must also have been many patrons whose influence was greater than that of the sophist of Antioch and whose success rate was greater too.

---

[1] *Ep.* 374–8, 281–2.

[2] Petit, *Libanius*, 397–400, lists 58 councillors of Antioch. Of seventeen men known to have obtained immunity from curial duties three senators spent money on Antioch after their elevation (Celsus I, Alexander X, Callimachus), and two men only received imperial office in old age (Antiochus II, Panolbius); one, Theotecnus, was excused the council because of age; cf. below, p. 277.

[3] R. Pack, '*Curiales* in the correspondence of Libanius', *T.A.P.A.* lxxxii (1951), 176–92.

[4] See Appendix III.

More quantitative analysis is provided by Petit. Of his list of fifty-eight councillors of Antioch, seventeen achieved positions usually associated with immunity from curial service.[1] Out of seventy-seven councillors of other cities, eighteen gained such posts.[2] But out of these thirty-five 'immune' men at least eleven either had performed their duties already, or continued to perform them, or were succeeded in the council by a son. Forty-seven per cent of the students of Libanius whose origin is known to us were sons of councillors, but of those whose careers are known only twenty-two per cent served in councils.[3] Again the decline is less drastic than it looks, because it is to a considerable extent accounted for by young men who became advocates and thus were not necessarily lost to their council.[4] By no means all the new posts were filled with men of curial origin. Of the forty-one pupils of Libanius who took up posts in the imperial civil service, five are known to have been of curial origin while the fathers of nine were already officials.[5]

These figures appear to establish that men were being lost to the council at a comparatively moderate rate. In fact the precision of their statistical form is quite misleading. The figures could only be fully meaningful if they were based on complete biographies of the men concerned. As it is, the careers of most of the men are quite obscure except for the one or two episodes which happen to be mentioned by Libanius. It is possible that many a councillor, of whom we read that he gained an immune position, in the end failed to preserve this immunity. It is likely that some of the men who did not seek—or who failed to find—an immune post during the years for which Libanius' correspondence happens to be preserved obtained such a post

---

[1] Petit, *Libanius*, 397–400; Alexander X, Antiochus II, Callimachus, Calliopius V, Celsus I, Euagrius IV, Eusebius XXII, Eutropius V, Gaudentius, Gemellus II, Hilarius VII, Miccalus, Olympius II, Panolbius, Silvanu, Libanius, Theotecnus.

[2] Ibid. 400–3; Achillius III, Aristophanes, Carterius, Dianius, Domnus, Faustinus, Firminus, Fraternus, Gerontius, Heraclitus, Hyperechius, Megistus, Seleucus, grandsons of Sopater, Pannychius, Pelagius I, Sidonius.

[3] Petit, *Étudiants*, tables on pp. 170 and 172.

[4] Ibid., table on p. 169, Agroecius, Asteius, Chrysogonus, Cimon, Dianius, Eusebius XI, Hermolaus are sons of *curiales* who became advocates—7 out of the 18 sons of *curiales* who are not recorded as following their fathers into the council (Petit, *Étudiants*, 175 n. 149). Nine pupils are sons of advocates but 25 became advocates, ibid. 174.

[5] Ibid. 166 and Appendix II.

in later years. Finally, there is no means of estimating the proportion of socially mobile *curiales* who are not mentioned in the writings of Libanius. All these uncertainties limit the value of quantitative deductions from the prosopographical material.

In fact there are reasons to believe that Petit's figures greatly understate the loss of men suffered by the council at Antioch.[1] In the *Misopogon* of 362, Julian claims that he enlarged the roll of the council of Antioch by two hundred names.[2] It is unlikely that Julian's action was intended to enlarge the council beyond its previous full strength. At the time many councils were below strength.[3] The council of Antioch had suffered severely in the Persian wars.[4] Many of the two hundred new councillors— military officers,[5] officials of the mint,[6] and men who only belonged to Antioch through their mother's side[7]—would surely not have been pressed into service except to fill up vacancies. Julian would never have enrolled so many people who genuinely felt themselves exempt,[8] if there had not been an urgent need for new councillors. It is likely that the council had been heavily under strength and that the two hundred new men were needed to restore numbers.

In the 380s, Libanius insists that there had been a dramatic decline in the membership of the council. 'We were once six hundred, or rather, by Zeus, twice as many, now we are not even sixty.'[9] In the sister speech he makes the fall in numbers appear even larger, from twelve hundred councillors to twelve.[10]

---

[1] The very large number of names known from Libanius' writings seems to demand statistical evaluation. But this is very difficult. Incompleteness and vagueness of information undermines all totals. The character of the evidence changes. In the fifties and sixties the bulk of it comes from letters, in the eighties and nineties from speeches. These difficulties strictly limit the value of even Petit's very careful work. The calculations on the careers of the students of Libanius (ibid. 168 *ad fin.*) are well based, but their significance is doubtful. The calculations of the strength of the council of Antioch at different periods (Petit, *Libanius*, 322–5) and of the proportion of councillors of different degrees of wealth (ibid. 330–1) are only made possible with the help of assumptions so uncertain as to make the calculations meaningless.

[2] Julian, *Misop.* 367D.   [3] *Ep.* 62, 627, 696, *Or.* xviii. 146–7.
[4] *Or.* xlix. 2.   [5] Ibid. 19, xlviii. 42.
[6] *Officiales*: Julian, *Misop.* 368; Lib. *Ep.* 1365.
[7] *C.T.* xii. 1. 51 (362).   [8] Amm. xxii. 9. 12, xxv. 4. 21.
[9] *Or.* xlviii. 4; cf. ii. 33; a heavy decline without figures: xxxii. 8, *Ep.* 851.

[10] *Or.* xlix. 8. Petit, *Libanius*, 323, takes these 12 to be the *principales* only. But as *principales* were men who had completed their civic liturgies, and these 12 claim to be performing all liturgies that have to be performed, they are unlikely to be only

Now the six hundred is clearly the original complement of the council. The status of the second six hundred is obscure, but since they only did what they were ordered and had no opportunity to display public spirit through expenditure they were not full councillors.[1] But while the statement of the full establishment of the council must be exact, the figures given for its reduced membership are not likely to be so.

Libanius' figures look as if they had been chosen because they form a neat series: six hundred, twice six hundred, sixty and twelve hundred, twelve. In any case it must often have been very difficult to establish whether a man whose name appeared on the roll of councillors was still genuinely available for curial duties, or already firmly ensconced in the imperial service. The figures are not to be taken literally, but they must mean that the shrinkage of the council had been very large indeed. The council must have been reduced to a small fraction of its former size, and the reserve six hundred must have disappeared completely.

Decline of numbers on such a scale cannot be explained by upward movement into the senatorial order and the central departments of the civil service. There simply were not enough posts available. In addition to the flow of councillors into the imperial civil service, there must also have been a large-scale loss of councillors who found their way into positions of security, after selling the property on which membership of the city council depended. There was no legal obstacle to prevent this, for until 386[2] the right of councillors to sell their land was unrestricted. Having sold it, a councillor might buy (according to the sum involved) a provincial governorship, or codicils of honorary rank, or a humble place in a provincial *officium*, or an education for his son. Alternatively he might sell his estate to a powerful patron, often no doubt a senator, but sometimes a *principalis*,[3] or he might settle in a remote village, trusting to luck and bad

principales. Libanius is giving an exaggeratedly small figure for the total of all active councillors. These might include *principales* who volunteered for duties from which they were now exempt.

[1] See Jones, *G.C.* 180, n. 47 on public services performed by non-councillors. Cf. below, p. 221.

[2] First restriction on sale of land: *C.T.* xii. 3. 1 (386); purchase of governorship xxviii. 22, xlviii. 11; education: (Libanius himself) *Or.* i. 26, 58.

[3] *C.T.* xii. 1. 50; thus Megistus, agent of the family of Thalassius (see above, p. 42), and Heraclitus, agent of Libanius' family (see above, p. 45), perhaps also Julianus XVII (*Or.* liv. 45).

communications that he would not again be troubled with curial service. The laws show that sometimes it was not even necessary to sell estates. Certain councillors sought security merely by moving their home from the city to the countryside.[1]

Much selling of curial land did take place. We have seen how some of Libanius' ancestral land was sold, ostensibly to pay for his studies, but perhaps also to free him from the risk of being recalled to the council. During the years of Constantius' Persian wars, many councillors were obliged to sell their lands. They found purchasers who were in the imperial service and thus immune from the council.[2] Libanius claims that the death of Julian brought about a crisis of confidence among councillors that led to widespread selling of estates.[3] In the course of time a marked change in land-ownership seems to have resulted. In 381 Libanius deplores the ruin and impoverishment of the councils. Everywhere the councils of cities with poor-quality land have been ruined, since councillors who were obliged to sell their lands found no purchasers. Cities with more fertile territory, among which no doubt Antioch is to be included, have been only a little more fortunate. There, councillors have sold their houses or their land, or both, to men of no family at all, who have become proud and flattered members of high society.[4]

Libanius usually explains the selling of curial land by the impoverishment of its curial owners.[5] This is unlikely to be altogether wrong, since at certain periods, notably during the Persian wars and in the 380s, pressure of government demands on councillors was very heavy.[6] Nevertheless the fact remains that we hear of very few cases of individual councillors bankrupted either by civic or by imperial demands. One suspects therefore that in many cases the urge to escape from the council, rather than

---

[1] *C.T.* xii. 18. 1–2 (Eastern laws). Councillors have moved their *lares* from the city without selling their estates.

[2] *Or.* xlviii. 3, xlix. 2, ii. 54, xxxvi. 5.

[3] *Or.* xviii. 288–9.

[4] *Or.* ii. 35 (general); *Ep.* 846 (388) on Emesa. 'Poor' is a relative term. *Ep.* 471 (355–6) shows Hierocles building, while according to *Ep.* 346 and 466 (355–6) he was poor; cf. also *Ep.* 375, Dianius is 'poor', i.e. too poor to perform liturgies, but wealthy enough not to have to do anything ταπεινόν to live.

[5] General: p. 183 n. 2 above. Individual cases: Julianus XVII (*Or.* liv. 22. 45), Hermeias (xxvii. 13, xxviii. 6), Anonymous (xlvii. 8), Olympius V (*Ep.* 1397), Acontius (*Ep.* 1495).

[6] See above, pp. 162 ff.

the need to raise money for compulsory public services, moved councillors to sell their land.

We have already noted Libanius' claim that the leading men of the council consolidated their own power, and the scope for personal enrichment it provided, by conniving at the escape of other councillors and thus keeping membership of the council low.[1] 'There is need to heat the water in the public baths for intending bathers. It is possible to approach this man or that but they (the leading councillors) do not want to. There is need for someone to keep horses that will provide entertainment at race meetings. Men exist who would undertake the liturgy if called upon, but they shamelessly nominate themselves. Then they blame the times for sinking the councils, when it is they who sink them, and drown them, and prevent their resuscitation.'[2]

These tactics could be advantageous only if the financial burden laid on the council as a whole was as a rule a moderate one. Had the burden been really crushing, the leading councillors would have been glad to have as many colleagues to share it as possible. If the burden was less heavy than might be expected, the explanation may well lie in the tendency for the curial contribution to the civic services—as opposed to army and empire—to be reduced.[3]

Oration xlix is obviously an attack on certain elements in the council of Antioch, and statements in it should not be accepted uncritically. Nevertheless much of the detail of Libanius' account is in accord with independent evidence. His description of the formation of a ruling clique looks like the rise of the *principales* seen from a civic rather than imperial point of view. There is plenty of evidence that implementation of the legislation binding councillors to their councils depended on the co-operation of the councillors themselves and particularly of the ruling group. It was the duty of the councillors to provide information about would-be fugitives and to start proceedings against them in the governor's court. The governor's part was merely to judge the ensuing case. Only quite occasionally did a governor take the initiative; perhaps only when a general review of the membership of the council

[1] *Or.* xlviii. 4, xlix. 4.   [2] Ibid. 10 (reading αὐτοὺς with Reiske in 1.20).
[3] See above, p. 158.

had been ordered by his superiors at Constantinople.[1] The *principales*, as leaders of the council, were therefore in a position to co-
operate with councillors who were escaping into other walks of
life simply by not reporting them.

Libanius' claim that the leading councillors attacked the
property of weaker colleagues, either with a view to winning the
favour of powerful men,[2] or for their own profit, also receives
independent confirmation. It was fear of this, so Libanius claims,
that prevented him from enrolling his son Cimon in the council.[3]
Moreover the distribution of liturgies provided plenty of opportunities for the abuse. If a man were given liturgies too heavy
for him, he would be obliged to sell his lands, and a powerful
man or a great councillor would be on the spot to buy them.
Libanius relates an alternative device. A councillor nominated
a colleague to perform a duty jointly with himself, knowing that
the other man, who was a student at Antioch, would be unwilling to carry out this obligation. If the man refused, the
nominator would be entitled to take over his property.[4] It is likely
that the powerful councillors frequently used pressure of this sort.
In 386 the government made it illegal for a councillor to sell
his land without the written approval of the governor. This was
the earliest law limiting a councillor's right to dispose of his
property. The purpose of the law was to prevent councillors
selling their land under compulsion of powerful persons. It is
significant that while this law does not mention the *principales* it
was generally assumed that its provisions were specifically directed
against them.[5] Evidently, leading councillors were well known to
be becoming richer at the expense of their weaker colleagues.

We may conclude that Libanius' description of the activities
of the leading councillors is essentially correct. If so, it provides an

---

[1] Councillors' task to inform governor of men who have escaped from council:
Or. xlviii. 7; cf. *Or.* xlix. 13, *Ep.* 870 (388). Councillors raise immunity of Eusebius
the Sophist in governor's court at Antioch, and at Constantinople: Seeck, *Briefe*,
143, s.v. Eusebius XXII. *Ep.* 293–4 Eusebius and Agroicius, two brothers claimed
by ψηφίσμασιν. Special intervention by governor or other agents of imperial government: *Or.* liv. 74 (388–9). In *Or.* xlviii and xlix Libanius mentions three occasions of
reform, instigated by the Emperor Julian and by the praetorian prefects, Cynegius
and Tatian.

[2] *Or.* xlviii. 37–8, xxxii. 8.   [3] *Or.* xlix. 8, *Ep.* 959 (390).

[4] *Ep.* 1496 (365); on *cessio bonorum* in third-century Egypt see E. P. Wegener,
Mnemosyne, ser. 4, no. i (1948), 115–29.

[5] *C.T.* xii. 3. 1 (386), 2 (423).

adequate explanation of the fact that so many councillors could escape from their duties in the face of determined opposition by the imperial government. Fugitives escaped prosecution because leading councillors either failed to prosecute them themselves or did not provide the information needed for a prosecution to be undertaken by the governors.

Libanius paints the conduct of the leading councillors in the blackest and most selfish terms. Perhaps a more impartial presentation of the situation would have pointed out an element of collusion in the relations between great and small councillors. The rate of decline of the council suggests that there was widespread eagerness to get out and this must have involved readiness to sell the property which tied a man to the council. To sell property that had perhaps belonged to one's family for generations must have been a desperate decision. But not more desperate than that other well-witnessed practice, by which decurions chose to have illegitimate sons by slave women rather than legitimate heirs who would inherit their father's property but also his curial duties.[1] These actions indicate the complete demoralization of what had once been the aristocracy of a region, the complete loss of that sense of responsibility for the city which Libanius had praised in the *Antiochicus*. The way the *principales* exploited the situation is as much a symptom of demoralization as the eagerness of others to escape. We have seen some of the causes: loss of power, loss of social prestige, loss of physical security, financial risks. The pressure of the powerful, from both outside and inside the council, destroyed the morale of the councillors, and built up such a pressure to be free from the burdensome institution that the imperial administration, riddled as it was with favouritism and corruption, could not resist it.

3. THE NEW ARISTOCRACY

We have seen that a principal factor behind the flight from the council was the growth of a new class whose prestige depended

---

[1] *Or.* xlviii. 30, ii. 72; Libanius himself: i. 278, *Ep.* 1063. 5. St. Augustine: Brown, *Augustine of Hippo*, 62. See also *C.T.* xii. 1. 6 (318). The motive was often—though not in cases of Libanius or Augustine—to gain the patronage of the slave woman's master: *Nov. Maj.* vii. 1–6. Illegitimate sons had no—or only a very limited—right of succession. To enable a bastard to succeed required risky and illegal arrangements: see *Or.* i. 195 and laws of *C.T.* iv. 6.

on wealth and rank acquired in the imperial service. We can still feel Libanius' resentment at this development. 'I have a right to be worried at the poverty of the councillors and the wealth of the *officiales*. Last year some of them sold meat, others bread, others vegetables. Now they have grown great through taking over the property of councillors. And they have so much gold they did not haggle over the price. Further they annoy their neighbours through the height of their houses, depriving them of unclouded enjoyment of daylight.' The governing class, the councillors, have become 'humble and few and not only poor but practically beggars. . . . The prestige of the council is reduced to nothing while the foreigners strut about and marry. We watch them and dine with them and wish them long life. Nobody would now marry his daughter to a councillor. No one hates his child so.'

The irritation is not surprising. It was not merely a matter of big houses and splendid marriages. The new class inevitably took over the councillors' role of exercising patronage over the mass of the inhabitants of city and territory. The men most favourably placed to do this were the *honorati*. These men, who had to bear none of the curial burdens and who had the same legal privileges as governors, were in a much stronger position to influence the imperial officials than the councillors.[1]

As the governors were judges of all matters, it was essential that they should be accessible to all, so that no man's case should go by default. Constantine endeavoured to make certain that this happened. He ruled that at the end of each court session a herald should ask the assembled public whether anyone else had business. Only if there was no reply to this announcement might the judge withdraw.[2]

In fact, this opportunity was not always available. It seems that during the fourth century the practice of hearing cases in secret became increasingly common.[3] When there was no open court, any opportunity to speak to the governor would have to be paid for.[4]

---

[1] See above, p. 175; quoted: *Or.* ii. 54–5, 35–6; cf. also 66.

[2] *C.T.* i. 16. 6 (331), to the provincials; cf. also ibid. 12. 1 (313), to proconsul of Africa.

[3] See s.v. Secretarium (O. Seeck) in *P.W.*, 2 Reihe, ii. 1, cols. 979–81. A law of Valentinian I, *C.T.* i. 16. 9 (364), stresses the public pronouncement of the verdict rather than the public hearing.

[4] *C.T.* xi. 16. 7 (331).

If access to the judge for most people was precarious and often expensive, there were persons for whom access was made very much easier. Morning audiences were held by all Romans of standing, including the emperor. This morning greeting, or *salutatio*, gave each client an opportunity to address a few conventional words to his patron, which would be answered more or less intimately according to the rank of the client.[1] Such audiences were held by the governors at Antioch. They were one of the ways of visiting the governor covered by the term εἴσοδος and attacked in *Orations* li and lii.[2] The audience was held before the opening of the court session. As each visitor was admitted a herald announced his name, so that all could hear who was being honoured.[3] The *ordo salutationis* of Timgad lists the men who might attend such an audience in order of precedence. Senators and *comites* are included in the first class. The second class comprises heads of the governor's office staff, together with members of the central departments of the administration. Former high priests of provinces and the highest ranking members of the council are placed in the third class. Most of the councillors, including the civic magistrates, together with the ordinary members of the governor's office staff, salute the governor only in the fourth class. There could be no clearer demonstration of the displacement from the head of civic society of the councillors by the *honorati*.[4]

In addition to the regular morning audience there was held four times a month a special audience for men of senatorial rank. Late in life, Libanius attended these audiences by virtue of his honorary praetorian prefecture. Since he claims that he never visited one particularly unpleasant *comes orientis* except on these occasions, it would seem that for men qualified

---

[1] J. Carcopino, *Daily Life in Ancient Rome*, 171–3. Also *P.W.* 2. Reihe, i. 2, cols. 2066–72.

[2] *Or.* li. 5 and 10, lii, 4 ff.

[3] Ibid. li. 10; cf. preamble to the inscription, *Syria*, xxiii. 173: the Emperor Caracalla was first saluted by the praetorian prefect and leading men, then sat down in the auditorium and asked the persons concerned in the day's judicial business to be brought in, cf. *C.J.* ix. 51. 1.

[4] L. Leschi, *R.E.A.* l (1948), 71 ff.; *C.I.L.* viii. 17896; Th. Mommsen, *Gesammelte Schriften*, viii. 478. *C.T.* vi. 7. 1 (372), *praef. urb.*, and *C.T.* vi. 28. 8. 2 (435), *mag. off.*, regulate precedence at audiences. Perhaps a specific summons was necessary before a man might attend. If so, this is the privilege that Libanius means, when he hopes that somebody will be given εἴσοδος, as in *Or.* xxvii. 10, liv. 7.

to attend, presence at the four audiences was practically obligatory.[1]

To judge by Libanius' behaviour in the years when he held his honorary rank, some *honorati* enjoyed almost unlimited access to the governor. Libanius was once asked to use his influence on behalf of some prison guards accused of conniving at the escape of prisoners. Immediately, so he tells us, he 'went in' to the consular Eustathius and put the guards' case.[2] Again Libanius expressly states that the same Eustathius never invited him for an evening.[3] Yet he also relates that one evening he called on the governor to ask him that a certain poet might be allowed to stay at Antioch.[4] Libanius was evidently entitled to visit Eustathius without an invitation.

We know that some grades of officials possessed this right. A law of 384 grants to officials of the imperial *scrinia* the right to *salutatio* of the governor, to a place beside him in court, and ends by threatening with fines members of the governor's *officium* 'if the *secretarium* of the judges should not be open to men who frequently come into the imperial consistory'. The right is further defined by a law of 396: they shall have the right, of their own volition and without any announcement, to enter the *secretarium* of any judge.[5] A law of 387, issued to the praetorian prefect of the East, gives the same privilege to all imperial procurators of perfectissimate rank.[6] The only civic dignitaries known to have the right are the high priests of provinces and the *defensor*.[7]

---

[1] *Or.* i. 212, Libanius did not 'go in' to Proculus at all. In *Or.* x he modifies this. He attended the audience that took place four times a month, but used it only for greetings (προσηγορία, *salutatio*). In *Or.* xlii. 36 Libanius makes it clear that he spoke to Proculus privately. How can these passages be harmonized? Perhaps the first passage means that Libanius never visited Proculus voluntarily. Then the other two would refer to more-or-less obligatory occasions. The four occasions a month would be functions which Libanius had to attend, the private talks might have followed a personal invitation from the governor which, as Libanius tells us in *Or.* lii. 42, it was never safe to reject. *Or.* lvi. 2, the governor Lucianus had allowed the *honorati* to 'greet' him only on four occasions a month. This the ex-governors resented. Evidently the ex-governors had a right to salute the governor in the morning. They normally made use of it more than four times a month, but four mornings in each month were particularly assigned to them. A very strict governor might not allow them to greet him at other times. Libanius took part in the audiences of the *honorati* as a result of his honorary praetorian prefecture. See Petit in *Byzantion* xxi (1951), 285–310.   [2] *Or.* liv. 42 ff.

[3] Ibid. 5–6.   [4] Ibid. 56.   [5] *C.T.* vi. 26. 7, *P.P.O.*

[6] Ibid. i. 32. 6, *P.P.O.*

[7] *Defensor*: *C.J.* i. 55. 4 (385). *Sacerdotes provinciae*: Th. Mommsen, *Gesammelte*

In addition to having privileged access to the governor by right of their status, *honorati* were also well placed to receive social invitations from the governor. The governor might be found in the company of these men when he was resting, or doing his paper work, or even when he was taking a bath. He might also spend the evening in their company.¹ There were loud protests when the consular Lucianus stopped such visits.²

The *honorati* were entitled to sit next to the governor during trials. Normally, they even sat on the same level as he. When the governor Lucianus raised himself on cushions above the *honorati*, they felt this to be an affront.³ The purpose of the privilege was no doubt to enable men with personal authority to advise and, if need be, restrain the governor when he was exercising his judicial functions. Libanius describes how on one occasion one of the παρακαθήμενοι got the governor to stop beating a man who was being interrogated under torture.⁴ On the other hand these men were in a very good position to influence the court in their own interest or that of friends and clients.

The abuses are fully described in *Orations* li and lii. Libanius professes to advocate the complete abolition of the right of access to the governor. But this is surely a rhetorical exaggeration. Libanius knew perfectly well that it was neither possible nor desirable to isolate the governor from his most powerful subjects.⁵ Presumably he would have been content if his pamphlets helped to reduce the opportunities for unwitnessed intercourse. The abuses described by Libanius were obvious to the central government also, and certain laws approach the problem in a similar

Schriften, vol. viii. 487, refers to *Coll. Conc.*, ed. Mansi, vol. iii. 802 ; = vol. iv. 501. At this time they acted as patrons not only with governors but even with the emperor: *C.T.* xvi. 2. 38 (407) *proc. Afr.* They were selected from advocates, *C.T.* xii. 1. 46 (358), *vic. Afr.*

¹ *Or.* li. 4–5, lii. 6–7, liv. 5–6, 69–70, xxvi. 16.

² Lucianus: *Or.* lvi. 2. Not only ex-governors benefited by social calls, schoolmasters commonly did so too, e.g. *Or.* lii. 29–31, *Or.* li. 13–17; also Libanius himself, before he held high honorary rank, in his relations with several high officials; doctors, too, were admitted, *Or.* lii. 32.

³ *Consessus*: ibid. 4. Laws regulating the privilege, *C.T.* i. 20. 1 = *C.J.* i. 45. 1 (408): *honorati* not to enjoy the privilege if they are themselves involved in the case. *Scriniarii* to enjoy *consessus*: *C.T.* vi. 26. 5 (389), *P.P. Gal.*, 7 (396), *P.P.O.*; *principes* of the *agentes in rebus*: *C.T.* vi. 28. 8 (435), *mag. off.*; decurions who have performed all *munera*: *C.T.* xii. 1. 109 (385), *P.P.O.*   ⁴ *Or.* lvi. 4.

⁵ *Or.* i. 170. Seeck, in the article cited, p. 187 n. 3, considers that *consessus* was introduced to counteract the growing tendency to hold court sessions *in camera*. Cf also *Or.* xxvi. 13–14.

manner.[1] But one suspects that in practice the need to respect the dignity of the ex-officials prevailed over the needs of justice. There also remained the intractable fact, that ordinary people needed a means by which they could bring grievances past greedy officials[2] to the notice of an inaccessible governor.

Unfair decisions in court were only one, if the most immediately harmful, consequence of the εἴσοδος. Another, also noted by Libanius but stressed less, was the opportunity given to men who had such access to influence government. It became customary for the men with access to determine a governor's decisions regarding the affairs of the city, instead of its traditional governing body, the council. While the *curia* continued to be responsible for the continuance of the municipal services, a considerable part of the advice given to governors on the subject will have come from the ex-governors and other magnates. Indeed even councillors might prefer to use these influential men as intermediaries—particularly when there was need to make excuses for errors and omissions.[3]

Often the aims and interests of *honorati* were diametrically opposed to those of the council. This was a fact that did not require demonstration: 'Who does not know of the continuous war which I have been waging on behalf of the council against the ex-governors? These men consider the council's good fortune their own misfortune, and its misfortune their good fortune. They have formed themselves into an armed camp, and they hurl missiles, they assault, they do wrong—now in word, now in deed. Although they have gained possession of the bulk of the council's property— now is not the time to explain how—they are dissatisfied that they do not have it all.'[4] Ex-governors supported councillors, or sons of councillors, who were trying to escape from their duties.[5] They had privileges as regards extraordinary levies and services which in times of pressure increased the burden of smaller landowners in the city.[6] In short, the *honorati* had power and influence without corresponding obligations of responsibility. The next

[1] *C.T.* i. 20. 1 = *C.J.* i. 45. 1 (408), *P.P. Ital.*; ibid. i. 16. 10 (368), *vic. hisp.*; *C.T.* i. 16. 13 (373). The praetorian prefect Cynegius published an edict which was quickly revoked, *Or.* lii. 46, cf. liv. 61, lvi. 2–4.

[2] *C.T.* i. 16. 7 (331) to provincials; *Or.* xxvi. 32; cf. *Or.* xlvi. 42; cf. *Or.* liv. 7.

[3] *Or.* lii. 11; Libanius patron of council: *Or.* xxxvii. 5; of councillors: xxxv. 25.

[4] *Or.* xxxvi. 5–6.   [5] *Or.* xlviii. 28, xlix. 13.

[6] Jones, *L.R.E.* 535–6.

chapter will show how this undermined the authority of the council in the city and its territory.

4. PATRONAGE[1] IN CITY AND TERRITORY

It was an ancient and universal custom in the Graeco-Roman world that men in public positions should not omit to let their private friends obtain some benefit from their public authority. There was no question of this being out of order, the only question was how far the claims of friendship might go. This difficult and important topic is discussed by Plutarch.[2]

Plutarch advises that a politician might properly help a friend to a magistracy or to some other notable administrative post. He might have him selected for an embassy.[3] Alternatively, he might hand over to a friend a case at law which would bring in a good fee, or introduce him to a rich man who was in need of legal advice, or help him to some profitable contract.[4] Lastly, a friend of the politician might be given favours which would result in his being praised by third persons; in other words, the politician is to listen to requests made by a friend on behalf of others.[5]

Plutarch's view of the duties of friendship was still very much alive in the time of Libanius, and the fact that it is held both by Libanius and by the powerful men he addresses in his letters is essential background to a large portion of his correspondence.[6] Very much of this is occupied with requests to friends, which, when fulfilled, would win praise from third parties. Sometimes he asks, as did Pelopidas in an anecdote related by Plutarch,[7] for an imprisoned person to be released. Often he requests a judge to decide in favour of a particular litigant, naturally asserting at the same time that the man has justice on his side.[8] He fre-

---

[1] L. Harmand, *Libanius, discours sur les patronages*; F. Martroye, 'Les patronages d'agriculteurs et de vici au 4ᵉ et au 5ᵉ siècles', *Revue historique de droit français et Étranger*, 4ᵉ série, vii (1928), 201 ff.; De Zulueta, 'De patrociniis vicorum', *Oxford Studies in Social and Legal History* i (Oxford, 1909), 1–78.

[2] Plutarch, *Praecepta gerendae reipublicae* (vol. x. 158 ff. in Loeb series, ed. H. N. Fowler). Treatment of friends, 806 ff. (ed. Fowler, 202. 13).

[3] Ibid. 808B–C (Fowler, 208).   [4] Ibid. 809A (Fowler, 212).

[5] Ibid. 808D–E (Fowler, 214–15).   [6] *Ep.* 503, *Or.* xiv. 1.

[7] Op. cit. 808E. Epameinondas had refused request to Pelopidas but granted it to his mistress. 'Favours of that sort are fit for courtesans to receive, but not for generals.' Libanius, *Ep.* 169, 204, 1369, *Or.* liv. 45, 65.

[8] *Ep.* 56, 83, 105, 110, 394, 400.

quently asks for men to be given posts in the government service.[1] Occasionally Libanius asks that a friend be given a building job.[2] In numerous letters he merely asks that a person should be assisted in his dealings with the administration.[3]

The background of all letters is the same. Libanius is a famous man and, what is more, the friend of many influential persons. These men held the same views as Plutarch on the duties of friendship and were ready to grant Libanius favours. So when someone was about to have dealings with a great man who was known to be Libanius' friend, he would approach Libanius and ask him to use his influence.[4] Then Libanius would either go to visit the powerful man himself, or if he was not at Antioch, he would write him a letter to be delivered by the man who had made the request.

From his surviving letters we can see that Libanius must have used his influence on behalf of hundreds of individuals. It is also clear that his efforts on behalf of clients, whether carried out by letter or by personal interview,[5] occupied a great deal of his time.[6]

Much of Libanius' activity as a patron was concerned with the making of requests to officials on behalf of former pupils. He advised Alexander, the governor of Syria appointed by Julian, that the best way he could further Libanius' school was to give preference to such of Libanius' former pupils as appeared as advocates in his court.[7] Similar requests were made to many another official. Pupils were to be given posts,[8] registered as advocates,[9] protected from the demands of their local council,[10] their property was to be safeguarded while they were at school;[11] they were to be 'known' by the governor when they returned home,[12] and so on. Libanius might even go to the extent of finding an old pupil a wife.[13]

---

[1] e.g. *Ep.* 1449, 545, 1260, 1224, 841.
[2] *Or.* xxvii. 3, *Or.* xiv. 63, *Ep.* 1392.   [3] *Ep.* 1344, 214, 152, 108.
[4] *Ep.* 1516, *Or.* liv. 4, *Or.* liv. 45–9.   [5] *Or.* i. 107–8.
[6] *Ep.* 701 (362). 589 (357): he spent hardly less time with governors than with pupils, cf. 351 (358–9). See also how busy Libanius was, even after the death of Julian, *Ep.* 1437.
[7] *Ep.* 838 (363); cf. *Or.* li. 13–17. Teachers spend much time making requests to governors. This causes the number of their pupils to grow.
[8] e.g. *Ep.* 1443.   [9] See above, p. 177.   [10] e.g. *Ep.* 1496.
[11] e.g. *Ep.* 288.   [12] e.g. *Ep.* 267–8.
[13] e.g. *Ep.* 1044 (392); 1095 for same man.

In addition to his pupils, Libanius would help a great variety of people:[1] relatives,[2] clients of his family,[3] school friends,[4] literary men,[5] Nicomedians,[6] Antiochene shopkeepers,[7] prisoners,[8] unfortunates generally.[9] Occasionally he used his influential connections on behalf of his city. He supported Antiochene embassies.[10] He negotiated an exchange of beasts for the arena between the council of Antioch and the governor and some decurions of Bithynia.[11] He pleaded for Antioch when Datian's estates near Antioch had been burned in a public disturbance.[12]

Many of the favours asked by Libanius were really unavoidable under the conditions of the Roman Empire. The government had to be informed in some way about the men who were candidates for posts in the government service, and in the absence of a system of examinations, patronage in the field of appointments was inevitable. Again, in view of the primitive nature of communications and of the corruption of the civil service, it was desirable that abuses and injustices should be brought to the notice of the government by men whose standing gave their information weight.[13] Nevertheless the system of favours raised moral issues.

---

[1] At times high-ranking members of the administration: *Ep.* 21 for an accused governor of Syria; *Ep.* 106–7 and 394–8 commend new governors to inhabitants of their province; cf. *Ep.* 457, 459. *Ep.* 1265–6 reconcile Clearchus, vicar of Asia, with Nicocles, a prominent citizen of Constantinople. In 390, Sapor, a former *magister militum* facing charges, expects Libanius to write on his behalf to the emperor, *Ep.* 957. This went beyond Libanius' power.

[2] For help with cousin's liturgy, see above, p. 141 n. 7.

[3] e.g. *Ep.* 152 (359–60).

[4] e.g. *Ep.* 763 (362), 585 (357), 184, 1032 (392).

[5] *Ep.* 382, special consideration shown to exponents of λόγοι; *Ep.* 312 (357) help for a teacher is a benefit to all Hellenes. Letters for family of his old teacher Zenobius: *Ep.* 101–2 (359–60), 532 (356), 118–19, 955, 931 (390). Client of Libanius' uncle taken over, *Ep.* 152. Commendations for poets: *Ep.* 1517, 1047, cf. *Or.* liv. 55, *Ep.* 816–17 (363). Commendations for sophists: *Ep.* 796 (362–3), 996, 997.

[6] *Ep.* 636, 641.   [7] See above, p. 53.   [8] *Or.* xlv.

[9] *Ep.* 1033 for orphans; 567 for a female slave; 244, aged official to be given easier work; 1339 for debtor to creditor; 1041 for a peasant who accidentally set fire to the house of a neighbour; 1253 for Manicheans; *Or.* xxix on an injustice suffered by a baker; *Ep.* 1360 for a youth and an old woman wronged by a powerful person.

[10] See Appendix I on embassies.   [11] *Ep.* 586–8, 598–9 (357).

[12] On Datian see Seeck, *Briefe*, 113–16. *Ep.* 1184 (364), Libanius' letter for Antioch; cf. 1173, 1186, 1197, 1259, Datian sends Libanius a letter announcing that he has pardoned Antioch, which Libanius reads to the council.

[13] Amm. xx. 5. 7, Julian, in his first speech as Augustus, promised not to allow patronage in connection with promotion to military or civilian posts.

Libanius sometimes interceded for men on trial, or pleaded for the reversal of the verdict pronounced against a man who had been found guilty. And such favours were asked in quite the same way as the others.¹ Clearly, neither Libanius nor the officials he addressed saw a sharp division between their obligations as friends and their duties as administrators or judges. This makes it possible for Libanius to ask an official to help a former governor of Syria now on trial, 'for justice and my sake'.² Of course Libanius always maintained that he was only asking for what the justice of his client's case required in any case. Perhaps he sincerely believed that this was true. But he also knew very well that favours might be disastrous to good government. At school he taught his pupils, if they should reach a position of authority, to govern strictly according to the law and to shun favour-giving.³ He composed two eloquent speeches about the corruption of justice by influence.⁴ Citizens of the empire would reap no benefit from victory over invading barbarians unless the rule of law was maintained within the empire.⁵ Moreover, when Libanius commended a litigant to a judge, he often included a phrase of apology, as for instance: 'If a judge is spurred on by his own nature to help the right, would it be a disgrace if he should listen to another person talking in the cause of justice?'⁶ Or: 'To help the accused is only wrong if to be accused and to be guilty are the same.'⁷ Nevertheless such scruples did not stop Libanius from asking favours. He continued to assume that his friends ought to oblige him, and to feel hurt if they refused.⁸

Indeed when Libanius encountered a governor who ruled with ἀκρίβεια,⁹ he had arguments ready to persuade him to take a more flexible view. He might ask him not to erase the Graces (τὰς χάριτας) from the number of the gods.¹⁰ Or he might remind him that to dismiss the Graces altogether is un-Greek,¹¹ or that a man who does not give good and just favours to friends is an enemy of the goddess Athena, who maintains the Graces in her porch.¹²

---

¹ *Ep.* 110, 151, 163.   ² *Ep.* 83.   ³ *Ep.* 696 (362).
⁴ *Or.* lii and li.   ⁵ *Or.* li. 2–3.   ⁶ *Ep.* 56 (359).
⁷ *Ep.* 105 (359–60).   ⁸ *Or.* lvi. 3, lvii. 21 ff.
⁹ e.g. Ecdicius, consular of Galatia addressed in *Ep.* 308 (360).
¹⁰ *Ep.* 221 (360) to Andronicus II. On his justice: *Or.* lxii. 7.
¹¹ *Ep.* 217, cf. 357.
¹² *Ep.* 673; see also *Or.* xiv. 1–3 to the Emperor Julian. We might also note that the practice of giving private persons permission to requisition the animals of

He argues, in other words, that it was traditional for men of education to give favours. He appeals to the tradition of Greek politics, as it had already been expressed by Plutarch two hundred years earlier.

Further, the ability to obtain favours showed to all the world that Libanius was honoured by men of power, and this was in itself a kind of insurance against attacks by unscrupulous persons. Libanius used to express pleasure at receiving letters from great men in the state, in a way which today would seem immoderate and undignified. It was his habit to read the letters aloud in public, pleasing his friends but angering his enemies.[1] Libanius would feel depressed when an expected letter from a great man failed to arrive, and he was reluctant to admit the non-arrival to inquirers. One might explain such behaviour as vanity, or an artist's longing for recognition, but this is inadequate. Letters from the powerful irrefutably demonstrated Libanius' influence. His standing in the town would rise when they arrived,[2] and in consequence the men he chose to help would receive greater benefit from his assistance, and his private affairs would be certain of greater respect, both from enemies who might want to harm him, and from officials, whose cooperation in many transactions was indispensable. Sometimes Libanius merely asks a governor either to invite the bearer of a letter, or to make his interest in his affairs manifest in some other way.[3] Such evident personal interest on the part of the governor, without any legal decision or further favour, was in itself a valuable form of protection. If an invitation from a governor might further a man's security, how much more would the ability to obtain a favour from him for a third person enhance a man's prestige? Libanius bore this in mind, and was keen not only that his help should be effective, but that it should be known to have been effective.[4]

peasants for rubble-carrying was justified—not by Libanius—as a 'favour' which the governor might reasonably grant, *Or*. l. 8.

[1] *Ep*. 1004 (391), Libanius has received a letter from Symmachus. *Ep*. 1117 (364), Libanius congratulated on having so powerful a protector as Datian. *Ep*. 963 (390), knowledge of letter from Siburius brings many to Libanius' house. *Ep*. 940 (390), the arrival of a letter from Proculus has improved Libanius' private affairs. See also *Ep*. 987, 1021, 1100.

[2] *Ep*. 991 (390), 556 (357).   [3] *Ep*. 585 (357), 108 (359–60).
[4] The reputation of being in a position to help is important, *Ep*. 284 (358–9), 293 (359–60) ... ἐμοί τε αἰσχύνη ἔχει τοῖς φίλοις εἰ μὴ δυναίμην βοηθεῖν.

When we consider all the reasons which induced Libanius to exercise patronage and to ask governors for favours, we realize that the giving and taking of favours played an essential part in social relationships at Antioch and, indeed, throughout the empire.¹ We can easily understand how Libanius, who was in the habit of preaching to his pupils the evils of favour-giving, should remind a pupil in an official position that Pericles had once asked the Athenians to transgress a law he had himself proposed, in order to confer the Athenian citizenship on his son by Aspasia.²

Libanius was only one of many patrons active at Antioch. Outstanding among the patrons were the *honorati*, who, as we have seen, had numerous opportunities of meeting and influencing the governor. But there were others who happened to enjoy social relations with the governor of the moment. They included teachers of rhetoric, who gained access to the governor to entertain him with their art, as Libanius himself had often done.³ A doctor is mentioned,⁴ perhaps the doctor of Tissamenes,⁵ who had exploited the intimacy given him by his professional duties so well, that he had become wealthier than great court officials and was lessee of a large portion of the council's land.

Certain men lived at Antioch whose rank was so high that they could afford not to visit the governor in person, and instead sent requests in writing.⁶ Even so, their demands carried more weight than requests made to the governors orally by others.

Libanius himself seems not to have charged clients for his help.⁷ But to many patrons their access to the governor was a source of income. Men had been known to rise from poverty to great wealth by exploiting their easy intercourse with governors.⁸ Formerly, patrons had been paid in kind. Clients filled the

¹ Amm. xxvii. 11. 3 remarks that the great Roman noble, Probus, was 'forced' to hold offices in spite of his naturally lazy character, because his clients wanted him powerful. Libanius, too, would be subjected to pressure by his clients to use what influence he had. Naturally, for if such humble persons as the baker's wife did not obtain justice through the intercession of an influential man, they would never obtain it. Libanius on case of baker's wife, *Or.* xxix. 13–14.

² *Ep.* 696 (362).

³ *Or.* lii. 29 ff., li. 13–17. Libanius himself did this, *Or.* i. 107.

⁴ *Or.* lii. 33.   ⁵ *Or.* xxxiii. 38.   ⁶ *Or.* li. 11.

⁷ *Or.* i. 109. He normally even refused the New Year presents (*Ep.* 1329) which were customarily exchanged between patron and client; ἐ. καλανδῶν, Foerster, (ed.), vol. 8. 473, l. 9.

⁸ *Or.* lii. 15 ff. *Or.* xxvii. 21, great wealth earned by father of assessor of *comes orientis* Icarius.

forecourts of their patrons' houses with rare foods, fish, wine, birds, and other luxuries of local origin, or brought by ship or camel from distant lands. They might also give wheat, barley, or clothing. But some time before 388 clients began to send presents of gold and silver.[1] The teaching profession, if not education, was among the beneficiaries. Libanius asserts that of the wealthy teachers of his day more had earned their wealth in the court-room than in the schoolroom.[2] This does not mean that the teachers earned their fortunes by appearing as barristers in the law courts. At this time the professions of advocate and sophist were separate.[3] The teachers' profitable advocacy derived from their opportunities for social intercourse with the governor.

The services of the patron were not paid by the client once and for all. Patrons were insatiable, and clients continued to feed them, paying a kind of insurance against the occasion when they would again need patronage.[4] The hold obtained by patrons over their clients was particularly tight in the case of certain shop-keepers.[5] 'And when they see their power, the craftsmen submit to them and even to their servants. For they, too, have power to whip them or bind them, to push them about, to throw them down and to disfigure their clothing. . . .' The effect of this was that the patrons and their servants bought the shopkeepers' goods for little or nothing, and in their great houses enjoyed abundance of everything, while the shopkeepers were short of bread. The patrons even obtained labour-services from the shopkeepers. They might, for instance, employ them on building work. The help given by a patron to a client was only the first stage in the business of favour-giving. The patron could also exploit his position of influence to bring the client into permanent depen-dence. We note that the consequences of the convention of favour-giving went beyond the aid given by patrons to clients. The same influence which enabled the patron to help his client also enabled him to subject the client to his will.

That this happened in the country is well known. Libanius provides an example in his *Contra Mixidemum*.[6] Mixidemus looks

---

[1] *Or.* li. 9. Libanius means that the patrons were becoming more shameless. We need not conclude with Piganiol that this was a consequence of greater abun-dance of money (*L'Empire chrétien*, 294).

[2] *Or.* lii. 29–30.

[3] Libanius himself never spoke in court, cf. Wolf, *Schulwesen der Spätantike*, 22–3.

[4] *Or.* lii. 14.   [5] Ibid. 16 ff.   [6] *Or.* xxxix.

like a fictitious name.[1] Perhaps it is a cover for the name of an individual too powerful to attack directly. But even if Mixidemus represents a particular individual, his career matches exactly that of the class of men who, according to Libanius, after starting at the bar poor proceeded to win power and wealth, through their access to the governor.[2] Mixidemus even managed to obtain several governorships and thus became an *honoratus*.[3] At some stage in his career he began to take certain country folk under his protection.[4]

Apparently these villagers had previously paid *officiales* to protect them.[5] That *officiales* might exercise patronage over villages is confirmed by an Egyptian law.[6] The fact that villagers approached *officiales* for protection should not be surprising. After all they were in the best position of all to influence their chief, the governor. What is surprising is that the *officiales* agreed to undertake the paid patronage of villagers. It is a good illustration of the failings of the imperial administrative machine. But in this particular case, the *officiales* were edged out of their perquisite by an *honoratus*, and Mixidemus was occupied, as Libanius says, 'slaving for the country folk', and no doubt drawing a satisfactory reward.

Moreover certain farmers farming good land 'under the hills', farmed their land for Mixidemus rather than themselves, for he exacted from them in good season and in bad a 'tax' of corn and other produce, and the wives of the peasants performed services in his household and at his banquets. In return, he promptly performed for the peasants whatever they asked of him. When they sent him letters with requests he would set aside all other business to perform what they required.[7]

At the same time Mixidemus was worming himself into other large villages. His practice was to buy one measure ($\pi\lambda\epsilon\theta\rho\sigma\nu$) of land in a village. He was then well set to obtain control of the whole village, for he was able to threaten its inhabitants and so make them submit to whatever he demanded.[8] We can see that Mixidemus was building up great estates for himself on the basis of patronage. The situation is very similar to that mentioned earlier of the shopkeepers and their patrons. The peasants needed

---

[1] Thus Foerster (ed.), vol. iii. 264, n. 3; Reiske (ed.), vol. ii. 353, n. 5. Petit, *Historia* v (1956), 503.

[2] Cf. *Or.* xxxix. 12 ff. and lii. 15.   [3] *Or.* xxxix. 6.

[4] Ibid. 10.   [5] Ibid.   [6] *C.T.* xi. 24. 3 (395).

[7] *Or.* xxxix. 10.   [8] Ibid. 11.

help and protection. The fact that this was previously supplied by officials suggests that it was help in their dealings with the administration, perhaps in disputes over taxation, perhaps in lawsuits with owners, if they had them. Certainly, the help was required at Antioch, where they sent the letters, not on the location of their farms. Such help Mixidemus was able to give as a result of his influence with the governor. Moreover this same influence also gave him the power to threaten[1] the men under his protection, and thus to subject them completely. This, according to Bell, was how the great estates we find in sixth-century Egypt were built up.[2]

Of the violence that powerful men could use Libanius gives examples. In his speech on behalf of Aristophanes he describes how Eugenius, an official under the Emperor Constantius, claimed land from the Corinthian decurion Aristophanes, apparently on the pretext that it was part of his wife's dowry. In the course of his efforts to get this land, not only did he involve Aristophanes in a lawsuit, but caused threats to be made against the managers of his estates. Eventually landlord and managers fled, and in their absence the land was not cultivated, the trees were cut, and the slaves either escaped or remained idle. Such behaviour, according to Libanius, was not uncommon among δυναστεύοντες in the reign of the Emperor Constantius.[3]

Eugenius was a man of high position. But much smaller men, if they had influence, could behave in a similar manner. Libanius describes how a sophist might punish parents who had failed to patronize his school. If the father was dead the sophist might arrange for the mother to be dragged into the market-place and handed over to 'soldiers'. If both parents were dead they would harry the servants on the estates of the son, until the young master gave up his schooling and returned home to help them.[4] It is not to be supposed that the sophist performed the acts of violence himself. He used his influence to get the authorities to make claims on the property of the men he wished to punish. This behaviour is typical. Patrons had no need to use violence themselves, since they could always move the state machine in their

[1] *Or.* xxxix. 11.
[2] H. I. Bell, *J.R.S.* xl (1950), 125, reviewing A. C. Johnson and L. C. West, *Byzantine Egypt: Economic Studies.*
[3] *Or.* xiv. 10–11, 45; Seeck, *Briefe,* s.vv. Aristophanes and Eugenius III.
[4] *Or.* lv. 11.

interest. Alternatively, they might get the authorities to condone acts of violence done by their clients.[1]

In various writings Libanius has occasion to mention different kinds of patronage but in the only speech entirely devoted to the topic, the famous *De patrociniis*, he restricts himself to one specific variety, that offered by soldiers to country folk. The first part of the speech describes patronage as it affects 'large villages each having many masters', which I have argued to be villages of peasant proprietors.[2] These villages were garrisoned, and the villagers made the commanding officer their patron. They rewarded the patron with wheat, or barley, or gold. Then they exploited the help he could give by raiding neighbouring villages. They cut off portions of land, diverted water courses, cut down trees, plundered and committed acts of violence against people, and then feasted their military friends in the midst of the ravaged village. The part of the soldiers in these activities was mainly passive, but their presence in the villages deterred the victims from retaliation. Another speech reveals a further benefit the patron might get out of these raids; the landowners of the raided villages might be compelled to sell him their land at token prices.[3]

The φύλακες τῆς χώρας, whose status has been discussed, watched the raids but failed to help the victims 'because of the patron'.[4] So it was not fear of violence from the soldiers which deterred them from intervening but the power of a distant patron, who would bring all serious counter-measures to nothing, and perhaps even obtain the punishment of their originators. In this connection there is an interesting law from the year 392, addressed to the praetorian prefect of the East, in which the *defensores* of the cities are asked to keep a particularly sharp supervision of legal proceedings connected with brigandage. The law ends by ordering 'that patronage (*patrocinium*) shall be abolished, which by bestowing favours on the guilty ones and aid on criminals, has made crimes increase'.[5] This phrase gives the most likely explanation of the operation of patronage in the case of these pillaging villages. On the other hand the military commander

---

[1] *Or.* lii. 18, village pays a patron to influence the judge to condone aggression against a smaller village.

[2] *Or.* xlvii. 4 ff. On various problems raised by this and other passages of *Or.* xlvii see L. Harmand, *Discours sur les patronages*, 126 ff.

[3] *Or.* lii. 12.   [4] *Or.* xlvii. 6.

[5] *C.T.* i. 29. 8 (392), *P.P.O.*

might just have given an assurance that he would not allow his troops to be used against the villagers under his protection.[1]

Villagers also use patronage against councillors who come down to their villages to collect taxes. They refuse to hand over the taxes. The councillors threaten the village headmen (ἄρχοντες). This too is to no purpose for the headmen are less powerful than the patron. Finally the councillors try force. The villagers resist. Thus the councillors are compelled to return to Antioch empty-handed. The imperial authorities of Antioch do not intervene on their behalf. The patron prevents it. So, at last, the councillors are left with no alternative but to sell their property to meet the tax they have been unable to collect. Again, we find that this had been brought about by the help given to the villagers by a patron who intrigued in the background and prevented the government machinery from being brought to bear against the defaulters.[2]

A patron might be sought by a dependent village no less than by a village of peasant proprietors.[3] It would, however, be a mistake to assume that such peasants were necessarily motivated by a dispute with their owner. It is quite clear from chapters 19–22 of the *De patrociniis* that to help the peasant to oppose the demands of his owner was not the original or even the most important function of the patron.[4] It would be absurd to suggest that a peasant should get in touch with a patron through his owner if it was precisely a dispute with the owner that had produced the need for a patron.[5] In fact the peasants' need was for help in a much wider field than that of landlord-and-tenant relations. It included protection against aggression,[6] or the diversion of irrigation,[7] and the settlement of disputes with other

---

[1] *P. Lond.* 234 = *P. Abinn.* 3.

[2] *Or.* xlvii. 7–10, cf. *C.T.* xi. 24. 3 (395), *comes Aegypti.*   [3] *Or.* xlvii. 11.

[4] The peasants claim that they chose patrons to save them from suffering wrong—even though the villages belong to men of distinction able to help the harmed. Only after a long time (πολλοῦ χρόνου προιόντος) did they begin to use patrons against their master. Significantly the parallels Libanius uses to discredit the peasants' recourse to patronage do not fit a peasant-owner dispute. The city which calls in the barbarians (ibid. 20) is in dispute with another city, not with the emperor. The slave who is wronged and looks to a patron has not been wronged by his master (ibid. 21). The deterioration in his attitude to his master is a result not a cause of his resort to a patron.

[5] Ibid. 22, the peasant to approach the master, the master the patron.

[6] Ibid. 11 : χεῖρα ὀρέξαι λυπουμένοις τὸ παθεῖν φεύγοντες.

[7] Ibid. 19: τὴν δι' ὑδάτων. Cf. ibid. 5, protected peasants divert water of other villages, cf. i. 53.

peasants;[1] also no doubt, although this is not mentioned, taxation. In some of these areas the landlord was unable to help, not because his own interest was involved, but because he was not sufficiently powerful.[2] In short, the peasants sought a patron in order to achieve objects which would have been performed by an efficient system of local government and justice.

In the absence of effective local government, the peasants retained a patron who would draw the attention of an imperial official to their situation, or failing this, remedy the grievance through his own power. But once they had obtained a patron, it was natural that sooner or later they should make use of him in disputes with their masters. Libanius himself had experienced this use of patronage. Some Jews, who had worked land of his family for four generations, shook off their ancient yoke and determined to fix their conditions of work themselves.[3] When Libanius took them to law over this, they placed their hope in the patronage of the general, probably the *magister militum per orientem*. At first the governor had imprisoned some of the men and let others go. The latter immediately went to the house of the general with offerings of wheat, barley, ducks, and fodder for horses. With the powerful man's help, they won the lawsuit. We note that the patron prevailed over Libanius, although he was a famous and well-connected man and an honorary praetorian prefect, and we may wonder, as Libanius did, what a man of lower standing would have to endure.[4]

In some areas peasants were unable to obtain a patron. Was this because there were no soldiers stationed near them? From these villages the peasants fled to the houses of powerful military men, quite often leaving their wives and children behind, and there enjoyed the benefits of protection. If any person should then lay an accusation against a fugitive, it would be enough for an officer to say that the general was interested in him for the accusation to be quashed.[5] What profit did the patron make in

---

[1] Ibid. xlvii. 19: ἤντ' αὖ δίκης που πρὸς ἀλλήλους δέωνται . . .

[2] Ibid. 22: εἰ τῆς χρείας ἐλάττων ὁ τὸν ἀγρὸν ἔχων.   [3] Ibid. 13.

[4] On the lawsuit, Harmand, *Discours sur les patronages*, 185–203. He is almost certainly wrong to place trial, general, and judge in the village. *Or.* xlv. 3–5 shows that cases of this kind were held before the governor at Antioch. The centralization of justice and the standing of Libanius make it most unlikely that an action brought by him was held anywhere but in the governor's court. *Ep.* 174 (359–60), Libanius as patron of a peasant writes to a governor.

[5] *Or.* xlvii. 17.

these cases? Perhaps he just gained labour for his own land.[1] Perhaps he sometimes became the owner of the land the peasants had deserted. In Gaul peasants are known to have fled to a patron, who placed them on land of his own; but only after they had given him their holdings.[2] As a result, both benefited at the expense of the taxes. The peasant on his patron's land would be safe from any arrears that the collectors might claim from him. The patron would probably be powerful enough to avoid paying a large part of his taxes altogether.

How widespread were the practices described in the *De patrociniis*? It can be argued that the speech was written in response to Libanius' own troubles with his Jewish peasants and that Libanius exaggerates the scale of the phenomenon in order to build up a personal grievance into a matter of public concern. But while personal considerations obviously played a part in the motivation of the speech, there is no need to reject the essential truth of its general description of patronage. After all, the landlord-and-tenant relationship is put forward as only one field out of many affected by patronage.

The speech concentrates on patronage provided by military commanders. These were not the only important patrons but there is every reason to suppose that military patrons were prominent. In areas where troops were stationed villagers had always treated the local commandant as the representative of the authorities, and sought his assistance in difficulties.[3] Often a local garrison commander was the only man of influence with whom peasants had regular contact. Moreover Libanius does not appear to be describing unfamiliar practices. He assumes for instance that payments from country folk form a recognized, if illegal, part of the income of a general.[4] The only development put forward as recent is that military support was made available against the landlord.[5]

Patronage was an institution of ancient standing. The disturbing development of this period was that it began to undermine established political and economic relationships not only

---

[1] Cf. the civilian patron Eulogius of *P. Thead.* 17.
[2] Salv. *Gub. Dei.* v. 8.
[3] E. G. Turner, *Greek Papyri*, 146 cites *P. Oxy.* xix. 2230, *P. Mich.* iii. 175, *P. Abinn.* 44, and introduction, 18–19.
[4] *Or.* xvii. 26.
[5] *Or.* xlvii. 11.

between city and country, but in many other spheres.[1] It was this which instigated Libanius to compose his speeches about rural patronage, about Mixidemus, and about the abuse of familiarity with governors. The same circumstance was responsible for the issue of six laws under the title *De patrociniis vicorum* in the Theodosian Code.[2]

Of the six laws, four date from the nineties of the fourth century. The situation was evidently getting worse. An important factor in the deterioration was the pressure of taxation imposed to meet the heavy military expenses of the empire in these years. The unhappy taxpayer had every incentive to seek means of lowering his tax burden. At the same time imperial officials, active and retired, were becoming steadily more privileged and, in the words of de Zulueta, 'it was largely by illicit extension of privilege that patronage throve'.[3] It was inevitable that ordinary men should seek the assistance and protection of the privileged.

But there was another development that induced ordinary people to retain privileged patrons. The tightening of the governor's control over the government of the city and its territory meant that the traditional authorities were losing the power to solve problems and settle disputes that arose in the territory of the city. Redress could come only from the governor, and, since he was not easily or cheaply available to ordinary folk, it was inevitable that peasants should seek the intercession of men to whom he was accessible.

This aspect of the problem was recognized by the imperial government. The Emperors Valens and Valentinian had tried to solve it by setting up in each city an official patron, the *defensor*. The description of the *defensor*'s function in one of their laws provides an excellent account of the circumstances which were responsible for the spread of patronage in the countryside.

Wise provision has been made that the innocent and peaceful rustics should enjoy the benefit of special *patrocinium*. Thus they shall not be exhausted by the fraudulent practices of court trials and be

---

[1] *C.T.* xiii. 1. 15 (386), *P.P.O.*, also 21 (418); *C.T.* xii. 1. 76 (371), *P.P.O.*, also 146 (395, *P.P. Ital.*); *C.T.* xii. 1. 50. 2 (362), *P.P.O.*; *C.T.* xii. 1. 6 (319); *C.T.* xiv. 3. 3 (364), *P.U.R.*; *C.T.* xiv. 4. 5 (389), *P.U.R.*; *C.T.* xiii. 7. 1 (399), *P.P.O.*, also 2 (406).

[2] *C.T.* xi. 24. Libanius' writings on related topics: *Or.* xxxix, xlvii, li, lii.

[3] F. de Zulueta, 'De patrociniis vicorum', 12. Some privileges which patrons might exploit for benefit of protected peasants: Jones, *L.R.E.* 774.

harassed even when they demand satisfaction, while they either provide for a very avaricious advocate or win over the chief of the office staff with very large bribes, as he blocks the threshold, while the *acta* of the case are purchased from the *exceptores*, and while as a tip the *intercessor* demands more from the winner of a suit than the loser will pay. The dignity of a senator does not allow such practices but with a speedy decision he settles the controversies that have arisen. For if anything has been wrongfully and violently taken away he eliminates all dilatoriness and restores the property to its owner. . . .[1]

The laws introducing the *defensor* were about twenty years old when Libanius wrote his *De patrociniis*. The new[2] office had not ended the demand for unofficial patrons. This is not surprising. A single officer could not satisfy the needs of so large a territory. In any case an official patron could hardly be asked to obtain unlawful favours, such as relief from taxation. Given the conditions of the time, one cannot see how people could be stopped from seeking the services of powerful patrons.

The eventual consequences of patronage could be extremely far-reaching. There is plenty of evidence that the patron often ended as the owner of the lands protected by him.[3] Patronage might therefore produce fundamental changes in the character of land-ownership. Patronage also interfered with the rents of the smaller landowners and with the taxes of the empire. In this way it provided a potential threat to the existence both of the council and of the imperial administration. Unfortunately it is very difficult to estimate quantitatively how far these effects of patronage had been realized in Syria. If one takes a comprehensive view of the evidence of Libanius' writings as a whole, one is not left with the impression that patronage had as yet become a crucial factor in the fields of curial finance and taxation. The example of Mixidemus shows that large estates were being built up on the basis of patronage. On the other hand the *De patrociniis* does not mention that the generals were actually becoming owners of the lands protected by them. It is likely that the full

---

[1] *C.T.* i. 29. 5 (370) from the *Theodosian Code* translated by C. Pharr (Princeton, 1952).

[2] On history and prehistory of the *defensor*, B. R. Rees, 'The *Defensor Civitatis*', *J. Jur. Pap.* vi. (1952), 73–102. I assume that the function, if not the title, of the *defensor* of 370 was new.

[3] Jones, *L.R.E.* 775–7; *C.T.* xi. 24. 6 (415), *P.P.O.*; *C.J.* xi. 54 (468); *C.T.* xi. 1. 32 (423), *P.P. Illyr.*; Augustine, *Ep.* 96.

effect of patronage only became apparent in Syria after Libanius' time.

We lack the evidence to study the conditions in the territory of Antioch during the fifth and sixth centuries. In Egypt papyrus evidence reveals a great increase in the importance of estates. In the fourth century there were numerous small peasant holdings at Oxyrhynchus; in the sixth century two-thirds of the combined territory of Oxyrhynchus and Cynopolis were occupied by the estates of the Apions, a great senatorial family.[1]

There have also been changes in the government of the countryside. The collection of taxes is no longer, or no longer entirely, in the hands of councillors who can be defied by patron-supported villagers. The officials who were responsible for divisions of the city-territory, the *praepositi pagorum*, continued to function but they were now known as pagarchs,[2] and the office was held by great landowners who were powerful in their own right.[3] They completely overshadow the council which had once been the source of their authority. They are now appointed and deposed by the governor, whose decision has to be confirmed by the praetorian prefect.[4]

This development evidently weakened the administrative machinery. Justinian remarks, no doubt with some exaggeration, that the corn collected in Egypt for dispatch overseas disappears on the way, and that pagarchs, councillors, and governors manage matters so that no one can find out what is going on, while they alone derive any profit.[5] At least part of the trouble seems to have been that the pagarchs were less easy to control than the former collectors had been. This is suggested by the vicissitudes of the village of Aphrodito. The Emperor Leo (457–74) had granted the village the privilege of *autopragia*, the right to pay its taxes

---

[1] Jones, *L.R.E.* 780; see also H. I. Bell, 'The Servile State in Byzantine Egypt', *J.E.A.* iv (1917), 86–106; E. R. Hardy, 'The Large Estates of Byzantine Egypt', (Diss. Columbia, 1931); G. Diosdi, 'Zur Frage der Entwicklung des Patrociniums in Ägypten', *J. Jur. Pap.* xiv (1962), 57–71.

[2] Pagarch = *praepositus pagi*: *C.T.* vii. 4. 1 (325); *P. Oxy.* xvii. 2110 (370). On the later pagarchy: G. Rouillard, *L'Administration civile de l'Égypte*, 54–5. A study of the institution is needed.

[3] Rouillard, op. cit. 54, nn. 2, 3.   [4] Justinian, *Ed.* xiii. 12, 25.

[5] Ibid. xiii (*praef.*): ἀλλ' οἱ μὲν συντελεῖς καθάπαξ ἰσχυρίζοντο πάντα εἰς ὁλόκληρον ἀπαιτεῖσθαι, οἱ παγάρχαι δὲ καὶ οἱ πολιτευόμενοι καὶ οἱ πράκτορες τῶν δημοσίων καὶ διαφερόντως οἱ κατὰ καιρὸν ἄρχοντες οὕτω τὸ πρᾶγμα μέχρι νῦν διετίθεσαν, ὡς μηδενὶ δύνασθαι γενέσθαι γνώριμον, αὐτοῖς δὲ μόνοις ἐπικερδές.

directly to the imperial authorities, and, provided the payments were made in time, to by-pass the regular collectors, in this case the pagarch of Antaeopolis.[1] The pagarch nevertheless continued to demand taxes from the village. Eventually the villagers gave their village to the Empress Theodora in the hope that she would protect it as her property. Later, when their difficulties came to a crisis, they sent an ambassador to Constantinople to seek help from the emperor himself. After three years the ambassador went a second time to secure a second imperial letter. But this did not prevent a later pagarch from attacking the village with a force of brigands, local levies, and soldiers. We do not know the end of the story but it is obvious that, compared with fourth-century Syria, there has been a break-down of orderly administration.[2]

5. DIRECT CONTACT BETWEEN THE URBAN POPULATION AND THE GOVERNORS

In the *Antiochicus* Libanius likens the relationship of people and council at Antioch to that of children and parents.[3] The comparison implies that the people would bring their grievances to the councillors and the councillors would—as the case might be—remedy them or place them before the governor. We may doubt whether the people's confidence in the council was ever as great as Libanius would have his readers believe. In any case, given the fact that all coercive power lay in the hands of the imperial officials, it was inevitable that protests should be addressed to them directly. In fact the regular ceremonial that accompanied the movements of a governor enabled him to keep in close touch with public opinion and public grievances.

Whenever a governor entered the city he would expect the leading citizens to meet him outside the gates. If the council did not turn up in strength this might have serious consequences for

---

[1] *Autopragia*: M. Gelzer, 'Zum αὐτόπρακτον σχῆμα der P. Aphrodito Cairo', *Arch. f. Pap.* v (1913), 188–9. The privilege granted to Aphrodito: *P. Cairo.*, Maspero i. 67019, ll. 1–6.

[2] The story of Aphrodito: Jones, *L.R.E.* 407–8; Hardy, op. cit. 135–9; H. I. Bell, 'An Egyptian village in the Age of Justinian', *J.H.S.* lxii (1942), 21–36; R. G. Salomon, *J.E.A.* xxxiv. (1948), 98 ff., on *P. Hamb.* 410; V. Martin, *J.E.A.* xv (1929), 96–102, on *P. Genev.* 210.

[3] *Or.* xi. 150–2.

its members.¹ The councillors in turn would be entitled to expect that the governor should descend from his carriage to greet them.² The crowd that welcomed the governor mirrored the social order of the town. In turn, he would pass senators and ex-governors, *officiales*, councillors, advocates, and teachers,³ and after passing the gates he would hear the acclamations (εὐφημίαι) of the people.⁴

It was a paradoxical feature of these acclamations that they formed a continuous accompaniment of public life. Acclamations were heard whenever the governor entered or left the city. The governor was greeted with shouts whenever he appeared in the theatre⁵ and even when he was merely driving through the streets.⁶ A governor thought it right and proper to be received by the people with acclamations, just as he expected the leading citizens to escort him when he was coming into the town or leaving it, or proceeding on a pleasure drive.⁷ He would treat acclamations as genuine evidence of the feelings of his subjects,⁸ and might worry if the shouting was not sufficiently loud.⁹ A governor received in complete silence by a theatre audience had been known to turn pale.¹⁰

Acclamations had a semi-constitutional status. Written record of acclamations was regularly sent to the capital so that the emperor might promote or punish his officials accordingly.¹¹ Carriers of this record were entitled to use the public post.

Acclamations could and often did contain material that was far from laudatory. In fact, an acclamation might easily turn into a demonstration. A demonstration made at a public spectacle was a privileged occasion. This is illustrated by a decision of the Ostrogothic King Theoderic (493–526). Shouts abusing certain senators had been raised during public games at Rome. The senators retaliated by arranging for some members of the Green

---

¹ *Or.* lvi. 1–2, 6, 9–12; punishment for failure to attend: *Or.* xxvii. 42.
² *Or.* xlvi. 40; cf. notes of Reiske (ed.), vol. ii. 490.
³ See (on reception of emperor): E. Kantorowicz, *Art. Bul.* xxvi (1944), 207–31; E. Peterson, *Zeit. syst. Theol.* vii (1930), 682–702.
⁴ *Or.* lvi. 15; also on welcoming acclamations: xx. 17, xv. 19.
⁵ *Or.* xxxiii. 12, xlvi. 17.   ⁶ *Or.* xli. 12.
⁷ *Or.* lvi. 1, liv. 54.   ⁸ *Or.* xli. 10, xlvi. 10 ff., 39, xlv. 22.
⁹ *Or.* xli. 3.   ¹⁰ *Or.* xxxiii. 12.
¹¹ *C.T.* i. 16. 6 (331), *ad provinciales* = *C.J.* i. 40. 3. Right to public post of carriers, *C.T.* viii. 5. 32 (370). The emperor's interest also implied in *Or.* xlv. 4: τὰς εὐφημίας ὑμῶν, i.e. of the emperors.

Faction, whom they thought responsible for the demonstration, to be attacked in the street. The affair was taken before the king. Theoderic ruled that the attackers were in the wrong. Abuse at the games should be tolerated. Abuse in the street was a different matter. Theoderic was a late and a barbarian ruler, but his attitude towards public demonstrations was the same as that shown by officials of the Later Empire.[1]

A governor could not avoid acclamations. He was obliged by law to attend public spectacles on certain occasions.[2] Moreover an invitation to come to the theatre issued to the governor by the assembled people had some formal significance. It might be carried by the *defensor* of the city and was entitled to courteous acknowledgment.[3]

Invitations were issued to the governor precisely in order to make him listen to complaints. So it is likely that a demonstration which induced the *comes* Icarius to come to the theatre twice on the same day was connected with the famine which was afflicting Antioch.[4] About this time, demonstrations in the theatre became so bad that the *comes* stopped performances.[5] But he also took notice of the complaints and fixed the price of bread. Another time, when the people protested that the water in the baths was not hot enough, Icarius had the responsible councillor beaten.[6] We frequently hear that demonstrations induced governors to take measures against the groups or individuals who had been demonstrated against. Food,[7] prices,[8] the employment of false measures,[9] were the topics which were regularly raised in demonstrations, and shopkeepers were the crowd's commonest victims.

But demonstrations were held on a great variety of issues. An emperor was asked to pardon certain foreign decurions under sentence of death. In the last days of the Emperor Valens there were 'rixae' and 'tumultus vulgares'; attempts were made to burn the baths which that emperor had built, and men who thought themselves wronged, shouted, 'Let Valens be burned

---

[1] Cass. *Var.* 1. 27; cf. *C.T.* i. 16. 6 (331): 'iustissimos ... iudices publicis adclamationibus conlaudandi damus omnibus potestatem e contrario iniustis et maleficis querellarum vocibus, accusandi. ...'

[2] *Or.* xlv. 8, 21, xxvi. 18; cf. *C.T.* xv. 5. 2.   [3] *Or.* xxvii. 32.

[4] *Or.* xxvi. 17. On the famine *Or.* i. 226 ff.   [5] *Or.* xxix. 2.

[6] *Or.* xxvi. 5, xxvii. 13.   [7] *Or.* xlv. 4, xlvi. 5, 7, 17.

[8] *Or.* xxix. 2.   [9] *Or.* xlvi. 10, cf. xxix. 22.

alive'.[1] In view of the personal nature of the attacks on the emperor, it is likely that his Arian religious policy and his suppression of the orthodox supporters of Meletius was being attacked. It is well known that the Riot of the Statues began as a remonstrance against the imposition of new taxes.[2] Only slightly later there took place yet another demonstration against the imperial authorities. The former consular Lucianus returned to Antioch after having been on trial at Constantinople on charges arising out of his governorship. Misled by the *defensor*, the citizens believed that he was returning as governor, and Lucianus was received with the customary ceremonies of welcome and the regular acclamations. The acclamations made to welcome this supposed governor began with shouts against the pagan gods, included attacks on the pagan praetorian prefect who had re-called Lucianus and put him on trial, and culminated in abuse of the young Emperor Arcadius. As it happened, this demonstration had no violent consequences.[3]

The acclamations consisted of rhythmical phrases, and were delivered in standardized form and order.[4] A complete record survives of acclamations made in 449 by the people of Edessa to welcome their governor. Seeck has compared this with the acclamations in honour of Lucianus and shown that the order of applause and abuse was the same in each case.[5] The people of Edessa began with the cry 'God is one' and continued with a long sequence of rhythmical phrases, extolling first the emperor, then the praetorian prefect, then in that order, the consul, two *magistri militum*, and the *comes orientis*. Last of all, there was a series in praise of the governor in whose honour the whole litany was being chanted. After the words of praise came the grievance. 'A new bishop for the metropolis!' 'Nobody wants Ibas!' and a long list of execrations directed against the unfortunate Ibas, whom the citizens of Edessa would no longer tolerate as their bishop.

The chanting of a long, rhythmical piece could not be done without preparation. The performance needed learning and leadership. This leadership, according to Libanius, was provided

---

[1] Demand for pardon: *Or.* xi. 155–6; Valens abused: Amm. xxxi. 1. 1–2.

[2] *Or.* xix. 25, xxii. 4.

[3] *Or.* lvi. 9, 2, 15; words of acclamation: ibid. 16.

[4] O. Seeck, 'Libanius gegen Lucianus', *Rh. M.* lxxiii (1920), 84–101.

[5] *Or.* lvi. 16; Procop. *Bell. Goth.* i. 64, the order of acclamations at Rome under Gothic rule was laid down in a treaty.

by about four hundred¹ men employed as a claque in the theatre. These men regularly led the people of Antioch in the acclamations, and this, no less than their role in the theatre, could be described as their profession, τέχνη.²

The claque was not formally employed by the imperial officials for the purpose of leading applause, but it used its control over the acclamations to extort concessions from governors. When a new governor came to the theatre for the first time, the claque would arrange for him to be received in absolute silence. Evidently the leaders of the claque were able to intimidate the rest of the audience.³ The disconcerted official would then have some popular announcement made, by means of which he might hope to win some cheers. This too would be to no purpose; finally, the governor would be compelled to negotiate with the leaders of the claque, and to win their support and cheers, at a price. This price might be a direct payment to the claque; or it might consist in increased employment for the claque's employers, the actors.⁴

But the fact that the members of the claque were in the first place employed by the actors, and not by the governors, gave them a degree of independence which they would have lacked had they simply been employed by the authorities. The claque might support a great variety of causes. Even councillors might make use of it in order to escape the wrath of a governor.⁵ The claque led the demonstration against the new taxes which set off the Riot of the Statues.⁶ The claque led demonstrations in favour of two deposed governors, Proculus⁷ and Lucianus.⁸ In

---

¹ *Or.* xli. 9.

² *Or.* lvi. 2, men whose 'skill' is to applaud the governors; ibid. 15 identifies them with followers of 'pantomimi'; xlvi. 17–18, men who lead applause of governors identified with the 400 of the claque. On earlier claques see R. MacMullen, *Enemies of the Roman Order*, 170 n. 10.   ³ *Or.* xxvi. 8 and xli. 3.

⁴ Payment to claque: *Or.* xli. 3–4; increased employment for actors: *Or.* lvi. 2, 16; Tissamenes, to please claque, interferes in management of shows: *Or.* xxxiii. 8; *Or.* xlv. 20–3 probably refers to the same activities. Claque obtained resumption of immoral festival at Daphne, *Or.* xli. 16, l. 11. The Council opposed the revival: *Or.* xli. 17. The claque might ask for money for an individual actor: *Or.* xlviii. 40.

⁵ *Or.* xlv. 22.

⁶ R. Browning in *J.R.S.* xlii (1952), 13–20, especially 14 and 20. After the riot we are told (*Or.* xxii. 37) that Senate and people of Constantinople pleaded for Antioch. The plea was surely included among acclamations of that city.

⁷ *Or.* xxvi. 2–4, 6–7.

⁸ *Or.* lvi. 16. The claque might be bought, to serve the private feuds of lesser men: *Or.* xlvi. 5, xxvi. 8; the claque could not be terrified by ruthlessness: *Or.* lvi. 25.

fact, the claque is associated with practically every public demonstration described by Libanius during the last decade of his life.[1]

This is a remarkable picture. That an unofficial body should exercise effective power in the city, and nevertheless not become the victim of counter-action by the imperial officials, is a phenomenon that strains belief. The strongest argument in favour of the truth of Libanius' account is that at a later date at Constantinople and Antioch the circus factions fulfilled a function very similar to that which Libanius assigned to the claque. The factions certainly led applause in theatre and hippodrome. They had control over the spectators, and the ability to produce disturbances on a very large scale. They showed remarkable independence of the government and ability to bargain even with the emperor.[2] The factions themselves did not, as I have argued, exist at Antioch in the fourth century, but the conditions which were to give such influence to the factions gave a similar role to an older and less comprehensive organization of the entertainment world: the dancers and their claque.

How long had the claque played this remarkable role? Acclamations had been officially recognized by Constantine but they are certainly very much older.[3] They must always have been organized and the claque of the theatre must always have been eminently qualified to lead them. Nevertheless the evidence of Libanius suggests that the situation he describes in his later speeches had only developed in his lifetime.

Such as it is, the evidence does not suggest that the claque was already taking a leading part in public disturbances in the reigns of Constantius or Julian. The lynching of the consular Theophilus was personally instigated by the Caesar Gallus.[4]

---

[1] See Appendix IV.

[2] Manojlović, 'Le peuple de Constantinople', *Byzantion* xi (1936), 617–716; A. Maricq, 'Factions du cirque et partis populaires', *Bull. de l'Acad. roy. de Belgique, Classe des Lettres*, 5ᵉ série xxxvi (1950), 396–421; H. G. Beck, 'Konstantinopel, zur Socialgeschichte einer frühmittelalterlichen Haupstadt', *B.Ƶ.* lviii (1965), 11–45; J. R. Martindale, '*Public Disorders in the Late Roman Empire*' (Oxford, unpublished B.Litt. thesis, 1960).

[3] On acclamations see s.v. Akklamation in *D.f. Ant. Chr.*, 216–33 (Th. Klauser); E. Kantorowicz, *Laudes regiae* (Berkeley, 1946); P. Maas, 'Metrische Akklamationen der Byzantiner', *B.Ƶ.* xxi (1928), 49–50; J. Colin, *Les Villes libres de l'Orient gréco-romain et l'envoi au supplice par acclamations populaires* (Brussels, 1965), 109–12.

[4] Greg. Naz. *V. Bas.* i. 57; Lib. *Or.* xix. 47–9, cf. xi. 153 ff.; Julian, *Misop.* 363C, 370.

Under Julian the polemical psalm-singing that accompanied the reburial of S. Babylas was presumably organized by the Church.[1] Disrespectful ditties sung by young revellers in the course of a nocturnal procession did not require organization of the kind provided by the claque.[2] When the shortage of food became serious, Julian was received in the hippodrome by shouts of 'Everything plentiful, everything dear'.[3] This was the kind of demonstration later led by the claque, but when Libanius discusses the misbehaviour of his fellow citizens during Julian's stay in the city, he blames a poor shiftless immigrant minority for the troubles. Neither dancers nor claque are mentioned.[4]

The claque is mentioned for the first time in a speech of 384. A disturbance was started in the theatre by some deserters and by the ὄχλος ἐν τῇ σκηνῇ τοῦ βίου τὰς ἐλπίδας ἔχων,[5] surely the claque. The better elements in the audience were compelled by the riff-raff to join in the mischief. On this occasion Libanius still takes a lenient view. He asks the governor to imprison the guilty but does not demand the death penalty or even corporal punishment.[6] In the ensuing years the claque and popular demonstrations become a central preoccupation of Libanius. The speech addressed to Timocrates[7] has no other purpose than to warn that newly appointed consular of Syria to disregard the acclamations and the men responsible for them. Their baneful influence had recently achieved the restoration of an immoral festival at Daphne,[8] which a wise emperor had abolished. The restoration of the festival had been opposed by the council but the claque had favoured it, and the claque had prevailed. These

---

[1] Soz. *H.E.* v. 19–20, Soc. *H.E.* iii. 18, Theodoret, *H.E.* iii. 6.

[2] Mocking of Julian: Julian, *Misop.* 357A, 360D, 354D, Amm. xxii. 3, Lib. *Or.* xv. 75, xvi. 28, 35; cf. a festival at Edessa: *Or.* xx. 27, xix. 48.

[3] First received with enthusiasm: *Or.* xv. 48. Soon after shouts of hungry people in the hippodrome: Julian, *Misop.* 368c, Lib. *Or.* xviii. 195.

[4] *Or.* xvi. 31, 32, 33.   [5] *Or.* xxvi. 8.   [6] Ibid. 9–12.

[7] *Or.* xli. I have seen no certain indication of date. It is certainly after 382, the date of Comitiva of Philagrius mentioned in 18, and in my opinion, earlier than the Riot of the Statues, which is not mentioned, although it would have given strong support to Libanius' argument. I would conclude that Timocrates was consular between 382 and 387. *Or.* xli also mentions the restoration of the immoral festival of Daphne (16). This is also mentioned in *Or.* l. 11, dated in 384–5. See Foerster's note, vol. iii. 469. Thus, *Or.* xli is not likely to be very much later than *Or.* l, i.e. than 385. It is probably earlier, for the events of Icarius' administration in which the claque played a part are not mentioned in the speech. This suggests that it preceded them.

[8] *Or.* xli. 16–17 and *Or.* l. 11.

men are spoiling the reputation of Antioch all over the world. Libanius would like to see the city freed from this pest. This evidently is impossible. He can only ask Timocrates to make the claque harmless by ignoring it.[1]

Tissamenes, perhaps the successor of Timocrates, but at any rate consular of Syria in 386, courted the applause of the crowd by accepting invitations to come to the hippodrome and to the theatre,[2] and by actively interfering in the management of shows.[3] When the crowd led by the claque had raised shouts against shopkeepers, he committed a number of shopkeepers to prison.[4] By thus displaying his conspicuous eagerness for the acclamations,[5] Tissamenes induced the people to believe that they governed the governor.[6]

A few months later, as if to prove Libanius right, came the Riot of the Statues. The crowd, led by the claque, got out of hand. The imperial images were broken and the city brought to the verge of disaster. In the trial following the riot a number of the guilty persons, probably including a portion of the claque, were executed.[7] Nevertheless the claque remained active. Scarcely a year later the claque led the daring acclamation of Lucianus, which included phrases against the Emperor Arcadius and the praetorian prefect Tatian. Thereupon Libanius advises the council to 'separate the well-behaved among the resident aliens from those who ought to have been rooted out long ago, to congratulate the city on the continued residence of the former and to free it from the latter, throwing them out, pushing them out, banishing them. What is the criterion? With foreigners who have house, wife, children, and craft it is right that we should share the city; for these possessions establish their respectability. But foreigners for whom services provided by the dancers are a substitute for all these things, we should order to look for another city—and to carry the dancers away with them on their shoulders.'

It is significant that Libanius did not believe that the problem could be solved by routine police measures. 'Let no one think that this thing can be stopped by sword and executions. If there was such deterring force in executions even the present outrage

---

[1] *Or.* xli. 19.   [2] *Or.* xxxiii. 8, xlv. 20–1.   [3] *Or.* xxxiii. 8; cf. xlv. 22.
[4] *Or.* xlv. 4: ... ταῦτα παρὰ τῶν τὰς εὐφημίας ὑμῶν ἐγκεχειρισμένων identifies the claque.
[5] *Or.* xxxiii. 12.   [6] Ibid. 11.   [7] *Or.* xix. 36.

would not have been committed, because of earlier executions. In fact, at the same time as people in the theatre talk about the men who have been executed for such offences, the more recent disturbances put the earlier ones in the shade. For the dancers take away their senses, being considerably more powerful than formerly, since they have many ready to die for them.'[1]

Libanius' advice was not heeded. In what may well be his last speech, written about 392, the influence of the claque is still a central issue. The consular Florentius had deposed a curial official in charge of markets, and beaten a number of shopkeepers in response to a demonstration led by the claque.[2]

On the evidence it looks as if the claque-led demonstrations were a phenomenon that developed during the last decade of Libanius' life.[3] What explanation can we offer? A possible one is that there was increasing tension within the city. The eighties of the fourth century were, as we have seen, a period of severe pressure of taxation. Further, the population of the city was increasing and perhaps outrunning its food supply. The two phenomena will certainly have made tempers rise. Nevertheless the general prosperity of the Syrian countryside in the fifth century was not accompanied by a decline of this tension in the city. The riots that are recorded from the reigns of the Emperors Zeno[4] and Anastasius[5] were far more severe than anything recorded from the fourth century.[6]

It is likely that the demonstrations led by the claque were not so much the expression of new tensions as a new form of political behaviour. The fact that acclamations were officially recognized as an occasion for making complaints[7] opened up a new means of communication between population and governor, by-passing the usual channels, whether official, curial, or provided by patrons. This in turn gave new power to any group that was in a position to organize acclamations. This possibility was first

---

[1] *Or.* lvi. 22–3.   [2] *Or.* xlvi. 5, 17–18, 31–2.

[3] Disturbances organized by claque getting steadily worse: *Or.* lvi. 25. In 361 Libanius could write about dancers παρ' ὧν ἡ τέρψις ταῖς πόλεσιν ἀμιγὴς κακῶν (*Or.* lxiv. 118, *Ep.* 615 for date).

[4] Malalas 389; also a fragment edited by Th. Mommsen, *Hermes* vi (1872), 572.

[5] Malalas 395.

[6] Note also the intensification of religious conflicts: R. Deveresse, *Le Patriarcat d'Antioche* (Paris, 1945).

[7] Cf. Cass. *Var.* i. 27, abuse of Roman senator at the Games should be tolerated, in the streets punished.

exploited by the claque and later by the factions of the hippodrome, but it was available to others also. A bishop, for instance,
might sometimes employ a claque to applaud his sermons or to
give the impression of massive public support for his doctrinal
positions.[1] The men who led applause in church could be used
to lead a demonstration in the theatre.

At Alexandria the governor used to publish his regulations to
the people assembled in the theatre. On one such occasion, the
Jews in the audience recognized among the crowd a number of
supporters of the bishop, including one Hierax, a conspicuous
applauder of the bishop's sermons. They at once concluded that
he was there to make trouble,[2] no doubt by leading a demonstration. The governor too felt that the bishop was trying to put
pressure on his administration.[3] Thus the scene was set for the
succession of disturbances which led to the expulsion of the Jews
from Alexandria.

The acclamations from Edessa mentioned earlier show a bishop
in the role of victim of a religiously motivated demonstration.
A strong faction had formed in opposition to Ibas. It included
many monks but also a number of councillors, officials, and
honorati, including the powerful *comes* Theodosius, perhaps an
active military commander.[4] The group gained control of the
acclamations and proceeded to make an endless series of demonstrations against the bishop. The acclamations took place where
Libanius would have led us to expect them, at the gates to welcome the new governor[5] into the city,[6] but also in church,[7] and
in the governor's own audience hall.[8] As a result, the governor
was first induced to send a protocol of the acclamations to Constantinople,[9] and then to follow this up with two formal petitions
for the deposition of Ibas.[10] Eventually Ibas was deposed. It

[1] At Antioch: *Akten der ephesinischen Synode vom Jahre 449*, ed. J. Flemming, with
a German translation by G. Hoffmann (Göttingen, 1917), 59, cf. 61 and 119. The
lectors and funeral staff (*lecticarii* and *copiatae*) lead a demonstration against the
imperial letter.

[2] Socrates vii. 13. Later use of claque for anti-pagan demonstration connected
with acclamations: Zach. Myt. *V. Sev.* 25, 35.

[3] Socrates vii. 13: ἐποπτεύειν αὐτοῦ τὰς διατυπώσεις.

[4] List of signatories: *Ephes. Synode*, 37–9.   [5] Ibid. 15–17.

[6] Ibid. 25, it is not stated whether in streets or in theatre.

[7] Ibid. 36.   [8] Ibid. 17–21.

[9] The reports of the acclamations read at the synod had come from Constantinople: ibid. 13. The reports are also mentioned ibid. 21, 27.

[10] Ibid. 23–5, 39–55.

appeared only much later that the impression which had been created by the demonstrators, that the citizens were virtually unanimous in their opposition to Ibas, was quite misleading.[1] Ibas returned to Edessa after the Council of Chalcedon in 451 and remained as bishop until his death in 457.

It will be seen that the acclamations were in fact a highly effective way of influencing the imperial representatives. Their importance was therefore bound to grow with the scope and frequency of the officials' interventions in the administration of the city. The development of the acclamations is quite parallel to that of patronage.

Significantly at Edessa the opponents of Ibas used both approaches: they organized acclamations and then exploited them with the aid of a powerful man, the *comes* Theodosius. They also made use of a new force whose influence was only just beginning to make itself felt in the lifetime of Libanius: the monks. Equally significantly, the council as such did not take part in the agitation. At least six councillors appear among the supporters of the petition, and one of these claims the additional support of the civic officials (ἄρχοντες).[2] But the petitioners do not produce a resolution of the council to support their claim, and the governor does not require one. Since the governor has direct contact with the city on the one hand through acclamations, on the other through influential individuals, there is no room for the council in the role of intermediary.

The Ibas affair at Edessa reveals a more advanced stage in the decline of curial government than do the speeches of Libanius. But the speeches quite unmistakably reveal the same tendency. When Libanius encourages young councillors to take the title of 'administrators' (πολιτευόμενοι) more seriously, it does not mean that they should strive to make sure that the council as a whole should reach the right decisions and that a sensible resolution should be presented to the governor on behalf of the city. Libanius looks upon the councillors as individuals and urges them not to

[1] Two hundred clerics of Edessa witness orthodoxy of Ibas in letter to Domnus of Antioch: *Act. Chalc.* (Mansi) vii. 227; 13 presbyters, 37 deacons, 12 subdeacons and lectors deny that Ibas had made the statements attributed to him: ibid. 250–5.

[2] *Ephes. Synode*, 39: Konstantinos, Bios, Gainas, Asklepios, Andreas, Eusebios. I take it that the 'Prinkips' Aurelianos is the *princeps* of the governor's *officium*; but he could be the *primus curiae*. Abgarios the σχολαστικός could also be a councillor, so might Palladios who refers to his 'colleagues'.

remain silent on occasions when the governor has summoned councillors, as well as others, to hear their individual advice.[1]

6. ORGANIZATION OF THE CRAFTSMEN AND SHOPKEEPERS

That craftsmen following the same craft should group themselves in guilds was already common practice in the Early Empire.[2] That all urban craftsmen all over the empire should be organized was a development of the Later Empire. It was a corollary of the systematic conscription of members of the shopkeeper class for services for city and imperial administration.[3]

Guilds were used to collect a great variety of levies from their members, of which the most notorious was the *collatio lustralis*.[4] They were also liable to various other compulsory services. At Antioch the innkeepers were required to maintain a hostel for the imperial post.[5] They provided all the equipment and personnel. Their contribution included couches, tables, mugs, cooks, cleaners, grooms, pimps, and if need be, doctors. Smashed equipment had to be replaced, and if an attendant was killed by a traveller, the shopkeepers were obliged to compensate the relatives. Whenever a general retired, he would seize and sell the eatables and everything would have to be furnished anew to his successor, only to be sold again when this general retired in turn.[6] Shopkeepers also owed certain services on behalf of the city. The transport of new pillars that were needed to replace old ones was their task. So also was the cleaning of the drains; dangerous work, in the course of which a man might be choked to death. A shopkeeper would be obliged to do his share personally, unless he could afford to hire a substitute. Shopkeepers also provided monthly assistance to beggars.[7]

---

[1] *Or.* xxxv.

[2] Jones, *G.C.* 256, n. 9; E. Ziebarth, *Das griechische Vereinswesen* (Leipzig, 1896); F. Poland, *Geschichte des griechischen Vereinswesens* (Leipzig, 1909); J. P. Waltzing, *Étude historique sur les corporations professionnelles* (Louvain, 1896–1902); *P.W.* suppl. vol. iv, cols. 155–211, s.v. Berufsvereine (Stöckle).

[3] Jones, *L.R.E.* 858–9; F. Dölger, 'Die frühbyzantinische und byzantinisch beeinflusste Stadt', *Atti del 3 congresso internazionale di studi sull'Alto Medioevo* (Spoleto, 1959), esp. 91–6.

[4] See above, p. 54; also Johnson and West, *Byzantine Egypt*, 154; 319–20; *P.S.I.* 1265.

[5] *Or.* xlvi. 19, cf. *C.T.* xi. 10. 1–2, Jones, *G.C.* 154–5 n. 109.

[6] *Or.* xlvi. 20, cf. *C.T.* viii. 6. 1 (368). [7] *Or.* xlvi. 21.

The Codes provide some information on the way these services were organized. In the imperial legislation, all guilds figure as *collegia* and their members as *collegiati* or *corporati*. However, the great *corpora* that served the provisioning of Rome were made up of landowners, and their membership was not really comparable with that of the shopkeeper and craftsmen guilds with which we are here exclusively concerned. In so far as the members of tradesmen's guilds were obliged to perform important public services, their status resembled that of decurions.[1] But *collegiati* were in every way the inferior of the decurions and performed their duties under the decurions' direction.[2] Some services were no doubt specific to a particular *collegium*. Demands for extraordinary supplies of bread would no doubt be made to the bakers' guild.[3] But many services were common to all. At Alexandria the *corporati* as a whole were responsible for the dredging of the Nile.[4] At Carthage *collegiati* had to supply materials to factories.[5] At Rome *corporati* provided the only police force.[6] At Constantinople men chosen from various corporations served as a fire brigade.[7] Within each guild the members performed the duties in turn in the same way as decurions did and there is at least one reference to *collegiati* who have performed the complete series of duties owed by them.[8]

One passage of Libanius suggests that at Antioch guilds were not the original, or at least not the only, means of organizing compulsory services. In *Oration* xlviii Libanius recalls that in the good old days the council had had six hundred members and in a sense even twice as many, for while six hundred councillors performed liturgies out of their property, another six hundred performed 'what they were ordered' with their bodies.[9] Who were these other six hundred, and what were they ordered to perform? It looks as if in addition to the register of the council there was a second list of six hundred men liable to humbler,

---

[1] e.g. *C.T.* vii. 21. 3 (390), cf. xvi. 2. 39 (408), xii. 1. 179 (415).

[2] *Nov. Maj.* vii. 3.   [3] *C.I.L.* viii. 8480 (Sitifis).

[4] *C.T.* xiv. 27. 2 (436); also the *parabalani*, the attendants of the sick; in fact the bishop's police force, were chosen from the guildsmen of Alexandria: *C.T.* xvi. 2. 42–3.

[5] *C.T.* xi. 24 (395).

[6] *Coll. Avell. Ep.* 14, 23; Jones, *L.R.E.* 693–4; see also Wilcken, *Chr.* i. 474 on night watch at Oxyrhynchus.

[7] *Not. Const.* ii. 25; Joh. Lydus, *De Mag.* i. 50; Jones, *L.R.E.* 694.

[8] *Nov. Val.* xx.   [9] *Or.* xlviii. 3.

plebeian rather than curial, liturgies.[1] The same passage also shows that at the time of writing the second list belonged to the past. Its functions will have been shared out among the guilds, as elsewhere in the empire.

The use of guilds to organize compulsory services would have been impossible if tradesmen had been allowed to work without belonging to a guild. Compulsory guild membership made possible very close control of the commercial activities of each trade. This development too has left some traces in the writings of Libanius.

As we have seen the food crises of the late fourth century differed from earlier ones in that price control, which had once been a strongly resisted emergency measure, had become a permanent feature. This development can also be observed elsewhere than at Antioch.[2] It is surely not chance that the guilds, which played no role at all in the Julianic famine, figure more prominently in the later troubles: the intensified control over individual shopkeepers was made possible by the existence of guilds. An earlier stage in this development can only be observed in Egypt. During the first half of the fourth century, when prices were rising rapidly, the guilds of Oxyrhynchus made regular reports to the *curator* of the city concerning the prices they would charge. Price competition between individual retailers was thus eliminated.

Control of the guilds was exercised by means of supervisors, usually councillors. We know most about the supervisor of the bakers. In 384 the *comes* Icarius appointed to this post one Candidus, a leading member of the council, who had given the Olympic Games and had been Syriarch. His office required him to ensure that the bakers observed the prices laid down by the *comes*[3] and sold loaves of regulation size. Candidus had 'soldiers' at his disposal.[4] He interrogated offenders himself, and though he might not inflict punishment without the governor's permission,

---

[1] Petit, *Libanius*, 53–4; Jones, *G.C.* 180 n. 47 on curial and non-curial liturgies.

[2] See above, p. 132 n. 3. Price reports: Jones, *L.R.E.* 859 on *P. Oxy.* 83, 85, *P.S.I.* 202, *P. Ant.* 38.

[3] *Or.* xxix. 2. In addition to the curial supervisors appointed by the governor, guilds probably had a leader elected by members from members to be responsible for the finances of the guild and the observance of its rules, as in *P.S.I.* 1265. Such leaders are not mentioned by Libanius, but the flight and return to work of the bakers are likely to have been directed by an 'internal' leader of the trade.

[4] *Or.* xxix. 22.

he had considerable latitude in choosing what punishment to inflict.[1] He was also concerned with the internal affairs of the guild, for he was able to exploit the rivalries among the bakers for his own profit.[2] Supervisors are also mentioned in connection with stonemasons,[3] greengrocers,[4] actors,[5] and perhaps metal-workers.[6] Presumably the main function of all these functionaries was to ensure that the members of each guild observed the regulations made for it. But at least one of the men mentioned, the supervisor of the greengrocers, felt some responsibility for the welfare of the tradesmen in his charge. When they were being prosecuted by the governor, he called on Libanius to use his influence on their behalf.

The indispensability of the services provided by the shopkeepers, combined with a hundred-per-cent guild membership, should have greatly increased the guilds' ability to further the interests of their members. There is some evidence that this was the case all over the empire.[7] At Antioch Libanius noted the strong sense of solidarity of sailors, peasants, tanners, and smiths,[8] but it is the cohesion of the bakers that figures most prominently in his speeches.[9] They regularly opposed the imposition of price

---

[1] *Or.* xxix. 10, 22–5.   [2] Ibid. 9.   [3] *Ep.* 1176 (364).
[4] *Or.* liv. 42.   [5] *Or.* xxxiii. 4; cf. above, p. 145.
[6] *Ep.* 197 (360); Petit, *Libanius*, 73, 398, thinks this an imperial post connected with the arms works.

[7] G. Mickwitz, *Die Kartellfunktion der Zünfte und ihre Bedeutung in der Entstehung des Zunftwesens* (Helsinki, 1936), esp. 198 ff.; R. MacMullen, 'A note on Roman strikes', *Classical Journal* lviii (1963), 269–71. I have not seen the evidently very important Russian work of I. F. Fichtmann, 'Fragen des Handwerks im byzantinischen Ägypten' (Diss. Leningrad, 1962), summarized in *Bibliotheca Classica Orientalia* x (1965), 281–3; articles by Fichtmann are summarized, ibid. viii (1963), 136 ff., 325; ix (1964), 159 ff. The restrictive practices attacked in *C.J.* iv. 59. 2 (483) and regulated in the oaths of the stonemasons of Sardes (see below, p. 223 n. 4) were made possible by full organization of trades. At Edessa in the fifth century the bakers had a legal monopoly of the baking of bread for sale: Josh. Styl. 31, 40. Monopolies in Ostrogothic Italy: Cass. *Var.* ii. 4, 26, x. 28. Monopolies might simply be established by court intrigue (*C.J.* iv. 59. 1), and yet often they will have been in the interest of government and tradesmen alike, facilitating supervision and eliminating competition.

[8] *Ep.* 226. 3–4 (360). The solidarity of peasants is no doubt that shown by village communities, whether free or tenant. In *Or.* xlvii. 13 ff., Libanius has trouble with his Jewish tenants as a whole, not with individuals.

[9] Libanius' use of ἔθνος by itself means no more than a collection of men following the same profession. In *Or.* i. 206 or 228, the meaning 'corporation' or 'guild' would fit, but in xxvii. 25 'trades' would be better, since the man is in charge of the market, not of guilds. In *Or.* li. 13 ἔθνος = profession (the teachers).

control by threatening to flee from the city. The threat was made good on at least one occasion.[1] They returned only after that attempt to fix prices had been abandoned, and they had been given assurances of safety through the agency of Libanius, their patron.[2] Thus the bakers' union was capable of taking corporate action on behalf of its members and of negotiating on their behalf.[3]

At Antioch there was a supervisor of stonemasons but we have no information about the activities of the guild which he supervised. An inscription recording an oath taken by stonemasons of Sardes enables us to conjecture what the concerns of the guild at Antioch may have been. The guild binds itself to ensure the completion of work undertaken by its members. In case of any breach of the terms of the declaration the guild as a whole agrees to pay a fine and accepts responsibility for the fine imposed on the defaulting member. So far this declaration safeguards the public interest and the union appears an instrument of control. But the declaration also asserts certain rights of the stonemasons. A man is allowed to interrupt work for up to twenty days on grounds of illness. It also seems to be assumed that work begun by a member of this guild would not be completed by workmen outside the guild.[4]

The evidence about guilds and their supervision at Antioch is very thin, and even when it is supplemented with evidence from elsewhere, only a very fragmentary picture emerges. But certain tentative deductions are possible. In the East the guilds were not decaying and the government was not obliged to force children to follow their parents in membership. On the contrary, their indispensability and cohesion gave them new power,[5] which among other things enabled them to bargain with the authorities. At the same time, the period of unrestricted competition between individuals was coming to an end. The members of the guilds accepted price control and other regulations with a consequent gain in security for both the consumer and themselves. A

---

[1] *Or.* i. 206, 226, xxix. 2, 19.   [2] Ibid. 5–6, 16–17.

[3] Cf. the edict issued about A.D. 200 to the bakers of Ephesus: W. H. Buckler, 'Labour Disputes in the Province of Asia', *Studies presented to Sir William Ramsay*, 30; also *B.C.H.* vii (1883), 504, and *E.S.A.R.* iv. 847.

[4] Buckler, op. cit., 36 ff. = *Sardis*, i. 1. 18.

[5] The guilds take part in the agitation against the patriarch Gregory of Antioch in 585 (Euagr. vi. 7); also against Ibas of Edessa (*Akten der ephesinischen Synode vom Jahre 449*, 21, 25).

summary of a succession of agreements like that of the stonemasons of Sardes would look very much like a chapter in the tenth-century *Book of the Prefect* of Constantinople. The bargaining power of the guilds might foreshadow the political situation in the Arab city, where guilds formed the only element of local self-government to face the representative of the central authority.[1]

7. RELIGIOUS CHANGES AND THEIR SOCIAL EFFECTS

Among the changes which transformed traditional civic institutions in the fourth century perhaps the most conspicuous were the effects of the replacement of the old pagan cults by Christianity. In this transformation the increased activity of the imperial administration played a part: the policy of the Emperor Constantius was actively anti-pagan, while the reign of Julian saw a brief but very energetic intervention on the pagan side. But in the field of religion, unlike that of administration, creative developments could and did take place in the provinces, and essentially religious developments at Antioch had local roots. There had been a strong Christian community at Antioch long before the conversion of Constantine. Already in the third century a bishop of Antioch had been in a position to incur unpopularity by surrounding himself with the ceremony of an imperial official.[2] Moreover, Antioch was a centre of theology. Its school of biblical interpretation insisted on the literal sense of biblical passages (one is reminded of the pagan Libanius' distrust of allegory) and opposed the figurative interpretation of Alexandria. The Christian community was already very large at the time of the Great Persecution. It must have grown further after the conversion of Constantine. The citizens' response to Julian revealed unmistakably that by the middle of the century the city was effectively Christian. The Emperor Julian and Libanius himself were quite aware that the majority of citizens opposed their revived paganism.[3] In his sermons of the last quarter of the century John Chrysostomus seems to take it for granted that the bulk of the

---

[1] G. E. von Grünebaum, *Islam* (London, 1955), 150–1.
[2] Eus. *H.E.* vii. 30. 6–9.
[3] Julian, *Misop.* 361D, 357D, 363. Lib. *Ep.* 1220, *Or.* xvi. 47–50, *Ep.* 1119. 4.

population is Christian.[1] In comparison with Jews and heretics
he treats pagans mildly.[2] In view of the links between paganism
and higher education, it is not surprising that John Chrysostomus is from time to time preoccupied with the paganism
of the philosophers, and concerned to contrast the universality
of Christianity with the class-bound character of intellectual
paganism.[3] Yet, on the whole, he is more concerned with the
survival of pagan practices among men who were already Christians. He warns his congregation against visits to the sanctuary
at Daphne, to that of Saturn in Cilicia, or to the grotto of Matrona
at Daphne.[4] He attacks the wearing of pagan amulets, and condemns the perpetuation of pagan customs at marriage festivals, or
during the New Year procession.[5]

But the number of professed pagans remained considerable. A
very large proportion of the country folk must have been pagan,
before the growth of monasticism around the middle of the century. Paganism of the countryside was weakened but still important in the eighties of the century. About the same time we
hear that the impressive behaviour of Bishop Flavianus after the
Riot of the Statues could still produce a number of conversions
to Christianity in the city.[6]

Paganism retained a significant hold in the upper classes.
While in the speeches he wrote under Julian, Libanius seems to
assume that the council was composed of at least nominal
Christians, a high proportion of pagans was still to be found
both among his pupils and among his acquaintances of curial
rank.[7] The sense of solidarity had probably developed during
the years when paganism was being attacked by Constantius,

---

[1] J. M. Vance, 'Beiträge zur byzantinischen Kulturgeschichte aus den Schriften
des Johannes Chrysostomos' (Diss. Jena, 1901), 19, 66; *Hom. contra Julianum et
Gentiles* 3 (*P.G.* l. 537); *Hom. in Matth.* 33–4 (*P.G.* lvii. 392).
[2] Baur, *Johannes Chrysostomus*, 273; Joh. Chrys. *Hom. in Ep. I ad Cor.* 4. 6 (*P.G.*
lxi. 38–40).
[3] Joh. Chrys. *Hom. in Matth.* 1. 5 (*P.G.* lvii. 19–20); *Hom. de mut. nom.* 4. 5 (*P.G.*
li. 152–3).
[4] Joh. Chrys. *Adv. Jud.* 1. 6 (*P.G.* xlviii. 851; 855); *Hom. in Ep. ad Titum* 3, 2
(*P.G.* lxxii. 679).
[5] e.g. engraved with head of Alexander the Great: *Hom. ad illumin. catech.* 2
(*P.G.* xlix. 240). Marriage festivals: *Hom. in Genes.* 48 (*P.G.* liii. 442–3); Vance,
op. cit., 77; A. Puech, *Jean Chrysostome et les mœurs de son temps*, 103–9. New Year:
Joh. Chrys. *Hom. in Kalendas* (*P.G.* xlviii. 953–62).
[6] Joh. Chrys. *Hom. de Anna* 1. 1 (*P.G.* liv. 634), cf. Downey, *Antioch*, 433.
[7] Figures: Petit, *Libanius*, 201.

and pagans were hoping that Julian would succeed to the throne.[1]

In the course of the century the pagan minority in the upper classes is likely to have shrunk further. At the time of the Riot of the Statues the council behaved as if it was solidly Christian. The councillors who protested against the new taxes called on the Christian God to help the city.[2] John Chrysostomus gives the impression that the councillors whom he visited in prison were Christians to a man.[3] But the correspondence of Libanius shows that even now some of the great curial families remained pagan, and adherents of the old religion were still to be found among Libanius' pupils and acquaintances.[4]

Intellectual paganism survived into the fifth century. At about 450, the pagan sophist Isocasius occupied a position comparable to that of Libanius in the previous century.[5] But at the same time Theodoret, the highly educated bishop of Cyrrhus, who was a friend of Isocasius, could refer to the 'insignificant remnants of the pagans' at Antioch,[6] and Isocasius himself was eventually compelled to become a Christian. Nevertheless there is evidence for pagans in the city as late as the mid sixth century.[7]

While Libanius' silence on specifically Christian topics suggests that he felt a considerable antipathy towards Christianity as such, his writings do not suggest that at Antioch or indeed in the other cities of the East there was great personal animosity between pagans and Christians. Perhaps the majority of Libanius' most intimate friends and pupils were pagans,[8] but among his correspondents and the fathers of his pupils there were not a few Christians, some perhaps Christians for convenience, others

---

[1] On the pagan 'underground': Petit, *Libanius*, 204–5; Dagron, *Empire romain d'Orient*, 68–9.

[2] *Or.* xix. 27.

[3] *Hom. ad pop. Ant.* 21. 1 (*P.G.* xlix. 211–12); ibid. 18. 4 (*P.G.* xlix. 187).

[4] Petit, *Libanius*, 201: of 19 *curiales* 3 or 4 are known to be pagans, 4 Christians; of 53 pupils, 21 are pagans, 2 Christians.

[5] Downey, *Antioch*, 483.   [6] Theodoret, *H.E.* v. 35.

[7] Downey, *Antioch*, 555, mentions a story in the Acts of the 2nd Council of Nicaea (ed. Mansi, xiii. 76) according to which pagans objected to a statue of Symeon Stylites the younger, presumably in mid sixth century. Two pagan priests from Antioch were prosecuted in 562 at Constantinople: Michael the Syrian (trans. Chabot), 2. 271.

[8] The figures of Petit, *Libanius*, 201, *Étudiants*, 116–18, suggest that in Libanius' school and among his friends pagans were much more strongly represented than in society as a whole.

certainly by conviction.[1] The point to note here is not Libanius' own toleration and friendship of Christians, which he so generously revealed in the letters he wrote to protect Christians during Julian's pagan reaction,[2] but that the Christians did not withdraw their friendship, or even the responsibility for the education of their sons, from a man who made no secret of his adherence to the pagan gods.

The same impression is gained from the treatment which Libanius received from governors and officials. Christian officials were not necessarily ill disposed towards the outspokenly pagan rhetor. There was no official with whom Libanius was on better terms than the Christian praetorian prefect of the East, Strategius Musonianus.[3] In his case, as indeed in others, common enthusiasm for rhetoric laid the foundations of the relationship. Rhetoric was neutral ground,[4] prized highly by Christians and pagans alike. Christians and pagans of the upper classes did not stand opposed as members of hostile camps. Indeed, the orthodox bishops and many members of their congregations might well have been more hostile towards heretics than towards pagans. At Antioch many families comprised adherents of both religions. While most of Libanius' relatives were still pagan, the most powerful branch of the family, the descendants of the praetorian prefect Thalassius, were Christians, and required Libanius' help under Julian.[5] His life-long friend Olympius was probably a pagan, but Olympius' brother, Euagrius IV, whom Libanius assisted when he was being tried on a criminal charge, was a Christian. A friend of Jerome, he ended his life as a schismatic bishop.[6] In short, Christians and pagans in the civic aristocracies were connected by so many ties of family, education, social life, and politics, that real antagonism was out of the question. A comparable state of

---

[1] e.g. *Ep.* 645–6. Eudoxius I was probably nephew of a bishop, grandson of a martyr; see Seeck, *Briefe*, under Caesarius I and II. The mother of John Chrysostomus was a firm Christian, yet she sent her son to Libanius' school; *Ep.* 647 may show St. Basil sending Libanius pupils. See also *Ep.* 1543–4 congratulating newly appointed bishops, cf. Petit, *Étudiants*, 128 n. 179.

[2] *Ep.* 724, 763, 819, 1411.

[3] *Or.* i. 106–8.

[4] J. Bidez, *Vie de l'empereur Julien*, 48.

[5] See Seeck, *Briefe*, under Thalassius I, Bassianus, Thalassius II.

[6] See ibid., under Euagrius IV. The pagan councillor Asterius (*Ep.* 1376, 1432) had a Christian son, Eusebius XXI (1411), and a pagan one, Olympius V (1432).

affairs existed among pagans and Christians in the senatorial aristocracy of Rome.[1]

The triumph of Christianity did not immediately revolutionize the cities' festival calendar. While sacrifices were ended, first through indifference, and at last through prohibition, the great public holidays continued, and in the case of one of them, at least, we can still feel the atmosphere of the occasion.

The civic year began with the riotous celebration of the New Year.[2] The night of the New Year was celebrated with feasting, drinking and dancing, processions, the chanting of ribald ditties, general licence, and a host of surviving pagan practices, against which John Chrysostomus raised his voice in vain. As might be expected, the moderate pagan Libanius gives us a sympathetic picture. He tells us that the New Year is celebrated all over the Roman Empire. Men give each other gifts and receive each other in hospitality. Friends living in different towns visit each other. Presents are given, and giver and receiver have the same pleasure. It is a general holiday. Schoolboys need not fear masters or pedagogues, slaves are given as much freedom as is practicable. Servants may be idle. The courts are shut. The prosecutor is silent. Even prisoners feel the benefit of the feast. Men make up their quarrels. A mediator need only mention the feast and the antagonists are shamed out of their hostility.[3] The festival teaches contempt for money, for everyone from the emperor downwards lessens his store with present-giving.[4] Donors add to the value of their gift by giving with their own hands, instead of sending a servant. There is, however, one change compared with the olden times: sacrifices and incense no longer burn on the altars.

In one of his model descriptions Libanius gives an account of the festival. The New Year festival is a great occasion for buying and selling. The market is never busier. On the day before the New Year gifts are carried through the town. The powerful send them to each other, and persons of lower rank send them to the powerful, and receive others in their turn. The weak nurse the patronage of the strong; the strong give pleasure to their

[1] P. R. L. Brown, *J.R.S.* li (1961), 6 ff.

[2] *Or.* ix; ἐ. καλανδῶν, Foerster (ed.), vol. 8, 472 ff.; Baur, *Johannes Chrysostomus*, i. 208.

[3] *Or.* ix. 14.   [4] Ibid. 9; ἐ. καλανδῶν 3–5, 10.

clients.[1] We observe that not all this gift-giving was altruistic. It is noteworthy that Libanius on principle did not accept New Year presents from strangers.[2] Perhaps acceptance would have put him under a kind of moral obligation to assist the giver. That night few go to bed. There is much singing and dancing. Processions invade the artisans' quarters. There is knocking at doors and jesting and scoffing. All is usually taken in good part, but it was not so taken by the Emperor Julian. He resented the mocking verses he was obliged to hear that night and they contributed towards his disillusionment with the city.[3] But then Julian was not used to the customs of Antioch and felt more at home with the sober and austere inhabitants of Gaul. At cock-crow some decorate the entrances of their houses with garlands, others conduct the councillors who are providing the horses for the day's chariot races to the temple. The men are dressed in purple. Their followers throw money to the crowd. Torches light the scene. Traditionally they then sacrificed and prayed that their horses might be victorious.[4] Libanius describes this ceremony as if it were still being performed, but in view of the abolition of sacrifices and incense burning, we must suppose that the sacrifice had been abandoned. Next the men who are going to produce the races pay a formal visit to the two governors, giving presents of gold to members of their office staff. The remaining councillors are present too and in their turn give gold to the officials. The *comes orientis* welcomes the members of the council with a kiss.[5] Resentment is felt if he does not kiss every man.[6] The *comes* and the consular too exchange kisses and gifts of gold. Finally, gold-giving becomes general.

Meanwhile it is growing light, and those who have spent the night drinking, sleep. Others accompany the procession of gifts through colonnades and along passages. On the second day of New Year people remain at home, and master and servant play at dice together; the savage pedagogue is not savage, and the bad-tempered teacher is mild. The season gives equal right of speech to all, and all alike enjoy freedom, peace, and content. On this day none is so poor that he does not get a filling meal. On the third day there are chariot races, and after the races

---

[1] Ibid. 5.   [2] *Ep.* 1329, perhaps 257.   [3] See above, p. 214.
[4] ἑ. καλανδῶν 7–8, liturgants visit temples; *Or.* ix. 18, sacrifices have ceased.
[5] Ibid. 8–9.   [6] *Or.* xxvii. 12.

people enjoy the pleasures of the baths, and then those of the table, and finally dice through the night. On the fourth day the feast comes to an end and reluctantly men return to work.

Beside the New Year the other festivals are shadows. We can scarcely do more than give a list. One surviving pagan festival early in the year was that of Poseidon, celebrated with chariot racing. We know this because in the commotion of this festival a councillor Candidus, who had incurred unpopularity through his control of the bakers, nearly had his house burned over his head.[1]

On the seventh day of the month of Artemis (May) the festival of Artemis was celebrated at Meroe on the east side of the town, where the temples of Artemis and of the Persian Sun-god were situated. On this occasion a boxing competition was held. Each of the eighteen tribes provided a boxer and the competitors fought fiercely, not for a prize but consecrating their ferocity to the service of the divinity. In Libanius' time this custom was going out of fashion. The day was no longer a school holiday. But once, when Libanius' boys stayed away from school to watch the fighting, the goddess rewarded them by saving their lives, for on that day part of their school building collapsed, raining stones that would have crushed an elephant.[2]

Early in summer came the festival of Calliope, which was celebrated with theatrical shows and chariot races.[3] These probably continued into the Christian era, as the people would not have agreed to part with their spectacles. When Julian was emperor, the sacrifice to Calliope was reintroduced and the applause included shouts for the gods. Also in May was the Maiumas, which according to Malalas lasted thirty days and was held every three years.[4] It was held in honour of Dionysus and Aphrodite, and was celebrated with nocturnal stage shows. The edict of Commodus, which established the Olympic Games, also contained regulations concerning endowments, the income from

---

[1] *Or.* i. 1, 230.   [2] *Or.* v. 43–51.

[3] *Ep.* 811 (363). Under Julian there were sacrifices in the theatre. Soon after the festival was prohibited or restricted, *Ep.* 1175 (364). Calliope as patron goddess of Antioch: *Or.* i. 102, xx. 51, lx. 13, *Ep.* 825 (363), 1182 (364), 1456 (363); cf. Downey, *Antioch*, 216–17.

[4] Malalas 285. 12–21, expensive private banquets: Julian, *Misop.* 362D, *C.T.* xv. 6. 1–2, *P.W.* xiv. 610, s.v. Maiumas. According to Theodoret, *H.E.* iii. 14 it lasted fourteen days.

which was to be spent on the Maiumas. The Maiumas may have been the immoral festival, strongly condemned by Libanius, for which men went down to Daphne for five days or more. This festival, Libanius tells us, had been prohibited by a good emperor, perhaps Julian, who we know was not very keen on it. But it had been revived and again permitted.[1] It is not surprising that the claque should have used its influence in favour of this festival, which profited its employers, the actors and dancers.

From 17 to 19 July was the festival of Adonis.[2] This was still sufficiently alive in Antioch for the Emperor Julian, arriving in the city on 18 July, to be met by women wailing the death of the young god, a bad omen. A little later came the old festival of Apollo at Daphne. This was practically dead when Julian came to Antioch, for the only sacrifice he saw was that of a goose, which the priest of Apollo had provided at his own expense.[3] Forty-five days in July and August every leap year were occupied by the Olympic Games, dedicated to Zeus.[4] They were held at the time of an older festival of the 'Offerings'.[5] At the time of the wine harvest, came the festival of Dionysus, perhaps at the same time as the Jewish festival of Tabernacles. At this season Dionysus was hymned everywhere, particularly in the countryside.[6]

We note that even in a largely Christian city a fair number of traditional festivals continued to flourish and to provide the citizens with holidays and entertainments. But Christianity was beginning to take over this function also. Christmas, celebrated on the day of Sol Invictus, came to Antioch in 376, and in a Christmas sermon of 386 John Chrysostomus[7] is concerned to show that Jesus was really born on that day. The Church was about this time developing a calendar of feasts, which, like the

---

[1] *Or.* xli. 16, l. 11; cf. x. 14.

[2] F. Cumont, 'Les Syriens en Espagne et les Adonies à Séville', *Syria* (1927), 330–41; Amm. xxii. 9. 14, xix. 1. 11.

[3] Julian, *Misop.* 362.

[4] See above, 114 ff. Libanius consistently stresses the religious character of the festival.

[5] Malalas 284.

[6] *Ep.* 661 (361), 1480 (363), 1288 (364), 1212 (364); οἱ ἄνδρες οἵδε τῶν περὶ τὸν Διόνυσόν εἰσιν ὑπηρετοῦντες καθ' ἕκαστον ἔτος τῷ μύθῳ τῷ περὶ τοῦ θεοῦ; cf. 1213. See also Theodoret, *H.E.* iv. 24. 3; Festugière, *Antioche*, 186, n. 2. *Ep.* 962 (390), image (of Dionysus?) carried in procession at Athens.

[7] *Hom. in nat. Christi* (*P.G.* xlix. 351–63).

pagan one, followed the course of the seasons.[1] Festivals of martyrs[2] were coming to be celebrated in many places, and enabled men to continue to celebrate, in honour of worthy Christians, the holidays of their old local deities. Perhaps there survived too some of the older excesses of merry-making.[3] There is also plenty of evidence that people who had trusted in the protection of amulets relying on pagan magic, now satisfied the need for security with Christian—or Jewish—amulets, inscribed with verses from the Bible often jumbled into anagrams.[4]

Paganism, it would appear, no longer presented a real problem. Significantly, John Chrysostomus can compare the pagans to children who are happy to spend their lives playing on the floor and who merely laugh when a grown-up tries to talk to them about serious matters.[5] Topics which roused Chrysostomus to passionate eloquence or violent abuse were the great prestige of Jewish practices, and divisions within the ranks of the Christians themselves. He was also profoundly influenced by that extraordinary phenomenon, the rise of monasticism. These were the burning religious issues of the age.

In the fourth century Syria had some wealthy and flourishing Jewish communities. Of these the new civic synagogue built in 391 at Apamea is evidence.[6] The inscriptions of the non-figurative mosaic floor show that the Jews spoke Greek and had Greek or Hellenized names. The fact that a large part of the mosaic was given by the Archisynagogus of Antioch witnesses the sense of solidarity of the Jewish communities in Syria. Antioch had a large Jewish community[7] and the prestige of Jewish rites was

[1] Bidez, *Vie de l'empereur Julien*, 27, n. 3.

[2] Scoffing at veneration of martyr's tombs: Julian, *Misop.* 344A; cf. Lib. *Or.* lxii. 10; attacks on tombs under Julian: *Misop.* 357C, 361A.

[3] H. Delehaye, *Les Origines du culte des martyres* (Brussels, 1933); *D.A.C.L.* x. 2359–512, s.v. Martyr (H. Leclercq); V. Schultze, *Antiocheia* (Gütersloh, 1930), 271–7.

[4] Schultze, op. cit. 176–83; M. Simon, 'Polémique antijuive de S. Jean Chrysostome', *Annuaire de l'Institut de philologie et d'histoire orientales et slaves* iv (1936) (*Mélanges Cumont*), 403–21, esp. 407–8.

[5] *Hom. in Ep.* 1 *ad Cor.* 4. 6 (*P.G.* lxi. 38–40), echoing Plato, *Tim.* 22.

[6] E. L. Sukenik, 'Mosaic Inscriptions in the Synagogue at Apamea on the Orontes', *Hebrew Union College Annual* xxiii (1950–1), 541–51.

[7] On the Jewish community: V. Schultze, *Antiocheia*, 176–83; S. Krauss, 'Antioche', *Rev. ét. juiv.* xlv (1902), 27–49; C. H. Kraeling, 'The Jewish Community at Antioch', *J. Bibl. Lit.* li (1932), 130–60; E. Bikerman, 'Les Maccabées de Malalas', *Byzantion* (xxi) (1951), 63–83. Malalas 290: a Jewish councillor *c.* A.D. 190. Lib. *Ep.* 914 (388), 317, 373, 374 (390), 1084, 1097–8 (393) addressed to

high. This was no doubt partly a side effect of the triumph of Christianity.[1] The fact that the Old Testament was part of the Christian Scriptures increased the prestige of the religious practices of the people of the Old Testament.[2] There were in John Chrysostomus' congregation men who would celebrate Jewish festivals,[3] or observe the Sabbath or fasts.[4] Some even accepted circumcision. Christians might consider an oath taken in a synagogue more binding than one taken in church,[5] and put their disputes before a Jewish communal tribunal rather than that of the secular administration.[6] Most important of all, rabbis had a reputation for being able to effect remarkable cures.[7]

The relationship between the two religions is symbolized by the fate of the tomb of the Seven Maccabee Brothers. This was situated in a synagogue, but Christians venerated the tomb of the brothers, who had long been regarded as forerunners of the Christian martyrs. No doubt the tomb of the Maccabees, like the tombs of other martyrs, was visited for the sake of miraculous cures. Some time after 363 this state of affairs induced the Christian authorities to take the synagogue away from the Jews and to turn it into a church. The Maccabee Brothers were included among the martyrs of Syria and a festival established in their honour.[8]

The ruthlessness of this confiscation is also reflected in the tone of the sermons against the Jews which John Chrysostomus preached in 386 and 387, during the Jewish festival season, when Judaizing was at its height.[9] It is also surely not chance that the new synagogue at Apamea was in use for only a short time and that before the end of the fifth century its site was occupied by a church.[10]

Jewish patriarch Gamaliel; cf. Seeck, *Briefe*, 162; Syme, *Ammianus and the 'Historia Augusta'* (Oxford, 1968), 61–4. Joh. Chrys. *Adversus Judaeos* (*P.G.* xlviii. 843 ff.); also *Contra Judaeos et Gentiles quod Christus sit Deus*, ibid. 813–38.

[1] Joh. Chrys. *Adv. Jud.* 4. 3 (*P.G.* xlviii. 874–6).

[2] Ibid. 1. 5 (*P.G.* xlviii. 850); 6. 6 (913 ff.).

[3] Ibid. 1. 1 (*P.G.* 814–15), 7 (853).

[4] Ibid. 1. 8 (855); ibid. 8. 1 ff. (927).

[5] Circumcision: ibid. 2. 1 (*P.G.* xlviii. 858); ibid. 1. 3 (847 ff.).

[6] *C.T.* xvi. 8. 22 (415).   [7] *C.T.* viii. 5, i. 7.

[8] Simon, op. cit., 412–19; Bikerman, loc. cit.

[9] On rhetorical abuse of these sermons, see above, pp. 34–5.

[10] Sukenik, loc. cit. For fifth- and sixth-century anti-Jewish riots see Downey, *Antioch*, 460, 499, 505 ff., 571, 573, 586 ff. Bishop leads action against Jews: E. W. Brooks, *The Select Letters of Severus of Antioch* (London, 1903–4); *Ep.* 15–16. On the deteriorating condition of the Jews of the empire in the fifth century see M. Simon, *Verus Israel* (Paris, 1964), 264–74.

The divisions in the great Christian community of Antioch must have been a continuous cause of strife in the public life of the city. The dispute as to who was the rightful bishop had broken out over the consecration of Bishop Eustathius in 324 and continued through the century. For a time Antioch had as many as four bishops simultaneously. The schism was exacerbated by the religious policies of the Emperors Constantius and Valens. By the time of the late speeches, the Emperor Theodosius' support of orthodoxy had achieved the elimination of the Arian sect, and Flavian was recognized as bishop by most important people at Antioch, but there remained a rival orthodox bishop. This difference was settled provisionally in 414, and finally only in 482.[1]

Unfortunately the evidence for these events is very scanty. Neither Libanius nor John Chrysostomus throws much light on the motives of the various parties. Historians of the schism depend for information on the bare outline provided by later ecclesiastical historians. As Lietzmann observed, the full story of this schism, one of the most important chapters in the ecclesiastical history of the fourth century, cannot be written.[2]

We are better informed about the growth of solitary and communal monasticism in Syria. The movement reached Syria some time before the middle of the fourth century. The earliest hermit known from Syria appears to have settled between Imma and Beroea in the reign of Constantius. The development was very rapid.[3] Though the monks are still not mentioned as playing a significant part in the opposition to Julian's pagan revival, they began to exert an influence on religious policy in the city in the reign of Valens. By the 380s monks were settled in large numbers in the desert just beyond the inhabited areas of Syria. In the next hundred years or so Syria was covered with monasteries.[4] Libanius describes the monks as peasants who had fled the land, and craftsmen who had forsaken their crafts. He is using a commonplace of abuse,[5] but he is not altogether misleading. As a rule, the monks came from the humble

---

[1] On the schism see Downey, *Antioch*, 351–3, 369–70, 410–19, 457 (with bibliography). See also R. Devreesse, *Le Patriarcat d'Antioche* (Paris, 1945).

[2] H. Lietzmann, *Geschichte der alten Kirche*, vol. iii. 115.

[3] *P.W.* 2. Reihe, iv. 2, cols. 1705 ff., s.v. Syria (E. Honigmann); Festugière, *Antioche*, 245–66.

[4] Tchalenko, *Villages*, ii, pl. cliii.   [5] *Or.* xxx. 31, 48.

classes. Typical monks would appear to have been countrymen, Syriac-speaking, and ignorant of Greek, like the old 'Syrian' hermit whom young John Chrysostomus joined and imitated.[1] Learning or even literacy was not required by a monk. Indeed they might be obstacles to his spiritual progress. A monk strove to purify his soul by a continuous course of asceticism and prayer, and expected to receive by the gift of God a wisdom far superior to any acquired in the world, whether through reading or experience.[2]

The belief that the life of the ascetic was the highest form of Christian life spread through all classes. Young John Chrysostomus, the son of a military official,[3] rejected the public career for which his education had fitted him to live the life of a hermit, and he was not alone among young men of his generation. This tendency among the young alarmed Christians and pagans alike, notably the parents of the youths who had left the city for life in a monastery or hermit's cell. Fathers had been known to lead parties to seek out the monks, to assault, and even to prosecute them.[4]

Nevertheless, the monastic idea impressed the older generations too. St. Nilus, who became a monk in the Sinai about 380, had perhaps previously been *praefectus urbi* of Constantinople.[5] The monastic life came to be rated at the monk's own valuation, even by men who had no intention of renouncing the world for it. Even among pagans asceticism was widely accepted as evidence of religious authority. A pagan philosopher too had long been expected to be abstemious and possibly miracle-working,[6] as well as learned in philosophy. This made it easier to see the ascetic life as an alternative and superior form of philosophy.[7] The writings of John Chrysostomus show how a man who had

[1] Pall. *Dial.* 5. 18; Festugière, *Antioche*, 287 n. 1, 288 ff., 291 ff. on Joh. Chrys. *Hom. in Ep. ad Eph.* 21, 162D–E; Theod. *H.R.* xiii (*P.G.* lxxxii. 1401): Macedonius; ibid. viii (1368B–C): Aphraates; ibid. xxviii (1488): Thalelaeus. See also references in Jones, *L.R.E.* 994 n. 21.

[2] Athanasius, *V. Anton.* 72–3; cf. R. Reitzenstein, *Historia Monachorum und Historia Lausiaca* (Göttingen, 1916).

[3] A. H. M. Jones, *H.T.R.* xlvi (1953), 171–3 on Pall. *Dial.* 5.

[4] Joh. Chrys. *Adv. oppugnatores vit. mon.* 45–7.

[5] F. Degenhart, *Der heilige Nilus Sinaiticus* (Münster, 1915), 27; based on Nicephorus Callistus, not a good authority.

[6] *Or.* xlii. 7–9; Eunapius, *V. Philosoph., passim.*

[7] e.g. Theod. *H.R.* 1348; Festugière, *Antioche*, 257, n. 3; 291 n. 1; 399 n. 4, φιλοσοφία became a technical term for the monastic life.

fully absorbed the classical education could nevertheless describe
the quite un-Hellenic phenomenon of monasticism in terms that
were long familiar as descriptions of the philosopher-sage. Like
the sage, the monk despises wealth. He is greater than a king, he
is alone powerful, alone happy, alone capable of consoling the
miserable, alone able to despise pleasures.[1] The monk is able to
speak out to the mighty.[2] Alternatively, the monk is shown to
enjoy all the moral benefits of the simple life, far from the crowds
and dissipations of the city, which poets since the Hellenistic
period had associated with life in the countryside.[3]

Biographies of hermits[4] draw vivid pictures of the influence
these men acquired among the country folk, who consulted them
about their many difficulties and especially sought to be healed
from disease. Hermits were also visited by people from the city,
including members of the households of the well-to-do and
wealthy wives. But their influence, particularly in religious
questions, extended further. When the Emperor Valens was
trying to force his Arian views on all his subjects, the hermit
Julian came to Antioch, proclaimed his orthodoxy, worked
miracles, and so, it is said, drew all the population of the city
to orthodoxy.[5] A few years later the hermit Aphraates dared
to scold the emperor for his persecution of the orthodox. 'You
have set fire to our father's house.' Valens did not change his
policy.[6]

A few years later the hermit Macedonius, who had for many
years lived an open-air life on Mount Silpius just to the east of
Antioch, had become so influential that Bishop Flavian thought
it worth while to ordain him. The hermit who was totally without
Greek did not understand the significance of the ceremony and
was extremely angry when it was explained to him. He feared
that he would now be compelled to leave his beloved mountain.[7]
The same Macedonius acted as spokesman of the monks who
pleaded for the city with the imperial commissioners after the

---

[1] Festugière, *Antioche*, 184, n. 1, 194–5.
[2] On monk's παρρησία: ibid. 274–6, 286–7.   [3] Ibid. 338–46.
[4] See ibid., *passim*; id., *Les Moines de l'Orient*, vols. 1–4 (Paris, 1961–5); H. Lietzmann, *Das Leben des heiligen Symeon Stylites, mit einer deutschen Übersetzung der syrischen Lebensbeschreibung und der Briefe von H. Hilgenfeld*, in *Texte und Untersuchungen* xxxii. 4 (1908).
[5] Theod. *H.E.* iv. 24 (*P.G.* lxxxii. 1187).
[6] Theod. *H.R.* viii (*P.G.* lxxxii. 1368).
[7] Theod. *H.R.* xiii (*P.G.* lxxxii. 1401–4).

Riot of the Statues.[1] Monks might cause a stir in the city in less dramatic circumstances. It was their custom to come into the town during the summer singing hymns. When the monks' arrival was reported, the governor Tissamenes would immediately adjourn the court over which he was presiding.[2]

It cannot be a coincidence that the years which saw the establishment of monks on the fringe of the inhabited areas of Syria also saw great progress of Christianity among country folk. In the hill area to the north-east of Antioch the two earliest known Christian inscriptions date from 336 to 337. In the following decade there is a steady growth in the proportion of Christian as opposed to pagan inscriptions. During the first stages of his campaign against the Persians, Julian noticed that the inhabitants of the countryside between Antioch and Beroea were significantly less enthusiastic about paganism than the inhabitants around Batnae, one day's march closer to the Euphrates.[3] An inscription of 367–8, recording the restoration of the temple of Zeus Koryphaios, is the latest known pagan inscription from that area. All later dated inscriptions are Christian.[4]

At first the monks' influence was exercised through the impact of their manifest holiness on men around them. But in 385 they were carrying out a systematic campaign against pagan temples. They were most active in the countryside,[5] where temples still played an important part in village life, and village festivals retained pagan characteristics.[6] But they also entered cities. Libanius mentions the destruction of a statue of Asclepius in Beroea[7] and of a great fortified temple on the Persian border at Edessa.[8] But the destroying monks did not enter Antioch itself. There the temples remained intact and pagan cult continued to be celebrated subject to legal restrictions.[9]

---

[1] Joh. Chrys. *Hom. ad pop. Ant.* 17 (*P.G.* xlix. 172 ff.); Theod. *H.E.* v. 19.

[2] *Or.* xlv. 26; Theod. *Ep.* 42, authority of a hermit supports reduction in taxation; cf. *H.R.* xvii, Abraames (*P.G.* lxxxii. 142). Monks intervene in judicial cases in cities: *C.T.* xvi. 3. 2 (392), ix. 40. 16 (398).

[3] Julian, *Ep.* 58 (Loeb) = 98 (Bidez).

[4] Epigraphic evidence on progress of Christianity on the limestone plateau, Tchalenko, *Villages*, 145 n. 2.

[5] *Or.* xxx. 9.

[6] Ibid. 17; cf. hymns to Dionysus: *Ep.* 1288, 661.　　　　　　　[7] *Or.* xxx. 39.

[8] Ibid. 44–5. On this temple: *C.T.* xvi. 10. 8 (382).

[9] *Or.* xxx 15. On survival of temples see Petit, *Libanius*, 199; Lassus, *Sanctuaires*, 245. Under Constantius pagans had to struggle to save their temples: *Or.* xv. 53.

The monks' campaign was not entirely spontaneous. They claimed to be enforcing the law of the Emperor Theodosius which had made sacrifice illegal. Libanius counters this claim by arguing that the peasants, who were after all not even councillors, would never dare to break an imperial law. Moreover the accusation of illegal sacrifice had in the past been made frequently before Bishop Flavian but had never been substantiated.[1] In any case, accusation against law-breakers should be made in the court of the governor and not of the bishop. This line of argument suggests that the activities of the monks were stimulated by the bishop of Antioch.[2] If pagan practices were reported to the bishop, the monks would raid the village where the offence had been committed. They do not appear to have hurt individuals unless they resisted, but destroyed the temple[3] and carried off any stores found in it.[4] They are also reported to have confiscated land, perhaps in the first place land belonging to the temple,[5] but also private land.[6] What happened to this land? Was it given to monasteries? Was it presented to the church of Antioch? At any rate, the fact that the monks effected permanent changes in the ownership shows that there was organization and powerful backing behind their activities.[7]

In the *Pro templis* Libanius links his attack on the monks with an attack on the praetorian prefect Cynegius,[8] and there can be little doubt that the campaign against the temples was encouraged, if not actually promoted, by the prefect who in 385 travelled from Constantinople to Egypt closing temples on the way.[9] The activities described in the *Pro templis* only mark the beginning of the final campaign against rural temples. In 388 the gods were able to watch the misdeeds of the governor Lucianus

---

There survived at least those of Hermes, Pan, Demeter, Fortuna, Ares, Calliope, Apollo, Zeus (both on the mountain and in the city): *Or.* xv. 79. In the 380s only the temples of Zeus, Athena, Dionysus, and Fortuna survived: *Or.* xxx. 51.

[1] Ibid. 15.

[2] Destruction of temples by bishop of Apamea: Sozomen vii. 20 (*P.G.* lxvii. 1453).

[3] *Or.* xxx. 8.   [4] Ibid. 11, 20.

[5] On temple lands: Tchalenko, *Villages*, 41, 177, 398.

[6] *Or.* xxx. 11; cf. Zos. v. 23.

[7] But the σωφρονισταί of *Or.* xxx. 12 are simply the monks.

[8] Ibid. 46.

[9] Zos. iv. 37; *Chron. Min.* 1, 244; Theod. *H.E.* v. 21, Soz. vii. 15, Jones, *L.R.E.* 167, P. Petit, 'Sur la date du *Pro Templis* de Libanius', *Byzantion* xxi (1951), 285–310.

from their still intact sanctuaries on the hills around Antioch.[1] But in the longer run the monks were completely successful. The hill country of north-eastern Syria which is so rich in ruins has scarcely any remains of temples. Even on so famous a site as Mount Casius nothing remains except a heap of ashes telling of the sacrifices for Zeus of long ago.[2] We see that the monks represented a new power in the countryside. Campaigns, whether directed against pagan temples, or in support of some doctrinal position, must always have been exceptional occurrences. But at all times the monks, either as solitary holy men, or gathered in large communities possessing considerable estates, were in a position to influence people in all classes of society. In other words they could assist or harm in the same way as patrons whose influence was purely secular. While we cannot watch the process in detail, the existence in the countryside of this new kind of patron must have had an influence on the perennial struggle between city and countryside, between city-based landowner, or tax collector, or official, and the peasantry.[3]

In the city too the triumph of Christianity produced a new centre of authority beside the old organs of local or imperial administration. By the end of the fourth century the bishop, apart from the imperial representatives, was by far the most powerful resident of the city. Leaving aside the more intangible authority of his religious office, he was the head of an organization whose size and complexity had no equal outside the imperial administration. He controlled a large charitable organization, which fed three thousand virgins every day and succoured prisoners.[4] It maintained hostels for travellers and hospitals for the sick and crippled.[5] It provided food and clothing to men whose names were entered on a register and who presented themselves day by day.[6] John Chrysostomus complains that so many of the

---

[1] *Or.* lvi. 22.   [2] Lassus, *Sanctuaires*, 247–8.
[3] Cf. Abraames and the tax collectors: Theod. *H.R.* xvii (*P.G.* lxxxii. 1420–1) or the stories told of Symeon Stylites in the Syriac Life: Lietzmann, op. cit. (p. 236 n. 4 above), 57, 92, 95, 130–1. On patronage exercised by Egyptian abbots: A. Steinwenter, 'Die Stellung der Bischöfe in der byzantinischen Verwaltung Ägyptens', *Studi in onore di P. Francisci* (Milan, 1954), 77–99, present ref. 88, nn. 1–3. P. *Cairo.*, Maspero 67297: προστασίας μήτε μοναχικοῦ μήτε στρατιωτικοῦ.
[4] Joh. Chrys. *Hom. in Matth.* 66 (*P.G.* lvii. 658), cf. *Or.* xlv. 10.
[5] Ibid. 630; *Hom. in Ep. I ad Cor.* 15 (*P.G.* lxi. 179–80) ; Philostorg. iii. 18.
[6] *Hom. in Ep. I ad Cor.* 15 (*P.G.* lxi. 179).

clergy were occupied for so much of their time in administration and almsgiving that few were left for the care of souls. The Church owned lands and horses; the clergy were busy renting dwellings and doing the work of shopkeepers, excise men, accountants, and treasurers; they spent time with wine merchants, corn merchants, and shopkeepers, and were occupied with mules and carriages. If we want to visualize the charitable activities of the Church, we must read the descriptions of St. Basil's vast new charitable institution outside Caesarea. This was a city in itself, with a church in the centre and around it the house of the bishop, streets of houses for the clergy, hostels for strangers, and hospitals for the sick.[1] Archaeology has revealed traces of similar complexes elsewhere, including Syria.[2]

His position involved a bishop in many of the activities of a secular magnate.[3] He was expected to intercede for members of his flock not only in heaven but with secular judges. Christians traditionally suspected secular courts, and secular justice was slow, expensive, and often corrupt. Christians had long preferred to have their disputes settled by the bishop. Constantine had given this practice official sanction with a law which allowed contestants in a civil case to agree to have their case heard by a bishop. He even amended this later to the effect that if only one of the parties wished the case to go before the bishop, he would have his way.[4] Criminal cases were outside the bishop's jurisdiction, but if a bishop were charged, he could only be judged by other bishops.[5] The bishop's jurisdiction may have

[1] *Hom. in Matth.* 85 (*P.G.* viii. 761–2); cf. Baur, *Johannes Chrysostomus*, 126–30; on Caesarea: Greg. Naz. *Or.* xliii. 63, Soz. *H.E.* vi. 34, Bas. *Ep.* 94, 140, cf. 142–4.

[2] Lassus, *Sanctuaires*, 233–4, 238–41; Tchalenko, *Villages*, 18, 396. C. A. Ralegh Radford on complexes of Christian buildings at Salona and Aquileia in *Christianity in Britain 300–700*, ed. M. W. Barley and R. P. C. Hanson, 23–7. Other examples in Claude, *Byzantinische Stadt*, 96–7.

[3] Incomes of bishops: Jones, *L.R.E.* 905–6 (on same scale as governors). Joh. Chrys. *Hom. in Matth.* 66. 3, the revenue of the church of Antioch compared with that of wealthy—but not the wealthiest—private individuals. One suspects an understatement; but cf. *Select Letters of Severus of Antioch, Ep.* 17, on poverty of see.

[4] Jurisdiction of bishop, *C.T.* i. 27. 1 (318); *Const. Sirm.* i (333); but *C.J.* i. 4. 7 (398), *C.T.* xvi. 11. 1 (399) restate that consent of both parties is required. On the jurisdictional privileges of clergy: Jones, *L.R.E.* 491–2. Sanctuary: *C.T.* ix. 45. 1–5; *C.J.* i. 12. 3 (431). Intercession: Syn. *Ep.* 67, Sid. Ap. *Ep.* vii. 9. 2; cf. Brown, *Augustine of Hippo*, 195–6, on Augustine's activities as judge, arbitrator, or patron. Supervision of prison and prisoners: *C.T.* ix. 3. 7 (409), Steinwenter, op. cit. (p. 239 n. 3), 91–2.

[5] *C.T.* xvi. 2. 12 (355).

grown out of traditional practice of Christians, but, established by imperial decree, it marked a definite sharing of the function of the imperial government.

This was not inappropriate. After all the bishop was the representative of the greater part of the population. He was, in a sense, the elected representative, even if he had not in fact been chosen by the whole body of his congregation.[1] The bishop was thus the real heir of the tradition of local autonomy, and it was as natural that the imperial government should recognize this, as it was that the crowd in 387, protesting against the taxes, should assemble outside the house of Bishop Flavian when they had failed to get relief from the governors. So too it was Flavian who travelled to Constantinople to plead for his city with the emperor.[2]

As the council declined in number, wealth, and reputation its representative function could be taken over by none other than the bishop. And there were plenty of occasions in numerous places for bishops to act as leaders of their city.[3] But it would be a mistake to assume that the change made no practical difference. A bishop with any sense of religious vocation, particularly if he had been a monk, had a very different sense of values from a curial magistrate. He would condemn many of the traditional objects of civic expenditure—games, shows, public display. He would look upon the motivation of traditional public munificence as a seeking after vain glory.[4] He would strive for religious unity rather than for political co-operation, and in so doing might provoke bitter divisions. In any case, the main object of his office

[1] Jones, *L.R.E.* 915–19, on election of bishops. The ordinary man probably had no part in the election: Zach. Myt. *V. Sev.* 110 ff., 238 ff., shows that Severus was elected bishop of Antioch at a meeting of bishops, clergy, and monks at Sidon. But clearly much pressure might be exercised by candidates and their supporters. In 413 Porphyrius could only be consecrated at Antioch when the bulk of the people had gone to Daphne to watch the Olympic Games: Pall. *Dial.* 16. 53. Popular pressure might also be exercised on individuals to compel them to become priests or bishops, Brown, *Augustine of Hippo*, 139.

[2] *Or.* xix. 28; Joh. Chrys. *Hom. ad pop. Ant.* 3. 1 (*P.G.* xlix. 4), 21 f. (211).

[3] e.g. Theodoret at Cyrrhus: Theod. *Ep.* 79, 81. The council of Cyrrhus was in a poor state, Lib. *Ep.* 1071, 1974 (393). Synesius of Cyrene led opposition against an oppressive governor: Syn. *Ep.* 57–8. Lacombrade, *Synésios de Cyrène*, 237–43. He organized action against a powerful law-breaker who had defied the police: *Ep.* 47. He concerned himself with the defence of the province: *Catastases* i and ii, cf. Lacombrade, op. cit. 230–6. See also *Chr.* I. 6, a bishop petitions the emperor for troops.

[4] Cf. Joh. Chrys. *De ed. lib.* 3–11.

would be to minister to the souls of members of his flock. It has been noted that Augustine and his episcopal colleagues used their diplomatic gifts, and their opportunities for exploiting influence, to further the interests of their church or of particular protégés. They left the mass of laymen to fend for themselves.[1] They might intervene in extreme cases of injustice but did not concern themselves with routine exploitation or oppression.[2] Even the most well-meaning bishop would show only intermittent concern for political issues. An emergency would normally be required to make them his central concern.

8. THE RIVAL STUDIES

In the writings of all periods of his life Libanius complains that the position of Greek rhetoric in education was threatened by shorthand,[3] Latin, and Roman Law.[4] The imperial government perversely gave preference to men skilled in the rival disciplines when appointments were to be made to the imperial service, with the result that fathers who had themselves been brought up on 'logoi' had their sons taught shorthand or Latin and law.

In the reign of Constantius or soon after, Libanius' most bitter complaints were directed against the preference given by the government to men skilled in shorthand. The teachers of rhetoric were earning little, the shorthand teachers were wealthy. The government was appointing shorthand writers to the highest positions in the imperial service, even to the highest rank of all, the praetorian prefecture of the East.[5] Naturally fathers made their sons learn shorthand. This would not necessarily mean that sons of good family would learn no Greek rhetoric at all, but that their course would be cut short, before they had obtained the full benefit from their study.[6] Inevitably, both the subject and its professors lost prestige.

---

[1] Brown, *Augustine of Hippo*, 420.   [2] Frend, *Donatist Church*, 329.

[3] *Or.* xxxi, a bibliography on ancient shorthand: Marrou, *Histoire de l'éducation*, 414 n. 22.

[4] On Latin and law: *Or.* xliii. 3 ff., *Or.* lxii. 21.

[5] *Or.* lxii. 8–10, 51. *Or.* xviii. 158 contrasts Julian's appointment of men trained in rhetoric with the appointment of stenographers by his predecessor, also *Ep.* 1224. The ὑπογραφεῖς, about whom Libanius complained, were members of the *officium* of notaries, *Or.* ii. 58.

[6] Wolf, *Schulwesen*, 80–2.

While these observations of Libanius are not disinterested, they have a considerable basis in fact. In the reign of Constantius the corps of the 'notaries', whose basic duty was to act as a secretariat for the imperial consistory,[1] had not yet gained the high social prestige it was to enjoy in later days, and might be recruited from the shopkeeper–artisan class or from even humbler levels of society. Hence many notaries lacked the full rhetorical education of young men of the landed aristocracy. It was nevertheless Constantius' policy to employ members of the corps for a great variety of responsible tasks and to promote them to the highest offices. Three of these men rose to be praetorian prefect.[2] Another, Datian, never held high office but was known to have great influence with the emperor.[3] Libanius' fellow citizens, therefore, had good reason to suppose that possession of the technical qualifications for service in the notaries might set their sons on the road to wealth and power.[4]

There undoubtedly was a demand for instruction in Latin and Roman Law at this time. Libanius himself tried to persuade a teacher of law to settle at Antioch. He failed.[5] In 360 a civic chair in Roman Law was established, and again Libanius was concerned with finding a man to fill it.[6] Libanius also tried to appoint a Latin teacher to his own school.[7] Another Latin teacher, Celsus II, appears to have taught independently.[8] We have no idea of the scale of the instruction in these Roman subjects at Antioch, but at this period it was not sufficiently large to arouse Libanius' indignation.

The law school at Berytus was another matter. A number of letters show that pupils of Libanius either cut short their studies of Greek rhetoric[9] to attend the law school of Berytus, or began to study law after they had completed their course in rhetoric.[10]

[1] Jones, *L.R.E.* 572.

[2] Philippus I (cf. Seeck, *Briefe*, 237 ff.), *P.P.O.* 341–51. Domitian, *P.P.O.* 353–4. Taurus, *P.P. Ital.* 351–61. Helpidius, *P.P.O.* 360–1. For their biographies see *P.W.* That they rose through shorthand: *Or.* xlii. 23–5.

[3] *Or.* xlii. 24; Seeck, *Briefe*, 113–17.

[4] Jones, *L.R.E.* 127–8; Petit, *Libanius*, 368.

[5] *Ep.* 433 (355), 478 (356), 486, 507. Silanus did not come.

[6] *Ep.* 209, again unsuccessfully. [7] *Ep.* 534 (356), 539 (356–7).

[8] *Ep.* 363 (358): Celsus II.

[9] Wolf, *Schulwesen*, 80–2, purely legal study was rare.

[10] *Ep.* 1431 (361); an older student, 1170–1, 1203 (364); another, 652–3 (361); other students of law: 1528–9 (365), Palladius; 339, Theodore; 87 (359), Silvanus; 1539 (365), boy learns rhetoric, then law; 1375 (363), boy runs away from

Libanius comments that it is impossible for anybody to benefit from taking both these courses. As a man learns the law, he will inevitably forget his Greek rhetoric.[1] As usual, he only half believes in his generalization, and his view of the incompatibility of rhetoric and law does not prevent him from commending a person for being skilled in both branches of knowledge.[2]

Although Libanius does not wish his pupils or anyone else of good family to study law on principle, he is quite ready to make allowances in individual cases. He was evidently on good terms with Domninus I, a teacher of law at Berytus, and wrote several letters recommending pupils to him. He also wrote letters for students going home and looking for appointments after they had finished their legal studies. He even wrote such a testimonial for a youth who had never been a student of his own, on the request of the teachers (γέροντες) at Berytus.[3] As in other matters, Libanius treats individual cases on their merits, and in a spirit quite different from the rhetorical and partisan aggression of his writings.

The preferment given to men who might be thought educated in nothing but shorthand came to an end with the death of Constantius. But the popularity of Latin and law continued to grow for the rest of Libanius' life, and the rivalry was more severe in the eighties of the century than ever before. About 374 Libanius complained of the weakness and disgrace of λόγοι,[4] since other subjects offered better prospects of preferment. He himself did not yet suffer from this rivalry. Some years later Libanius criticizes Eumolpius for advising his brother, the praetorian prefect Dometius Modestus (370–7), to appoint as his assessor a young man who had just returned from studies in Italy. Though this passage is the earliest mention of the practice, it had evidently gone on for some time.[5] In the following years it loomed largely in the mind of Libanius as the chief cause of the decline of Greek Letters. According to a passage of the *Autobiography* written about

Libanius' school to study law at Berytus. The frequency of law studies: *Ep.* 1203 (364); cf. P. Collinet, *Études historiques sur le droit de Justinien*, vol. 2, *Histoire de l'École de droit de Beyrouth* (Paris, 1925), 85–91.

[1] *Ep.* 1375 and elsewhere, cf. Wolf, op. cit. 81.
[2] *Ep.* 339, 871.
[3] *Ep.* 117, 1131, 1171, 653, 533 for a student of another Sophist, 1528–9.
[4] *Or.* i. 154.
[5] *Or.* xl. 5 ff. See Seeck, *Briefe*, s.vv. Eumolpius and Modestus.

384, the sailings to Italy had reached such an extent that people had advised him to retire from teaching. Some teachers had done this and had left Antioch to settle in various towns of Asia.[1] In the *De pactis* of 386 the migration of students to Italy is given as evidence of the low esteem into which Greek Letters had fallen.[2] It is mentioned in the two speeches dealing with the condition of the council of Antioch,[3] and in one of four letters concerned with the withdrawal from Greek education between 390 and 393.[4]

The advantage of these Roman Studies was that they provided a chance for sons of decurions to escape from curial duties in their home towns. This was already recognized by the imperial government in 370. The prefect of the city receives instructions that a record be kept in the office of tax assessment, in which are to be entered every month the names of the newly arrived students, together with their country of origin, and also the names of students who are due to return home because they have finished their studies. No student may stay at Rome beyond his twentieth year. If the need should arise, the prefect is authorized to use force to send the youths home.[5] The law is directed explicitly against students from Africa but, as we have seen, ten years later the journey to Rome was a common practice among the youth of Syria also.

Nevertheless, the evidence of Libanius shows that study at Rome continued to be an effective means of escaping from curial duties. The law of 370 itself shows why this was so. 'Similar registers, moreover, shall be dispatched each year to the bureaux of our Clemency in order that we may learn of the merits and education of the various students and may judge whether they may be necessary to us.' In other words, if men are thought suitable for employment in the imperial service they will be employed. As a large proportion of the students are likely to have come from curial families, and most forms of service in the imperial administration carried immunity from curial duties, the last clause reopens the door which the earlier clauses had closed. Here is a particularly striking example of the self-contradictions

[1] *Or.* i. 214, date shown by *c.* 233.
[2] *Or.* xliii. 5, dated by Foerster, vol. iii. 334.
[3] *Or.* xlviii. 22 ff., xlix. 27.
[4] *Ep.* 951 (390), *Ep.* 955 (390), 961 (390), 963 (390), cf. *Or.* i. 234.
[5] *C.T.* xiv. 9. 1.

forced upon the government, when it tried at the same time to establish an efficient civil service and to maintain the strength of the councils.

The later writings of Libanius suggest that the 'flight' from λόγοι was much more general than before. Now for the first time Libanius was obliged to treat a teacher of Latin rhetoric as a serious rival in his own city of Antioch.[1] Previously his only rivals at home had been sophists of Greek.[2] The rivalry of the Latin sophist plays an important part in three speeches written around the year 388. It appears that while some pupils changed over from Greek to Latin completely, more attended classes in both subjects and showed more interest in Latin than they did in Greek. The lack of zeal for Greek showed itself in unruly behaviour while Libanius was declaiming speeches, and in general apathy. No longer were students eager to learn portions of his speeches by heart, nor did they now come together after Libanius had spoken to reconstruct Libanius' declamation from memory. The Latin rhetor had his own students' organization, and youths who had never given battle on Libanius' behalf fought for his rival. Hooliganism reached its climax when the boys vented their anger on a pedagogue, tossing him in a blanket, because he had committed his charges to devote more time to Greek Letters than they liked.

We notice, therefore, throughout the lifetime of Libanius, a steady increase in the popularity of Latin and legal studies, which was caused by the government's policy of giving preference, when making appointments to the civil service, to applicants who had knowledge of Latin and Roman Law. The government's motives are not far to seek; Latin was still the official language of the Roman Empire in the East.[3] Until about 440 the edicts

---

[1] *Or.* i. 255, xxxviii. 6, iii, *passim.* Latin teacher orders tossing in blanket of pedagogue, *Or.* lviii. 29; his motive, ibid. 21.

[2] *Ep.* 363 (358).

[3] H. Zilliacus, *Zum Kampf der Weltsprachen im oströmischen Reich* (Helsingfors, 1935). Latin was used particularly in the business of the central departments at Constantinople, also in their communications to the provinces. See U. Wilcken, 'Über den Nutzen der Lateinischen Papyri', *Atti del IV Congresso di papirologia* (Milano, 1936), 101–22. Also from higher to lower officials in Egypt, P. Jouguet in *R.E.L.* iii (1925), 43. So *P. Gen.* 45 = *Chr.* 464 from *comes et dux Aegyptii* to Abinnaeus, dismissing him. But this is a military document, and Latin remained the language of command in the army for a very long time, cf. F. Lot, 'La Langue de commandement dans les armées romaines', in *Mélanges Félix Grat.*, vol. i (Paris,

of the praetorian prefect were issued in Latin.[1] Only with the Novels of Justinian did Greek become the normal language in which Imperial Constitutions were issued.[2] Of course, Latin could not be used in relations with the local populations, who understood only Greek. The coexistence of the two languages in the practice of the imperial administration is well illustrated by some papyrus protocols of hearings held before governors. The framework of the document, the description of the place, date, and circumstances of the audience are in Latin, while almost all the speech recorded, both that of the governor and that of his subjects, is Greek. The fact that this is theoretically a Roman court proceeding in Latin may or may not be apparent in the sentence, which is sometimes stated in Latin, with a Greek translation added.[3] But while most of the relations between governors and governed were of necessity carried out in Greek, the internal relations of the administration, particularly the correspondence with the central administration and the business in the central bureaux remained in Latin.

While this was so, it is not surprising that the government valued highly officials with a knowledge of Latin. They cannot have been easy to find. Most officials in the eastern half of the Empire came from the Greek-speaking provinces.[4] There seems to have been little work on the extent of knowledge of Latin in the East;[5] but Libanius gives the impression that the knowledge of Latin was not widespread.[6] He himself needed an interpreter to read a letter of Symmachus.[7] Libanius' uncle, Phasganius, had none and was proud of his ignorance.[8] A great-grandfather

1946), 203–9; and Z. von Lingenthal, 'Wissenschaft und Recht für das Heer', *B.Z.* iii (1894), 437 ff., especially 441 on use of Latin in sixth century; also Turner, *Greek Papyri*, 75 n. 2.   [1] Joh. Lydus, *De mag.* ii. 12, iii. 68, 42.

[2] L. Wenger, *Die Quellen des römischen Rechts* (Vienna, 1953), 657 ff. Even among the Novels exceptions were issued in Latin because they were addressed to central offices where Latin was still officially in use.

[3] Zilliacus, op. cit. 97; Lallemand, *L'Administration civile de l'Égypte*, 160.

[4] This is suggested by governors mentioned with their provinces in Seeck, *Briefe*. There were exceptions. Rufinus, *comes orientis* 363–4, was an Italian, and the praetorian prefect, Rufinus (392–5), a Gaul or Spaniard, and the prefect Cynegius (384–8), a Spaniard. Both were appointed by a Spanish emperor, Theodosius. The law that men should not govern their home province was not always enforced. Among contraventions, Celsus I, governor of Syria in 363.

[5] Marrou, *Histoire de l'éducation*, 348 and 544 n. 7, bibliography; also p. 246 n. 3 above.

[6] Commendations for knowing Latin are not frequent, *Ep.* 668 an example.

[7] *Ep.* 1004.   [8] *Or.* xlix. 29.

had once made a speech in Latin and this deceived people into thinking that he had been of Italian origin.¹ Evidently fluent knowledge of Latin was unusual among the *curiales* of Antioch.² The rarity value conferred by knowledge of Latin is illustrated by Ammianus' comment that Strategius Musonianus, the prae-torian prefect of Constantius, had risen higher than was ex-pected, because he knew both languages.³ What happened when (as must have been quite frequent) a man who had no knowledge of Latin was appointed governor, we can only imagine. He will have been extremely dependent on his officials. Not only would they have to carry out his correspondence with his superiors, but he would have to rely on them if he wanted to look up old imperial edicts or legal decisions, on which his own administra-tion and jurisdiction must be based. After all, since the *Constitutio Antonina* the inhabitants were all Roman citizens and, as such, subject to Roman Law.⁴

It therefore must have happened quite frequently that neither judge nor litigants in a lawsuit knew Latin, nor could they read the Roman Law according to which the case should have been decided. Further, ancient court practice made a division between the professions of advocate and lawyer, and in court the position of the advocate, usually trained in nothing but rhetoric, was far more prominent than that of the lawyer. In the good old days, Libanius relates, the men skilled in law stood silent before the advocate, waiting for his command to read.⁵ Such men must have lived in every town, and their ability to write out contracts and wills according to the forms of Roman Law will have been indispensable.⁶ Nevertheless they were traditionally the social

---

¹ *Or.* i. 3. A notable exception was Euagrius, brother of Libanius' friend Olympius and friend of St. Jerome, who translated Athanasius' *Life of St. Anthony* into Latin. That family descended from Pompeianus Francus, general of the Emperor Aurelian and probably a westerner, cf. Seeck, *Briefe*, 128–30.

² Shouts in Latin in the enlarged plethron: *Or.* x. 14 (384).

³ Amm. xv. 13. 1–2.

⁴ On the effect of the *Constitutio Antoniana* on legal practice, see Mitteis, *Reichsrecht und Volksrecht*, 180, 187–8.

⁵ *Or.* ii. 44.

⁶ Mitteis, *Reichsrecht und Volksrecht*, 176, on *notarii* and *tabelliones*, cf. Libanius, *Ep.* 115, 152. The Syriac Law book of Hierapolis, text in S. Riccobono, *Fontes Iuris Romani Anteiustiniani* (Florence, 1940), vol. 2, 759 ff., is a commentary on imperial constitutions for school use originally composed in Greek. See W. Selb, *Zur Bedeutung des syrisch-römischen Rechtsbuches* (Munich, 1964), (*Münchener Beiträge zur Papyrusforschung* xlix), conclusions: 242, 249.

inferiors of the rhetorically trained advocates. Councillors' sons studied rhetoric and became advocates; the sons of shopkeepers or craftsmen might study law.[1]

Under these circumstances we cannot expect that Roman Law was dispensed in the courts of the governors at Antioch in a very pure form. Libanius does not throw much light on this matter. In one case (of 388) he claims that the law allows the accuser in an action to withdraw, whereas the governor insists that he should resume the prosecution, even if he does not want to.[2] There is nothing in this passage incompatible with the principle of Roman Law, as expressed in Mommsen's *Strafrecht*,[3] according to which the accuser can only withdraw with the judge's permission. The judge will bear in mind the motives which guided the accuser in the first place, and accordingly either permit him to drop the prosecution or punish him.

In another passage of the same speech Libanius appeals to the legal principle that there must be no revival of the accusation after the verdict, and this, too, is justified in Roman Law.[4] Three letters of the year 365 deal with a lawsuit over the property of a woman who married a second time, after her first husband had died.[5] The only child of her first marriage was dead also. The second husband sought to claim the property for his wife on the ground that there was no surviving child from the first marriage. His opponents claimed that the second marriage was invalid because it was contracted within one year of the husband's death. The defence to this was that imperial exemption had been granted. All these arguments seem to fall within the laws of the Theodosian Code iii. 8. 1–2, both published in 381. If my interpretation is true, these laws restate, rather than proclaim, legal principles. This case is, however, less significant for conditions at Antioch, as it was finally fought at Constantinople.

In *Oration* lvii, of uncertain date, Libanius claims that according to the law, the judge may lay down the time within which a debtor must make payment. I am not certain whether there is such a principle in Roman Law or not.

Leaving questions of law for questions of procedure, we find reference to the practice of holding some trials at night.

---

[1] *Or.* lxii. 21.　　　　　　　　[2] *Or.* liv. 46.
[3] Th. Mommsen, *Strafrecht* (Leipzig, 1899), 452 and 499 ff.
[4] *Or.* liv. 50, *Strafrecht*, 450.　　　[5] *Ep.* 1511, 1512, 1513.

Ellebichus made a show of following this custom after the Riot of the Statues,[1] but its universality is suggested by the procedure of Maximinus in the course of the magic trials of Rome.[2] Then, in the trial after the Riot of the Statues, Ellebichus, the judge, was very keen to extort confessions from the accused,[3] and this seems to agree with the spirit of legislation in the Code, according to which confession is more certain than proof and might rule out appeal.[4]

These passages suggest that the law enforced at Antioch was basically Roman, but the information is quite insufficient to form any picture of its detailed working, or of its Greek or Oriental accretions.[5]

Given the position of Latin and of Roman Law in the administration of the empire, and the fact that the inhabitants knew neither Latin nor Roman Law, the Eastern government was confronted with a choice between two policies. Either it could systematically adopt Greek as the language of administration, or it could try to make the knowledge of Latin and Roman Law as widespread as possible among its officials. The evidence of Libanius shows that it adopted the second course.[6]

Another means of improving the administration of law was by control of the profession of advocate. This was possible because in the fourth century it was no longer open to anyone who wanted to speak as advocate in court. Each court had a number of advocates registered with it, and according to a law of Constantine, no man might practise advocacy at more than one court.[7] There is no clear evidence that the necessity for registration was in fact used to force would-be advocates to study law.

---

[1] Law of debt: *Or.* lvii. 31. Trials at night: *Or.* xxii. 21; xxv. 43 refers to same practice.

[2] Amm. xxviii. 1. 54.   [3] *Or.* xxii. 23.

[4] Cf. *C.T.* ix. 40. 1 (Constantine) and *Strafrecht*, 437.

[5] Cf. remarks of G. von Beseler, 'Libaniana', in *Byzantinisch-neugriechische Jahrbücher* xiv (1937–8), 1–40; also Harmand's examination of Libanius' lawsuit with his Jewish tenants, *Discours sur les patronages*, 193–200.

[6] Cf. *Ep.* 1539.

[7] There was no fixed limit to the number of advocates allowed at any court: *C.T.* ii. 1. 1 (319) but advocates were not allowed to practise at more than one, ibid. 2 (319). Antioch had three 'choruses' of advocates, those respectively of the *comes orientis*, consular, and *magister militum per orientem*: *Or.* xi. 191. An attempt to limit career of advocates to 20 years: *Ep.* 857 (388); its abandonment: 916 (390). It was re-enacted soon after, Jones, *L.R.E.* 509 n. 89; on status of advocates in general: ibid. 507–16.

It is likely that one purpose of the registration was to prevent too many men from enjoying *de facto* immunity from curial duties.[1] It is significant that Julian who increased the number of councillors also reduced the number of advocates.[2] Nevertheless the view began to prevail both in the administration and among the public at large that it was not enough for a barrister to be a persuasive speaker: he ought also to have an expert knowledge of law.[3]

The final stage in the development was that the government made knowledge of the law a condition of the registration of advocates. As far as we can tell from our evidence, this stage was reached only seventy years later, when the Emperor Leo ordered that men who wished to join the bar of the praetorian prefecture must bring the sworn testimony of their professors as to their skill in law.[4] Also the length of the law-course to be attended by a would-be advocate was fixed.[5] By then advocacy was no longer a free profession, but the groups of advocates at the various courts were government-controlled bodies of limited size, with seniority, recognized heads, fixed fees, and retirement honours. At this time, too, certain groups of advocates had real understanding of law, as is shown by questions on matters of law sent by them corporatively to the emperor.[6] This was much later than Libanius and goes beyond anything suggested in Libanius' writings, but the tendency towards this state of affairs was already strong in his time.

When we survey the passages in Libanius witnessing to the advances made by Latin and law in education, we must

---

[1] Cf. above, p. 177. [2] *Ep.* 1353 (363).

[3] *Or.* ii. 43–5, *Ep.* 1170, 1203. The legal expert was also favoured by changes in court procedure: see Jolowicz, *Historical Introduction to Roman Law*, c. 26. The stress is on written rather than oral evidence: the judge, not the advocate, examines witnesses. There are no concluding speeches. The advocates take up individual points as they arise. There is no longer necessarily a 'day in court'. The trial might be broken up into a number of separate investigations. In accordance with this is the description of the trial of the case between Libanius and his Jewish tenants, *Or.* xlvii. 13–16; cf. Harmand, *Discours sur les patronages*, 193. There, too, the judge calls witnesses, there is no 'day in court', but prolonged investigation in private, and the judge finds the verdict in private, some days after the close of formal proceedings. Perhaps he sought out more information—in accordance with a judge's new task of supplementing evidence of the party that is too weak to bring it itself; cf. M. Lemosse, *Cognitio* (Paris, 1944), 240. [4] *C.J.* ii. 7. 11. 2.

[5] Ibid. 7. 24. 4–5 (517; bar of consular of Syria); ibid. 22. 4–6 (505; bar of *comes orientis*).

[6] *C.J.* vi. 58. 12 (advocates of Caesarea), vi. 38. 5 (advocates of Illyricum).

conclude that we are faced by a deliberate and sustained attempt of the Roman government to make the Roman character of the empire prevail against all difficulties. This impression is confirmed by the evidence of the papyri in Egypt.[1] According to Wilcken, there was a noticeable increase in the use of Latin in administrative documents from the reign of Diocletian onwards.[2] Most strikingly, the protocols of the proceedings of the law courts were now drafted in Latin, although they had previously been in Greek, and although most of the speeches recorded inevitably remained in Greek.[3] The forms of the reports, according to Bickermann, changed from the form of Greek ὑπομνηματισμοί to that of Latin *gesta* or *acta*.[4] The period sees an increase in the number of Latin words in Greek documents and perhaps even a Latin influence in the script. It is also notable that a large proportion of the bilingual literary Greek and Latin texts, as well as purely Latin texts, date from this time, and seem to bear witness to the activities of Latin teachers, the Egyptian colleagues of the men who gave such pain to Libanius.[5] Latin managed to hold on to these gains throughout the fourth century, and even into the fifth century, although they fade out in the sixth.

Taken by itself, the evidence from Egypt might be explained as a consequence of the acts of Diocletian, which abolished the separate status of Egypt in the Roman Empire, but when seen together with the passages in the writings of Libanius, it confirms that a very real effort was made over a long period by the imperial government to keep the Eastern Empire a Roman Empire.[6] Indeed inscriptions on coins continued in Latin into the reign of Heraclius (610–41) and beyond.[7]

Yet, in spite of this, Libanius' worries about the progress of Latin may seem excessive. The fact that the overwhelming majority of the educated inhabitants of the East spoke Greek only could not be overcome, and in fact concessions were made. Thus, in spite of the definite rulings of Roman Law that contracts

---

[1] See bibliography of Latin papyri in *Scriptorium* iv (1950), 119–31; R. Cavenaile, *Corpus Papyrorum Latinarum* (Wiesbaden, 1958).

[2] Wilcken, op. cit. (p. 246 n. 3 above), 100 ff.

[3] Survey of evidence: Lallemand, *L'Administration civile de l'Égypte*, 160.

[4] E. Bickermann, '*Testificatio Actorum*', *Aegyptus* xiii (1933), 333–55.

[5] Wilcken, op. cit. 105.

[6] The dividing line between the two halves of the empire was not drawn along the linguistic boundary: Jones, *L.R.E.* 986.

[7] Zilliacus, op. cit. 54.

or transactions involving persons must be in Latin, Greek wills were made. Again, a law of 397[1] allows judges to pronounce the sentence in Greek. In 439 a law of Theodosius II shows that at this time wills might legally be written in Greek. Laws and imperial letters, whether addressed to individuals or communities, were drafted in both languages, but the Greek version was dispatched and published and might even be cited in court.[2]

In the second decade of the fifth century a professor of law at Berytus wrote a textbook of Roman Law in Greek. It seems likely that Greek became the language of instruction at the law school about this time; it certainly was in the later fifth century.[3] How it would have pleased Libanius to hear this! About 440 the prefect Cyrus first published edicts of the praetorian prefecture in Greek[4] and the other government departments followed. Justinian made a grand gesture when he had his *Corpus Juris Civilis* published in Latin, but he published his own legislation in Greek.

Again, the fact that the government tried to maintain the Latin and Roman character of the empire did not mean, as Libanius often implied, that it did not value Greek rhetoric. The honours and salaries paid by the government to sophists like Themistius and Libanius, and also to lesser lights in smaller places, show how highly it rated the value of 'logoi' to the empire. The comparative freedom of speech allowed to these great sophists is evidence of the same esteem. Altogether, the honours, visits, and tributes Libanius received from all manner of people, for no other reason than that he was the most celebrated representative of 'logoi' in his day, does not suggest that 'logoi' were despised. Further, while it may have occurred that men obtained high office purely because of their knowledge of Latin and of law, and though at some periods and in some offices promotion on these grounds may have been more common than at others, nevertheless, as Petit has shown, on the whole the men brought up on 'logoi' continued to get the governorships, although sometimes they may have learned Latin as well.[5] There is in Libanius scarcely any evidence that men studied law without having studied Greek rhetoric before. As in many respects, so in this, John Lydus represents the outlook of the imperial civil

---

[1] *C.J.* vii. 45. 12. [2] Jones, *L.R.E.* 988–9.
[3] Collinet, *L'École de Beyrouth*, 212 ff. [4] Joh. Lydus, *De mag.* ii. 12, iii. 42.
[5] Petit, *Libanius*, 368.

service: at the same time pedantically antiquarian and imbued with love of the rhetorical tradition. John Lydus regretted the action of Cyrus in ceasing to publish his edicts in Latin, and considered this to have been the cause of great evils to the state.[1] At the same time, however, he was proud of his own literary skill in Greek and of the recognition which he met as an exponent of literature and learning.[2]

Further evidence of the strength of the Greek rhetorical tradition is that it obtained a firm footing in the preaching of the Church. Men like John Chrysostomus and the Cappadocians had views on good language and speech-making closely akin to those of Libanius, and the applause they earned with their sermons shows that members of their congregations appreciated good speaking too. The Greek of the Bible continued to need apologetics. Certainly, if one includes the Christian literature, the fourth century was a Golden Age for Greek writing.[3] Libanius' fear of Latin appears to have been exaggerated: he may nevertheless have had good grounds for his worries about the future of Greek education. After all, Greek did not survive very long in Syria after the Arabs had conquered the country, and especially when Arabic had become the language of the administration. Arabic quickly achieved what Libanius had feared Latin would do.[4] Greek speakers had always been a minority in Syria and rhetorically educated speakers of Greek a minority within the minority. The correspondence of Libanius shows that the educated few were as keen as ever that their sons should receive the traditional education. At the same time the emotional impact of Greek letters may well have been declining. That the gymnasia were allowed to disappear surely reveals a steep decline in the valuation attached to Hellenism. This in turn would reduce the social incentive for Hellenization among rising individuals from the lower classes. At the same time, the translation of part of the liturgy into Syriac had reduced the religious

[1] Joh. Lydus, *De mag.* ii. 12, iii. 42.

[2] Ibid. iii. 29–30. On the high esteem for Greek rhetorical education on the part of the government, see Marrou, *Histoire de l'éducation*, 410–14.

[3] On the close relationship between Christianity and classical education, Marrou, op. cit. 416–35: 'La religion chrétienne exige impérieusement au moins un minimum de culture lettrée . . . Les chrétiens . . . n'ont pas creé d'écoles qui leur fussent propres . . . Même prêché à des Chinois ou à des Bantous, l'Évangile ne peut oublier qu'il a d'abord été rédigé en grec', etc.

[4] Jones, *L.R.E.* 968–9, 996.

incentive.[1] We might also note that the council was not worried by reductions in the cultural expenditure of the city.[2] The book trade was on a small scale. Libanius and other authors arranged for the copying and distribution of their writings themselves.[3] Libanius' own speeches are addressed to a small and select group. Their allusiveness[4] is incompatible with a wide appeal. Thus Greek civilization was vulnerable. Libanius was surely aware of these trends, even though his professional struggles against the rival studies blinded him to the deeper causes of them.

[1] J.-B. Chabot, *Littérature syriaque* (Paris, 1934). In Egypt, where the scriptures and much theological literature was translated into Coptic, it has been observed that illiteracy in Greek seems to have slowly penetrated into higher reaches of the social scale during the Later Empire: R. Calderini, 'Gli ἀγράμματοι nell'Egitto greco-romano', *Aegyptus* xxx (1950), 14–41 (summary 26–7).

[2] *Or.* xlix. 32.

[3] A. F. Norman, 'The book trade in fourth-century Antioch', *J.H.S.* lxxx, (1960), 122–6.

[4] Id., 'The Library of Libanius', *Rh. M.* cvii (1964), 158–75, esp. 159–60.

CONCLUSION

THE FOURTH CENTURY AND AFTER

'THE cities were ruined in the third century both by barbarian invasions and by exactions of the government.' So Piganiol begins the chapter on the decurions in his work on the Christian Empire.[1] Our discussion has shown that this was not true of Antioch in the fourth century. Antioch was a prosperous city. It had many wealthy citizens and a comparatively small proportion of absolute paupers. The economy of the city was based on money. The regional aristocracy continued to live in the city and spent little time on estates in the country.

Many basic problems remain unsolved. The city had a very large population but we have no idea of the relative strength of the various occupational groups that comprised it. We know little about the way ordinary citizens of Antioch earned their living. We know that Libanius thought that Antioch was a flourishing city. We lack criteria which would enable us to compare the prosperity of Antioch in the fourth century with that which the city enjoyed under the Early Empire. Nevertheless we can be certain that the economic and social foundations of city life in Syria remained secure.

From an economic or social point of view the condition of Antioch was strikingly different from that of cities in the provinces of the West,[2] especially from the cities of transalpine provinces.[3] There the aristocracy moved into the countryside[4] and

---

[1] A. Piganiol, *L'Empire chrétien* (Paris, 1947).

[2] E. Ennen, *Frühgeschichte der europäischen Stadt* (Bonn, 1953); also 'Les différents types de formation des villes européennes', *Le Moyen Âge* lxii (1956), 399–411.

[3] On the more complete survival of city communities in N. Italy and Spain: Ennen, op. cit. 229 ff., 241 ff. On civic institutions in Spain under the Visigoths: E. A. Thompson, *The Goths in Spain* (Oxford, 1969), 118–21. Where civic institutions survived at all in the West their development continued to resemble that of Eastern cities to a surprising extent even under barbarian rule. F. Dölger, 'Die frühbyzantinische und byzantinisch beeinflusste Stadt', *Atti del 3 Congresso internazionale di studi sull'alto Medioevo* (Spoleto, 1959), 66–100.

[4] S. Dill, *Roman Society in the Last Century of the Western Empire* (London, 1899), chapters on the society of Ausonius and of Sidonius Apollinaris; K. F. Stroheker, *Der senatorische Adel im spätantiken Gallien* (Tübingen, 1943).

craftsmen followed the aristocracy.[1] The urban population was greatly reduced. Eventually a remnant might survive around a cathedral or other religious centre, or around the residence of a barbarian court.[2]

From a political point of view the condition of Antioch was less happy. Rostovtzeff reached the conclusion that the self-government of the cities of the Roman Empire was destroyed by the long period of third-century anarchy,[3] and the evidence in favour of this view is impressive. Nevertheless at Antioch the process was much more gradual. There is practically no evidence for the developments that took place in the city's institutions during the third century.[4] But we can observe that the system of provincial government which Diocletian set up to restore stability after the anarchy greatly narrowed the scope of civic self-government. Finance, food, public works, eventually even entertainment came to be controlled very closely by the agents of the imperial administration.

The imperial administration was carried on by paid officials and their subordinates: it was quite independent of local landed power. Antioch was the residence of three important officials: the *comes orientis*, the consular of Syria, and the *magister militum per orientem*. The general had little influence on life in the city but the two civilian governors interfered constantly in every aspect of local government. The high concentration of officials was of course peculiar to Antioch. Ordinary cities will have felt the pressure of the imperial administration less.

The intense control exercised by the governors produced far-reaching changes in the pattern of political behaviour at Antioch. While the city council was rarely, if ever, called upon to make collective decisions of policy, councillors were still required to perform numerous duties for city or empire. These were always

---

[1] Jones, *L.R.E.* 861; Ennen, op. cit. 89–90, on rural glass and pottery industries.

[2] E. Ewig, 'Résidence et capitale dans le haut Moyen Âge', *Rev. hist.* (1963); H. von Petrikovits: 'Das Fortleben römischer Städte an Rhein und Donau', *Trierer Zeitschrift* (1950), 72–81; S. S. Frere, 'The End of Towns in Roman Britain', *The 'Civitas Capitals' of Roman Britain*, ed. J. S. Wacher (Leicester, 1966), 87–100.

[3] M. Rostovtzeff, *The Social and Economic History of the Roman Empire*, 2nd edn. (Oxford, 1957), 513–14.

[4] According to Libanius, measures of Constantine *began* the decline of the council (*Or.* xlix. 2), but his writings reveal little knowledge—or at least interest—concerning the calamities of the later third century.

burdensome and might occasionally be dangerous. The compensating social prestige attached to membership of the council was much reduced. Imperial officials, active and retired, occupied the summit of the social pyramid. Hence there developed a strong pressure to escape from curial duties. The council was reduced to a fraction of its former establishment. At the same time leadership in the council fell into the hands of a small number of very rich families. The government favoured the development of a ruling oligarchy within the council by conferring legal privileges on the *principales*. It was convenient for the administration to do business with a small permanent group. Members of the group exploited their position for their own financial advantage.

There is no evidence that these developments had a deleterious effect on popular entertainment and related services. It is likely that, as the number of councillors available for duties was reduced, the proportion of civic expenditure that had to be paid out of the pockets of the councillors was reduced also, but the loss to the civic services may well have been compensated by an increase of the imperial contribution to the regular expenses of the city.

The reduced membership and prestige of the council made it less effective as the representative of the city *vis-à-vis* the imperial officials. This role was increasingly taken over by new institutions. The ceremony of acclamation enabled a governor to keep in touch with public opinion directly, and without consulting the local authorities. This in its turn gave new political importance to anyone favourably placed to organize applause, first the stage artists and perhaps the bishop, later in the fifth century the factions of the hippodrome.

Many of the complaints voiced as part of the acclamations were concerned with the food supply of the city. As a result, governors were induced to exercise close control over the shopkeepers. This was made easier by the full organization of trades in guilds. The governor appointed supervisors over the various trades organizations and through them watched over such matters as weights and measures and prices. Towards the end of the century price control appears to have become permanent.

The period also saw new and important developments in the field of patronage. The humble inhabitants of the empire had never been able to obtain justice without the support of patrons, but in this period the character of the patrons was changing. When all important decisions were made by the governors, the only patron worth having would be a man who could influence decisions in the governor's court. But the most effective intercessors with imperial officials were other officials, officers, or privileged ex-officials, rather than the civic councillors or local landowners who had previously acted as patrons of the small man in town or country. Hence new ties of clientage came to supersede older loyalties. There developed a threat both to landownership and to taxation. It is very difficult to assess the scale of the phenomenon, but it must have undermined the way in which the countryside had traditionally been governed by the civic authorities, and thus furthered the disruption of the city-state.

Ideological changes were working in the same direction. The public entertainments, through which members of the curial class had traditionally expressed their civic spirit, were under strong attack by the Church, so was the motivation which had impelled generations of liturgants to munificence for the sake of honour and applause.[1] In another sphere the fact that the government began to require technical qualifications for appointment to its service temporarily lowered the prestige of the traditional education. Of more lasting significance was the propagation of a non-classical and other-worldly ideal through the enormous impact of the ascetic movement. Preachers like John Chrysostomus urged rich men to give their wealth to the poor, but they did not preach an ideal of public service to replace the one which they helped to destroy.[2]

The available evidence does not allow us to study the evolution of the institutions of Antioch through the fifth and sixth centuries. But it is possible to gain an impression of the direction in which cities were developing by looking at the evidence for the East as a whole.

During the fifth century and for at least part of the sixth, the imperial administration remained extremely powerful, able to extract—in some areas of Egypt at least—an ever-increasing volume of taxation.[3] At the same time, the imperial governors

---

[1] Cf. Brown, *Augustine of Hippo*, 198 ff., 205.
[2] Jones, *L.R.E.* 982–5, deals with lack of guidance for governors rather than councillors, but the problem is the same.
[3] Jones, *L.R.E.* 464.

interfered in the smallest detail of municipal administration.[1] At Edessa, the capital of the province of Osroene, a newly appointed governor has the streets cleaned. He orders the destruction of cabins which artisans had built between pillars of a colonnaded street. He also orders shopkeepers to hang an illuminated cross over their shop on Sundays.[2] A later governor has all porticoes whitewashed.[3] In short the governor acted as the head of the city even in the most trivial things, and when he had occasion to leave the city he appointed a deputy.[4]

The cities were thoroughly Christianized. Their appearance came to be dominated by churches.[5] For the inhabitants the security provided by the circuit of walls was reinforced by faith in the supernatural defence assured by relics.[6] A bishop who had the support of his congregation was inevitably extremely powerful. The most formidable bishop of all was the bishop of Alexandria; through his influence over the Alexandrian crowd and over Egyptian monks he was able to use force against opponents even in defiance of the prefect of Egypt. Examples of the abuse of his powers are the murder of the pagan philosopher Hypatia[7] and the expulsion of the Jews from Alexandria.[8] So is the campaign against manifestations of paganism carried on by students later in the century and described by Zacharias of Mytilene.[9] But the bishops of Alexandria also came to exercise some ordinary functions of local government.[10]

The bishop of Alexandria's position was exceptionally powerful but there is evidence of secular activity by bishops elsewhere. In the small and poor city of Cyrrhus in the province of Euphratensis, Bishop Theodoret (423–60) put up great public works and

---

[1] Jones, *L.R.E.* 758–9.

[2] *Chronicle of Joshua the Stylite*, ed. and trans. by W. Wright (Cambridge, 1882), 29; on this Claude, *Byzantinische Stadt*, 148–9.

[3] *Chronicle of Joshua the Stylite*, 32.

[4] Ibid. 40.   [5] Claude, op. cit., 85–99.

[6] Ibid. 139–44; N. Baynes, 'The supernatural defenders of Constantinople', *Anal. Boll.* lxvii (1949, *Mélanges Paul Peeters*), 165–77 = *Byzantine Studies*, 248–60.

[7] E. Stein, *Histoire du Bas-Empire* (French edn. by J.-R. Palanque, 1959), 277, Soc. *H.E.* vii. 15.

[8] Soc. *H.E.* vii. 13, John of Niciu lxxxiv. 89–99.

[9] Zach. Myt. *V. Sev.* 25–36.

[10] *V. Joh. Eleem.* (*Anal. Boll.* xlv (1927), 19–73), 16, supervision of tavern-keepers; in dispute over market monopoly: ibid. 15; supervision of weights and measures: ibid. 3; cf. G. R. Monk, 'The church of Alexandria in the city's economic life in the sixth century', *Speculum* xxviii (1953), 349–62.

used his influence at court to protect his city from the fiscal demands of the government.[1] At Edessa too we hear of bishops who performed secular tasks. One took a leading part in famine relief. He went on an embassy to Constantinople in order to ask for a reduction in taxation. He received gold from the emperor for the task of repairing fortifications.[2] Ibas, one of his predecessors, had even provided a chariot race.[3]

The evidence shows that a bishop was in a position to take a leading part in the government of his city. In the sixth century he was even encouraged by the imperial government to do so. It nevertheless remains uncertain whether bishops under normal conditions felt it to be their duty to take a responsible and continuous part in local government. It may well be that as a rule the bishops only became fully engaged in the secular sphere during emergencies. There was the additional complication that after 451 the Eastern Church was split between followers and opponents of the council of Chalcedon and a bishop might be an agent of division rather than unity.[4]

When a city was not united behind its bishop it was more fragmented than ever before. *Honorati*, clergy, monks, the remaining councillors, the guilds, and sometimes the mass of the people grouped in support of the factions of the hippodrome, could all make themselves heard separately, but no body was in position to express the will of the city as a whole. When the opponents of Bishop Ibas of Edessa wished to persuade the imperial authorities that the city rejected its bishop, they organized a series of acclamations and followed these up with signed petitions. The signatories included clergy, monks, *honorati* and decurions, soldiers, teachers, and artisans; but the significant

[1] E. Frézouls, 'Recherches historiques et archéologiques sur la ville de Cyrrhus', *Annales archéologiques de Syrie* iv–v (1954), 89–128; Theodoret *Ep.* (*P.G.*) 81 (public works), 42–7 (taxation); Claude, *Byzantinische Stadt*, 137–8, cites secular activities of bishops from several other cities.

[2] Josh. Styl. 38, 78, embassies to Constantinople; 42, famine relief; 87, 91, bishops build fortifications; see also *Edessa Chron.* 67.

[3] *Akten der ephesinischen Synode vom Jahre* 449, 27, 25; cf. Joh. Ephes. *H.E.* v. 17, patriarch Gregory of Antioch asks the Emperor Maurice for orders to build a hippodrome.

[4] The laws of *C.J.* i. 4 show that the administration was trying to involve the bishop in local government. His responsibilities progress from the welfare of prisoners (law 9 of 409) to civic finance (law 22 of 529). See Claude, *Byzantinische Stadt*, 122–3. On consequences of Chalcedon see A. Grillmeier, H. Bacht (eds.), *Das Konzil von Chalkedon* (3 vols., Würzburg, 1951–4).

fact from our point of view is that the petition was accepted by the governor as an expression of the will of the whole city, even though it was signed only by individuals and not supported by corporative decisions of any of the classes concerned.[1] This was convenient for the petitioners. It enabled them to ignore the considerable support for Ibas which was later shown to exist. But the situation reveals the decay of the political organization of the city.

The cities were too important for the empire for their institutions to be allowed to collapse. The Emperors Anastasius and Justinian made a real attempt to involve powerful individuals outside the council in the administration of their city. Anastasius formed bishop, clergy, and all the principal landowners of the city into an assembly which was to elect the corn-buyer, and probably the *curator* (*pater*) and the *defensor*. Justinian made this body responsible for public works and civic finance. He also built up the powers of the *defensor* to make the office one of real importance, which would be held by the principal landowners in turn on nomination by the notables of the city. Councillors continued to exist and to figure in legislation, but they were now little more than hereditary tax collectors.[2]

It is not clear how far these reforms succeeded in restoring initiative and independence to local government. The fact that Justinian published some laws forbidding governors to appoint deputies to govern cities,[3] and others to prevent intervention by officials of the praetorian prefecture, suggests that the reforms met with only limited success. This is confirmed by the anonymity of the notables, other than bishops, in the narrative histories of the sixth century. When the patriarch of Antioch had been killed in the earthquake of 526 the city was left with no one to provide for its exigencies.[4] When the Persians invaded Syria in 540 the civil and military organization of the empire largely collapsed, and the notables of the cities were left with the decision whether

[1] See above, pp. 217–18.

[2] Jones, *L.R.E.* 758–9, nn. 104–5; Claude, *Byzantinische Stadt*, 106–23; H. Jaeger, 'Justinien et l'*episcopalis audientia*', *Nouv. rev. hist. de droit franc. et étr.*, 4ᵉ sér. xxxviii (1960), 214–62.

[3] Jones, *L.R.E.* 759 n. 105; C. Kunderewicz, 'Les Topotérètes', *J. Jur. Pap.* xiv (1962), 33–50.

[4] Intervention by the prefecture: Jones, *L.R.E.* 759, n. 106. Death of Euphrasius: Evagr. iv. 5.

to face a siege or buy the enemy off. Many cities offered ransom. The man who negotiated with the Persians was almost invariably the bishop.[1] Bishops were to play the same part at the time of the Arab conquest.[2] At Antioch the man appointed to negotiate with the king of Persia was Megas, bishop of Beroea.[3] But the bishop of Antioch too appears to have been in favour of the decision to buy the Persians off. At any rate, when representatives of the Emperor Justinian forbade the payment of money to the enemy the bishop of Antioch was charged with treason and left the city.[4]

There is little evidence that the notables of Eastern cities provided active leadership in other fields than that of negotiations with the invaders. When the Persians broke into Antioch they were resisted by the young men of the circus faction. These were not a civic militia. The majority were unarmed and fought with stones.[5] The cohesion of the supporters' clubs provided a substitute for communal organization.

Government by notables and the bishop did not in the long run bring about a revival of civic self-determination. When the Arabs conquered the Near East they seem to have allowed a certain amount of self-government by the notables at first, but before long the Arab Empire,[6] just like the revived Byzantine Empire, concentrated all power in the central authority.[7]

The fully developed Muslim city was, and is, superficially very different from the Graeco-Roman city. The Muslim city as a unit had no institution of local self-government at all. The prince appointed a governor, who in turn appointed his principal assistants. There was no civic cohesion. Different racial or religious groups lived in separate quarters, often divided by walls and

[1] Procop. *B.P.* ii. 5. 13 (Sura), 29 (Sergiopolis); ibid. 13. 13 (Constantina).

[2] Claude, *Byzantinische Stadt*, 135, on role of bishops of Jerusalem and Alexandria.

[3] Procop. *B.P.* ii. 6. 17.

[4] Ibid. 14 ff.; cf. Downey, *Antioch*, 533–44. I assume that the Antiochenes who took counsel concerning this matter (Procop. *B.P.* ii. 6. 16) were the notables.

[5] Procop. *B.P.* ii. 8. 7, 25; also 9. 8–9. That factions were not a militia is shown by H.-G. Beck, *B.Z.* lviii (1965), 37–8. S. P. Vryonis, 'Byzantine circus factions and the Islamic *futuwwa* organisations', ibid. 46–59, suggests, but does not prove, continuity between the 'young men' of the factions and the Islamic organization.

[6] C. Cahen, 'Zur Geschichte der städtischen Gesellschaft im islamischen Orient des Mittelalters', *Saeculum* ix (1953), 59–76, esp. 64–5.

[7] G. Ostrogorsky, *History of the Byzantine State*, trans. J. Hussey (Oxford, 1956), 217, on Novels xlvi, xlvii, lxxviii of Leo VI (886–912).

gates, possessing their own mosques, baths, and market. Self-government existed only at this ward level and in the organization of the numerous guilds of traders and craftsmen. Guilds too were organized on a religious or racial rather than a civic basis. Trades were systematically organized, and each trade was likely to have one of the markets completely to itself.[1]

Many of these features can be seen developing in fourth-century Antioch. Enough has been said about the weakening civic institutions and the ever-growing control of the governor. We have also noted the complete organization of trades into guilds. At Beroea this period saw irregularly laid-out quarters rising around the regularly planned Hellenistic city.[2] The shops built between the pillars of street colonnades at Antioch and elsewhere mark the beginning of the development of the colonnaded street into an Arab 'soukh'. Nevertheless it appears that the regular geometrical street plan of Antioch was maintained to the end of the Byzantine period.[3] The legislation of Justinian shows that attempts were made to maintain control over the siting of private buildings but the laws also reveal the conflicting interventions of civic officials, governors, and agents of the praetorian prefecture, which made the law difficult to enforce.[4]

In the fourth century the religious and racial segregation of the citizen body had scarcely begun. Antioch was of course the scene of religious conflicts, both between Christians and pagans and

---

[1] G. E. von Grünebaum, *Islam*, 141–58; cf. structure of modern Antioch: J. Weulersse, 'Antioche', *Bulletin d'études orientales* iv (1934), 27–79, esp. 37 ff., 74 ff. E. Ashtor Strauss, 'L'Administration urbaine en Syrie médiévale', *Rivista degli studi orientali* xxxi (1956); B. Lewis, 'The Islamic Guilds', *Ec. H. Rev.* viii (1937), 20–37; E. Wirth, 'Die soziale Stellung und Gliederung der Stadt im osmanischen Reiche des 19. Jahrhunderts', in Th. Mayer (ed.), *Untersuchungen zur Gesellschaftlichen Struktur der Mittelalterlichen Städte in Europa* (Stuttgart, 1966), 403–26.

[2] Sauvaget, *Alep* (Paris, 1941), 66–7, and 'Esquisse d'une histoire de la ville de Damas', *Rev. Ét. Islam.* viii (1934).

[3] See above, p. 56 n. 1. Evidence cited by Claude, *Byzantinische Stadt*, 58–9, suggests that the blocking of main thoroughfares by private building only made real progress in the post-Byzantine period. The conclusion that the Hellenistic chessboard pattern was maintained at Antioch during the whole history of the ancient city was reached by J. Lassus on the evidence of his excavations. See Lassus's forthcoming book on the main street of Antioch (Princeton U.P.).

[4] *C.J.* viii. 10. 12 (Zeno) addressed to *praefectus urbi* of Constantinople; 13 (531) extends Zeno's law to all cities, *governors* are made responsible for enforcement. But x. 30. 4 (530) had forbidden intervention by the provincial administration—the *pater* and notables were solely responsible. *Nov.* xxv. 4. 2 (535) forbids intervention by agents of the praetorian prefect.

among sects within the Church; but certainly at the social level represented by Libanius and his friends division between Christians and pagans was bridged by a common concern for the city and its traditional and largely secular civilization. But for the future the position of the Jewish community was more significant. This had existed in the city almost since its foundation but had retained its own communal institution and never became fully integrated into the citizen body. In the fourth century sermons like those of John Chrysostomus must have widened the gulf between the Jews and the Christian majority.[1] His anti-Jewish sermons bear witness to an intensification of division caused by the rivalry of monotheistic religions. It was presumably this phenomenon, exacerbated by the arrival of privileged Muslims, that produced the ultimate fragmentation of the citizen body. All inhabitants accepted the principle that community life should be shaped by religion, and their adherence to different religious groups made it impossible that they should hold any common concept of citizenship.[2]

[1] On the Jewish community of Antioch see above, p. 223. On Jewish quarters elsewhere see Claude, *Byzantinische Stadt*, 178–9; on the Alexandrian community, the most important of all: H. I. Bell, *Jews and Christians in Egypt* (London, 1924).

[2] Von Grünebaum, op. cit. 142–4; N. Baynes, 'The Thought-World of East Rome', in his *Byzantine Studies and Other Essays* (London, 1955), 24–46.

APPENDIX I

EMBASSIES[1]

No. 1. A.D. 345–50.
The ambassador Obodianus passes through Nicomedia during Libanius' stay there, *Ep.* 381.

No. 2. 351.
Occasion: the accession of the Caesar Gallus? Letoius I was ambassador, *Ep.* 551 (356–7). Date of embassy follows from *Ep.* 552 (357), (517. 17) and *Ep.* 551 (514. 14–15). Themistius was at Constantinople, Libanius was at Constantinople, the emperor was west of Constantinople. Letoius was about to give Olympic Games. All this taken together points to 351 or early 352. Otherwise, Petit, *Libanius*, 416.

No. 3. 355.
Ambassadors: Antiochus II, Pompeianus II to Milan. Occasion: the proclamation of Julian as Caesar? Other business:
(*a*) Request for Imperial help for Olympic Games in 356, *Ep.* 440, 439, and 449.
(*b*) Permission for Libanius to stay at Antioch, *Ep.* 440.
(*c*) Some private business of Pompeianus, *Ep.* 441 and *Ep.* 35.

No. 4. 357.
Ambassador Letoius I, who volunteered in place of Phasganius, when the governor insisted that Phasganius should be replaced by a man of the same standing. Occasion: the *vicennalia* of the Emperor Constantius. *Ep.* 550, 552, 555–9, and 567. Certain unstated requests were made, to which opposition was expected, *Ep.* 554. The assembly of Syria τὸ κοινόν was concerned, *Ep.* 556. Later in same year, probably for the same occasion, Pelagius travelled as ambassador to Italy for his city Cyrrhus of Euphratensis, *Ep.* 562–3.

When the embassies came to Rome there was much speech-making, *Ep.* 566. At Antioch the *vicennalia* were a holiday, *Ep.* 559.

No. 5. 359–60.
Obodianus ambassador. Occasion: to ask Constantius to return to Antioch, *Ep.* 114. Some other business required that the *magister officiorum* should be well disposed towards Antioch. Presumably Obodianus was also asking for the subsidy for the beast-chases his son was about to produce.

[1] Cf. Petit, *Libanius*, 415–19.

No. 6. 362.
Obodianus and others ambassadors, *Ep*. 697, 702. Occasion: Julian's arrival at Constantinople, and no doubt his succession to throne of Constantius. Julian, *Misop*. 367D records that the embassy arrived latest of all the embassies, but was nevertheless granted the remission of much taxation.

No. 7. 363.
Embassy to congratulate the new emperor, Jovian, *Ep*. 1432. Ambassador Olympius V, a pagan, but favourable to Christians, and brother of a very strong Christian, Seeck, *Briefe*, 224–5. He was therefore a 'safe' ambassador. At same time an embassy was sent by Ancyra. Strategius (*Ep*. 1436) and Bosporius (*Ep*. 1444) were ambassadors. They carry gold crowns, *Ep*. 1436. They also hope to counter sermons of a Christian influential at court, perhaps Athanasius, cf. Amm. xv. 7. 7 and *P.W.* s.v. Jovian (ix. 2, cols. 2006–11). They also defend governor of Galatia from charges, *Ep*. 1439.

No. 8. 364.
Ep. 1184–6: embassy takes crowns to the new emperor, Valentinian I.

No. 9. 365 (Spring).
Occasion: the accession of Valens? Business: to invite emperor to Antioch, probably also to bring gold wreaths. There was more, for Libanius asks Jovinus to make the way smooth for ambassadors, *Ep*. 1499, 1505. The embassy arrived late. Perhaps the gold could not be collected in time.

No. 10. 387.
Or. xxxii. 2–7. Ambassadors: Thrasydaeus, ibid. 6; Eusebius XXII (the sophist) ibid. 3, *Or*. i. 258, Norman, *Libanius' Autobiography*, 223–4; Hilarius VII, Zos. iv. 41. 2. A fourth ambassador, *Or*. xxxii. 3.

This is not one of the embassies mentioned in the letters, as proposed by Pack, *Studies*, 123. The letters begin in 388 while this embassy must belong to the previous year. Reasons:

1. A general in charge at Antioch. This must be Ellebichus, but he did not remain very long. When Libanius wrote *Or*. xxii in his praise he had already gone, ibid. 41. In summer 388 he was certainly no longer there, *Ep*. 868 (date: Seeck, *Briefe*, 450).
2. The embassy apologizes for the riot, the city being not yet quite out of danger. It replaces an embassy omitted through the riot, therefore it will not have been very much later than the riot, *Or*. xxxii. 2.

The embassy which it replaced, and which was not sent on account of the riot, was no doubt occasioned by the celebration of the *decennalia* of Theodosius and the *quinquennalia* of Arcadius, cf. R. Browning, *J.R.S.* xlii (1952), 14.

No. 11. 388.
Purpose: to carry the council's complaints against the consular Lucianus.

According to *Or.* lvi. 14, Tatian was *P.P.O.* The date must therefore be after March 388. I would suggest fairly soon after, and earlier than the first of the surviving late letters. For when the letters resume, Libanius has just been cleared of a charge of treason, *Ep.* 840. *Or.* i. 273 relates the circumstances of this charge as brought about, not in the governorship of Lucianus, but in that of his successor Eustathius, cf. *Or.* liv. 39–41.

No. 12. 388.
Embassy sent to congratulate the Emperor Theodosius on victories, perhaps not yet the final victory, over the usurper Maximus, Seeck, *Briefe*, 449–50.

The embassy consisted of three men (*Ep.* 867 and 852), for whom *Ep.* 864–8 and 850–2 were written. It is probable that, like the embassy of Emesa, at about the same time, *Ep.* 846, the embassy of Antioch carried gold wreaths for the emperor.

Further, the embassy had the purpose of asking help from the emperor, to save the council from attrition, *Ep.* 851. It appears that the suggestion that an embassy be sent for this purpose had come from the praetorian prefect Tatian himself, *Ep.* 851. The embassy of Emesa also requested help to restore the desperate condition of their city. Evidently, Tatian was at this time inaugurating his policy of restoring the councils, cf. *Or.* xlix. 31.

No. 13. Autumn 388.
A two-man embassy. Cynegius and Eusebius were the ambassadors, *Ep.* 878–9, 880, 883. I follow Seeck, *Briefe*, 451 against Petit, *Libanius*, 419 in assuming that the Eusebius who is the bearer of *Ep.* 878 must be a member of the embassy described in the first sentence of the letter as crowning Theodosius after his victory over Maximus. Who of the many known holders of the name was this Eusebius? Seeck, *Briefe*, 143–4 and 451, and Petit, *Libanius*, 419 identify him as Eusebius XXII, the sophist, Libanius' assistant. I disagree for the following reasons:

(a) Libanius does not identify Eusebius of this embassy as 'the sophist', which is his normal practice.

(b) Libanius does not praise this Eusebius' great rhetorical skill, praise he would scarcely omit if he were commending his assistant.

(c) Libanius does not commend this Eusebius to his most powerful acquaintances. Indeed, he writes remarkably few letters for him.

Normally the number of letters of recommendation is proportional to the closeness of his friendship for the bearer.

(*d*) Eusebius was a very common name. Seeck lists at least 36 distinct and identifiable men of that name (*Briefe*, 137–46).

(*e*) Seeck, *Briefe*, 144, makes the point that, according to *Ep*. 880, Eusebius the ambassador was engaged on his second embassy. This would be true of Eusebius the sophist (cf. No. 10). Yet, if Libanius was writing for Eusebius the sophist, he might praise him not only for being an ambassador twice, but for agreeing to be an ambassador twice, when he was legally exempt from all such duties. Libanius does not make this point. I would conclude that Eusebius the ambassador was not Eusebius the sophist.

Seeck, *Briefe*, 144, Pack, *Studies*, 123, and Petit, *Libanius*, 419, concluded that it was the three-man embassy of 388 (our No. 12) which attacked the curial immunity of Eusebius XXII, the sophist, when it passed through Constantinople a second time on its return journey from Italy. I would suggest that the immunity of Eusebius XXII was attacked by the two-man embassy of Eusebius and Cynegius.

My reasons are as follows:

(*a*) Proceedings to force the sophist into the council seem to have started while the second embassy of 388 was already on its way. At any rate, Libanius in *Ep*. 870, i.e. a letter written a little later than those for the second embassy, wrote that it seemed to him that the action against the sophist would be made a duty of the embassy. But surely the embassy that had already started had received its instruction? In this letter Libanius must mean an embassy which was still being prepared at Antioch, i.e. the third embassy of 388.

(*b*) Libanius used all possible influence on behalf of the earlier embassy, the second of 388. This suggests that he was sincerely in accord with its purpose. He wrote fewer letters to less influential men for the later embassy. This suggests that he was less well disposed towards it, which would be natural if they intended to claim Libanius' assistant for the council.

(*c*) I have argued earlier that Eusebius the sophist did not travel to Constantinople as an ambassador in 388. When he travelled in winter 388–9, he did so as a private individual to obtain the reversal of the decision won by the third embassy of 388. *Epp*. 904–9 were written for this journey. These letters were written to Libanius' most influential friends, and identify their bearer, Eusebius, as 'the sophist'. Eusebius was successful, but not totally, for in 390, he travelled to Constantinople again to obtain formal confirmation of his immunity, *Ep*. 918–21.

APPENDIX II

THE DATES AND CIRCUMSTANCES OF
ORATIONS XLVIII AND XLIX

PACK concluded that the two speeches belong together, and were
both written by Libanius to defend the immunity from curial duties
of himself, his son, and his assistant, in 388. According to Pack, the
argument of each speech is the same: the council was dwindling, but
there were a number of ways in which its leaders could halt and reverse
the drift, without calling on sophists or their sons. One of the speeches
was intended to combat Libanius' opponents at Antioch, the other
those at Constantinople.[1]

But the general tone of the two speeches does not favour this view
of their purpose. If it was Libanius' aim to protect men associated with
education from enrolment into the council,[2] it was not sufficient for
him to show that councillors were still escaping, and that it was the
council's duty to bring back the fugitives. He would also have to show
that the attempts of the council to enrol sophists and their assistants
were unnecessary and misguided. In fact, he not only omits any
reference to attempts to enrol the wrong people, but very strongly
implies that the council was not enrolling anybody, and that no action
of any kind to remedy the situation had originated from it. Such
passages as *Or.* xlviii. 4, 6, 15, 17, do not carry the implication that
the council was enrolling sophists, but that it did nothing while its
numbers declined.

All passages so far cited are in *Oration* xlviii, but the same argument
can be applied to *Oration* xlix as well. For instance, in that speech,
Libanius advises the emperor to whip the councillors, if they will not
enforce the laws regulating membership of the council more zealously.[3]
This would be extremely dangerous advice to give for a man who was,
at that moment, and by means of this very speech, defending men of
undeniably curial descent from the claims of their council. Thus,
Pack's explanation of the origins of *Orations* xlviii and xlix is inadequate, and further examination of the evidence is desirable.

Any attempt to date these two speeches must start from the one
certain datable fact contained in either of them. *Oration* xlix was

---

[1] Pack, *Studies*, 121–4.
[2] See below, p. 272, for Libanius' efforts on behalf of Cimon, Thalassius IV, and
Eusebius XXII, the sophist.
[3] *Or.* xlix. 27.

written after the death of the praetorian prefect Cynegius, which is implied in its contents.[1] It is likely that the man mentioned as the present praetorian prefect was Cynegius' successor, Tatian. Since Cynegius was buried on 19 March 388, it is evident that *Oration* xlix was written after this date. The other limit can be put, less certainly, as the summer of 392, when Tatian was deposed from the prefecture.[2] It is almost certain that *Oration* xlix was written between those dates.

It is possible to make conjectures about a more precise date. The speech was written at a time when Tatian's attempts to enlarge the council lay in the past and could be seen to have succeeded to only a very limited extent.[3] There is some independent evidence about Tatian's reforms. The governor Eustathius, we are told, set about enlarging the council in accordance with a recent law.[4] This must have been within the ten months Eustathius ruled Syria, i.e. between summer 388 and spring 389.[5]

Some time during this interval a law on the subject of the enlargement of the council must have come to Antioch. There is reason to suppose that it came rather late in this period. An embassy carrying a request for such a law[6] travelled in summer 388.[7] Since the law would only have been issued after lengthy negotiations, it would only have been issued in autumn or winter. No law on the subject of the councils appears between June 388 (*C.T.* xii. 1. 119) and December 389 (*C.T.* xii. 1. 120). There is, however, evidence that Tatian made legislation specifically for Antioch. This included a clause requiring senators to contribute to the heating of the baths and possibly the games of the Syriarch.[8] I would suggest that these regulations were part of the now lost enactment, prepared by Tatian in response to the requests of the embassy of summer 388.

Of the effect this legislation had at Antioch Libanius tells us little. The attempt to claim Eusebius the sophist for the council had been begun, probably at the instigation of the councillors, before the new legislation came to Antioch. The extremely long time taken to reach a decision in this case, possibly considerably more than a year, may have been the result of the atmosphere created by this

---

[1] Ibid. 4 brings us to events very close to Cynegius' death. 31 refers to the *present* praetorian prefect, evidently not the same as the man mentioned in 4. The present prefect has held his office for some time. Since Libanius died not very long after the accession of Rufinus, the second prefect after Cynegius, it is likely that the prefect at the time of *Or.* xlix was Cynegius' successor, Tatian.

[2] Seeck, *Briefe*, 287.   [3] *Or.* xlix. 1, 13–14, 31.

[4] *Or.* liv. 74.   [5] Seeck, *Briefe*, 147–8.

[6] *Ep.* 851–2.

[7] Before the defeat of the usurper Maximus was known at Antioch. Maximus was executed on 28 August 388, Seeck, *Briefe*, 449–50.

[8] *C.T.* xii. 1. 131, vi. 3. 1 from the law of 397 annulling Tatian's regulations.

legislation.¹ The attempt to force Thalassius IV to undertake a corn transport liturgy² may have been part of the enforcement of Tatian's laws. Certainly, he travelled to Constantinople in the course of 390 in an unsuccessful attempt to win immunity in the senate,³ and his case may have dragged on into 391.⁴ This might be a reason for proposing a very late date for the speech. But since Libanius had been half-hearted in his original support of Cimon, and does not appear to have given him sustained help in the later stages,⁵ and since the opposition to Cimon's efforts appears to have come from men at Constantinople, who objected to his illegitimacy, and not from the councillors at Antioch, we may suppose that Libanius felt safe to send his speech to Constantinople before Cimon's return and death in 391. Perhaps the receipt of the presents Tatian sent him, in celebration of the consul-ship which he entered on the first day of 391, encouraged Libanius to send *Oration* xlix to the prefect.⁶

Let us now turn to the sister speech, *Oration* xlviii. The similarity of the two speeches might suggest that they were written about the same time.⁷ But this conclusion is not inevitable. Libanius' speeches are written according to certain school-learned principles, which govern both the composition of the speech and the arguments used in it. Consequently, speeches on similar topics are very much alike.⁸

Foerster thought that *Oration* xlviii was later than *Oration* xlix. It contains the statement that Libanius has already addressed the em-peror on behalf of the councillors. Foerster took this to be a reference to *Oration* xlviii.⁹ But this is not necessarily so. Already in 386 Libanius claimed in very similar terms that he had helped the council with consulars, counts of the East, praetorian prefects, and even the em-peror.¹⁰ Indeed, we have a number of speeches written on topics of public concern, certainly before 388, and addressed to the emperor.¹¹

Arguments for making *Oration* xlviii the earlier of the two speeches and for dating it well before 388 have been put forward by Sievers¹² and are, to my mind, decisive. The speech contains no reference to

---

¹ *Ep.* 870 (388), cf. Seeck, *Briefe*, 451; *Ep.* 904–9 (388), Seeck, op. cit. 453; Ep. 918–21 (390), Seeck, op. cit. 454.
² *Or.* liv. 47.
³ *Or.* xlii, *Ep.* 922–30 (390), Seeck, *Briefe*, 455.
⁴ *Ep.* 959–60 (390), 1000–3 (391), on date Seeck, *Briefe*, 459–60; *Or.* i. 279.
⁵ We have only two letters (*Ep.* 959–60) written in his support. In *Ep.* 1000–3 Libanius claims that Cimon travelled against his advice.
⁶ *Ep.* 1021.
⁷ So R. Foerster (ed.), vol. 3. 450 n. 2.   ⁸ See above, pp. 37–8.
⁹ Foerster (ed.), vol. 3. 425 on *Or.* xlviii. 1.   ¹⁰ *Or.* xxxvi. 5.
¹¹ *Or.* l, xlv, xxxiii, perhaps xxx. In any case xlviii. 1 πρὸς αὐτῶν ἐκείνων τὸν ἄριστον could refer to Julian.
¹² Sievers, *Leben*, 194 n. 33.

the curial legislation which the Emperor Theodosius made on the advice of the praetorian prefect Cynegius between 384 and 387.[1] We know that the legislation in favour of the councils, published on the advice of the praetorian prefect Cynegius, was enforced at Antioch. We know that the prefect himself came to Antioch to enforce it, and we know of at least two men who were placed in the council by him,[2] and of another whose exemption he confirmed.[3] Moreover, Cynegius' successor, Tatian, also made legislation which was intended to fill the council,[4] and this, too, was applied with limited and temporary success at Antioch.[5]

In *Oration* xlviii Libanius not only fails to mention this legislation and its consequences, but he very strongly suggests that there had been no legislation and no active intervention on behalf of the council by the imperial government for some time. Throughout the speech Libanius is concerned to show that the councillors have been very slack indeed in their efforts to prevent colleagues escaping. If there had been recent legislation, and a visit of the praetorian prefect, without any permanent improvement being achieved, the failure would have provided the strongest possible support for Libanius' argument. He would surely have used it.

In fact, Libanius mentions only one law which the councillors might have enforced had they wanted to. Of this law, he says that so far from being enforced, it was not even promulgated at Antioch.[6] This law was certainly not part of Cynegius' legislation, for, as we have seen, he came to enforce his laws in person. Since Libanius accused the council of gross negligence in the enforcement of only this one law, the implication is very strong that there were no others; in fact, that the speech was written before Cynegius had come to Antioch to enforce his own legislation.

In favour of this view are the defensive arguments which Libanius puts into the mouths of councillors. They argue, for instance, that Antioch has only had bad governors, who have not supported efforts on behalf of the council.[7] Surely this could not have been said after Cynegius' visit, or after a real, if not prolonged, attempt had been made to enforce Tatian's legislation? Then, the councillors are made

---

[1] But *Or.* xlix. 5–6 mentions this legislation, referring to a change in policy whereby *curiales* were admitted into the senate without being freed from membership in their council; *C.T.* xii. 1. 111 (386), 118 (387), 122 (390).

[2] *Or.* xxxviii. 20 (Silvanus), iv. 20 (Eutropius).

[3] Eusebius XXII, the sophist. I conclude that the prefect of *Or.* liv. 52, was Cynegius, because he was the prefect who had regulated the membership of the Council most recently.

[4] *C.T.* xii. 1, laws: 119–23, 127, also 131 and *C.T.* vi. 3. 1.   [5] *Or.* xlix. 31.

[6] *Or.* xlviii. 15. The law is *C.T.* xii. 1. 51 = *C.J.* x. 32. 22 of Julian, or a restatement of the same rule by a later emperor.   [7] *Or.* xlviii. 10.

to say that a time is coming which will restore the councils.[1] After the efforts of Cynegius and Tatian, this time would no longer have been in the future. They continue that they did their best under Julian. Surely if the time of writing is after Cynegius, they would have mentioned his favourable attitude towards them, rather than Julian's, since it was more recent? All this suggests that the speech was written before Cynegius had come to Antioch.

In spite of the general similarity in the arguments of *Orations* xlviii and xlix, there is one notable difference which makes it likely that there was a gap of years between the writing of the two speeches. *Oration* xlix is very much more severe than xlviii in its condemnation of the councillors. The accusation of deliberate sabotage, which is mentioned but at once dropped in xlviii,[2] is sustained throughout *Oration* xlix. One explanation of this springs to mind. When Libanius wrote *Oration* xlviii, the councillors had allowed the council to decline without doing much about it, but also without the imperial government having encouraged a more energetic policy. When he wrote *Oration* xlix, the government had just made a strong effort to restore the council, and this had failed—failed, as Libanius thought, because the councillors did not want it to succeed.

We can now proceed to a closer dating of *Oration* xlviii. The speech was certainly written after the death of the Emperor Valens,[3] that is later than 10 August 378 when Valens was killed in the battle of Adrianople.

The speech was also written at a time when some persons were thinking of benefiting the council of Antioch. No active steps had yet been taken, but it was the known intention of these unnamed men that had given Libanius the occasion for his speech.[4]

Some light is thrown on the identity of these men by an imaginary objection which Libanius raises on behalf of the councillors of Antioch. This begins with the enigmatic sentence ὁ δ' ἀνὴρ αἴρεται ἡμῶν and feels that his inability to come to Antioch has been his loss.[5] He will wish to honour the city by issuing a law on behalf of the councils which owes its origin to his stay among the citizens of Antioch. Foerster has taken this to be a reference to the Emperor Theodosius, since his wish, confirmed by oath, to see Antioch is also mentioned in one of the sermons of John Chrysostomus on the Riot of the Statues.[6]

---

[1] *Or.* xlviii. 17.
[2] Ibid. 4–5.
[3] Ibid. 36.
[4] Ibid. 1, cf. 17.
[5] Ibid. 27 and Foerster's critical note. Sievers, *Leben*, 194 amended this to ὁ δ' ἀνὴρ ἱμείρεται. Foerster prefers ὁ δ' ἀνὴρ (i.e. βασιλεὺς) ἐρᾷ τε ἡμῶν.
[6] 'Foerster cites Joh. Chrys. *Hom. ad pop. Ant.* 21. 2, 217B (*P.G.* xlix. 214) and *Or.* xx. 45, i. 220 for Theodosius' expressed desire to come to Antioch. Strictly only the emperor could 'issue' laws, cf. *or.* lii. 46.

This is a reasonable hypothesis only if we suppose, as Foerster did, that a phrase referring to the emperor has dropped out of the evidently corrupt text. If we do not make this assumption, it seems remarkable that an emperor should be described merely as ὁ δ' ἀνήρ. It is surely more likely that these words do not refer to the emperor at all. If not he, who else could be described as making a law but the praetorian prefect? Sievers took the view that 'the man was the praetorian prefect, Cynegius. This is reasonable, for we know that while he held the office of *quaestor sacri palatii* Cynegius had been given the special mission of restoring the councils of the cities, and that when he travelled to Egypt as prefect the restoration of city councils was one of his main concerns.[1]

If this identification is correct, it follows that the speech was written at a time when Cynegius was planning his journey but had not yet set out. Petit[2] and Seeck[3] consider that Cynegius only started on his journey after the publication of the law against pagan sacrifices which he was to enforce so fanatically. If so, the speech was written before, but not very long before, summer 385.

To sum up, the most likely date of the speech is between the summer of 384 and of 385. Reform of the councils was then in the air. Much legislation had been published, though evidently so far with little practical effect at Antioch.[4] Perhaps none of the earlier laws went to the root of the matter.[5] Perhaps governors were waiting for the praetorian prefect to enforce the laws in person. It would be perfectly in character that at this moment Libanius should endeavour to further the cause of curial reform. His standing, moreover, was such that he might expect to be able to speak with greater effect. He had been invited by the consul Richomer to attend his inauguration on 1 January 384.[6] The invitation was accompanied by a letter from the emperor himself. About the same time, Proculus placed a picture of Libanius in the town hall of Antioch.[7] Petit has argued plausibly that these honours were accompanied by the grant of the honorary rank of praetorian prefect.[8] In addition, Libanius was on good terms with all three of the great officials at Antioch. Eumolpius, consular of Syria, was a relative and old friend.[9] Ellebichus, the *magister militum per orientem* after 31 December 383, was on good terms with Libanius,

---

[1] *Or.* xlix. 3.

[2] *Byzantion* xxi (1951), 299 ff. Another view: *Prosopography of the Later Roman Empire*, s.v. Cynegius (3).

[3] Seeck, *Untergang*, vol. v. 218–19; Anhang to vol. v, 526–8.

[4] *C.T.* xii. 1. 105 (May 384)–110 (May 385).

[5] The radical change in policy is *C.T.* xii. 1. 111 (April 386); cf. Jones, *L.R.E.* 742.

[6] *Or.* i. 219–20.   [7] *Or.* xlii. 43.

[8] 'Sur la date du *Pro Templis* de Libanius', *Byzantion* xxi (1951), 285–310.

[9] Seeck, *Briefe*, 135.

and received a panegyric from him.[1] During the early part of his governorship, which began in summer 384, the *comes orientis* Icarius, was on excellent terms with Libanius, who could advise him 'as a father a son'.[2] It is reasonable to conclude that Libanius, being in this very strong position in the city, took the opportunity to speak on a topic which had always been close to his heart.

---

[1] Seeck, *Briefe*, 167.   [2] *Or.* i. 225 ff.

APPENDIX III

SOME FUGITIVE COUNCILLORS

PACK's presentation of the evidence is inevitably incomplete. There are a number of cases of men seeking or obtaining immune jobs without our being told whether they belonged to curial families. Thus Honoratus, son of ex-governor and sophist Quirinus, *Ep.* 358–9, 365, 366; the two sons of the doctor Marcellus, *Ep.* 362 (358); the son of Marianus, *Ep.* 875–6 (388); Eusebius XXVIII, *Ep.* 884–7 (388); Olympius VI, Seeck, *Briefe*, 225; Saturninus II, *Ep.* 1489–90 (365); some are likely to have been *curiales*.

I interpret the following cases differently from Pack:

Pack's No. 11. (Gerontius III.) Probably successful, since Gerontius did settle as a teacher at Apamea.

13. (Hyperechius.) Successful, since Hyperechius was in the *officium* of *castrensis sacri palatii* at time of Procopius' rebellion: Amm. xxvi. 8. 5.

18. (Thalassius IV.) Failure. *Or.* xlii expresses disgust with persons responsible for it.

17. (Severus V.) Failure. Severus claimed immunity as a philosopher. This was not granted in the fourth century. We last hear of him travelling to Palestine. This does not look as if he could settle in peace at home.

I would add the following cases to Pack's list:

I. *Ep.* 1385–1401. Theotecnus claims immunity on account of old age—granted.

II. *Ep.* 1318 (364). Gemellus, a relative of Libanius, has obtained a post under the *comes orientis*, where he avoids the tears and chains of the council. He obtained this on Libanius' advice, therefore probably with his support. Escape successful.

III. Libanius asks Salutius, the praetorian prefect, for governorship for old councillor, Antiochus II—granted? (*Ep.* 1387.)

IV. Carterius of Arke in Armenia (*Ep.* 245 and 656) eventually escaped into the army without Libanius' help.

The following 'immune' men had either performed duties already or were still performing them or left a son in the council: Antiochus II, Panolbius, Theotecnus, Alexander X, Callimachus, Celsus I, Libanius, Firminus II, Pelagius I, Sidonius, Fraternus.

APPENDIX IV

THE CLAQUE

It may be argued that I have given to the claque as a body, distinct from the general mob of Antioch, more influence than the evidence of Libanius allows. My answer to this is that, even when Libanius does not expressly mention the 400 men employed to act as the claque in connection with a demonstration, he implies that they were, in fact, responsible.

The following passages are relevant to this problem:

1. *Or.* xxvi. 5, 8 ff., 17 (384–5).
2. *Or.* xli (382–6?).
3. *Or.* xxxiii. 8, 11–12, xlv. 4, 22. Both speeches concern Tissamenes, consular of Syria in 386.
4. *Or.* xix. 28 (387).
5. *Or.* lvi. 2, 15, 16–17, 22–5 (especially 23 ff.) (388).
6. *Or.* xlvi. 5, 17, 18, 31, 39 (392–3).

Of these series of passages, no. 2 certainly deals with the claque. The argument of *Or.* xli is that governors should not consider the acclamations in the theatre to be the opinion of the city. In fact, they only represent the actors and dancers and their claque, about 400 in all (*Or.* xli. 6–7, 9). In the case of no. 6 the reference to the claque is no less definite. Libanius is opposing a governor, who has followed the demands made in the theatre by dismissing a curial official and punishing certain shopkeepers. Libanius argues that the actors and their 400 parasites, not the people, have made these demands. The figure 400 is mentioned at 387, l. 20.

In the case of no. 5 the reference to the claque is scarcely less certain, cf. *Or.* lvi, vol. 4. 132, ll. 10–12, with *Or.* xlvi, vol. 3. 387, ll. 4–6. Also *Or.* lvi, vol. 4. 139, ll. 5–7, with *Or.* xlvi, vol. 3. 381, ll. 13–14 and ibid. 394, ll. 11–14; *Or.* lvi. 23 with *Or.* xli. 6. No. 4 describes men held responsible for the Riot of the Statues in terms strongly recalling Libanius' descriptions of the claque—cf. *Or.* xix, vol. 2. 398, ll. 5–7 with *Or.* lvi, vol. 4. 139, ll. 5–7 and ibid. 23. In both cases Libanius stresses the absolute and shameful dependence of the trouble-makers on the dancers, as well as the fact that they were strangers. Moreover, John Chrysostomus, *Hom. ad. pop. Ant.* 17 (*P.G.* xlix. 176) confirms that the guilty few were the claque: Ἐντεῦθεν αἱ ῥίζαι τῆς πονηρίας ἐβλάστησαν τῇ πόλει οἱ τὰς αὐτῶν φωνὰς τοῖς ὀρχουμένοις πωλοῦντες . . .

οἱ πάντα ἄνω καὶ κάτω κινοῦντες. Cf. also *Hom. ad pop. Ant.* 2 (*P.G.* xlix. 38).

The passages of group 3 belong together, since all refer to the governorship of Tissamenes. Of these, *Or.* xlv. 4, vol. 3. 361, ll. 4–7 surely refers to the claque, cf. *Or.* xlvi, vol. 3. 387, ll. 5–6 ff. The τινες ... ἐφ' ὅσοις ἄν τις ᾐσχύνθη of *Or.* xxxiii. 12, vol. 3. 171, ll. 15–16 might, of course, just be random members of the mob. On the other hand the situation described in *Or.* xxxiii. 11–12 is basically that described in *Or.* xli. 2–4, the claque attempts to extort concessions from a governor by withholding applause.

Then, *Or.* xxxiii. 8 and xlv. 22 describe the efforts made by Tissamenes to obtain εὐφημίας in the theatre. Again, when Libanius writes ἀφ' ὧν ἡγοῦνται τοὺς ἀργοὺς τουτουσὶ καὶ κηφῆνας ἐπισπᾶσθαι, ταῦτα χαρίζονται ... κἂν τύχωσι τῆς κλαγγῆς τῶν γεράνων εὐδαιμονίζουσι ἑαυτούς. He might just refer to applause of the rabble, but the situation is precisely that of *Or.* xli. 16 and of *Or.* xlvi. 39 and elsewhere. Like Florentius, Tissamenes considered τὰς παρὰ τῶν κακίστων εὐφημίας ἀπόδειξιν ἀρχῆς ἀρίστης, and if in *Or.* xli and xlvi Libanius squarely identified these worst of men with the claque, there is little doubt that he had the claque in mind also when he wrote about 'idle drones' and 'screaming of cranes' courted by Tissamenes.

No. 1 is the earliest of these groups of passages, and the one which identifies the claque least clearly. Yet, here too, there is good reason to believe that Libanius was of the opinion that at least part of the blame went to the claque. *Or.* xxvi, vol. 3. 6, ll. 10–13 shows that the demonstration in the baths grew out of εὐφημίαι which, as we have seen, it was the claque's task to lead. Ibid. 7, ll. 18–19 describes the part of the demonstrators as ὄχλος ἐν τῇ σκηνῇ τοῦ βίου τὰς ἐλπίδας ἔχων. The phrase suggests that the demonstrators were making a living out of selling their applause and other favours to the dancers and actors. But if we cannot be certain that the demonstration against Icarius in the baths was organized by the claque, there can be no doubt that the claque did organize a disturbance in the theatre about the same time, *Or.* xxvi. 17, vol. 3. 11, ll. 7–8; cf. also *Or.* xli, vol. 3. 296, ll. 1–2, where the claque is certainly meant.

The conclusion of this examination of groups of passages relevant to the problem of the claque at Antioch is that in four out of six cases, there is definite reference to the claque, as distinct from the mob, in influencing governors, and leading a variety of demonstrations. In the remaining two cases reference to the influence of the claque as a separate body is likely. Of course, that Libanius ascribed such importance to the claque is not proof that it was important. But if we provisionally accept his view of the role of the claque, we gain a stimulating hypothesis to guide our researches into early

Byzantine municipal government, and particularly into the origins of the circus factions.

The acclamations, as we have seen, dated from the time of Constantine at least, but their use for demands and criticism was newer. It probably had not yet begun when Julian was at Antioch, and in my opinion, the claque's political role was becoming steadily more important, even within the period covered by the late speeches, i.e. 382–93.

That, at the time of the Timocrates speech, the claque's bargaining with governors was fairly recent is stated in *Or.* xli. 15. That disturbances caused by the claque were getting steadily worse, is stated in *Or.* lvi. 25: καὶ τὰ πρότερα κρύπτεται τοῖς δευτέροις τῶν ὀρχηστῶν πλέον τι τῶν προτέρων δυνηθέντων ἐχόντων πολλοὺς ἑτοίμους ὑπὲρ αὐτῶν τελευτᾶν. Also Libanius became increasingly severe in his judgement of the claque. He counselled Icarius to mild punishment, *Or.* xxvi. 9–10. But four years later he advised expulsion of all foreign residents without house, family, or craft in the city, in his *Contra Lucianum*, *Or.* lvi. 22–3. We might also remark on the number of the speeches written in these years in which the acclamations play an important part, i.e. *Or.* xxvi, xli, xxxiii, xlv, xlvi. Strong evidence that in the first half of Libanius' life the claque was not yet a danger to peace is provided by *Or.* lxiv. 118–19, which, referring to the dancers, asserts παρ' ὧν ἡ τέρψις ταῖς πόλεσιν ἀμιγὴς κακῶν. This speech is mentioned in *Ep.* 615, and was therefore written in 361. Libanius could not have written this in the eighties.

SELECT BIBLIOGRAPHY

THE following lists contain titles which the author found most helpful or to which he wishes to draw the reader's attention. Fuller bibliographies are to be found in Foerster, R., and Münscher, K., s.v. Libanius, *P.W.* xii. 2, cols. 2485–551; Petit, P., *Libanius et la vie municipale à Antioche* (Paris, 1955); Downey, G., *A history of Antioch in Syria* (Princeton, 1961); Ganghoffer, R., *L'Évolution des institutions municipales en Occident et en Orient au Bas-Empire* (Paris, 1963).

SOURCES

Acts of Second Council of Ephesus, Syriac text by Flemming, J., German translation by Hoffmann, G., *Abhandlungen der K. Gesellschaft der Wissenschaften zu Göttingen*, Phil.-hist. Kl. xi, N.F. 15. 1 (1917).

Ammianus Marcellinus, *Histories*, with English translation, 3 vols., ed. Rolfe, J. C. (Loeb Classical Library, London, 1935–9).

Codex Theodosianus, 6 vols., with commentary by Gothofredus, J. (Lyons, 1665); 3 vols., ed. Mommsen, Th. (Berlin, 1905); translated by Pharr, C. (Princeton, 1952).

Euagrius, *Historia Ecclesiastica*, eds. Bidez, J., Parmentier, L. (London, 1898, repr. 1964).

Eunapius, *Lives of the philosophers and sophists*, with English translation, ed. Wright, W. C. (Loeb Classical Library, London, 1922).

John Chrysostomus, *Opera*, cited from Migne, *Patrologia Graeca*, vols. xlvii–lxiv.

Joshua Stylites, *The Chronicle*, Syriac text and translation, Wright, W. (Cambridge, 1882, repr. 1968).

Julian, *Œuvres complètes*, 4 vols., eds. Bidez, J., Rochefort, G., Lacombrade, C. (Paris, 1932–64).

—— *Epistulae et leges*, eds. Bidez, J., Cumont, F. (Paris, 1922).

—— *Works*, with English translation, 3 vols., by Wright, W. C. (Loeb Classical Library, London, 1949–53).

Libanius, *Opera*, ed. Foerster, R., 12 vols. (Leipzig, 1903–22).

—— *Orationes et Declamationes*, ed. Reiske, J. J. (Altenburg, 1791–7). The notes are still helpful.

—— *Libanius' Autobiography*, *Oration I*, with translation and commentary, Norman, A. F. (Oxford, 1965).

—— *Selected works*, 3 vols., text, translation, notes, Norman, A. F. (Loeb Classical Library, London 1969–).

Malalas, John, *Chronographia*, ed. Dindorf, L. (vol. xv of the *Corpus Scriptorum Historiae Byzantinae*, Bonn, 1831).

—— *Die römische Kaisergeschichte bei Malalas* (Stuttgart, 1931) contains text of books ix–xii and studies on it by A. Schenk von Stauffenberg.

Malalas, John, Fragments in Mommsen, Th., 'Johannes von Antiochia und Malalas', *Hermes* vi (1872), 523–83.
—— *Church Slavonic version*, books viii–xviii, translated by Spinka, M., and Downey, G. (Chicago, 1940).
Marc the Deacon, *Vie de Porphyre*, text, translation, and commentary by Grégoire, H. and Kugener, M.-A. (Paris, 1930).
Notitia Dignitatum, ed. Seeck, O. (Berlin, 1876, repr. 1966).
Palladius, *Dialogus de Vita S. Joannis Chrysostomi*, ed. Coleman-Norton, P. R. (Cambridge, 1928).
Socrates Scholasticus, *Historia Ecclesiastica*, *P.G.* lxvii (Paris, 1859).
Sozomen, *Historia Ecclesiastica*, *P.G.* lxvii (Paris, 1859).
Theodoret, *Historia Religiosa*, *P.G.* lxxxii, 1283–1496.
Zacharias of Mytilene, *Vita Severi*, ed. with French translation, Kugener, M.-A., *Patrologia Orientalis* ii. 1.

GENERAL AND CULTURAL HISTORY

Arnim, H. von, *Dio von Prusa* (Berlin, 1898).
Baynes, N. H., *Byzantine studies and other essays* (London, 1955).
Behr, C., *Aristides and the sacred tales* (Amsterdam, 1968).
Bidez, J., *La Vie de l'empereur Julien* (Paris, 1930), cited: Bidez, *Vie de Julien*.
Boulanger, A., *Aelius Aristide* (Paris, 1923, repr. 1968).
Brown, P. R. L., *Augustine of Hippo* (London, 1968).
Cameron, A., 'Wandering Poets', *Historia* xiv (1965), 470–509.
—— 'Agathias on the early Merovingians', *Annali della Scuola Normale di Pisa*, ser. ii, vol. xxxvii (1968), 95–140.
Chastagnol, A., *Le Sénat romain sous le règne d'Odoacre* (Bonn, 1966).
Dagron, G., 'L'Empire romain d'Orient au IVe siècle et les traditions politiques de l'hellénisme, le témoignage de Thémistios', *Travaux et Mémoires* iii (1948), 1–242.
Dawes, E., and Baynes, N. H., *Three Byzantine saints* (Oxford, 1948).
Dvornik, F., *Early Christian and Byzantine political philosophy* (Washington, 1966).
Hahn, I., 'Der ideologische Kampf um den Tod Julians des Abtrünnigen', *Klio* xxxviii (1960), 225–32.
Kaegi, W. E., *Byzantium and the decline of Rome* (Princeton, 1963).
Lacombrade, C., *Le Discours sur la royauté de Synésios de Cyrène*, text, translation, commentary (Paris, 1951).
—— *Synésios de Cyrène* (Paris, 1951).
Laistner, M. L. W., *Christianity and pagan culture in the Later Empire* (Cornell, 1951, paperback 1967); contains English translation of John Chrysostomus' *De educandis liberis*.
Marrou, H. I., *S. Augustin et la fin de la culture antique* (Paris, 1938).
—— *Histoire de l'éducation dans l'antiquité*, 2nd edn. (Paris, 1950); English translation by Lamb, G. (London, 1956).
Nilsson, M. P., *Die hellenistische Schule* (Munich, 1955).

Peeters, P., *Le Tréfonds oriental de l'hagiographie byzantine* (Subsidia Hagiographica xxvi, Brussels, 1950).

Piganiol, A., *L'Empire chrétien (325–395)* (Paris, 1947).

Ruether, R. R., *Gregory of Nazianzus* (Oxford, 1969).

Seeck, O., *Geschichte des Unterganges der antiken Welt*, 5 vols. (Berlin, 1910–13, repr. 1966).

Stein, E., *Geschichte des spätrömischen Reiches*, vol. 1 (Vienna, 1928); French 2nd edn., translated by Palanque, J.-R., *Histoire du Bas-Empire*, vol. 1 (Paris, 1959).

Thompson, E. A., *The historical work of Ammianus Marcellinus* (Cambridge, 1947, repr. 1969).

Walden, J. H. W., *The universities of Ancient Greece* (New York, 1912).

SOCIAL, ECONOMIC, ADMINISTRATIVE, AND
URBAN HISTORY

van Berchem, D., *L'Armée de Dioclétien et la réforme constantinienne* (Paris, 1952), criticized by Seston, W., in *Historia* iv (1955), 284–96.

Boak, A. E. R., *Manpower shortage and the fall of the Roman Empire in the West* (Ann Arbor, 1955).

Buckler, W. H., 'Labour disputes in the province of Asia', *Anatolian studies presented to Sir William Mitchell Ramsay* (Manchester, 1923), 27–50.

Cahen, C., 'Zur Geschichte der städtischen Gesellschaft im islamischen Orient des Mittelalters', *Saeculum* ix (1953), 59–76.

Claude, D., *Die byzantinische Stadt* (Munich, 1969).

Coleman-Norton, P. R., ed., *Studies in Roman economic and social history in honor of Allan Chester Johnson* (Princeton, 1951).

Colin, J., *Les Villes libres de l'Orient gréco-romain et l'envoi au supplice par acclamations populaires* (Brussels, 1965).

Courtois, C., Leschi, L., Perrat, C., Saumagne, C., *Tablettes Albertini* (Paris, 1952).

Déléage, A., *La Capitation du Bas-Empire* (Mâcon, 1945).

Dill, S., *Roman society in the last century of the Western Empire* (London, 1905).

Dölger, F., 'Die frühbyzantinische und byzantinisch beeinflußte Stadt', *Atti del 3 Congresso internazionale di studi sull'alto Medioevo* (Spoleto, 1959), 66–100.

Duncan-Jones, R., 'An epigraphic survey of costs in Roman Italy', *P.B.S.R.* (1965), 189–306.

—— 'Wealth and munificence in Roman Africa', *P.B.S.R.* (1963), 160–77.

—— 'City population in Roman Africa', *J.R.S.* liii (1963), 85–90.

—— 'Human numbers in towns and town organisation of the Roman Empire', *Historia* xiii (1964), 198–208.

Ennen, E., *Frühgeschichte der europäischen Stadt* (Bonn, 1953).

Friedländer, P., *Darstellungen aus der Sittengeschichte Roms*, 10th edn. by Wissowa, G. (Leipzig, 1921–3); an English version by J. Freese and Magnus, L., *Roman life and manners* (London, 1913).

Ganghoffer, R., *L'Évolution des institutions municipales en Occident et en Orient au Bas-Empire* (Paris, 1963).

Grosse, R., *Römische Militärgeschichte* (Berlin, 1920).

Hands, A. R., *Charities and social aid in Greece and Rome* (London, 1968).

Hardy, E. R., 'The Large Estates of Byzantine Egypt' (Diss. Columbia, 1931).

Hauser-Meury, M.-M., *Prosopographie zu den Schriften Gregors von Nazianz* (Bonn, 1960).

Hirth, F., *China and the Roman Orient* (Leipzig, 1855, repr. 1966).

Hombert, M., and Préaux, C., *Recherches sur le recensement dans l'Égypte romain* (Brussels, 1952).

Johnson, A. C., *Egypt and the Roman Empire* (Ann Arbor, 1951).

—— and West, L. C., *Byzantine Egypt: economic studies* (Princeton, 1945, repr. 1967).

Jones, A. H. M., *Ancient economic history* (London, 1948).

—— 'The date and value of the Verona list', *J.R.S.* xliv (1954), 21–9.

—— 'Inflation under the Roman Empire', *Ec. H. Rev.* v (1953), 293–317.

—— *The cities of the eastern Roman provinces* (Oxford, 1937, 2nd edn. 1970).

—— *The Greek city from Alexander to Justinian* (Oxford, 1940).

—— *The Later Roman Empire, 284–602*, 3 vols. (Oxford, 1964).

Kirsten, E., 'Die byzantinische Stadt', *Berichte zum XI. internationalen Byzantinisten-Kongress*, v. 3 (Munich, 1958).

Kurbatov, G. L., 'La désagrégation du régime esclavagiste et les problèmes du développement intérieur de la cité byzantine au Vᵉ–VIᵉ siècles a. J.-C.', *V.L.U. ist.* iii (1965), 62–72 (Russian with English summary).

—— 'Quelques problèmes concernant la désagrégation de la polis antique dans les provinces orientales de l'Empire romain au IVᵉ siècle', *V.L.U. ist.* ii (1960), 47–61 (in Russian).

Lallemand, J., *L'Administration civile de l'Égypte* (Brussels, 1964).

Leo the Wise, *Book of the Prefect* (τὸ ἐπαρχικὸν βιβλίον), ed. Nicole, J., (Geneva 1893); English translations by Freshfield, E. H., *Roman law in the Later Roman Empire* (Cambridge, 1938), and Boak, A. E. R., *J. Econ. Business History* i (1929), 600–19.

MacMullen, R., *Enemies of the Roman order* (London, 1967).

—— *Soldier and civilian in the Later Roman Empire* (Harvard, 1963).

—— 'A note on Roman strikes', *Classical Journal* lviii (1963), 269–71.

Manojlović, G., 'Le peuple de Constantinople', *Byzantion* xi (1936), 617–716.

Maricq, A., 'Factions du cirque et partis populaires', *Bull. de l'Acad. roy. de Belgique*, Classe des Lettres, 5ᵉ série, xxxvi (1950), 396–421.

Martindale, J. R., 'Public Disorders in the Late Roman Empire' (Oxford B.Litt. thesis, 1960, unpublished).

Mazzarino, S., *Aspetti sociali del quarto secolo* (Rome, 1951).

Mickwitz, G., *Geld und Wirtschaft in dem römischen Reich des vierten Jahrhunderts* (Helsingfors, 1932, repr. 1965).

—— *Die Kartellfunktion der Zünfte* (Helsingfors, 1936, repr. 1968).

Mitteis, L., *Reichsrecht und Volksrecht in den östlichen Provinzen des römischen Kaiserreiches* (Leipzig, 1891 repr. 1963).

Monneret de Villard, U., 'Antiochia e Milano nel VI secolo', *Orientalia Christiana Periodica* xii (1946), 374–80.

Pearce, J. W. E., *Roman imperial coinage*, vol. ix (London, 1962).

Pigulewskaya, N., *Byzanz auf den Wegen nach Indien* (Berlin, 1969).

Riccobono, S., and others, *Fontes Iuris Romani Ante-Iustiniani*, 3 vols. (Florence, 1940–3).

Robert, L., *Les Gladiateurs dans l'Orient grec* (Paris, 1940).

Rostovtzeff, M., *Caravan cities* (Oxford, 1932).

—— *Social and economic history of the Hellenistic world* (Oxford, 1941).

—— *Social and economic history of the Roman Empire* (1st English edn., Oxford, 1926; 2nd edn. 1957).

Rougé, J., *Recherches sur l'organisation du commerce maritime sous l'Empire romain* (Paris, 1966).

Rouillard, G., *L'Administration civile de l'Égypte byzantine* (Paris, 1928).

Ruggini, L., 'Ebrei e orientali nell'Italia Settentrionale fra il IV e il VI secolo a. Cr.', *Studia et documenta historiae et iuris* xxv (1959), 186–308.

—— *Economia e società nell''Italia annonaria'* (Milan, 1961).

Russell, J. C., 'Late Ancient and Medieval population', *P.A.P.S.* xlviii. 3 (1958).

Stöckle, A., *Spätrömische und byzantinische Zünfte* (*Klio*, Beiheft ix, 1911; repr. 1963).

Turner, E. G., *Greek papyri* (Oxford, 1968).

Vasiliev, A. D., 'Monument of Porphybrius', *Dumbarton Oaks Papers* iv (1948), 29–49.

Warmington, E. H., *The commerce between the Roman Empire and India* (Cambridge, 1928).

SYRIA AND ANTIOCH

Baur, P. C., *Der heilige Johannes Chrysostomus und seine Zeit* (Munich, 1929–30), cited: Baur, *Johannes Chrysostomus*.

B.R. 513 Geographical Handbook: Series Syria (Admiralty, London, 1943).

Brooks, E. W., *The select letters of Severus of Antioch* (London, 1903–4).

Butler, H. C., and Prentice, H. K., *Publications of the Princeton archaeological expedition to Syria, 1904–5 and 1909*.

Chevallier, D., 'De la production lente à l'économie dynamique en Syrie', *Annales* xxi (1966), 59–70.

Cumont, F., 'The population of Syria', *J.R.S.* xxiv (1934), 187–90.

Devréesse, R., *Le Patriarcat d'Antioche* (Paris, 1945).

Downey, G., *A history of Antioch in Syria* (Princeton, 1961).

—— *A study of the 'Comites Orientis' and the 'Consulares Syriae'* (Princeton, 1939).

Dussaud, R., *Topographie historique de la Syrie antique et médiévale* (Paris, 1927).

Elderkin, G. W., and Sillwell, R., *Antioch on the Orontes*, Publications of the Committee for the excavation of Antioch and its vicinity (Princeton, 1934–52).

Festugière, A. J., *Antioche païenne et chrétienne* (Paris, 1959).

Février, J. G., *Essai sur l'histoire politique et économique de Palmyre* (Paris, 1931).

Frézouls, E., 'Recherches historiques et archéologiques sur la ville de Cyrrhus', *Annales archéologiques de Syrie* iv–v (1954), 89–128.

Garrett, R., Butler, H. C., Prentice, W. K., Littmann, E., *Publications of an American archaeological expedition to Syria in 1899–1900* (New York, 1903–14).

Goossens, G., *Hierapolis de Syrie* (Louvain, 1943).

Grünebaum, G. E. von, *Islam* (London, 1955), esp. 141–58 on the Islamic town.

Harper, G. M., 'Village administration in the Roman province of Syria', *T. Cl. St.* i (1928), 103–68.

Heichelheim, F. M., *Roman Syria*, vol. 4 in *E.S.A.R.*, 121–257.

Honigmann, E., 'Syria', *P.W.*, 2nd ser. iv. 2, cols. 1549–1727.

Jalabert, L., and Mouterde, R., *Inscriptions grecques et latines de la Syrie* (Paris, 1929).

Kraeling, C. H., 'The Jewish Community at Antioch', *J. Bibl. Lit.* li (1932), 130–60.

Lassus, J., *Inventaire archéologique de la région au nord-est de Hama* (Damascus, 1935).

—— *Sanctuaires chrétiens de Syrie* (Paris, 1944).

Levi, D., *Antioch mosaic pavements*, 2 vols. (Princeton, London, The Hague, 1947).

Liebeschuetz, W., 'The Syriarch in the 4th century A.D.', *Historia* viii (1959), 113–26.

—— 'The finances of Antioch in the 4th century A.D.', *B.Z.* lii (1959), 344–56.

—— 'Money economy and taxation in kind in Syria in the 4th century A.D.', *Rh. M.* civ (1961), 242–54.

Mouterde, R., and Poidebard, A., *Le 'Limes' de Chalcis, organisation de la steppe en haute Syrie romaine* (Paris, 1945).

Norman, A. F., 'Gradations in later Municipal Society', *J.R.S.* xlviii (1958), 79–85.

—— 'The book trade in fourth-century Antioch', *J.H.S.* lxxx (1960), 122–6.

—— 'The family of Argyrius', *J.H.S.* lxxiv (1954), 44–8.

—— 'Notes on some *Consulares* of Syria', *B.Z.* li (1958), 73–7.

Puech, A., *Saint Jean Chrysostome et les mœurs de son temps* (Paris, 1891).

Sauvaget, J., *Alep* (Paris, 1941).

Selb, W., *Zur Bedeutung des syrisch-römischen Rechtsbuches* (Münchener Beiträge zur Papyrusforschung xlix, Munich, 1964).

Tchalenko, G., *Villages antiques de la Syrie du nord*, 3 vols. (Paris, 1953).

Waagé, D. B., *Antioch on the Orontes*, vol. iv. 2, Greek, Roman, Byzantine and Crusaders' coins (Princeton, 1952).

Weulersse, J., 'Antioche, essai de géographie urbaine', *Bulletin d'études orientales* iv (1934), 27–79.

LIBANIUS

Downey, G., 'Libanius' Oration in Praise of Antioch' (*Or.* xi), translation, introduction, and commentary, *P.A.P.S.* ciii (1959), 652–86.

Foerster, R., and Muenscher, K., s.v. Libanius, *P.W.* xii. 2, cols. 2485 ff.

Harmand, L., *Libanius, Discours sur les patronages* (Paris, 1955).

Kurbatov, G. L., 'Les esclaves et l'esclavage dans les œuvres de Libanius', *V.D.I.* lxxxviii (1964), 92–106 (in Russian).

—— 'Le terme δῆμος dans les œuvres de Libanius et la question des δῆμοι byzantins', *XXVe Congrès international des orientalistes* (Moscow, 1962), 504–10.

van Loy R., 'Le *Pro Templis* de Libanius', *Byzantion* viii (1933), 7–39, 389–404, a translation and commentary.

Norman, A. F., 'Philostratus and Libanius', *Cl. Phil.* xlviii (1951).

Pack, R. C., 'Studies in Libanius and Antiochene society under Theodosius', includes translation and commentary of *Or.* xlv (Diss. U. Michigan, 1935), cited: Pack, *Studies*.

—— 'Curiales in the correspondence of Libanius', *T.A.P.A.* lxxxii (1951), 176–92.

Petit, L., *Essai sur la vie et la correspondance du sophiste Libanius* (Paris, 1866).

Petit, P., *Les Étudiants de Libanius* (Paris, 1957).

—— 'Les sénateurs de Constantinople dans l'œuvre de Libanius', *L'Antiquité classique* xxvi (1957), 347–83.

—— *Libanius et la vie municipale à Antioche au IVe siècle après J.-C.* (Paris, 1955), cited: Petit, *Libanius*.

—— 'Libanius et la *Vita Constantina*', *Historia* i (1950), 562–82, criticized by Moreau, J., *Historia* iv (1955), 234–55.

—— 'Recherches sur la publication et la diffusion des discours de Libanius', *Historia* v (1956), 479–509.

—— 'Sur la date du *Pro Templis* de Libanius', *Byzantion* xxi (1951), 285–310.

Seeck, O., *Die Briefe des Libanius zeitlich geordnet*, in Gebhardt–Harnack, *Texte und Untersuchungen*, N.F. 15 (Leipzig, 1906, repr. 1967), cited: Seeck, *Briefe*.

—— 'Libanius gegen Lucianus', *Rh. M.* lxxiii (1920), 84–101.

Sievers, G. R., *Das Leben des Libanius* (Berlin, 1868).

Wolf, P., *Libanios, autobiographische Schriften*, German translation and notes for *Or.* i–v (Zürich, 1967).

—— *Vom Schulwesen der Spätantike, Studien zu Libanius* (Baden-Baden, 1950).

de Zulueta, F., 'De patrociniis vicorum...', *Oxford Studies in Social and Legal History* i (1909), 1–78, largely on *Or.* xlvii.

ADDENDA

The following works add to our knowledge of topics treated in *Antioch*, but I read them only after I had completed the text of the book.

Ammianus Marcellinus, *Römische Geschichte*, text and commentary by W. Seyfarth, vols. 1–2 (Berlin, 1968).

Brown, P. R. L., 'The diffusion of Manichaeism in the Roman Empire', *J.R.S.* lix (1969), 92–103.

—— 'The Later Roman Empire', *Ec.H.R.* xx (1967), 327–43.

Bruck, E. F., *Kirchenväter und soziales Erbrecht* (Heidelberg, 1956), on influence of Syrian customs in the West.

Bullough, D. A., 'Urban change in early medieval Italy: the example of Pavia', *P.B.S.R.* xxx, N.S. xvii (1962), 47–115.

Cambridge History of Islam, 2 volumes, eds. P. M. Holt, Ann K. S. Lambton, and Bernard Lewis (Cambridge, 1970).

Cameron, Averil and Alan, 'Historiography of the Late Empire', *C.Q.* N.S. xiv (1964), 316–28.

Ceran, W., 'Stagnation or fluctuation in Early Byzantine Society', *Byzantinoslavica* xxxi (1970), 192–203: references from John Chrysostomus to social mobility and condition of shopkeeper-craftsmen.

Chastagnol, A., 'La Préfecture urbaine à Rome sous le Bas-Empire' (Paris, 1960).

Ciocan-Yvanescu, R., 'Sur le rôle d'Antioche au point de vue économique, social et culturel au VIᵉ siècle', *Byzantion* xxxix (1969), 53–73.

Crawford, D. J., 'Kerkeosiris: an Egyptian village in the Ptolemaic period' (Cambridge, 1971).

Downey, G., '*Polis* and *civitas* in Libanius and St Augustine', *Académie royale de Belgique, Bulletin de la classe des lettres* lii (1966), 356–66.

Hansen, H. and Th. Schiøler, 'Distribution of land based on Greek–Egyptian papyri', *Janus* (1952), 181–92.

Hoffmann, D., *Das spätrömische Bewegungsheer und die Notitia Dignitatum*, 2 vols. (Düsseldorf, 1971).

Jones, A. H. M., Morris, J., and Martindale, J. R., *The Prosopography of the Later Roman Empire*, vol. 1 (260–395).

Lauffer, S., *Diokletians Preisedikt*, Texte und Kommentare: no. 5 (Berlin, 1971).

Matthews, J. F., 'Maternus Cynegius and his family', *J.T.S.* N.S. xviii (1967), 438–46.

Mayerson, P., 'The first Muslim attacks on Southern Palestine', *T.A.P.A.* xcv (1964), 55–199.

Percival, J., 'Seigneurial aspects of late Roman estate management', *E.H.R.* lxxxiv (1969), 449–73.

Pigulewskaya, N., *Les Villes de l'État iranien aux époques parthe et sassanide* (Paris, 1963).

Segal, J. B., *Edessa, 'The Blessed City'* (Oxford, 1970).

Szilágyi, J., 'Zur Entwicklung des Preis- und Lohnverhältnisses in der römischen Kaiserzeit', in *Neue Beiträge zur Geschichte der alten Welt*, ed. E. C. Welskopf, vol. 2 (Berlin, 1965), 133–9.

Thompson, E. A., *The Goths in Spain* (Oxford, 1969).

Wypszycka, E., 'Les Factions du cirque et les biens ecclésiastiques', *Byzantion* xxxix (1969), 180–98.

—— 'Textilhandwerk und der Staat im römischen Aegypten', *Archiv für Papyrusforschung*, xviii (1966), 1–22.

INDEX OF GREEK TERMS

GENERAL INDEX

Roman numerals refer to the prosopography in Seeck's *Die Briefe des Libanius*, arabic numerals in brackets to Jones, Martindale, and Morris, *The Prosopography of the Later Roman Empire*.

Abbossos, Syrian village, 119
Abinnaeus, Flavius, *praefectus alae*, 118
Abraames (Abraham), hermit, 62, 239
acclamations, 209 ff.
Achaea, building finance, 153
Achillius III (2), doctor, 180
Acontius, councillor of Antioch, 183
actors, 222; attitude of church, 145; rewards of, 145–6
actuarius thymelae et equorum currulium, 160
adaeratio, 89–90
Addaius, general, 114
Adonis, 231
Adrianople, battle of, 5, 13
advocates, 177; wealth, 50; former students of Libanius, 180; knowledge of law, 248–9, 251; registration, 250–1
Aegae (Cilicia), fair of, 77
Africa, effect of Vandal invasions, 81
agentes in rebus, 58; abuse of, 33; children enrolled, 178
agriculture, feeding a city, 96; crop yields, 151
Agroecius I, Armenian, 180, 185
Aila (Aquaba), 76
Alaric, King of Visigoths, ransom paid to, 78
Alexander III (5), consular of Syria in 363, 20, 130, 179
Alexander X (6), senator, 59, 179, 180; Olympic Games of 364, 137
Alexander XIII (13), fugitive colonus, 176
Alexandria, merchants, 83; population and corn supply, 95; civilian control, 118; police, 125; food distribution, 129; corn supply, 129; budget, 158; leading councillors, 172, 173; expulsion of Jews, 217; *corporati*, 220; power of bishop, 260
Alexandria ad Issum (Cilicia), 99
allegory, 9
Alytarch, 127, 143

Amanus, mountain near Antioch, 41
ambassadors, selection, 167
Ambrose, bishop of Milan, 36
Ammianus Marcellinus, historian, 115; portraits of villains, 33
Anastasius, emperor, 125; reforms civic government, 262
Anatolius I (3), praetorian prefect, correspondent of Libanius, 20
Ancyra (Galatia), 17
Andronicus, governor of Pentapolis, 33
Andronicus II (3), governor of Phoenicia, 195
annonae civicae, 127
Antaeopolis (Egypt), pagarch of, 208
Anthesterion, 63
Antioch, *see also* table of contents; imperial residence, 3–4; era of, 40; notables of, 41; proportion of poor, 41; 'agora', 55; citizens' rural links, 73; communications, 73–4, 77; provisioning, 73–5; area, 92; church of, 93, 94; source of food supply, 96; immigration, 97; householders, 97; riots, 97; poverty, 97–8; walls, 97, 98; military base, 117; and villages, 121–2; distribution of food, 127 ff., 129; imperial subsidies, 155–6; captured by Persians, 263; colonnaded street, 264
Antioch, bishop of, and territory, 121; power of, 239 ff.; wealth of church, 240
Antioch, plain of, land-tenure, 69
Antiochicus, Or. XI of Libanius, 137, 170
Antiochus II, councillor of Antioch, 42, 137, 177, 179, 180, 266, 277
Apamea (Syria), 40, 45, 120, 140; emigrants, 81; inscriptions from territory, 99; destruction of, 100; pagans kill bishop, 108; villages of, 119–20; councillors frightened, 175; destruction of temples, 238; synagogue, 232, 233

Julianus XVII, impoverished councillor of Antioch, 38, 147, 182, 183

Justice, jurisdiction of civic magistrates and of governors, 113; public and secret, 187; influence of *honorati*, 198–9; intercession with judges, 195; location of Libanius' case, 203; court protocols, 247; court procedure, 249–50, 251

Karanis (Egypt), 89
kingship, theory of, 9–10

labourers, 63
Lactantius, Christian rhetor, 13
Lamachus, councillor of Antioch, 166
landowners, scattered estates, 42; precariousness of ownership, 43; commercial transactions, 45; form the upper class, 48; lend money, 49; and commerce, 48–9, 82–3; interest in retailing, 61; orders to peasants, 63; agents of, 63; usury by, 64; labour services for, 64; supported by authorities, 66; gain land of debtors, 67; church-building, 72; transport facilities, 74; trade in corn, 74; own ships, 75; resisted through patron, 202; estates grow through patronage, 206; and monks, 239

landscape, appreciated, 51
Laodicea (Syria), 56, 140; an inscription, 99
Latin, at Antioch, 1, 11; knowledge in East, 247; use in administration, 246–7; wider use in 4th C., 252; Greek prevails, 252–3

law, not observed, 107; obtained by influence, 109; drafted for ambassadors, 109; 'living law', 109–10; evaded, 179; conflict of rival authorities, 264

lecticarii, 217
Letoius I, councillor of Antioch, estates near Cyrrhus, 42; Olympics of 352, 136, 143; embassy, 266

Letoius II, nephew of Letoius I, 143; Olympic Games of 388, 137
letter-collections, 22
Libanius, *see also* table of contents; attitude to empire, 10–11; reform speeches, 5–6; praetorian prefecture, 6; concubine, 7; compared with

Aristides, 8; attitude to Rome, 10; *Antiochicus*, 10, 137; justification of rhetorics, 11–12; religious and educational views, 11–16; on divine intervention, 13–14; speeches on the council, 28; courage and caution, 29–30; publication of speeches, 30; Atticism, 31; the *Pro templis*, 39; mother sells land, 43; salaries, 44, 89–90; *De patrociniis*, 119, 201–5; on price control, 132; moralist, 139; *De rhetoribus*, 152; pagan and Christian pupils, 226–7; Or XLIII (De pactis), 245; treason charge, 268

lighting, use of olive oil, 79
limes of Chalcis (Syria), olives not grown, 80; military occupation, 117
limestone plateau (Syria), villages of, 71–3; causes of prosperity, 79–81; date of decline, 80
linen garments, 58, 60, 79
lions, cost of, 157
Litarba (Tērib), 40
litter, 47
Lollianus, 46
'lots', 147, 149–50, 153
Lucianus (6), consular of Syria, 36; dismissal, 115; and *honorati*, 189; demonstration for, 211; embassy complains against, 268
Lucianus, minor official, 19
Lupicinus (6), general, 114
Luscus, *curator*, 169
Lycia, timber from, 75

Maccabees, tomb of, 233
Macedonius, hermit, 62, 236
magic, 14, 32, 33, 106; Theodore trials, 5, 22; amulets, 225, 232
magister militum per orientem, 115–16
magistrates (civic), 168
Maiumas, pagan festival, 230
Malalas, John, chronicler, value of, 127
Mancian tenure, 72
Manichaeans, 29
manufacture, 52, 54–5
Marcellus (2), doctor at Antioch, sons of, 177, 178, 277
Mardonius II (2), eunuch at court, 27
Marianus, inscribes son in *officium*, 177, 277
marriage, 225
martyrs, veneration, 232

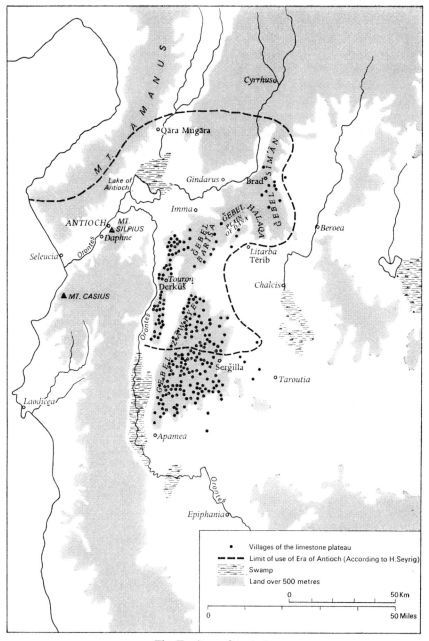

The Territory of Antioch